The easy Guide to Your First Walt Disney World Visit 2016

Dave Shute & Josh Humphrey

Theme Park Press

Theme Park Press publishes its books in a variety of print and electronic formats. Some content that appears in one format may not appear in another.

Editor: Bob McLain
Layout: Artisanal Text
Cover Design: Emily White

"Jim Gem's" content © Jim Korkis

ISBN 978-1-941500-61-3
Printed in the United States of America

Theme Park Press | www.ThemeParkPress.com
Address queries to bob@themeparkpress.com

To my mom and dad, for introducing me to Disneyland, Disney World...and everything else —Dave

To my mom, dad, brother, and friend(s)—without your help and guidance this would probably be a prison memoir rather than a Walt Disney World guidebook —Josh

Contents

How to Use This Book

This chapter has two purposes: introducing the topics of the rest of the book and boiling down our recommendations into an easy-to-digest list. The chapters that follow it offer detailed information on the whys and hows behind our recommendations. For example, you may be interested only in eating at one or two sit-down restaurants. Instead of forcing you to read through a hundred reviews, we've listed the best values and the most immersive experiences here in an effort to speed up and simplify the planning process. And you never know, as you read the later reviews of our favorite restaurants, something else might catch your eye.

While you can skip around the book, we do suggest consuming the full text from beginning to end—perhaps a chapter per night with the help of a glass of wine and a roasty, toasty fire. The chapters build on each other, with decisions made during Chapters 2 and 3 affecting the choices you make in Chapters 4 and following. Chapters 8 and 9 come full circle and serve as the road map for your entire trip.

Changes, corrections, updates, links to larger color versions of key charts, and such, can be found at YOURFIRSTVISIT.NET/EASY-GUIDE-2016-CHANGES or at EASYWDW.COM/EASY-GUIDE.

Why Age and Height Matter [Chapter 2]

Children of all ages enjoy wonderful visits to Walt Disney World every single day of the year. However, if this may be your kids' only childhood visit, consider going when your youngest child is at least 8 or 9, and your shortest child at least 48 inches tall.

Many of Walt Disney World's best and most popular attractions require riders to be 48" tall, and kids around the third-grade-age are mature enough to appreciate the layers and nuances of each Disney experience. Those already planning to return may want to start earlier, when the kids are younger and all aspects of the Disney magic are open to them. While toddlers and younger kids are charmed by and enamored with the

Disney princesses, older kids may be less enthusiastic about a sit-down meal with Belle and Cinderella. Starting young offers an opportunity to enjoy many varied trips as the kids get older. But starting too young and too short on a once-in-a-lifetime trip means passing on several of Disney World's best rides. Chapter 2 describes how easy it is to design an itinerary with kids (or adults) of any age.

How Long to Stay [Chapter 3]

Wonderful Walt Disney World vacations come in all shapes and sizes, with guests enjoying trips that last anywhere from just one day to as long as several weeks. However, for a once in a lifetime trip, we recommend spending nine days in Orlando.

Guests planning to return enjoy the ability to ease into visiting the theme parks with shorter trips of four or so days, knowing they can catch missed attractions and experiences in the future. Those planning once-in-a-lifetime style vacations are best served pushing their stay to eight or nine days. This affords the opportunity to enjoy most of the best of Walt Disney World, and also allows a mixture of longer days in the theme parks tempered by more relaxing downtime back at the resort. While a longer trip will be more expensive than a shorter one, fixed travel costs and the way Disney prices tickets make the per-day costs of a longer trip significantly lower.

Shorter stays are often rewarding and enjoyable for everyone involved, but the limited time necessitates skipping key experiences and often requires a more ambitious schedule with fewer opportunities to relax.

When to Go [Chapter 4]

If you can, visit Disney World at some point between the day after the Martin Luther King Day holiday in January until the Thursday before President's Day in February, or the two weeks beginning the Sunday after Thanksgiving.

In picking dates, it's important to consider crowd levels, pricing, weather, possible refurbishments, and special events. Our specialty is honing in on the less crowded times to visit, when wait times are lower at attractions, lines are shorter at stores and dining venues, and there's less congestion inside the parks. Lower crowds means being able to do more in a less stressful environment. From there, we typically prioritize lower resort pricing, followed by weather, refurbishments, and special events.

Based on these factors—but especially low crowds and lower prices— we recommend the following weeks:

- From the day after the Martin Luther King Day holiday in January until the Thursday before President's Day in February
- The Sunday after President's Day through the first week of March
- The week that begins the Sunday after Easter until mid-May
- From the day after Labor Day through the rest of September
- The last two weeks of October
- November after Veterans Day until the Saturday before Thanksgiving
- The two weeks beginning the Sunday after Thanksgiving

Among these, Josh recommends the late January and early February dates, with the lowest prices (prices go up February 7), comfortable daytime temperatures, and some of the lowest crowds of the year. Dave prefers the two weeks after Thanksgiving, which marry below average-crowds and prices with Disney World's astonishing Christmas displays and offerings like Holidays Around the World and Mickey's Very Merry Christmas Party.

Those embarking on a possible once-in-a-lifetime trip should note that the peak of the hurricane season ends in early October, and that a few rides are almost invariably closed for refurbishments in January and early February.

If these dates won't work, Chapter 4 offers a blow-by-blow overview of everything to expect all year long.

Where to Stay [Chapter 5]

Stay at Disney's Art of Animation, Pop Century, Port Orleans French Quarter, Port Orleans Riverside, Grand Floridian, Wilderness Lodge, Contemporary Resort, or the Polynesian Village Resort.

We suggest that you stay in a Disney-owned resort hotel. While more expensive than hotels operated by third parties, they are also typically:

- Much more fun
- Much more convenient
- Much more "Disney"

The Disney-owned hotels also offer unique perks. The most advantageous perks include:

- Free airport transport to and from your hotel via Disney's Magical Express.
- Free and frequent transport from your hotel to the parks, waterparks, and Disney Springs.

- Free parking at both your hotel and the parks.
- The right to book dining ten days further out than non-Disney guests, which can be critical for high-demand meals like dinner at Be Our Guest Restaurant.
- The right to book FastPass+ reservations for key attractions beginning 60 days in advance of arrival. At press-time, non-Disney guests (except those at the Swan or Dolphin) can only book these 30 days in advance.
- Access to the various Disney Dining Plans, which are a convenient budgeting tool even if they often don't present much actual savings.

Perhaps even more important than any of these quantifiable perks is the comfort and safety of staying inside the "Disney bubble", far removed from the hustle, bustle, and worry of the outside world. Staying on property is the easiest way to forget about life's problems and truly enjoy an immersive experience together. While a vacation staying off-site is generally less expensive at first blush, consider additional expenses like resort fees, car rental, and the price of your time. There is no more convenient way to experience Walt Disney World for the first time than staying at one of their resorts. There is a reason Disney commands premium prices and why so many return visitors stay on property over and over again. Strongly consider the additional cost of an on-property stay and find out for yourself.

Specifically, we recommend, depending on budget:

VALUE RESORTS

Art of Animation, Pop Century

These resorts are among the least expensive on property, offer dedicated bus service, have great food courts, and offer newer rooms. Art of Animation is the newest Disney resort on property, and Pop Century is a short walk away.

MODERATE RESORTS

Port Orleans French Quarter, Port Orleans Riverside

French Quarter enjoys the smallest footprint of the moderate-level resorts and all rooms are just a few minutes away from the resort's amenities, including the bus stop, food court, boat dock, and resort concierge. Riverside is much larger, but offers better amenities, including a table service restaurant, a more robust feature pool, several quiet pools, and prettier surroundings.

DELUXE RESORTS
....

Grand Floridian, Wilderness Lodge, Contemporary, Polynesian Village

The Grand Floridian is Disney's flagship resort and its most opulent, providing several of its nicest restaurants, beautiful pool and garden areas, and a convenient location to Magic Kingdom. Wilderness Lodge is considerably less expensive and its woodsy atmosphere and stunning lobby may be more appealing to some guests, but its rooms are smaller and it's a bit less convenient across Bay Lake from Magic Kingdom. We love its lush public areas and variety of restaurants. The Contemporary is a magical space and just a short walk away from Magic Kingdom. Theme park view rooms in the tower look over Cinderella Castle and the monorail zooms through the center of the resort all day. The Polynesian Village combines South Seas theming that kids find fun and adults find charming with great convenience and strong dining.

Chapter 5 includes in-depth reviews of every Disney-owned hotel.

How to Spend Your Time [Chapter 6]

Set daily plans from the example itineraries and "cheat sheets" we provide.

Planning your time at Walt Disney World can be easily broken down into three parts:

- Dividing your days among the parks
- Picking the best parks for each day
- Setting your plan for each park day

There are two different easy ways to use this book to plan your time at Walt Disney World, each designed around Disney's new FastPass+ program:

- For those who can use them as a starting point, we provide sample 9-day, Saturday-arrival itineraries, and
- For everybody else, we provide "cheat sheets" for designing your visits that work for both younger and older kids, and for longer and shorter trips.

Here's an excerpt from one of the example itineraries:

Meals	Wednesday	Thursday
Breakfast	*Hotel Room*	*Hotel Room*
Lunch	**Chef's Mickeys 11am**	Hotel Counter
Dinner	Magic Kingdom or Hotel Counter	Hollywood Studios Counter
Parks, Etc.		
Early Morning	Off	Off
Late Morning	Off	Off
Early Afternoon	At Magic Kingdom by noon	At Hollywood Studios by noon
Late Afternoon	Magic Kingdom	Hollywood Studios
Evening	Magic Kingdom	Hollywood Studios
Late Evening		
Notes		
Parade	Afternoon Parade	
Fireworks	Wishes	Fantasmic
Park-Open Target	n/a	n/a
FastPass+ Target	Space Mountain	Toy Story Midway Mania

And here's an example from one of the Cheat Sheets:

Late Arrival Touring at Animal Kingdom (with 6pm or later close)

1. Arrive between 10:30am and 11am. Schedule FastPass+ at Expedition Everest (12:30–1:30pm), Adventurers Outpost Mickey and Minnie Meet (1:30–2:30pm), and Kali River Rapids (2:30–3:30pm).
2. Visit Oasis Exhibits until 11am.
3. See It's Tough to be a Bug on Discovery Island: 11:15–11:30am.
4. See Finding Nemo the Musical: 11:40am–12:45pm (12pm start).
5. Ride Expedition Everest in Asia with FastPass+: 12:50–1:05pm.
6. Have lunch. Yak & Yeti and Flame Tree Barbecue are closest.
7. Meet Mickey and Minnie at Adventurers Outpost with FastPass+: 2pm–2:15pm.
8. Walk Maharajah Jungle Trek in Asia: 2:20–2:45pm.
9. Ride Kali River Rapids with FastPass+: 2:50–3:10pm.
10. Grab a snack (carts and kiosks are all around): 2:50–3:10pm.
11. See Festival of the Lion King in Africa: 3:40–4:30pm (4pm start).
12. Ride Kilimanjaro Safaris: 4:35–5:10pm.
13. Ride Primeval Whirl in DinoLand: 5:25–5:40pm.
14. Ride DINOSAUR: 5:50–6:10pm.
15. Return to Asia for Expedition Everest or a skipped attraction with a 7pm or later close.

Chapter 6 includes in-depth reviews of all the theme park attractions and explains theme park touring strategy in detail.

Where to Eat [Chapter 7]

Target your dining venues based on our recommendations, our reviews, or simply where you are when you're hungry!

First-time family visitors to Walt Disney World need to know three things about dining:

1. Several dining venues are among the most memorable and delightful experiences Walt Disney Word has to offer.

2. Table service reservations open 180 days in advance. Availability at the most sought-after restaurants is taken almost immediately.

3. Disney World dining is expensive. Expect to pay 25 to 40% more on-property than you would for comparable meals off-property. For most (but not all) visitors, the Disney Dining Plan won't save any money.

For families, we recommend:

- The Princess meals: **Cinderella's Royal Table** at the Magic Kingdom and **Akershus Royal Banquet Hall** at Epcot. The first has the better setting, the second is much less expensive.

- Dining with Tigger, Pooh, and friends at the **Crystal Palace** in the Magic Kingdom.

- Dining with Mickey and Friends at **Chef Mickey's** at Disney's Contemporary Resort and **'Ohana** breakfast at Disney's Polynesian Village Resort.

- Dining in the Beast's Castle at **Be Our Guest Restaurant** in Magic Kingdom.

- Various degrees of wait-staff induced silliness at **50's Prime Time Café** at Disney's Hollywood Studios and **Whispering Canyon Café** at Disney's Wilderness Lodge.

- **The Hoop-Dee-Doo Musical Revue**, a fun, energetic dinner show with interactive elements and plenty of audience participation at Disney's Fort Wilderness Resort.

- Exotic settings in the local versions of national chain restaurants like the **Rainforest Café**, in both Disney's Animal Kingdom and Disney Springs, and **T-REX** in Disney Springs.

For couples looking for the most romantic atmosphere and the best food, we suggest:

- **California Grill**—located on the 15th floor of the Contemporary Resort, it offers breathtaking views of Magic Kingdom during the evening fireworks, in addition to a great menu focused on fresh ingredients, sushi, and contemporary cocktails.

- **Artist Point**—nestled inside Wilderness Lodge, it is themed to the restaurants found in the great National Park lodges of the Northwest. Buffalo, salmon, and a terrific mushroom soup and berry cobbler are menu mainstays.
- **Victoria & Albert's**—offering impeccable service and astonishing attention to detail, dinner at this Grand Floridian restaurant is a truly memorable experience.

Chapter 7 includes advice on the Disney Dining Plan and in-depth reviews of all the major Disney World dining options, plus suggestions on the best quick service options.

Which Tickets to Buy and How Much to Budget [Chapter 8]

Big budgets allow for more extravagances, but a vacation can be tailored to just about any budget. Realistically, a family of four is looking at spending more than $4,000.

"What should we budget?" is the hardest simple question for this book to answer. This is because smaller families, families whose kids are younger, families staying at a less expensive hotel, families going during a less expensive week, and families on shorter trips will pay less. Larger families, families where everyone is older than nine, families staying at a more expensive hotel, families going during a more expensive week, and families on longer trips will pay more.

- A parent and one younger child with three days of tickets and three nights in a value resort during one of the less expensive price seasons could spend as little as $1,300 in Orlando.
- Add another parent and another younger child and this trip jumps to $2,100.
- Stretch the visit out to the 8 nights we recommend for "only visits" and the in-Orlando price exceeds $4,000.
- Stay this long in one of the more expensive deluxe resorts instead, and the price is more than $7,500.
- Shift to the most expensive times to visit at this deluxe resort and add $1,700 more.

(Prices will likely increase 3-5% during 2016. All the figures are before transportation costs and souvenirs.)

The good news is that budgeting for a specific trip is relatively straightforward, once you've made the key decisions that are outlined in this book.

How to Set Everything Up and Get Everything Done [Chapter 9]

Your plans should be firm at least 181 days before your arrival date. Then see the To-Do List for exactly what to do, and when, to prepare for your trip.

There are three key dates to consider:

- Restaurant reservations open for booking 180 days before a potential dining date

- For those staying at a Disney-owned resort or the Swan or Dolphin, FastPass+ reservations can be booked beginning 60 days before their arrival date

- For everyone else, FastPass+ reservations can be booked beginning 30 days before planned use

Building a To-Do List is keyed to these three dates because booking as early as possibly will result in the widest selection of experiences being available. Chapter 9 covers exactly how and when to make these decisions.

Disney World planning may feel like a daunting task. Don't worry. You're in good hands. The following chapters offer a step-by-step walkthrough of the entire planning process, offering just the right amount of detail so you can make informed decisions. When everything goes according to plan and the group asks, "How did you make this trip so wonderful?" you can respond with a smile, "It was pretty easy, actually."

Why Age and Height Matter

Children of all ages enjoy Walt Disney World in their own ways, whether by meeting the characters, riding the thrill rides, or blending both roller coasters and princess breakfasts into an overall itinerary. When deciding whether it's time to book a trip, consider the ages and heights of the kid(s) and what they can and will be able to experience once they arrive. If one or more of the kids are under 48 inches tall, they will run into attractions they aren't able to experience due to height restrictions. If they don't have the intellectual and emotional maturity of the typical eight year old, other rides for which they are tall enough may be too frightening, or just a little too sophisticated for them to fully enjoy.

If your kids aren't eight or older and over 48" tall, and this is a once-in-a-lifetime trip, you need to decide whether you should wait until they are tall enough and mature enough to enjoy everything Walt Disney World offers. Even with height restrictions and the possibility that the content of an attraction like Ellen's Energy Adventure will fly over their heads, younger and shorter kids typically have as much fun as their older counterparts. With a little planning, it's easy to design an itinerary around the unique needs of kids of any age.

This chapter first discusses trips with kids of various ages. It then covers handling a single visit with kids of wildly different ages.

Visits by Age and Height

PRESCHOOLERS

Preschool age children especially delight in the magic of meeting the Disney characters. They are young enough that they still believe they are meeting *the* Cinderella and *the* Winnie the Pooh. Pictures of the kids entranced with characters like Snow White and the Seven Dwarfs will turn into memories that last a lifetime. Some kids remain shy or apprehensive about meeting the characters. Mickey is, after all, an alarming five feet tall. Goofy, with his oversize top hat, stretches over six feet. With apprehensive and shy kids, run a search on YouTube for "Disney World characters" and watch some interactions leading up to the trip. This will familiarize the kids with what to expect and reduce many of the first-time jitters and the tears that accompany them. While preschoolers will be too short or young for many of the premier attractions, there's still plenty for them to experience, especially at Magic Kingdom.

But they shouldn't try everything. Some attractions are simply too scary or intense for preschoolers. To help you figure out what is what, we have sorted every attraction based on how well kids of varying ages are likely to enjoy them.

Comprehensive Guide to Rides

Key: **E**=Epcot, **AK**=Animal Kingdom, **HS**=Hollywood Studios, **MK**=Magic Kingdom
Underline: Favorite of older kids; *Italic*: Skippable for older kids

PRE-SCHOOL KIDS

Avoid	E: *Captain EO, Gran Fiesta Tour (Mexico)*, Innoventions, *Journey into Imagination with Figment*. MK: Carousel of Progress, Hall of Presidents.	E: Impressions de France, O Canada!, Reflections of China, Agent P's World Showcase Adventure. MK: Stitch's Great Escape.	E: The American Adventure, Mission: Space, Soarin', Test Track. AK: DINOSAUR, Expedition Everest. HS: Fantasmic!, Rock 'n' Roller Coaster, Tower of Terror. MK: Haunted Mansion, Space Mountain, Splash Mountain.
Other	E: *The Circle of Life*, Living with the Land. AK: *Conservation Station*, Primeval Whirl, *Wildlife Express Train*. MK: Country Bear Jamboree, *Enchanted Tiki Room*.	E: Ellen's Energy Adventure, The Seas with Nemo and Friends. AK: Pangani Forest Exploration Trail. HS: Lights Motors Action Stunt Show. MK: The Barnstormer, Swiss Family Treehouse.	E: Spaceship Earth. AK: It's Tough to Be a Bug, Maharaja Jungle Trek. HS: Great Movie Ride, Indiana Jones Epic Stunt Spectacular, Walt Disney: One Man's Dream. MK: Big Thunder Railroad, Pirates of the Caribbean, Seven Dwarfs Mine Train.
Best-Loved	AK: *The Boneyard*, Dinorama, Triceratops Spin. HS: *Honey I Shrunk the Kids Movie Set*, Disney Junior: Live on Stage. MK: Astro Orbiter, Prince Charming Regal Carrousel, Dumbo the Flying Elephant, Magic Carpets of Aladdin, Mad Tea Party, Tomorrowland Speedway, Tomorrowland Transit Authority PeopleMover, Tom Sawyer Island, WDW Railroad.	AK: Finding Nemo the Musical, Flights of Wonder, Rivers of Light*. EP: Frozen Ever After*. HS: Frozen Sing-Along Celebration, Voyage of the Little Mermaid. MK: It's a Small World, Liberty Belle Riverboat, The Many Adventures of Winnie the Pooh, Monsters Inc. Laugh Floor, Under the Sea: Journey of the Little Mermaid	E: Illuminations, Turtle Talk with Crush. AK: Festival of the Lion King, Kali River Rapids, Kilimanjaro Safari. HS: Beauty and the Beast, Muppet Vision 3-D, Star Tours, Toy Story Midway Mania. MK: Afternoon Parade, Buzz Lightyear, Enchanted Tales with Belle, Evening Parade, Jungle Cruise, Mickey's PhilharMagic, Peter Pan, Wishes Fireworks.
	Skippable	**Other**	**Favorite**

THIRD GRADERS AND UP

* Preliminary Ranking of Attractions Yet to Open

For example, in the bottom left box we have The Boneyard, which is a richly themed playground at Disney's Animal Kingdom. Younger kids love to play there, but most older kids will find it juvenile. The upper right box contains several of Disney's best attractions, many of which aren't suitable for younger children due to height restrictions or scary content. Most older kids (and their parents) love these attractions, which is why they fall into "favorites" for third graders and up, and into "avoid" for preschoolers.

With preschoolers, try to match their interests, stamina, and routines with what the family plans to accomplish...or you'll have the joy of experiencing the same tantrums every other parent is enjoying come 3pm.

When the meltdowns begin, it's not uncommon for Josh to turn to Dave and say, "It must be 3 o'clock." Indeed, even more common than Mickey bars and WDW t-shirts are the afternoon hissy fits. Be realistic about how long the kids are going to be able to go. While Disney World might be a magical place, pixie dust does not seem to increase kids' stamina or reduce their inclination to break down when they're overstimulated and ready for a nap. Plan a daily afternoon break for when crowds, wait times, and heat peak. This will rejuvenate the kids and their parents and prepare them for a fun and relaxing evening back in the parks.

YOUNGER SCHOOL-AGE KIDS

Kids between five and eight are young enough that they still enjoy most character meets and some of the other sillier entertainment that older kids may have lost interest in. They are also beginning to approach the height required to enjoy Disney's more thrilling major attractions.

The chart, below, illustrates which attractions shorter kids are disqualified from riding. Unfortunately, this chart could double as a list of Disney World's best and most popular attractions (with the exception of Stitch's Great Escape), including almost all of the headliners at each park. With a single trip on the horizon, if you can't wait until the kids are 48" tall, consider waiting until they are at least 44" tall. They'll then be eligible for every ride on property but two. And the two they aren't eligible for aren't necessarily deal breakers. Primeval Whirl is an off-the-shelf carnival ride at Animal Kingdom. Rock 'n' Roller Coaster is located inside a relatively nondescript building at the end of a long road on Sunset Boulevard at Hollywood Studios. Simply avoid it and the kids won't feel like they're missing anything.

Keep in mind that "tall enough for" doesn't necessarily translate into "ready for". Moreover, many of Disney World's best attractions are like a Pixar movie in that there are layers of substance and humor that guests of all ages enjoy for different reasons. Kids between 5 and 8 understand and enjoy the attractions on a basic level, but nuances and deeper meanings are often lost.

Disney World Rides Excluded by Height

Children Less Than **38"** Tall Can't Ride	Children Less Than **40"** Tall Can't Ride	Children Less Than **44"** Tall Can't Ride	Children Less Than **48"** Tall Can't Ride
Primeval Whirl	Primeval Whirl	Primeval Whirl	Primeval Whirl
Rock 'n' Roller Coaster	Rock 'n' Roller Coaster	Rock 'n' Roller Coaster	Rock 'n' Roller Coaster
Expedition Everest	Expedition Everest	Expedition Everest	
Mission: SPACE	Mission: SPACE	Mission: SPACE	
Space Mountain	Space Mountain	Space Mountain	
Big Thunder Mountain	Big Thunder Mountain		
DINOSAUR	DINOSAUR		
Soarin'	Soarin'		
Splash Mountain	Splash Mountain		
Star Tours	Star Tours		
Stitch's Great Escape	Stitch's Great Escape		
Test Track	Test Track		
Tower of Terror	Tower of Terror		
Kali River Rapids			
Seven Dwarfs Mine Train			

KIDS BETWEEN 8 AND 88

Kids who are eight or older are tall enough, old enough, and mature enough to enjoy all of Disney World's rides and entertainment. Unfortunately, they may be getting too old to be swept up in the magic of breakfast with Cinderella inside the Castle. Most remain happy to participate, if for no other reason than it makes mom happy.

With just one planned trip, consider waiting until the kids are around this age. Returning guests that begin visiting when their kids are younger enjoy the widest range of experiences over many years. Cherish the memories of their first visit with Mickey Mouse and look forward to pretending you're not afraid when junior first starts begging to ride Expedition Everest.

Trips with Children of Different Ages

There are several ways to cope with and plan trips around kids of wildly different ages and maturity levels. The underlying problem, as shown in the previous chart, is that kids of varying ages enjoy different things. This is not unique to Disney World. At home, young kids may like playing with Legos, while older kids have moved on to the Xbox and Playstation 4. At Disney World, kids may occasionally want to or need to split up in order to experience certain attractions. Disney has made this relatively easy by building playgrounds and diversions aimed at younger kids in close proximity to the thrillers. Here are a few other ideas:

Take advantage of Rider Switch. Commonly referred to as "Child Swap", Rider Switch allows those eligible and willing to experience an attraction with a height requirement to ride, while others either wait alongside them in line or do something else. Most attractions require the group to approach the attraction's entrance and present the child too short or too leery to board the ride. The Cast Member will hand the group a Rider Switch pass. The members of the group experiencing the attraction wait in line. Members not experiencing the attraction may wait at the same time or head elsewhere. Once the group has experienced the attraction, up to three people can use the Rider Switch pass to enter the FastPass+ line, eliminating much of the wait. This can include a member or two of the original group. For example, let's say a family of four wants to experience Test Track, but one child is too short. Parent 1 and the older child wait in line and ride, while Parent 2 and the younger child head off to Innoventions to play. Once Parent 1 and the older child are off Test Track, up to three members of the family may use the Rider Switch at the FastPass+ line. That means the older child that previously rode Test Track can ride again alongside Parent 2. Parent 1 can then take the younger child elsewhere—perhaps to the interactive play area at Mission: SPACE's exit.

Have part of the family focus on rides for older kids, and the rest on attractions designed for the youngest. Split the family up, with older kids and a parent on one set of rides, and the littler ones on another age-appropriate set. This works particularly well if one parent has little interest in the thrill rides and coasters anyway. You can build completely different itineraries and FastPass+ selections for the two groups, or have some experiences in common and some different.

Consider childcare services. Disney vets use an independent in-room babysitting service called "Kid's Nite Out" for kids between six months and twelve years old. Rates start at $18 per hour for one child and go up to $26 an hour for four children (four hour minimum). There's a $2/hour surcharge after 9pm and a one-time transportation fee of $10. Babysitters arrive armed with age-appropriate games, crafts, and books.

In addition, Children's Activity Centers are available for potty-trained kids between 3 (if potty-trained) and 12 at select resorts:

- Simba's Cubhouse at Disney's Animal Kingdom Lodge
- Lilo's Playhouse at Disney's Polynesian Village Resort
- Cub's Den at Disney's Wilderness Lodge
- Sandcastle Club at Disney's Yacht Club and Beach Club Resorts
- Camp Dolphin at Walt Disney World Dolphin and Walt Disney World Swan (child must be between 4 -12)

Rates are $15/hour with a two-hour minimum. Call 407-939-3463 for more information or to reserve. These services are available to all guests, but are most convenient for those staying nearby or for families that want to drop off a youngster before heading to some of Disney's finer dining choices.

Families visiting with kids of any and all ages thoroughly enjoy their Walt Disney World vacations, but keep in mind that the experience will be quite different depending on who it is you're taking. Groups consisting of families with kids of varying ages will need to make some compromises, but the good news is that the vast majority of your time can and will be spent together as a family.

How Long to Stay

This chapter addresses the decision-making process for how long to stay at Walt Disney World. Guests planning to return enjoy the ability to ease into visiting the theme parks with shorter trips of four or so days, knowing they can catch missed attractions and experiences in the future. Those planning once-in-a-lifetime style vacations are best served pushing their length of stay to eight or nine days. This affords the opportunity to enjoy much of the best of Walt Disney World, and also allows a mixture of longer days in the theme parks tempered by more relaxing downtime back at the resort. Shorter stays are often rewarding and enjoyable for everyone involved, but the limited time necessitates skipping key experiences and requires a more ambitious schedule with fewer opportunities to relax.

We'll first cover the basics: budgets, time, and the ages of the kids. Then, in the next section, we'll address the importance of taking time away from the parks to relax, followed by a section about allocating time for an "only" trip.

Budgets, Time Available, and Ages of the Kids

Most prospective guests will choose a length of stay based on three primary factors: budget, time constraints, and kids' ages. Mom might only be able to get a Monday through Wednesday off work, necessitating a shorter five-day trip that begins with travel early Saturday and ends with travel late Wednesday. A budget might be stretched too thin for a seven-night stay at a moderate resort, but work with fewer nights at a value (Chapter 5 explains the difference between "moderates" and "values"). A family with very young kids may find that a delightful trip lasts only three or four days.

The good news is that guests with a wide range of budgets and trip lengths can thoroughly enjoy their visits. The bad news is that, like most things, (within reason) more is better.

A longer trip means more relaxing, more theme park visits, more Mickey ice cream bars, and, ultimately, more flexibility. Longer trips also have lower per-day costs. Most travel costs are fixed regardless of how many days you spend in Orlando. If airfare and related costs are $1500, the per-day travel cost on a five-day vacation is $300. On a ten-day trip, the per-day travel cost drops in half, to only $150 per day. Second, at press time adding the fifth to tenth day on your Disney World theme park ticket is only an additional $10.65 (including tax) per day. A four-day child base ticket costs $304 with tax. That's $76 per day. An eight-day child base ticket costs $346 with tax. That's just $43 per day. Of course, days five through eight come with other costs like dining, souvenirs, and lodging, but one long stay is often much less expensive than two shorter stays.

If this is a once-in-a-lifetime visit, we recommend trying to stretch your vacation dollars to eight nights and nine days. This allows for the equivalent of a full day at Animal Kingdom and Hollywood Studios, in addition to two days at Epcot and two or three full days at Magic Kingdom. The longer trip length also offers flexibility in late arrivals and early departures. You may elect to leave Epcot one afternoon at 3pm to head off to the Grand Floridian Resort & Spa for afternoon tea with Alice from *Alice in Wonderland*. With an eight-night stay, there's plenty of time to return to Epcot without fear of missing anything. On a four-night trip, there's more pressure to stay in the park and tour until the last member of the family drops. It's either that or potentially miss out on key attractions that could be made up with a longer stay.

If time and budget don't allow, a shorter trip can be perfectly enjoyable, particularly if you're already planning a trip farther down the road. Two trips spread out over the years offer an opportunity to enjoy two potentially different experiences, while also providing more time to save for the hefty costs. (It also affords a great opportunity to purchase two of our guidebooks, which is pretty fantastic in itself.)

Deciding on a trip length that maximizes value and enjoyment varies a bit based on age:

KIDS FIVE AND YOUNGER tend to enjoy Magic Kingdom the most, where Fantasyland and most entertainment offerings cater specifically to their heights and maturity levels. Kids at that age may have no interest in visiting Disney Springs or Animal Kingdom. In this situation, a three- or four-day trip focused on visiting Magic Kingdom offers plenty of time to visit over multiple half days, in addition to affording opportunities to head back to the resort for naps.

MOST KIDS BETWEEN FIVE AND EIGHT will still prefer Magic Kingdom over the other major theme parks, but will get more out of trips to Animal Kingdom, Epcot, and Hollywood Studios. Plan to spend at least a half day at each of these three, pushing the number of theme park days up to five or six.

MOST KIDS EIGHT AND OLDER will be tall enough to ride every major attraction, including the thrill rides at each theme park, and mature enough to enjoy them all. Still plan at least two days at Magic Kingdom, but add full days at each of the other major theme parks (and, if you can, even more at Epcot) to take care of attractions like Soarin' and Rock 'n' Roller Coaster.

The Value of Time Away from the Parks

Many first-time visitors equate time away from the theme parks as time wasted or value lost. This seems logical on the surface. After all, if theme park tickets are going to cost $350 a pop, we sure as heck better be in the theme parks waiting in line for *something*. But don't make the most common rookie mistake.

Touring the theme parks in Florida, by their very nature, is exhausting—particularly during the unrelenting summer when it's 85 degrees by 10:30am. It's a lot of standing. It's a lot of walking. If the kids are in strollers, it's a lot of pushing. In fact, it's not uncommon at all for guests to rack up five or more miles a day walking through the theme park. Just a quick lap around Epcot's World Showcase Lagoon is 1.2 miles. And that's without doing anything!

Time spent together back at the resort hotel will likely be some of the most fun, most rewarding experiences of the trip. One of Josh's favorite memories from his first visit to Disney World is sitting on the beach at the Polynesian with his brother, mom, and dad holding a Mickey ice cream bar in one hand and a hot cocoa in the other. Dave has fond memories of playing on the beach at the Contemporary with his mom and sister while his dad napped back in the room. Spending time with loved ones is a big part of a vacation and spending relaxing time together with Walt Disney World as the backdrop is an integral part of the experience.

Afternoon breaks are particularly necessary with young kids (or dads) who will be bombarded with sensory overload virtually every moment they spend in the parks. A child that's spent a few hours back at the pool will be a much happier camper when it comes time to stake out a spot for IllumiNations that night. And, as an added bonus, those afternoons are also the busiest and hottest parts of the day at the theme parks. Where would you rather be? In a 25-minute-long line for a $4 Smartwater in the scorching afternoon sun, or back at the resort sipping a Mai Tai on the beach?

If It's Your Only Visit, Aim for Nine Days in Orlando

Returning visitors have the flexibility of choosing to spend less time at the theme parks and more time enjoying their resort and the other amenities Walt Disney World offers. But the four major theme parks—the Magic Kingdom, Epcot, Disney's Hollywood Studios, and Disney's Animal Kingdom—are the heart of a Walt Disney World experience. To fully appreciate the best they have to offer, you need about eight days:

- About a day each at the Animal Kingdom and Hollywood Studios
- At least a full day and an additional evening at Epcot
- Two to three days at the Magic Kingdom
- A couple of days taking it easy

Add it up and you're looking at about seven full days in Orlando with a travel day on both ends, bringing the total number of vacation days up to nine.

SHORTER "ONLY" VISITS

Shorter "only" visits are doable with some compromises:

FIVE FULL DAYS To see most of the best of Disney World, five full days in the parks are about the minimum—two in the Magic Kingdom, and one more in each of the other three parks. Working some of this park time into your arrival or departure days will give you some needed time off in the middle of your visit.

SIX FULL DAYS Adding another day lets you have more time off and more time at Epcot.

LONGER "ONLY" VISITS

If you are fortunate enough to enjoy more than nine days in Orlando, first prioritize time spent away from the parks. Time is a luxury at Walt Disney World, and more time means more sleeping in, more late park arrivals, and more time relaxing at the pool. Late arrivals are particularly advantageous with the invention of FastPass+, which offers the ability to schedule three high priority attractions for later in the day, far in advance of setting foot inside the theme park. For example, with two days of late arrivals at Epcot, you can schedule Soarin', Character Spot, and Spaceship Earth on day one, and Test Track, Mission: SPACE, and Turtle Talk with Crush on day two. Show up at 11am and you'll be able to walk on six of the most popular attractions over those two days with minimal waits. Experiencing Soarin', Test Track, Mission: SPACE, Spaceship Earth, Character Spot, and Turtle Talk with Crush over the course of just one day will require a very early morning, much more walking, and a carefully crafted plan. It's doable, but it requires a much longer, more intense day.

CONSIDERING ARRIVAL DAYS

If you are planning a nine-day visit, we suggest a trip that spans the nine days from Saturday to the following Sunday because it best fits the typical week off work. The sample itineraries presented in Chapter Six will guide you through planning such a visit.

Of course, flexible visitors may prefer to arrive another day of the week, for the sake of saving time and money. Disney World tends to be busiest on weekends as local passholders push up attendance. If possible, design your vacation to maximize the number of weekday theme park visits. As a bonus, Disney resort rates are typically higher on Friday and Saturday nights by $20 to $150. (The higher upcharges are in the more expensive rooms during the more expensive seasons.) Avoiding these nights will save money and reduce waits.

Airfare is typically cheapest on Tuesdays and Saturdays, and there may be other travel expenses that can be reduced by traveling on certain days. Guests with flexible schedules should use services like KAYAK.COM or GOOGLE.COM/FLIGHTS to search out the cheapest or most convenient itinerary possible.

When deciding how long to stay, keep in mind that most travel costs are fixed, and the per-day cost of theme park tickets goes down as more days are added. Longer vacations allow more flexibility, in addition to providing more opportunities to experience everything Walt Disney World has to offer. Shorter Walt Disney World vacations tend to be more of a whirlwind experience. That isn't necessarily bad, but the go, go, go mentality often leaves first-time visitors thinking they need a vacation from their vacation upon returning home.

When to Go

In picking dates, it's important to consider crowd levels, pricing, weather, possible refurbishments, and special events. Our specialty is honing in on the less crowded times to visit, when wait times are lower at attractions, lines are shorter at stores and quick service venues, and there's less congestion inside the parks. Lower crowds means being able to do more in a less stressful environment. From there, we typically prioritize resort pricing, followed by weather, refurbishments, and special events.

CROWDS Walt Disney World is the most crowded when hordes of U.S. school kids are out of school: from early June through the third week in August, Thanksgiving week, Christmas and New Year's weeks, President's Day week, the spring break month of March; and the weeks before and after Easter. Other dates see an ebb and flow of mostly low and moderate crowds, all noted in the month-by-month calendar that follows.

PRICING Disney resort pricing is constantly fluctuating, so much so that the same exact room can cost $224 one night and $261 the next night, as it does at Port Orleans Riverside from December 10-11. Picking less expensive dates may save $150–300 per night at the deluxe resorts. Disney calls periods of different prices "Price Seasons": value, regular, summer, fall, etc. Fortunately, the less crowded times are also often the least expensive.

WEATHER The main weather points that concern us are summer heat and humidity, erratic winter highs and lows, and the peak of the hurricane season from mid-August to early October. Many of the least crowded and least expensive stretches suffer from weather issues, but none of these issues is routinely as challenging as the heat and humidity of the crowded summer months.

REFURBISHMENTS Disney tends to announce refurbishments about eight weeks in advance, making it difficult to plan a vacation around an unexpected major refurbishment. Fortunately, refurbishments follow a pattern, and we've identified when they're less likely to occur. In addition, it's rare that more than one or two major attractions are closed at the same time.

SPECIAL EVENTS Certain guests, particularly those returning, may want to plan a vacation around a special event like Star Wars Weekends or the Epcot Food and Wine Festival. Our month-by-month calendar identifies these special events and offers some advice on taking advantage of them, or how best to avoid them, depending on your needs.

Based on these factors—but especially low crowds and lower prices—we recommend the following weeks throughout the year:

- From the day after the Martin Luther King Day holiday in January until the Thursday before President's Day in February
- The Sunday after President's Day through the first week of March
- The week that begins the Sunday after Easter until mid-May
- September after Labor Day through the end of the month
- The last two weeks of October
- November after Veterans Day until the Saturday before Thanksgiving
- The two weeks beginning the Sunday after Thanksgiving

Among these, Josh especially recommends the late January and early February dates, with the lowest prices (prices go up February 7), comfortable day-time temperatures, and some of the lowest crowds of the year. Dave prefers the two weeks after Thanksgiving, which marry below average crowds and prices with Disney World's astonishing Christmas displays and offerings like Holidays Around the World and Mickey's Very Merry Christmas Party.

Those embarking on a possible once-in-a-lifetime trip should note that the peak of the hurricane season ends in early October, and that a few rides are almost invariably closed for refurbishments in January and early February.

This chapter begins with summaries of what you can expect of weekly crowds, resort prices, and weather.

Next, it presents detailed overviews of each of the months of the year, discussing prices, weather, crowds, refurbishments, special events, and recommended times to visit that month.

Finally, for first timers who may never return, it presents Dave's chart that ranks all the weeks of the year based on crowds, pricing, weather, and other essential variables.

Crowds and When to Go

When considering "low crowds", it's important to remember that Walt Disney World comprises four of the top ten busiest theme parks in the world, by overall attendance. Magic Kingdom averages around 52,000 guests per day. The days with the lowest attendance tend to see slightly north of 30,000 guests, while anything over 55,000 will result in much longer lines. Epcot averages about 30,000 guests per day. It's rare that the park sees fewer than 20,000 people, while anything above 35,000 will result in longer lines.

Each park suffers from bottlenecks and narrow walkways, in addition to succumbing to periodic mass exoduses from shows throughout the day. From there, certain attractions are extremely popular, with demand far outstripping supply. For example, let's take a look at Toy Story Mania at Disney's Hollywood Studios, one of the most popular rides in any theme park and often the one with the longest peak waits. The attraction moves through about 900 people an hour and the Studios' average attendance is around 27,500 people a day. On an average day with the Studios open from 9am–8pm, there are 9,900 total rides to share among 27,500 people. And it only takes 900 of those 27,500 people (or just 3.2%) in front of you to hit a 60-minute standby wait. (Disney will be opening extra capacity at Toy Story Mania soon.)

With ony five rides and ten more shows and other attractions, the headlining Studios' attractions see 40- to 70-minute peak waits even on the least crowded days. Don't be too discouraged, however. Just because everyone else waits 75 minutes in line doesn't mean you have to. Our touring tips and the cheat sheets that follow in Chapter Seven will reduce waits to virtually nothing.

In the chart on the following page, don't focus on small differences. Try to go during a lower crowd week, with a crowd ranking of four or less, and avoid higher crowd weeks, with rankings of eight or higher.

Disney World 2016 Crowd Calendar

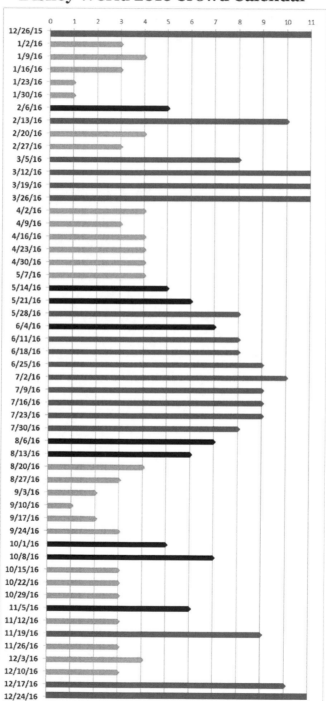

Prices and When to Go

The major prices at Walt Disney World that vary by season are hotel room costs. "Season" does not mean anything so simple as fall or winter. Disney changes prices much more frequently than that, and has a metastasizing group of invented seasonal names—e.g., not just Value Season, but also Value Season 1 and Value Season 2—to describe its price levels. Disney's price season names (excluding variants like Value Season 2 and some holiday and special event weekends) are

- Value
- Fall
- Regular
- Summer
- Peak
- Easter
- Holiday

The first two seasons are always the lowest-priced, and the last three always the highest. Disney groups hotels into value, moderate, and deluxe resorts (more on this in the next chapter). At Disney's value resorts, Summer rates are much higher than Regular rates; at its moderates, Summer and Regular are about the same over a multi-day visit; and at deluxe resorts, Summer rates are lower than Regular rates. Moreover, deluxe seasons change according to a different calendar in the summer and fall than value and moderate seasons do.

For exact prices by day, search for "Mousesavers 2016 Disney World Room Rates" and follow the links. The chart on the following page shows different resort prices at Walt Disney World over the year in 2016. It does not refer to the seasons themselves, as it's much more useful to show actual prices. The chart picks an example from each group, and to smooth out fluctuations that come from weekend upcharges, averages prices over an eight-night stay.

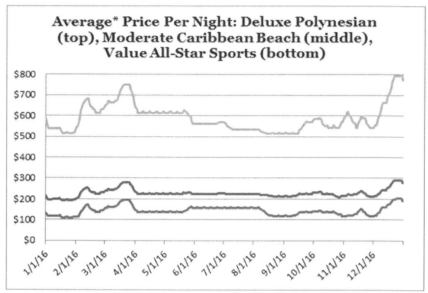

Average* Price Per Night: Deluxe Polynesian (top), Moderate Caribbean Beach (middle), Value All-Star Sports (bottom)

*Average of next 8 nights by arrival date, standard room, including tax

Weather and When to Go

This chart shows the range of high temperatures at Disney World. The middle line is the average high. There's a 20% chance highs will be lower than the lower line, and a 20% chance that highs will be higher than the higher line. Note the big range of temperatures in the winter months.

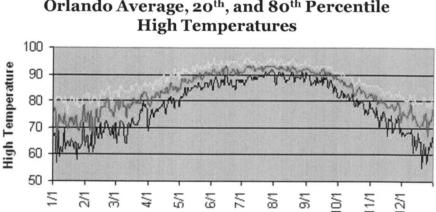

Orlando Average, 20th, and 80th Percentile High Temperatures

Month-by-Month
Comments on When to Go

JANUARY

COST Most of January enjoys the least expensive resort pricing of the year, but January 1–2, 2016, with Holiday season pricing, are among the most expensive nights of the year. The Friday-Sunday periods of the WDW Marathon (Jan. 7–9) and Martin Luther King Jr. weekends see average pricing. (See earlier in this chapter for more on pricing.)

WEATHER It's the coldest month in Orlando, with erratic temperatures and an average high of 69 and an average low of 50 degrees. Historically, it rains on 22% of days.

CROWDS Many U.S. school districts continue winter break through the first week, causing some of the highest crowds of the year to persist through the first Saturday of the new year. Crowds are low the rest of the month, with two major exceptions. Marathon Weekend brings in thousands of runners and their families, but they have surprisingly little impact on theme park crowds, resulting in only average crowds. Martin Luther King Jr. weekend crowds, from January 15–18, are well above average and the highest crowd level we'll see until President's Day weekend in the middle of February. It's best avoided.

REFURBISHMENTS January usually sees the most refurbishments, including brief closures at most resort pools and typically lengthier closures at a few other attractions. Splash Mountain usually closes for at least a month beginning the second week. The vast majority of attractions remain operating. Blizzard Beach will likely be closed through mid-March.

SPECIAL EVENTS THAT MAY AFFECT CROWDS OR YOUR STAY:

- The WDW Marathon impacts transportation on the morning of the half- and full-marathons. It's best to take Disney transportation.
- Several holiday events, including the Osborne Lights at Hollywood Studios, continue through the first week in January.
- Beginning in mid-January, avoid the large tour groups that become common.

BEST TIME TO VISIT January 19 and later has cool weather, some of the lowest crowds of the year, and the lowest Disney hotel prices of the year.

FEBRUARY

COST The lowest pricing of the year continues up until the Sunday a week before President's Day weekend, when prices rise to the average Regular season level. The Thursday before President's Day weekend prices rise again to the expensive Peak season. Peak pricing continues through the week following President's Day. Prices fall back to average February 21, 2016, and stay at that level into early March.

WEATHER The average high is 72 degrees and the average low 53, but temperatures are erratic and highs can get into the low 80s or dip well below 60. Precipitation is relatively low, but it does rain on about 23% of days.

CROWDS Crowds are below average to average through the Wednesday before President's Day weekend, when crowds are well above average (as well as on the week following it). Crowds return to average from the last week in February through the first week in March.

REFURBISHMENTS Most refurbishments will be completed by mid-February. A water park usually remains closed.

SPECIAL EVENTS THAT MAY AFFECT CROWDS OR YOUR STAY:
- The Princess Half Marathon (Feb. 18–21) is scheduled the weekend after President's Day. It affects transportation in the early morning on Sunday and keeps crowds above average until the Saturday following President's Day.
- Superbowl Sunday (Feb. 7) sees few locals visiting, reducing crowds.
- Valentine's Day (Feb. 14) makes it harder to secure dinner reservations, but does not affect attendance.
- The Atlanta Braves MLB baseball team returns to the ESPN Wide World of Sports Complex in mid-February for spring training.

BEST TIME TO VISIT A trip during the first week and a half before peak season pricing goes into effect is best, with the first week of February seeing the lowest prices and some of the lowest crowds of the year.

MARCH

COST March 1–4 is Regular season with average pricing across the resorts. The rest is Peak season and then Easter season with some of the highest prices of the year.

WEATHER Temperatures warm, but remain erratic. Expect highs anywhere from the mid-60s to the mid-80s with an average high of 77 and an average low of 57 degrees, with minimal precipitation.

CROWDS Expect average crowds the first week, followed by some of the heaviest crowds of the year the rest of the month due to spring breaks.

REFURBISHMENTS Pool closures remain common, and Blizzard Beach likely will remain closed through mid-March. Attraction closures are less common.

SPECIAL EVENTS THAT MAY AFFECT CROWDS OR YOUR STAY:

- The Epcot International Flower and Garden Festival will begin on March 2 and continue through May 15. The Festival brings millions of flowers, Disney-themed topiaries, and special activities around the Park, in addition to kiosks in World Showcase offering food and beverage samples that generally cost $2–$7 each. The Festival does not adversely affect daily crowds.

BEST TIME TO VISIT February 27 through March 5 will have the lowest crowds and prices of the month.

APRIL

COST The Easter weeks, which comprise Easter Sunday and the weeks before and after the holiday, are among the most expensive of 2016. Avoid March 20 through April 2 if possible. Prices return to average on April 3 and stay that way for the rest of the month.

WEATHER April warms up to some of the most comfortable weather of the year, with an average high of 82 degrees and an average low of 62. Precipitation remains low with chances at 18%.

CROWDS Heavy spring break crowds continue through one week after Easter Sunday. Beginning Monday, April 4, average level crowds return through early May.

REFURBISHMENTS Pool closures are rare, and few attractions are typically closed.

SPECIAL EVENTS THAT MAY AFFECT CROWDS OR YOUR STAY:

- The Star Wars Half Marathon weekend, new to Walt Disney World in 2016, is April 14–17. It affects transportation in the early mornings, but will have little impact on crowds.
- The Epcot International Flower and Garden Festival continues through April. See "March" for details.

BEST TIME TO VISIT Begin a trip at least one week after Easter Sunday when crowds and resort prices fall from some of the highest levels of the year to average.

MAY

COST May 1–26 is Regular season, with average resort pricing, before prices rise slightly from May 27–29 for Memorial Day. Then it's Summer season, when Value and Moderate resort prices are higher than Regular, but lower than Peak. Deluxe Summer prices are actually lower than Regular season by a few dollars.

WEATHER Temperatures rise significantly in May, with an average high of 87 and an average low of 69 degrees. The weather gets wetter and more humid as you move closer to June.

CROWDS Crowds are average to slightly above average through the Thursday before Memorial Day weekend. The earlier in May, the less crowded it will be. May 28–30 (Memorial Day weekend) is busier than the rest of May, but not as busy as other major holidays like Easter.

REFURBISHMENTS Rare.

SPECIAL EVENTS THAT MAY AFFECT CROWDS OR YOUR STAY:

- The Epcot International Flower and Garden Festival continues through May 15. See "March" for details.
- Star Wars Weekends brings *Star Wars* characters for meet and greets, special celebrity autograph sessions, a parade, and weekend fireworks to Disney's Hollywood Studios. The event runs Fridays–Sundays, beginning in mid-May. Hollywood Studios will see some of its heaviest crowds of the year on these days. With the exception of Memorial Day Weekend, when Friday is the best day to visit, Sunday is the least crowded day at the Star Wars Weekends due to people traveling and those attending on Friday or Saturday because they can't wait until Sunday.

BEST TIME TO VISIT Any time between May 1–14, with average crowds and resort pricing, cooler and drier days than later in the month, and the Flower and Garden Festival in full swing. You also won't need to worry about the Star Wars Weekend crowds at Hollywood Studios.

JUNE
....

COST All of June is Summer season. At the Values and Moderates, pricing is slightly lower than Peak Season. At the Deluxe Resorts, pricing is actually slightly lower than Regular Season and significantly less than Peak Season.

WEATHER June is hot, with an average high of 90 and an average low of 72 degrees. Precipitation inches up with a 38% chance and the highest accumulation of precipitation of the year.

CROWDS June is among the busiest months of the year as schools let out for summer and as South American tour groups drive crowds significantly upwards. Daily crowds are lower than Easter or Christmas weeks, but busier than just about any other time.

REFURBISHMENTS Rare.

SPECIAL EVENTS THAT MAY AFFECT CROWDS OR YOUR STAY:

- Star Wars Weekends continue through mid-June. See "May" for details.

- The "Sounds Like Summer" concert series will happen in June and July in Epcot outside the American Adventure Pavilion in the World Showcase. This series of cover bands doesn't make crowds any larger than they would be otherwise.

- Tour groups are common in June and July. If you see (or hear) a group of young kids walking around behind a 20-year-old carrying a flag, head in the opposite direction.

BEST TIME TO VISIT June 5–11 will have slightly lower crowds than later in the month, in addition to reduced precipitation and slightly lower temperatures.

JULY

COST All of July is Summer season at the Values and Moderates, with prices slightly higher than Regular Season and slightly lower than Peak Season. At the Deluxes, the first week and half is Summer season, with pricing slightly lower than Regular season. After Juy 9, deluxe pricing is reduced further to Value season 2. The only exception is July 1–3, with pricing $10–$40 more per night than the rest of the month.

WEATHER July is among the hottest months in Orlando, with an average high of 91 and an average low of 74 degrees. Even worse than the heat is the humidity, which averages about 75%. Rain showers also increase in July, with a 49% chance of precipitation on any given day.

CROWDS Fourth of July crowds are the largest of the summer. The rest of July is the first or second busiest month overall because almost all U.S. kids are out of school. International visitation is also at its highest point of the year. Most other months have at least some portion where crowds will be significantly smaller, but not July. It is crowded every day. Crowds are slightly lower towards the end of the month.

REFURBISHMENTS Rare.

SPECIAL EVENTS THAT MAY AFFECT CROWDS OR YOUR STAY:

- Magic Kingdom offers a special fireworks show on July 3 and 4. The July 3 show is slightly less crowded. Epcot hosts special events and meet and greets in the United States Pavilion throughout the Fourth, and offers a special IllumiNations show with several extra minutes of intense fireworks. Hollywood Studios also offers a special fireworks show. The Magic Kingdom show is the best, but Epcot and Hollywood Studios crowds are more manageable.

- The "Sounds Like Summer" concert at Epcot continues. See "June" for details.
- Tour groups remain common.

BEST TIME TO VISIT As late in July as possible is best. International visitation wanes and pricing at the Deluxes is lower.

AUGUST

COST Deluxe prices continue low throughout August, dropping even a bit more on August 14. Summer season at the Values and Moderates, with prices slightly higher than Regular season and slightly lower than Peak, continues through August 14. On August 15, the Values and Moderates drop to the Regular season, and then on August 19 drop again to the Fall season, one of the lower priced seasons.

WEATHER August is one of the hottest months in Orlando, with an average high of 91 and an average low of 75 degrees. Peak hurricane season begins in the third week. Hurricanes have not directly impacted Disney World since 2004, but they and lesser storms may affect flights and bring nasty weather. Showers and thunderstorms are common in the afternoons, with a 43% chance of precipitation.

CROWDS The first two weeks in August are as crowded as the rest of the summer. Crowds diminish beginning the third week in August as kids start the new school year and are the lowest of the summer in the final week. Guests with flexible schedules are best served waiting until September when crowds are significantly lower.

REFURBISHMENTS Rare.

SPECIAL EVENTS THAT MAY AFFECT CROWDS OR YOUR STAY:
- None.

BEST TIME TO VISIT The last week in August is the least crowded since early May.

SEPTEMBER

COST September sees a mixture of Value, Fall, and Regular price seasons. All prices are below average. Value and Moderate prices, while still low compared to most other dates, are higher earlier in the month than in prior years, as the price season then is now Fall instead of Value.

WEATHER September is just barely cooler than the summer months with an average high of 89 and an average low of 74 degrees. Humidity remains extremely high, and there is a good chance thunderstorms or rain will disrupt most afternoons and some evenings. Historically, it rains 40% of days in September. Peak hurricane season continues.

CROWDS Crowds are at their lowest levels of the year during the first three weeks in September. The only time you may find less people in the parks is certain days toward the end of January and the first two weeks in February, making it an excellent time to visit as far as crowds are concerned. September 5–7 will be the busiest days due to the Labor Day holiday, but even those three days will have significantly smaller crowds than any of the days over the summer.

REFURBISHMENTS The frequency of attraction refurbishments increases with the lower crowds. Expect a few rides to be down.

SPECIAL EVENTS THAT MAY AFFECT CROWDS OR YOUR STAY:

- *Mickey's Not So Scary Halloween Party* will include several dates beginning in mid-September. It requires a separate ticket to attend. The Party runs from 7pm until midnight, with ticket holders typically allowed to enter as early as 4pm. The Party's main features are a unique parade, fireworks show, and trick-or-treating throughout the park. Most rides are operating. This event closes the Magic Kingdom at 7pm for visitors without a ticket to the Halloween Party. The Magic Kingdom is actually less busy on days when there is a Halloween Party because it closes early. If you have park hopper tickets, you may want to start at Magic Kingdom and then hop to another park to end the day. Without a park hopper, consider a dinner reservation at one of the resorts connected by the monorail or watercraft and, then proceed to the beach or lookout area at the resort to watch the fireworks. Tuesday Parties are the least crowded.

- *Night of Joy* is a contemporary Christian concert series that is moving to the Wide World of Sports in 2016, after having taken place inside Magic Kingdom after-hours for years. Night of Joy participants will receive admission to Magic Kingdom during the day with bus transportation offered to Wide World of Sports for the event.

- *The Epcot Food and Wine Festival* will begin in later September. It runs every day through early November. There are also bands performing throughout the Festival outside at the American Gardens Theater for free. It's a fun event with interesting food, educational classes, and several expensive dinners. During the Festival, Epcot is extremely busy on weekends, and weekdays in World Showcase are also busier.

BEST TIME TO VISIT Any September date before Food and Wine begins will have low crowds and some of the lowest prices of the year, especially when considering the likelihood of significant discounts. Any date later in the month to the beginning of October is still more than do-able with well below-average crowds, other than the weekends at Epcot.

OCTOBER

COST Most of October is a mix of Fall season and Regular season 2, with pricing slightly below average. Columbus Day weekend (Oct. 8–10) is the exception, with average pricing.

WEATHER Weather cools slightly with an average high of 84 and an average low of 68 degrees. Precipitation is much lower than the summer months, with a 26% chance of showers on any given day. Peak hurricane season ends early in the month.

CROWDS Crowds are heavier in October than in past years with domestic school schedules moving towards week-long fall breaks. South American attendance is also higher in the first two weeks, culminating in the largest crowds of the month over Columbus Day weekend. Still, they won't be anywhere near as bad as summer or other holiday weekends. If you are flexible with your dates, hold off until after October 15.

REFURBISHMENTS Expect a couple minor attractions to be closed briefly throughout the month.

SPECIAL EVENTS THAT MAY AFFECT CROWDS OR YOUR STAY:

- *The Gartner Symposium* likely will return to the Swan, Dolphin, Beach Club, and Yacht Club in early October. All of the Epcot-area resorts will be sold out, and most of the restaurants in the area will be booked solid for those dates. The convention does not affect theme park attendance, except for Epcot, which is busier in the evenings.
- *Mickey's Not So Scary Halloween Party* includes many dates throughout October. See "September" for details.
- *Epcot's International Food and Wine Festival* continues daily through early November. See "September" for details.

BEST TIME TO VISIT October 22 through the end of the month is the best time to visit in October, with average crowds, cooler weather, and plenty of opportunities to enjoy Mickey's Not So Scary Halloween Party and the Food and Wine Festival.

NOVEMBER

COST With the exception of Thanksgiving week (Nov. 19–26), all of November is Fall season, with pricing slightly higher than Value season 2 and lower than Regular season. Thanksgiving week sees pricing about equal to a weekend during Regular season, which is less than Peak season and other major holidays.

WEATHER It's noticeably cooler than September and October, with an average high of 76 and an average low of 59 degrees. November introduces more variability in high and low temperatures than the summer. Humidity is also substantially lower, with a 23% chance of precipitation. For those who like warm, but not uncomfortably hot temperatures, November is the perfect month to visit.

CROWDS Crowds are surprisingly light for the majority of November, with two major exceptions. The first is November 10–13, due to a phenomenon known as "Jersey Week" combining with, we expect, the Wine and Dine Half Marathon. All New Jersey schools are off the Thursday and Friday of the first full week of November, and many families from the state travel to Disney World during that week and/or weekend. This raises crowd levels significantly, particularly at Epcot and Magic Kingdom. Second, Thanksgiving week is very crowded.

REFURBISHMENTS Typically a few minor attractions.

SPECIAL EVENTS THAT MAY AFFECT CROWDS OR YOUR STAY:
- *Mickey's Very Merry Christmas Party* begins in early November and happens several other evenings throughout the month. It requires a separate ticket to attend. Like Mickey's Not So Scary Halloween Party, this Party includes a unique parade, fireworks show, and several special stage shows. Cocoa and cookies take the place of trick-or-treating candy. The Party runs from 7pm–12am, with Party ticket holders allowed to enter as early as 4pm. Because of the 7pm closures for regular guests, other nights that have late closures, fireworks, and the evening parade are wildly crowded at the Magic Kingdom. Unlike the Halloween Party, where the first few parties are typically the least crowded, the first few Christmas Parties typically sell out due to elevated crowds for Veterans Day and the Wine and Dine Half Marathon.
- *Epcot's International Food and Wine Festival* continues daily through mid-November. See "September" for details.
- *Holidays Around the World* in Epcot begins on Friday, November 25. Disney brings in storytellers to tell holiday stories and explain unique traditions in many of the World Showcase countries. Santa Claus meets in the U.S. Pavilion. In addition, the Candlelight Processional is an amazing stage show featuring the voices of famous celebrities, a large choir, and a 50-piece orchestra. The show, which tells the story of Christmas, is put on three times throughout the night (5pm, 6:45pm, and 8pm) and lasts about 40 minutes. IllumiNations, the nightly fireworks and laser show, also includes several holiday-only effects that you won't want to miss. Holidays Around the World will increase crowds to the World Showcase in the evening, especially on the weekends.
- The Osborne Family Spectacle of Dancing Lights will not be shown in 2016.

BEST TIME TO VISIT November 13–19 is the best time to visit with the lowest crowds of the month and low resort pricing. You'll have plenty of opportunities to see the Magic Kingdom Castle Lighting and to attend Mickey's Very Merry Christmas Party. Consider a visit over the first week in November if you'd prefer to attend the Food and Wine Festival.

DECEMBER

COST Fall season continues with prices slightly below average through December 10, 2016. Peak season, with well-above-average pricing, begins December 11 and the highest prices of the year, the Holiday season, begin December 22.

WEATHER Expect erratic temperatures throughout December. It is not uncommon for one day to be in the low 60s and the next day to be in the high 70s. Nonetheless, the average high is 72 and the average low is 53 degrees, making most afternoons comfortable and most evenings a little chilly. Precipitation remains low with a 22% chance.

CROWDS Crowds are slightly below average to average through December 16. Beginning December 17, some of the heaviest crowds of the year arrive, with the highest crowds of the year from December 25–31.

REFURBISHMENTS Expect a few minor attraction closures for brief stints.

SPECIAL EVENTS THAT MAY AFFECT CROWDS OR YOUR STAY:

- The ABC Christmas Day Parade taping is likely to be scheduled for December 2 and 3. Most of Main Street will be closed off December 3. Expect additional delays in Frontierland and Liberty Square as the floats are moved to Main Street, on top of incredibly heavy crowds due to the fact it's a Saturday with long hours and night-time entertainment in the midst of Mickey's Party season. December 3 is best avoided, while the 2nd is less impacted as the bulk of the taping occurs before park opening.

- Pop Warner brings its youth football Super Bowl to Disney World over the first full week of December. Pop Warner does not have a substantial impact on theme park attendance, but it does have a serious impact at the resorts where kids and their families stay. Pop Warner families typically receive hefty discounts at the All-Stars, Coronado Springs, and Caribbean Beach. If planning a trip over the first full week of December, consider booking another resort to avoid thousands of largely unchaperoned kids.

- Mickey's Christmas Party continues through several dates in December, with the last party likely on December 16. See "November" for details.

- Holidays Around the World in Epcot runs through December 30. See "November" for details.
- The Osborne Family Spectacle of Dancing Lights will not be shown in 2016.

NEW YEAR'S EVE CELEBRATIONS Magic Kingdom hosts identical fireworks December 30 and 31. The 30th is slightly less crowded, but both days should fill to capacity in the afternoon. Epcot hosts a special IllumiNations on the 31st with several minutes of outstanding fireworks at the end. Dance parties throughout World Showcase continue into the late night. Hollywood Studios shoots fireworks off from behind and on top of the buildings around Hollywood Boulevard to live music. The Studios' show is the easiest to see, and Animal Kingdom is the least crowded park to visit during the day.

BEST TIME TO VISIT Try to end the trip by December 11 to take advantage of below-average crowds, below-average resort pricing, and everything the Christmas season has to offer.

When to Go If It's Your Only Visit

A family looking at a once-in-a-lifetime trip should aim to visit at a less-crowded time when refurbishments and weather are less likely to negatively impact the trip. Based on both this and the delights of the Disney Christmas program, Dave has ranked all the weeks of the year for first-timers who may never return, in the chart on the following page.

Choosing dates is easiest for those with flexible schedules. For vacationers with school-age children unwilling to take them out of school, or other date constraints, picking a date among the less desirable times of year may be a bit daunting. The good news is that you're in the best possible position to make an informed decision. From there, we'll help you save money and time in the following chapters, regardless of when you ultimately choose to visit.

2016 Weeks to Visit Rankings

Arrival Date	Week Rank	Crowd Ranking	Values Prices	Moderates Prices	Deluxes Prices	Other
Bold=Recommended Week for First-Time Visitors Who May Never Return						
12/26/15	46	11	Highest	Highest	Highest	Xmas Program
01/02/16	51	3	Low	Low	Moderate -	Ride Closures Common
01/09/16	52	4	Lower	Lower	Lower	Ride Closures Common
01/16/16	50	3	Lower	Lower	Lower	Ride Closures Common
01/23/16	48	1	Lowest	Lowest	Lowest	Ride Closures Common
01/30/16	49	1	Lowest	Lowest	Lowest	Some Ride Closures
02/06/16	53	5	Moderate	Moderate +	Moderate +	Some Ride Closures
02/13/16	41	10	Higher	Higher	Higher	
02/20/16	**14**	**4**	**Moderate**	**Moderate +**	**Moderate +**	
02/27/16	**8**	**3**	**Moderate**	**Moderate +**	**Moderate +**	
03/05/16	34	8	High	High	High	
03/12/16	43	11	High	High	High	
03/19/16	45	11	Highest	Highest	Highest	
03/26/16	44	11	Highest	Highest	Highest	
04/02/16	**15**	**4**	**Moderate**	**Moderate +**	**Moderate +**	
04/09/16	**7**	**3**	**Moderate**	**Moderate**	**Moderate +**	
04/16/16	**10**	**4**	**Moderate**	**Moderate**	**Moderate +**	
04/23/16	**11**	**4**	**Moderate**	**Moderate**	**Moderate +**	
04/30/16	**12**	**4**	**Moderate**	**Moderate**	**Moderate +**	
05/07/16	**13**	**4**	**Moderate**	**Moderate**	**Moderate +**	
05/14/16	16	5	Moderate	Moderate	Moderate +	
05/21/16	18	6	Moderate	Moderate +	Moderate +	
05/28/16	33	8	High	Moderate	Moderate	
06/04/16	21	7	High	Moderate	Moderate -	
06/11/16	32	8	High	Moderate	Moderate -	
06/18/16	31	8	High	Moderate	Moderate -	
06/25/16	38	9	High	Moderate	Moderate -	
07/02/16	40	10	Higher	Moderate	Moderate -	
07/09/16	37	9	High	Moderate	Lower	
07/16/16	36	9	High	Moderate	Lower	
07/23/16	35	9	High	Moderate	Lower	
07/30/16	30	8	High	Moderate	Lower	
08/06/16	20	7	High	Moderate	Lower	
08/13/16	29	6	Moderate -	Moderate	Lowest	Peak Hurricane Season
08/20/16	27	4	Low	Moderate -	Lowest	Peak Hurricane Season
08/27/16	25	3	Low	Moderate -	Lowest	Peak Hurricane Season
09/03/16	23	2	Low	Moderate -	Lowest	Peak Hurricane Season
09/10/16	22	1	Low	Moderate -	Lowest	Peak Hurricane Season
09/17/16	24	2	Moderate -	Moderate	Lower	Peak Hurricane Season
09/24/16	26	3	Moderate	Moderate	Moderate -	Peak Hurricane Season
10/01/16	28	5	Moderate	Moderate +	Moderate	Peak Hurricane Season
10/08/16	19	7	Moderate	Moderate +	Moderate	
10/15/16	**9**	**4**	**Moderate**	**Moderate**	**Low**	
10/22/16	**5**	**3**	**Moderate**	**Moderate -**	**Low**	
10/29/16	**6**	**3**	**Low**	**Low**	**Moderate -**	
11/05/16	17	6	Low	Moderate	Moderate +	Some Xmas Program
11/12/16	**4**	**3**	**Low**	**Moderate**	**Moderate -**	Some Xmas Program
11/19/16	39	9	Moderate +	High	Moderate	Some Xmas Program
11/26/16	**1**	**3**	**Low**	**Moderate -**	**Low**	Xmas Program
12/03/16	**2**	**4**	**Low**	**Moderate -**	**Low**	Xmas Program
12/10/16	**3**	**3**	**Moderate +**	**High**	**High**	Xmas Program
12/17/16	42	10	Higher	Higher	Higher	Xmas Program

Where to Stay

5

In this chapter we suggest that you stay in a Disney-owned resort hotel, either a value, moderate, or deluxe resort, based on your budget. Specifically, we recommend:

- **VALUE** Art of Animation, Pop Century
- **MODERATE** Port Orleans French Quarter, Port Orleans Riverside
- **DELUXE** Polynesian Village, Wilderness Lodge, Contemporary, Grand Floridian

The chapter begins by addressing the advantages and disadvantages of staying on-site in a Disney-owned hotel. We then discuss the key differences between Disney's value, moderate, and deluxe classes, and take a look at what specifically differentiates resorts within each class. Next we provide detailed reviews by resort class. The chapter finishes with alternatives to staying in a Disney resort.

Stay at a Disney World Owned Resort

More than 20 Disney-owned resorts dot the 40+ square miles that comprise Walt Disney World.

Another dozen hotels owned by third parties are also on Disney World property. Most are located in the far southeast corner of Disney World near Disney Springs (formerly known as Downtown Disney). Third-party hotels closer to the parks include the Swan and Dolphin, both about a 10-minute walk to Epcot and about 15 minutes away from Hollywood Studios. Another is Shades of Green, an armed forces recreation center with lodging for military personnel and their families, located right across the street from the Polynesian. Finally, the Four Seasons Resort Orlando, between Fort Wilderness and Port Orleans Riverside, is the first five-star resort on property, and it offers luxurious amenities (with pricing to match), including the best pool complex in all of Disney World. There's more on these non-Disney owned hotels on Disney World property, and also off-site options, near the end of this chapter.

The Disney-owned resorts are usually more expensive than hotels operated by third parties, but they are also typically:

- Much more fun
- Much more convenient
- Much more "Disney"

The Disney-owned hotels offer a laundry list of unique perks that third-party operators could never dream of providing. The most advantageous perks include:

- Free airport transport to and from your hotel via Disney's Magical Express.
- Free and frequent transport from your hotel to the parks, water-parks, and Disney Springs.
- Free parking at both your hotel and the parks.
- The right to book dining ten days further out than non-Disney guests, which can be critical for high-demand meals like dinner at Be Our Guest Restaurant.
- The right to book FastPass+ reservations for key attractions beginning 60 days in advance of arrival. All non-Disney guests except those staying at the Swan or Dolphin can book only up to 30 days before use—which may mean some attractions aren't available for pre-booking, and others may be available only at less convenient times.
- Access to the various Disney Dining Plans, which are a convenient budgeting tool if your family eats the way they are designed to feed you, and may save you a bit if your kids are younger than ten and you plan on several character meals.
- Keeping Disney magic real and definite: while it's easy to read a list of definable resort perks, it's more difficult to describe to a first-time visitor how it feels to be caught up in the completely immersive atmosphere of the Walt Disney World bubble. There are very few vacation destinations in the world that truly allow visitors to escape the harsh realities of life and instead be immersed in the fun and fantasy of a make-believe world. An inclusive on-property stay offers just that—from the time Magical Express picks you up at the airport to the moment they drop you off again, there's nothing to worry about at Disney World. Just keep your credit card handy.

The Perk We Rarely Recommend

Extra Magic Hours (EMH) are one of the best-known perks offered to guests staying at Disney-owned resorts, as well as at the Swan, Dolphin, and Shades of Green. (The Disney Springs Hilton no longer participates in EMH as of 2016.) EMH are early or late periods—most commonly at one park each day—when only guests at these hotels can ride the open Disney World attractions.

There are two varieties of Extra Magic Hours: morning and evening. Morning Extra Magic Hour is limited to one hour immediately before a park's regular open. Evening Extra Magic Hours are two hours long and begin immediately after a park's regular close. Most popular rides operate during both Morning and Evening Extra Magic, though the selection is wider during the evening. The participating attractions are indicated in Chapter 6. At least one park offers Extra Magic Hours virtually every day. Disney World experimented with multiple EMH schedules in 2015, and seems at press time to have settled on the following:

SUNDAY Hollywood Studios morning

MONDAY Animal Kingdom morning

TUESDAY Epcot evening

WEDNESDAY Magic Kingdom evening

THURSDAY Epcot morning

FRIDAY Magic Kingdom morning; Hollywood Studios evening

SATURDAY Animal Kingdom morning

Seasonal or special events may alter the schedule slightly, so check the park calendars. One good example is during Star Wars Weekends from the middle of May to the middle of June, when Hollywood Studios offers morning Extra Magic Hour on Wednesdays instead of Saturdays.

So why is the park with such a great benefit so rarely recommended? Over 25,000 rooms on property have the opportunity to "take advantage of EMH" and every guest checking in will receive a Times Guide with the Extra Magic Hours schedule for the week clearly listed. "Up to two exclusive hours inside the park" sounds so overwhelmingly positive that the majority of the 75,000+ resort guests staying on property choose the park with the "extra magic". In turn, the park(s) with Extra Magic Hours are usually the busiest from 10am–7pm because they attract so many extra people. Simply choosing a different park avoids these resort guests.

In addition, Morning EMHs begin at 8am or even 7am, and it's awfully hard to get the family up, bathed, clothed, fed, and on the way in time to actually take advantage of the extra time. Arriving late to the park with EMH completely negates any benefit. Evening EMHs are often late at night, making it more difficult to arrive at a park the next day before open when waits are often much shorter. Moreover, because Hollywood Studios and Epcot offer so few rides during EMH, wait times at them are usually just as long during evening EMH as they are during the day, negating much of the benefit.

There are a few ways to make Extra Magic Hours work:

- If you actually arrive in time to take advantage of the full morning EMH and can park hop (hopping, and its cost, is explained in Chapter 8) away from it in the afternoon, then you can have a tremendous amount of success during the extra hour, particularly at Magic Kingdom and Animal Kingdom. The morning EMH park will be busier than other days from 10am–7pm, and staying in the park during that time will lessen the benefit of the extra hour.

- Evening EMHs are less busy in the final hour, particularly at Magic Kingdom on nights its regular close is late. Those able to park hop to the evening EMH park at night and stay through EMH close often enjoy themselves if they begin with the "anytime attractions" we identify in Chapter 6.

It's easier to simply avoid the park with EMH and instead visit the less busy parks. You'll also be better rested and better able to enjoy the parks in the morning during a regular day.

How to Pick Your Disney Resort Hotel

The most important factor is budget. Standard value resort rooms range in price from $101/weeknight at the All-Stars during value season all the way up to $228/night at Art of Animation over Christmas. Standard rooms at the deluxes start at $325 at Animal Kingdom Lodge in the value season and go up to $886/night for a standard view at the Grand Floridian over the holidays. Larger rooms, better locations, and better views cost even more.

There are five different types of Disney resorts:

- **VALUE RESORTS** Lowest prices, smallest rooms, fewest amenities, no table service restaurants. (Value resort "Family Suite" rooms, available at Art of Animation and All-Star Music, come in at about twice the size of a standard room, but cost more than twice as much.)

- **MODERATE RESORTS** Middle-of-the-road prices, room sizes, and amenities. Table service restaurants at all but Port Orleans French Quarter.

- **DELUXE RESORTS** Highest prices, largest rooms, most amenities, plentiful dining.

- **DISNEY VACATION CLUB RESORTS** There are multiple deluxe-level room types: "Studios" are similar to deluxe rooms; "Villas" are larger and have full kitchens, and, at the two-bedroom and larger sizes, sleep eight people plus.

- **THE CAMPSITES AT DISNEY'S FORT WILDERNESS RESORT** Campgrounds for tent and RV campers (the Cabins at Fort Wilderness are grouped in the moderate class).

The vast majority of first time visitors stay in one of the first three resort types. The table below shows more detailed distinctions among them. Take heed of the notes at the bottom of the table...none of this is as easy as we'd all wish!

What You Can Expect by Price Class

Value Resorts	Moderate Resorts	Deluxe Resorts
Basic, small, ~260 square foot rooms	Good-sized ~314 square foot rooms	Lovely ~344-440 square foot rooms
Prices of $111–$148/night	Price of $206–$214/night	Prices of $367-$663/night
Two full beds sleeping 4	Most have two queen beds, sleep 4	Most sleep 5 on two queens and a daybed
Split baths	Split baths	Most have split baths
No coffeemakers	Coffeemakers	Coffeemakers
Basic exteriors	Lovely exteriors	Lovely exteriors
Basic landscaping	Lovely landscaping	Lovely landscaping
Basic pools	Nice pools with slides	Great pools with slides
Food court	Food court, plus table servcie at most	Food court at most; table service at all
Basic dining choices	Better dining at most	Best dining for adults and kids
Hourly luggage service	Bell luggage service	Bell luggage service
Buses to parks	Buses to parks	Room service
Pizza delivery	Pizza delivery	Fun park transport at most, also buses

NOTES

Excludes Family Suites, Cabins, DVC	Some rooms at CB and POR sleep 5	AKL and WL rooms sleep 4
Price: Weeknight Fall 2016 Price Season	Pirate rooms at CB have full beds	AKL has only bus transport to parks
Rooms can hold in addition one more child younger than 3 at check-in	POFQ has no table service	
	CS has room service	

Once you've set your budget, there's no one size fits all answer, but the material in this section, and detailed reviews later in this chapter, should help paint a clearer picture of which resort is the best fit for your group. The reviews focus on the standard room options at each of Disney's resorts, the Disney Vacation Club Studios, and also the popular family suites at Art of Animation and All-Star Music. For a more comprehensive look at the various Disney Vacation Club Villas and updates on the comings and goings of the resorts throughout the year, visit Dave's YOURFIRSTVISIT.NET.

Dave suggests picking hotels based first on overall kid appeal, mainly visual, and then on transportation convenience in a trip where the Magic Kingdom sees the most visits. Convenience to Epcot is prioritized second.

The chart below is derived from this methodology, with Dave's top picks at the top and on the right. Josh ranks resorts on a wider set of criteria, but largely arrives at the same results.

RESORTS SORTED BY CONVENIENCE AND KID APPEAL

Bold= Value Resort, *Italic* = Moderate Resort, <u>Underline</u> = Deluxe Resort

CONVENIENCE

Very Convenient	<u>Grand Floridian</u>	<u>Contemporary</u>	<u>Polynesian</u>
Convenient	<u>BoardWalk Inn and Villas</u> <u>Beach Club and Villas</u> <u>Yacht Club</u>		Wilderness Lodge and Villas Animal Kingdom Lodge and Villas **Art of Animation** **Pop Century**
Somewhat Convenient	*Port Orleans Riverside* *Port Orleans French Quarter* <u>Old Key West</u> <u>Saratoga Springs</u> *Fort Wilderness*	*Caribbean Beach* *Coronado Springs*	**All-Star Sports** **All-Star Movies** **All-Star Music**
KID APPEAL	Slight Kid Appeal	Some Kid Appeal	Great Kid Appeal

---

Jim's Gems
by Jim Korkis

When designing Walt Disney World, the Seven Seas Lagoon was to represent the seven major seas of the world and there would be several resorts associated with them. Asian, Persian, and Venetian resorts were planned, in addition to the Polynesian. Originally, the Polynesian was to look like a triangular island volcano twelve stories high with a South Seas restaurant at the top. For decorative purposes, real bamboo had been used in the resort, but it quickly split and rotted, forcing a replacement right before opening of fiberglass bamboo.

VALUE RESORTS

Art of Animation and Pop Century are the top two choices.

The distinctive features of the value resorts are their tiny 260-square-foot standard rooms, their terrific—but garish to the eyes of many adults—kid appeal, and their short list of resort amenities compared to what you'll find at the moderates and deluxes. For instance, a lot of first-time visitors are surprised that standard value rooms don't have coffeemakers. You also won't find bikes and other leisure activity rentals or table service restaurants at the values.

Standard value resort rooms sleep four in two full beds. You may also add a child younger than three in a crib. These rooms fit the needs of many first-time family visitors looking for low prices, as they won't be spending much time in them other than sleeping.

Family Suites at the All-Star Music (520 square feet) and Art of Animation (565 square feet) resorts are much larger, sleep six, and include coffee-makers in every room, but cost more than double the price of standard rooms.

Dave favors Art of Animation with its oversized icons of some of Disney's most popular contemporary properties like *Cars* and *Finding Nemo* that are sure to excite kids. Rooms are bright and cheery, from the deep red clam-shell-themed chairs to the oversize Ariel motif on the shower curtain. Josh loves Animation's detailed theming, but all its standard rooms are located in the Little Mermaid section, which is a five to seven minute walk from the main building. This is less of a concern if you're already planning to stay in one of its more convenient family suites. Pop rooms are blander and more generic looking with little in-room decoration. Some families and couples may prefer the subdued theming at Pop, while others favor the over-the-top décor at Animation. Otherwise, Pop standard rooms usually run $15–$30 less per night than standard rooms at Art of Animation. Both resorts are newer than the All-Stars, provide dedicated bus service, offer elevated fare at the quick services, and feature more robust Disney-inspired theming.

The other value resorts—All-Star Sports, All-Star Music, and All-Star Movies—cost about $10 per night less than Pop, but they're also significantly farther away from Magic Kingdom and Epcot. The three All-Stars sometimes share buses and none of their themes (except Movies) are overtly "Disney", though each features smaller character scenes around the resort. Finally, their food courts offer lower quality, less inspired fare.

MODERATE RESORTS

Port Orleans French Quarter and Port Orleans Riverside are the best choices.

Standard moderate rooms are found in all moderates except the Cabins at Fort Wilderness. They cost, on average, about $85/night more than the least expensive standard value rooms and about $350/night less than a standard room at the Polynesian Village. Your extra $85/night buys you about 50 more square feet than value rooms, in addition to queen beds (except in Caribbean Beach's "Pirate Rooms"), double sinks (except at Coronado Springs), a coffee-maker, a table service restaurant (except at French Quarter), an indoor lounge (except at Caribbean Beach), a pool slide, and hot tubs. The moderates also provide the most cost-effective way to sleep five (in the Alligator Bayou section of Riverside and in many Caribbean Beach rooms after its recent refurb), and the most cost-effective way to get a full kitchen (in The Cabins at Disney's Fort Wilderness Resort). Compared to the deluxes, the moderates have limited dining options, no character meals, are less convenient to at least one theme park, and have far fewer services and amenities. Fortunately, living areas are more comparable in size to those in the deluxes than you might expect, especially deluxe resorts with smaller room sizes like those at Animal Kingdom and Wilderness Lodges.

Of the moderates, all but Port Orleans French Quarter are large and spread out, with dozens of guest buildings spread out over hundreds of acres. All have multiple bus stops (including shared buses at POFQ). All have more amenities than the values, but fewer than the deluxes. Coronado Springs offers the most amenities, including a salon, gym, nightclub, a strong room service menu, and the largest hot tub on property. French Quarter offers the fewest, including the smallest feature pool, no quiet pools, and no sit-down restaurant. Luckily, all those amenities and more are a short walk or boat ride away at Port Orleans Riverside.

Moderate resorts favor tranquility and a more sublime atmosphere when compared to the values, but don't offer the lushness and detail of the deluxes. This may translate to less overt kid appeal. There are no 50-foot-tall Mickey Mouse icons at the moderates, and other than some subtle references, nothing about them screams Disney World. Of the moderates, the vast majority of kids prefer Caribbean Beach Resort, with its beautiful white sand beaches, hammocks, and colorful guest houses. It also features a pirate-themed pool and play area that kids adore.

Our preference for Port Orleans French Quarter comes largely from its being so much easier to get around than any other moderate, and the relative ease in getting from it to the Magic Kingdom. Among the less convenient moderates, Port Orleans Riverside beats out Caribbean Beach because of its better transportation and it beats out Coronado Springs because of its more family-friendly atmosphere and dining.

In a new development for 2016, the two Port Orleans resorts are typically more expensive than the other two traditional moderates, and Caribbean Beach is the least expensive.

(The Cabins at Fort Wilderness are so different than any other moderate that we refer you to the detailed review later in this chapter. However, we do not recommend them for first-time visitors.)

DELUXE RESORTS

The Polynesian Village, Wilderness Lodge, Contemporary, and Grand Floridian are the best choices.

Compared to other Walt Disney World options, the deluxe resorts are distinguished by having the:

- Most amenities, with the Contemporary and Grand Floridian at the top of this list.
- Nicest views, especially at the Contemporary, Polynesian, Grand Floridian, and Animal Kingdom Lodge.
- Best in-resort and nearby dining options, especially at the four Magic Kingdom-area resorts—the Contemporary, Polynesian, Grand Floridian, and Wilderness Lodge. The Epcot resorts—the BoardWalk Inn, Yacht Club, and Beach Club—have access to many nearby restaurants, but most of them are undistinguished for either kids or parents. The restaurants in the Animal Kingdom Lodge are marvelous, but there's no character dining, and no easy access to more dining at other resorts.
- Best pools, especially at the Beach Club, Yacht Club, Wilderness Lodge, and Animal Kingdom Lodge.
- Best transportation, especially at the Contemporary, Polynesian, and Grand Floridian that share the resort monorail. The Polynesian is most convenient overall. It has resort monorail and boat access to Magic Kingdom, and it's also possible to walk from the Polynesian to the Transportation and Ticket Center (TTC) to catch the Epcot monorail, which eliminates the lengthy monorail ride to the TTC before then having to switch monorails. The Contemporary is just a ten minute walk away from the Magic Kingdom, making it most convenient for a Magic-Kingdom-centric vacation. The Beach Club, located just a five minute walk or boat ride away from Epcot's International Gateway entrance, is the most convenient for an Epcot-centric vacation, particularly during the Food and Wine Festival in the fall.

- Largest standard rooms, with those in the monorail resorts the largest, and those at the Wilderness and Animal Kingdom Lodges the smallest.
- Highest prices for standard rooms, with the monorail resorts the highest, and Wilderness and Animal Kingdom Lodges the lowest.
- Mixed kid appeal, with the Wilderness Lodge and Animal Kingdom Lodge the highest, the Polynesian next, and the Yacht Club and BoardWalk Inn the lowest.

As perhaps is clear by now, there are much bigger differences across the deluxes than in the other price classes. The detailed reviews later in this chapter cover these differences.

We particularly recommend the Polynesian which combines kid-and adult pleasing South Seas theming with large, recently renovated rooms, great dining for both kids and adults, and a newly-renovated main pool. It also has the most convenient location for trips particularly focused on Magic Kingdom and Epcot. Next, we recommend the Wilderness Lodge. Its location across Bay Lake puts it a fun boat ride or just a short bus ride to Magic Kingdom. It offers one of the most family-friendly restaurants in Whispering Canyon Café. Artist Point is a delightful Northwest-inspired signature restaurant away from the hustle and bustle of the monorail resorts. And Territory Lounge, with terrific Northwest beer on draft and a menu that features appetizers that come out of the kitchen it shares with Artist Point, is among the best on property. The pool is fantastically themed and there's even a geyser that erupts throughout the day near the outdoor bar. One deterrent—rooms are smaller than at most other deluxes, but prices are in turn lower.

Among the rest, Beach Club is the best choice for an Epcot-focused visit—which most first visits aren't. It's closer to Epcot and less uppity than neighboring Yacht Club. It also shares with the Yacht Club the best pool complex at a Disney-owned resort on property (the pools at the new Four Seasons are the best overall on-property pool complex) and is more convenient to the limited Epcot-area quick service dining.

Value Resort Reviews

DISNEY'S ART OF ANIMATION RESORT

Disney's Art of Animation Resort ("AofA") is themed on four wildly popular Disney animated films—*Cars*, *The Lion King*, *Finding Nemo*, and *The Little Mermaid*. Like Disney's other value resorts, this theming is partly achieved with larger-than-life sculptures, but much more than the other values, the theming is also suffused into the landscape and into the rooms themselves. This makes it the most "Disney" of any Disney World hotel, wonderfully so to kids, and unrelentingly and garishly so to some adults.

You'll find at AofA four lodging areas, each with two or three buildings framed around one of the movies, and two distinct room types. Family Suites sleeping six are found in the Cars, Lion King, and Finding Nemo areas, and standard rooms similar to those at the other value resorts (except for their much deeper Disney theming) are in the more distant Little Mermaid area. Found in Animation Hall near the entrance to the resort are dining, shops, and guest services. The main "Big Blue" pool, just outside Animation Hall, is the best pool among the values. You'll find two smaller pools as well—a tiny one in the Cars area, and a larger one in the Little Mermaid section. (You need to bring towels from your room to any of these pools; housekeeping can get you more towels if you need them.)

All transport to theme parks, water parks, and Disney Springs is via bus. AofA is one of only two resorts at Walt Disney World with one bus stop and no shared buses, making total transit time shorter—nearby Pop Century is the other. Because at full capacity AofA holds fewer people than Pop does, AofA is the clear convenience winner among the values. AofA (and Pop Century) are just next to and south of the Epcot Area resort Caribbean Beach, but Disney way-finding identifies them as ESPN Wide World of Sports Area resorts. Regardless, these are the two most centrally-located of Disney's value resorts, though neither is particularly close to anything.

AofA's rich and detailed theming gives it the highest kid appeal, by far, among the values, and perhaps of any Disney World resort—at least for kids into one the movies it showcases. As with all the values, adult appeal is mixed, with some finding it fun, and others garish.

At AofA, there are two very different room types in four very different themed areas.

One room type is standard rooms sleeping four on two full beds (almost identical except in decoration to what you'll find at the other value resorts). These are all found in the Little Mermaid area, which is also the farthest area from the main pool, Animation Hall, and bus stops. At about 260 square feet, these standard rooms may be the smallest four-person rooms you will ever see in the U.S. outside of historic center-city hotels. Besides the two full beds, you'll find in the sleeping area a table and two chairs, a TV/dresser combo, and a mini-fridge. There are no coffee-makers in these standard rooms. In the divided bath, you'll find a clothes hanging area, hair dryer, and single sink separated from the rest of the room by a fabric curtain. Next to this you'll find the toilet and tub in their own room. Unlike the other value resorts, which

Disney's Art of Animation Resort
Standard Little Mermaid Room Floor Plan ~260 Square Feet

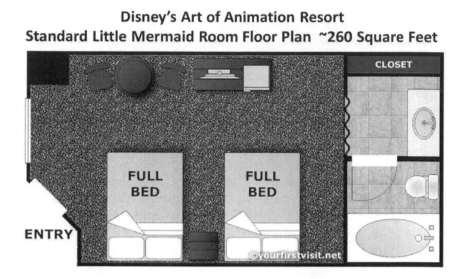

have little room theming, the *Little Mermaid* gang is quite present in these rooms. No rooms at Art of Animation have balconies. All Little Mermaid rooms are accessed from exterior corridors.

The rest of the rooms at AofA are Family Suites, found in three themed areas—Cars, Finding Nemo, and the Lion King. (No standard rooms are in these three areas, and no family suites are in the Little Mermaid area.) AofA Family Suites sleep six in more than twice the area of standard rooms, and contain a living room with a couch that folds out into a full bed, a dining area with a full bed that folds down, a master bedroom with a queen, two full baths (one connected to the master bedroom) and a kitchenette with a mini-fridge, microwave, and coffee-maker. Each of these rooms is deeply themed to its respective movie. Family Suites are accessed via interior corridors—more comfortable than exterior ones, but potentially more noisy.

Dining is in Animation Hall at the food court, Landscape of Flavors, the most ambitious of Disney's food courts in terms of adventuresome menus and fresh preparation. (Josh finds it unreliable and easily over-pressed by guests—if you do too, the food court at Pop Century is just over the bridge between the two resorts.) There's no indoor bar, but you'll find an outdoor bar by the main pool. There is no table service restaurant at any value, nor any character meals.

Amenities at the resort include nightly movies, jogging trails, play-grounds, and an arcade. Art of Animation and Pop Century are the only value resorts on a lake, but the only water recreation available is bird-watching.

At AofA there are no upcharges for views , but Finding Nemo suites as of 2016 are a little more expensive than Cars or Lion King suites, because of their convenience.

Standard four-person rooms are $148/night on weekdays and $173/night on Fridays and Saturdays during the 2016 Fall season. 2016 peak prices for these rooms are $228 and prices bottom out at $128/night. These prices are about $15–$30 per night more expensive than Pop Century, and around $25–$40 more per night than the All-Stars.

Six-person Lion King or Cars family suites are $327/night on weekdays and $372/night on Fridays and Saturdays during the 2016 Fall season. 2016 peak prices for these rooms are $522 and prices bottom out at $312/night. These prices are about $70–$90 per night more expensive than the only other value resort family suites at All-Star Music. Nemo suites average $10–12 more per night.

Disney's Art of Animation Resort
Family Suite Floor Plan ~565 Square Feet

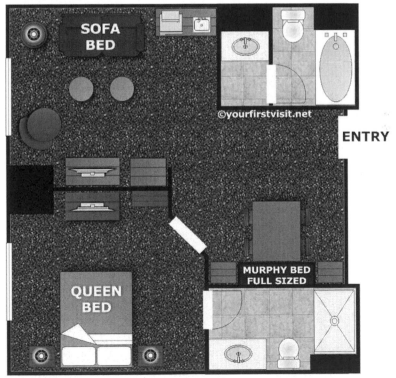

DISNEY'S POP CENTURY RESORT

Disney's Pop Century Resort ("Pop") is themed around the toys, cultural icons, and Disney characters popular in the second half of the twentieth century. Think larger-than-life icons of Roger Rabbit, yo-yos, and a Mickey phone with Mickey, too. Pop has five themed lodging areas, each with one to three buildings framed around one decade—the 50s, 60s, 70s, 80s, and one lonely building representing the 90s. All this is more fun than it sounds, and the icons of characters—Roger Rabbit, Mickey, Mowgli and Balou, Lady and Tramp—add Disney sparkle. Found in Classic Hall near the entrance to the resort are dining, shops, and guest services. The main Hippy Dippy Pool is just outside Classic Hall. You'll find two additional, smaller—but still plenty big—pools, the Bowling Pin pool in the 50s area, and the Computer Pool in the 80s and 90s area. Among these three pools, Pop has the largest area of pool and sunbathing space of any value. (You need to bring towels from your room to any of these pools; housekeeping can get you more towels if you need them.)

All transport to theme parks, water parks, and Disney Springs is via bus. Pop is one of only two resorts at Walt Disney World with one bus stop and no shared buses, making total transit time shorter (nearby AofA is the other). Because at full capacity AofA holds fewer people than Pop does, AofA is the clear convenience winner among the values, but Pop is a close second. Pop is just next to and south of the Epcot Area resort Caribbean Beach, but Disney way-finding identifies it as an ESPN Wide World of Sports Area resort. Regardless, Pop and AofA are the

Disney's Pop Century Resort
Standard Room Floor Plan   ~260 Square Feet

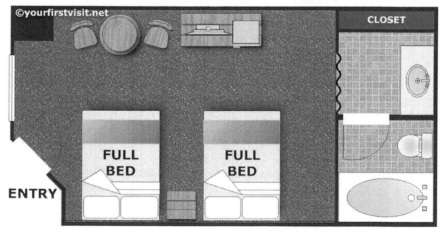

two most centrally-located of Disney's value resorts, though neither is particularly close to anything.

Not so deeply themed as Art of Animation, especially in the rooms, but more Disney than any of the All-Star resorts except, possibly, All-Star Movies, Pop has high kid appeal, and is a little less busy to parental eyes than AofA.

Standard rooms at Pop sleep four on two full beds (almost identical to what you'll find in the standard rooms at the other value resorts). At about 260 square feet, these standard rooms may be the smallest four-person rooms you will ever stay in. Besides the two full beds, you'll find in the sleeping area a table and two chairs, a TV/dresser combo, and a mini-fridge. There are no coffee-makers in these standard rooms. In the divided bath, you'll find a clothes hanging area, hair dryer, and single sink separated from the rest of the room by a fabric curtain. Next to this you'll find the toilet and tub in their own room. The rooms themselves have next to no theming. No rooms at Pop have balconies, and all are accessed from exterior corridors.

Dining is in Classic Hall at the food court Everything Pop. In terms of size and menu, Everything Pop is well above average among the values. There's no indoor bar, but you'll find an outdoor bar by the main pool. There is no table service restaurant at any value, nor any character meals.

Amenities available at the resort include nightly movies, jogging trails, playgrounds, and an arcade. Art of Animation and Pop Century are the only value resorts on a lake, but the only water recreation available is bird-watching.

At Pop, you can pay extras for "preferred" rooms closer to Classic Hall and for pool views. Standard view, non-preferred four-person rooms are $122/night on weekdays and $147/night on Fridays and Saturdays during the 2016 Fall season. 2016 peak prices for these rooms are $212 and prices bottom out at $111/night. These prices are about $15–$30 per night less expensive than AofA, and around $10 more per night than the All-Stars.

DISNEY'S ALL-STAR MOVIES RESORT

Disney's All-Star Movies Resort ("Movies") is themed around five movies—*Toy Story*, *The Mighty Ducks*, *Fantasia*, *The Love Bug*, and *101 Dalmatians*—with two accommodation buildings in each theme. These films are represented by much-larger-than-life icons of characters and objects from them. Found in Cinema Hall near the entrance to the resort are dining, shops, and guest services. The main Fantasia Pool is just outside Cinema Hall. You'll find a smaller—but still plenty big—hockey-themed pool in the Mighty Ducks area. (You need to bring towels from your room to any of these pools; housekeeping can get you more towels if you need them.)

All transport to theme parks, water parks, and Disney Springs is via bus. At lower demand times, Movies shares buses (except to Magic Kingdom) with sister resorts All-Star Music and All-Star Sports. Shared buses stop at Sports first and Movies last—which at times has meant the buses were filled by the time they got to Movies, making this resort the least convenient of the three. The All-Star resorts are Animal Kingdom Area resorts, and are the least conveniently located of the values.

Movies is much more Disney-themed than the other All-Stars, but does not have so rich a set of kid-appealing movies in its themes as AofA, nor are many of its movies as widely kid appealing as the Disney characters and the toys at Pop. The rooms themselves have only the lightest theming related to their area. Adults may find the theming garish, or may warm to the represented movies.

Standard rooms at Movies sleep four on two full beds (almost identical to what you'll find in the standard rooms at the other value resorts, although the All-Stars and AofA are a little less crowded at the entry door, and a little more crowded by the bath wall, than are standard rooms at Pop). At about 260 square feet, these standard rooms are very, very small. Besides the two full beds, you'll find in the sleeping area a table and two chairs, a TV/dresser combo, and a mini-fridge. There are no coffee-makers in these standard rooms. In the divided bath, you'll find a clothes hanging area, hair dryer, and single sink separated from

Disney's All-Star Movies Resort
Standard Room Floor Plan   ~260 Square Feet

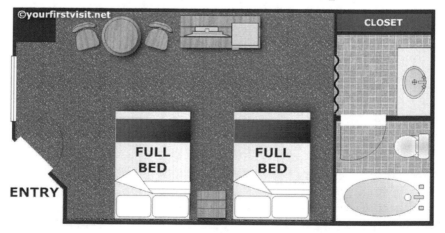

the rest of the room by a fabric curtain. Next to this you'll find the toilet and tub in their own room. No rooms at Movies have balconies, and all are accessed from exterior corridors.

Dining is in Cinema Hall at the World Premiere food court. Movies has the largest food court among the All-Stars, but its menu is a bit thinner than other All-Star food court offerings, making it below average among the values. The bar is set in the exterior wall between the food court and the pool, and serves guests from both areas. There is no table service restaurant at any value, nor any character meals.

Amenities available at the resort include nightly movies, jogging trails, playgrounds, and an arcade.

At Movies, you can pay extra for "preferred" rooms closer to Cinema Hall. Non-preferred rooms are $111/night on weekdays and $137/night on Fridays and Saturdays during the 2016 Fall season. 2016 peak prices for these rooms are $201 and prices bottom out at $101/night. These prices are the same as similar rooms at the other All-Stars, about $25–$40 per night less expensive than AofA, and around $10 less per night than Pop.

DISNEY'S ALL-STAR SPORTS RESORT

Disney's All-Star Sports Resort ("Sports") is themed around five sports—baseball, basketball, tennis, football, and surfing—with two accommodation buildings in each theme. These sports are represented by much-larger-than-life icons of sports objects, and by theming of the spaces between the two buildings of each theme to the playing field of the respective sport. Dining, shops, and guest services are in Stadium Hall near the resort entrance. The main Surf's Up pool is just outside Stadium Hall. You'll find a smaller—but still plenty big—baseball field-themed pool in the baseball area. (You need to bring towels from your room to any of these pools; housekeeping can get you more towels if you need them.)

All transport to theme parks, water parks, and Disney Springs is via bus. At lower demand times, Sports shares buses (except to Magic Kingdom) with sister resorts All-Star Music and All-Star Movies. Shared buses stop at Sports first and Movies last—which means that Sports guests are most likely to get a seat, making Sports the most convenient of the All-Stars, and of average convenience among the values. The All-Star resorts are Animal Kingdom Area resorts, and are the least conveniently located of the values.

Sports appeals to kids interested in its specific themes, but is otherwise thin on general kid appeal. The rooms themselves have only the lightest theming related to their area. Adults may find the theming garish, or may warm to the represented sports. All the All-Stars can be overrun with kids competing in events at ESPN Wide World of Sports, and this seems most common at Sports.

Standard rooms at Sports sleep four on two full beds in rooms pretty much identical to what you'll find at the other All-Stars. At about 260 square feet, these standard rooms are teeny but adequate for sleeping. Besides the two full beds, you'll find in the sleeping area a table and two chairs, a TV/dresser combo, and a mini-fridge. There are no cof-fee-makers in these rooms. In the divided bath, you'll find a clothes hanging area, hair dryer, and single sink separated from the rest of the room by a fabric curtain. Next to this you'll find the toilet and tub in their own room. No rooms at Sports have balconies, and all are accessed from exterior corridors.

Dining is in Stadium Hall at the End Zone food court. Recently ren-ovated, this space is still too small for the guests it tries to serve, and is below average among the values. The bar is set in the exterior wall between the food court and the pool, and serves guests from both areas. There is no table service restaurant at any value, nor any character meals.

Amenities available at the resort include nightly movies, jogging trails, playgrounds, and an arcade.

At Sports, you can pay extra for "preferred" rooms closer to Stadium Hall. Non-preferred rooms are $111/night on weekdays and $137/night on Fridays and Saturdays during the 2016 Fall season. 2016 peak prices for these rooms are $201 and prices bottom out at $101/night. These prices are the same as similar rooms at the other All-Stars, about

Disney's All-Star Sports Resort
Standard Room Floor Plan   ~260 Square Feet

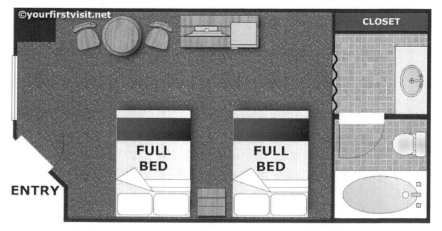

$25-40 per night less expensive than AofA, and around $10 less per night than Pop.

DISNEY'S ALL-STAR MUSIC RESORT

Disney's All-Star Music Resort ("Music") is themed around five musical genres—calypso, jazz, Broadway, rock, and country, with two accommodation buildings in each theme. These genres are represented by much-larger-than-life icons of musical instruments and other objects related to the theme, e.g., cowboy boots in the country music area, and by a bit of theming here and there of the spaces between the two buildings to the musical genre. Found in Melody Hall near the entrance to the resort are dining, shops, and guest services. The main Guitar pool is just outside Melody Hall. You'll find a smaller—but still plenty big—piano-themed pool deeper in the resort. (You need to bring towels from your room to any of these pools; housekeeping can get you more towels if you need them.)

All transport to theme parks, water parks, and Disney Springs is via bus. At lower demand times, Music shares buses (except to Magic Kingdom) with sister resorts All-Star Movies and All-Star Sports. Shared buses stop at Sports first and Movies last—which means that Music guest are less likely than Sports guests to get a seat, but more likely than Movies guests. This makes Music of average convenience among the All-Stars, and of below-average convenience among the values. The All-Star resorts are Animal Kingdom Area resorts, and are the least conveniently located of the values.

Disney's All-Star Music Resort
Standard Room Floor Plan   ~260 Square Feet

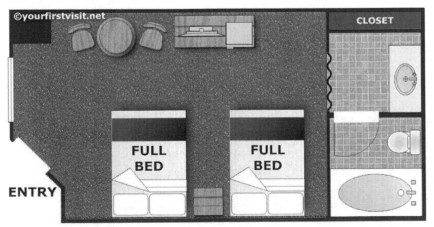

Music appeals to kids interested in its specific themes, but is otherwise quite thin on general kid appeal. The rooms themselves have only the lightest theming related to their area. Adults will find it the loveliest of the values, and its overall layout the easiest to understand and navigate.

Music has two very different room types: standard four-person rooms found in all its themed areas, and six-person family suites in the Calypso and Jazz areas.

Standard rooms at Music sleep four on two full beds in rooms pretty much identical to what you'll find at the other All-Stars. At about 260 square feet, these standard rooms are really small but adequate for sleeping. Besides the two full beds, you'll find in the sleeping area a table and two chairs, a TV/dresser combo, and a mini-fridge. There are no coffee-makers in these standard rooms. In the divided bath, you'll find a clothes hanging area, hair dryer, and single sink separated from the rest of the room by a fabric curtain. Next to this you'll find the toilet

Disney's All-Star Music Resort
Family Suite Floor Plan ~520 Square Feet

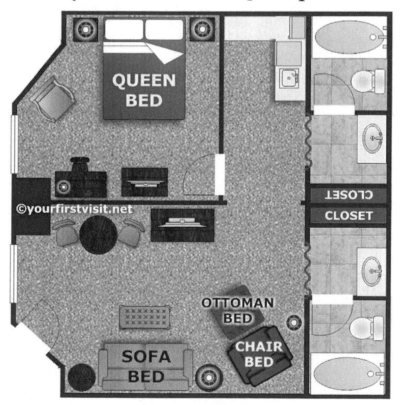

and tub in their own room. No rooms at Music have balconies, and all are accessed from exterior corridors.

Family Suites at Music sleep six in twice the area of standard rooms, and contain a living room with three furniture items that fold out into beds—a couch that folds out into a full, and a chair and an ottoman that each fold out into twins. It also has a master bedroom with a queen and two full baths, each accessible to anyone in the room, plus a kitchenette with a mini-fridge, microwave, and coffee-maker. These rooms are not nearly as much fun as the suites at AofA, and the fold-out beds are not nearly as comfortable for older/heavier guests. But some families will appreciate the more flexible number of sleeping spots, and others the fact that these suites are typically $70–$90 per night less expensive than those at AofA.

Dining is in Melody Hall at the renovated in 2014 Intermission food court. This space is too small for the guests it tries to serve, and is below average among the values. The bar is set in the exterior wall between the food court and the pool, and serves guests from both areas. There is no table service restaurant at any value, nor any character meals.

Amenities available at the resort include nightly movies, jogging trails, playgrounds, and an arcade.

At Music, you can pay extra for "preferred" standard rooms closer to Melody Hall. Non-preferred standard rooms are $111/night on weekdays and $137/night on Fridays and Saturdays during the 2016 Fall season. 2016 peak prices for these rooms are $201 and prices bottom out at $101/night. These prices are the same as similar rooms at the other All-Stars, about $25–$40 per night less expensive than AofA, and around $10 less per night than Pop.

Family Suites at Music are all the same cost, whether in Jazz or Calypso. Family Suites are $253/night on weekdays and $304/night on Fridays and Saturdays during the 2016 Fall season. 2016 peak prices for these rooms are $447 and prices bottom out at $244/night. These suites are about $70–$90 less per night than at AofA.

Moderate Resort Reviews

DISNEY'S PORT ORLEANS FRENCH QUARTER RESORT

Disney's Port Orleans French Quarter Resort ("POFQ") is one of two moderates with "Port Orleans" in the name—the other is Port Orleans Riverside Resort. Some mistakenly call these one resort. The only point of commonality most guests will ever notice is that guests at either are welcome to share the other's pools. The confusion comes from Disney shutting down, more than a decade ago, the table service restaurant and bike rentals at what was then known as Port Orleans Resort, and is now POFQ, and then renaming both resorts as Port Orleans—indicating to guests that these amenities weren't really missing, but just more distant, at Port Orleans Riverside, part of the same resort now...

Disney does not much bother with this distinction any more—other than making it clear to guests that they are welcome to partake in everything offered at both. It turns out that despite the missing amenities at Port Orleans French Quarter, it is the most highly valued of the Disney moderates—which is why alone among the moderates it is almost never included in Disney's discounts and other special offers.

POFQ has as its theme New Orleans and Mardi Gras, combining lacy wrought iron, lovely gardens, and cobblestoned streets. You'll also find Mardi Gras figures and decorations scattered about, especially in

Disney's Port Orleans French Quarter Resort
Floor Plan ~314 Square Feet

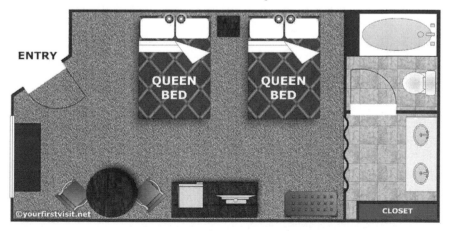

the food court and near the main pool. POFQ has half as many rooms as the other traditional moderates, and has—with no lake or river in the middle—a much more compact footprint for those rooms. As a result, it is, by far, the easiest moderate to get around. It has no real separate areas for its seven accommodations buildings, although you'll see North Quarter and South Quarter signage meant to help you find your building. Near the entrance at the center you'll find dining, shops, and guest services in the Port Orleans Mint building. The only pool, the Mardi-Gras themed Doubloon Lagoon, is just steps away, and the sole bus stop is right out front. One pool may seem like not enough, but the main pool area at POFQ has 65% of the area that Port Orleans Riverside's main pool has, but serves only half as many rooms. Most times of the year POFQ shares buses (except to the Magic Kingdom) with Riverside, but the single bus stop on the Magic Kingdom route makes it overall the most convenient of the moderates.

All transport to theme parks and water parks is via buses. Disney Springs is accessible by both boat and bus. POFQ, like Riverside, is labeled as a Disney Springs Area Resort in Disney's way-finding material, but is more centrally located than that implies. The Magic Kingdom, Epcot, and Disney's Hollywood Studios are all close.

There's no special kid appeal at POFQ, and in fact the Mardi Gras theming—including, for example, an enormous depiction of a dragon/snake at the pool—wigs some kids out. But POFQ is the loveliest and most romantic of the moderates, and that, when combined with the ease of getting around and to the parks, makes it a great favorite of adults among the moderates.

Jim's Gems
by Jim Korkis

Disney's Port Orleans Resort opened in May 1991. It was themed to the French Quarter of New Orleans around the mid-1800s and was situated by the Sassagoula River, a man-made Disney waterway named after the Native American word for Mississippi. The jester figure located near Doubloon Lagoon pool is based on the figure found next to the Canal Street / Algiers Ferry terminal in New Orleans. Mardi Gras legends Blaine Kern Artists Inc. collected and created special prop items such as the jesters. Some of the Mardi Gras decorations were purchased directly from warehouses in New Orleans.

Rooms at POFQ are typical of those at the traditional moderates. They sleep four on two queens in about 314 square feet, and all come with a table and two chairs, a dresser/mini-fridge, coffee-maker, hair-dryer, and a divided, family-friendly bath. In the bath, the two sinks and closet/dressing area are shielded from the sleeping part of the room by a curtain, and the tub and toilet have their own room. All buildings have elevators. No rooms have balconies. All rooms are accessed from exterior corridors.

The only dining at POFQ is at the food court Sassagoula Floatworks Food Company, which is well above average among the moderates, and has a nice sprinkling of themed offerings—for example, beignets, Po Boys, jambalaya, and BBQ ribs served with collard greens. (You can, of course, walk to the table service Boatwright's at Riverside.) The indoor bar, the Scat Cats Lounge, is not as rollicking as the River Roost Lounge at Riverside, but one should always have the option to not rollick. There are no character meals.

Amenities are thinner than at the other moderates, although most that are missing are nearby at Riverside. On site, you'll find (besides the pool) an arcade, playground, and nightly movies. (Some nights, movies are at Riverside or POFQ, but not both.)

At POFQ there are no "preferred" rooms—itself an indication of how easy it is to get around for a moderate—but you can still pay extra for king beds, for garden views, for pool views, and for water views. Standard view rooms are $214/night on weekdays and $237/night on Fridays and Saturdays during the 2016 Fall season. 2016 peak prices for these rooms are $299 and prices bottom out $197/night. Prices are the same as Port Orleans Riverside and typically about $10/night more than Caribbean Beach, and $5/night more than Coronado Springs.

DISNEY'S PORT ORLEANS RIVERSIDE RESORT

Disney's Port Orleans Riverside Resort ("POR") is one of two moderates with "Port Orleans" in the name—the other is Port Orleans French Quarter. Some mistakenly call these one resort. The only point of commonality most guests will ever notice is that guests at either are welcome to share the other's pools and other amenities.

POR has as its theme the 19th century American South, particularly the bayou and riverine areas of Louisiana and Mississippi. Rooms in the massive resort are in two areas, Magnolia Bend, with four large buildings meant to be reminiscent of plantation mansions, and Alligator Bayou, with many smaller buildings meant to evoke a more rural feel. Found in the Sassagoula Steamship Company area near the entrance to the resort are dining, shops, and guest services. The main pool, located on a central island, has a bit of saw-mill theming, and is average among moderate pools. Testifying to the sprawl of the resort and the distance of many rooms from Ol' Man Island, you'll find five additional smaller pools around the resort. The resort proper has four bus stops, but most times of the year shares buses (except to the Magic Kingdom) with nearby Port Orleans French Quarter, making it less convenient than either Coronado Springs or Port Orleans French Quarter. The overall accommodations footprint of POR is larger than that of Coronado Springs, but, because it has no lake, the main services at POR are more central than those at Coronado Springs.

All transport to theme parks and water parks is via bus. Disney Springs is accessible by both boat and bus. POR is labeled as a Disney Springs Area Resort in Disney's way-finding material, but is more centrally located than that implies. Before the Animal Kingdom and Blizzard Beach opened, the two Port Orleans Resorts were in fact the most centrally located moderates, and the Magic Kingdom, Epcot, and Disney's Hollywood Studios are still all close—at least after the buses finally get out of the resort. The resort itself is massive, and some rooms are a hike from the main services, and others from the main pool...some from both.

There's no special kid appeal at POR compared to that at Caribbean Beach, and no special adult appeal compared to that at Coronado Springs and POFQ. But even so, POR is likely the best-loved, most frequently recommended, and most loyally defended of all the moderate resorts.

Disney's Port Orleans Riverside Resort Standard Room Floor Plan ~314 Square Feet

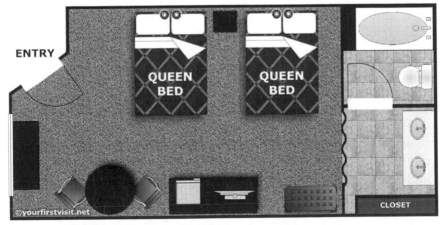

There are three very different room types at POR. All are about the same size as those at the other traditional moderates, about 314 square feet, and all come with a table and two chairs, a dresser/TV/mini-fridge combo, coffee-maker, hair-dryer, and a divided, family-friendly bath. In the bath, the two sinks and closet/dressing area are shielded from the sleeping part of the room by a curtain, and the tub and toilet have their own room. The two story buildings in Alligator Bayou have no elevators, but the taller Magnolia Bend buildings do. No rooms have balconies. All rooms are accessed from exterior corridors.

The Alligator Bayou section of POR is one of only two areas at Disney World with traditional moderate rooms that sleep five—two each in two queens, and the fifth in a small murphy bed (about 66 inches long by 31 inches wide, and meant for a kid ten or younger) that folds down beneath the TV. (Caribbean Beach is the other.)

Rooms in half the Magnolia Bend section have "Royal" theming, and are more expensive. These rooms sleep 4 in two queens, and have much prince and (especially) princess detail, including a lovely headboard light show based on the *Princess and the Frog* triggered by an easy-to-miss button on the side.

Rooms in the other half of Magnolia Bend also sleep 4 in two queens, but do not have the special royal theming—nor its extra cost. They are also largely more convenient than the Royal Rooms, and, if you don't need the fifth sleeping spot, more livable than the Alligator Bend rooms.

Dining is at Sassagoula Steamship Company, with a food court that's average among the moderates and a table service restaurant, Boatwright's Dining Hall, that's also average. The food court is too small for the crowds it faces, and has little special on its standard menu to reflect the theming other than grits at breakfast and a Cajun chicken sandwich. The indoor bar, the River Roost Lounge, has a widely loved family-friendly show from "Ye Haa" Bob Jackson most Wednesday through Saturday evenings. There's also a bar at the main pool. There are no character meals.

Amenities available at the resort include nightly movies, campfires, bike rental, fishing, jogging trails, playgrounds, and an arcade. (Some nights, movies are at Riverside or POFQ, but not both.) The main pool is far too small for the resort, and can't fit everyone who would like to be there.

At POR you can pay more for preferred locations that are a closer walk to the Sassagoula Steamship Company, for the Royal rooms, for king beds, for garden views, and for water views. Standard view, non-preferred rooms are $214/night on weekdays and $237/night on Fridays and Saturdays during the 2016 Fall season. 2016 peak prices for these rooms are $299 and prices bottom out at $197/night. Prices are the same as POFQ and typically about $10/night more than Caribbean Beach, and $5/night more than Coronado Springs.

DISNEY'S CARIBBEAN BEACH RESORT

Disney's Caribbean Beach Resort ("CB") is themed around Caribbean islands, their beaches, and the pirates who once voyaged among them. Rooms in the massive resort are found in six "villages" ringing a lake, all named after Caribbean destinations: Trinidad North, Trinidad South, Martinique, Barbados, Aruba and Jamaica. Each colorful village has palm-tree lined beaches, and each has its own pool and bus stop. The central Old Port Royale area includes the main pool at the resort, the pirate-themed Fuentes del Morro Pool—the best pool of the Disney World moderate resorts—as well as dining, shops, yet another bus stop, and some guest services. (Other guest services are located in the out-of-the-way Customs House.)

Seven pools and seven bus stops may sound like an abundance of riches. They are not.

Rather, there are this many pools and bus stops because of design flaws that make CB large and hard to get around—especially for guests staying at Trinidad South, and to a lesser extent, at Barbados. This is the resort's major negative. All transport to theme parks, water parks, and Disney Springs is via buses. Because of the number of required bus stops, CB is not particularly convenient to anywhere, but is closest to Disney's Hollywood Studios and Epcot.

Disney's Caribbean Beach Resort
Floor Plan   ~314 Square Feet

Many rooms at CB have Disney theming—a light touch in most, and deep pirate theming in the distant (and overly expensive) Trinidad South area. The combination of Disney-themed rooms, sparkling beaches, bright colors, swaying palms, and the pirate-themed main pool give CB high kid appeal among the moderates. Adults like most of this, too, but can be frustrated by the walking distances and all the bus stops.

After its 2014–2015 refurb, there are now three types of standard rooms at CB, all about 314 square feet: Pirate-themed rooms that sleep four, rooms that sleep four on two queens, and rooms that sleep five on two queens and a murphy bed under the TV that's about 30 inches wide by 64 inches long. (The floor plan, previous page, depicts a five person room.) At press time, refurb plans for the overly expensive and distant Pirate rooms in Trinidad South were not clear. We expect—but cannot confirm—their full beds to be replaced by queens.

Rooms come with a table and two chairs, a dresser/TV/mini-fridge combo, coffee-maker, hair-dryer, a smaller storage chest in four-person rooms, and a divided, family-friendly bath. In the bath, the sinks and closet/dressing area are shielded from the rest of the room by a curtain in the Pirate rooms and sliding solid doors in all other rooms, and the tub and toilet have their own room. The two-story buildings that hold these rooms have no elevators, and no rooms have balconies. All rooms are accessed from exterior corridors.

Dining is at Old Port Royale, with a food court that's a little below average among the moderates and too small for peak crowds, and a table service restaurant, Shutters, that's been revitalized with more Caribbean and seafood flair since new chef Mike Reitzler signed on. There's no dedicated indoor bar—the only bar is outdoors near the main pool. There are no character meals.

Other amenities available at the resort include nightly movies, camp-fires, bike rental, fishing, a Pirate Adventure cruise, great jogging trails, playgrounds, and an arcade. The main pirate-themed pool is not small, but is so popular that it can't fit everyone who would like to be there.

At CB, you can pay more for preferred locations that are closer to Old Port Royale, for the Pirate rooms that are quite a hike and still have full beds, for king beds, and for water views. Standard view, non-preferred rooms are $206/night on weekdays and $234/night on Fridays and Saturdays during the 2016 Fall season. 2016 peak prices for these rooms are $288 and prices bottom out at $187/night. This is on average about $10/night less than POR and POFQ, and a few dollars less than CS.

Preferred rooms and a rental car would make up for the inconveniences of CB, but may add $80 per night or more, depending on the hotel price season and seasonal rental car rates.

DISNEY'S CORONADO SPRINGS RESORT

Disney's Coronado Springs Resort's ("CS") theme is based on the American Southwest, Spanish-colonial Mexico, and the architectural remnants of Mesoamerican civilizations. Rooms in the massive resort are found in three areas surrounding a lake: the Casitas, elegant colonnaded three- and four-story buildings; the Ranchos, a sharply contrasting, desert-inspired area; and the Cabanas, a beach-house themed area with beaches, too—fewer than at Caribbean Beach, but more than at any other moderate. The El Centro area, between the Casitas and Cabanas, includes dining, shopping, and guest services, and leads to the Coronado Springs Convention Center. Away from El Centro, and near the actual center of the resort—and most convenient to the Cabanas and Ranchos—is the Mesoamerican-themed main pool, the Lost City of Cibola, in the Dig Site area, the second-best pool among the moderates. Each of the three room areas has its own smaller pool (the Casitas pool has the only lap pool at Disney World), as well as a bus stop. A fourth bus stop is at El Centro.

All transport to theme parks, water parks, and Disney Springs is via buses (or your rental car). CS is labeled as an Animal Kingdom Area Resort in Disney's way-finding material, but is in fact the most centrally-located of all the moderate resorts. This, combined with its "only" four bus stops, makes it the second most convenient of the moderates— among them, only Port Orleans French Quarter is more convenient for park travel. The resort itself is massive, and some buildings in the Ranchos in particular are quite distant from El Centro.

Disney's Coronado Springs Resort Floor Plan ~314 Square Feet

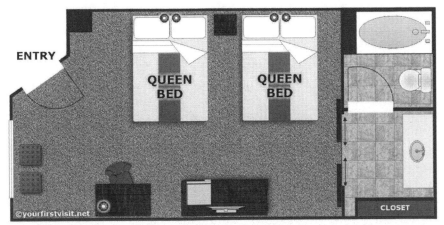

Coronado Springs is the only moderate with convention facilities. This has led to much fussing, largely unfair. The same number of rooms occupied by conventioneers rather than families means fewer people in total at the resort (because conventioneers average fewer people per room) and fewer people at the bus stops and pools (as the fewer conventioneers are in meetings, not going to the parks or the pools). Most of the time, except breakfast, there's also fewer people in CS's public dining spaces, as most meetings have meals served as part of the meeting program. However, when a thousand people leave a meeting at once, and all want to go someplace, things clot up quickly.

On the other hand, because of the demands of the business travelers at the convention center, Coronado Springs has a much higher level of services and amenities than at the other moderates. There are the usual nightly movies, campfires, bike rental, fishing, playgrounds, and arcade. In addition, uniquely at CS among the moderates, you'll find a health club, spa services, real room service, a main pool menu with real food, the largest hot tub at Disney World, multiple bars, and a business center. The effect of these extra services is to make Coronado Springs quite attractive to adults. Kids like the beach-themed Cabanas, the Dig Site area and main pool, and, if they aren't familiar with the geography, the exotic Southwest theming.

Standard rooms at CS hold four people on two queen beds in about 314 square feet. They are similarly sized to those at the other traditional moderates, but have no Disney theming—and are in fact the most stark rooms among the moderates. At press time, the scope and impact of an expected refurb were unclear. In a concession to convention travelers, they come with a desk rather than the table and two chairs you'll find in the other traditional moderates. Most other room amenities are similar—a dresser/TV/mini-fridge combo, coffee-maker, and hair dryer. The bath is divided and family friendly, but also designed so a conventioneer can use both parts at once. As a result, it has one sink rather than two, and sliding wooden doors separating it from the sleeping area, rather than the fabric curtains you'll find in the other traditional moderates except the refurbed rooms in Caribbean Beach. All buildings have elevators, and no rooms have balconies. All rooms are accessed from exterior corridors.

Dining is at El Centro, and, unless you are on the dining plan, is more expensive than at the other moderates. The food court, Pepper Market, used to be the best food court among the Disney World hotels, but while still good has gotten less interesting recently. The main table service restaurant, Maya Grill, has a menu suited to the Southwest theming of the resort, but is overpriced. A smaller table service venue,

Las Ventanos, offers a simpler menu. The indoor bar, Rix Lounge, is the closest thing to a club you'll find in a Disney-owned hotel; there's an additional outdoor lakeside bar, and yet another bar by the pool. There are no character meals.

You can pay more for preferred locations that are a closer walk to El Centro, for king beds, for suites, and for water views. Standard view, non-preferred rooms are $208/night on weekdays and $232/night on Fridays and Saturdays during the 2016 Fall season. 2016 peak prices for these rooms are $294, and prices bottom out at $191/night. Prices typically are a few dollars more than CB, and a few dollars less than POR and POFQ.

THE CABINS AT DISNEY'S FORT WILDERNESS RESORT

Disney has had some trouble over the years communicating what's in the Cabins at Disney's Fort Wilderness Resort. The cabins—each its own little building—are distinctive spaces, sleeping six in two rooms, and with full kitchens. There used to be a "home away from home" category which the Cabins were in, but everything else in this group was a "deluxe" class room, and the Cabins didn't match up well with them.

So to eliminate the confusion about amenities, in 2009 Disney re-classed these Cabins as "moderates". This is a fair description of room-level amenities and spaciousness, but there's really few other ways that the Cabins are like the other moderates (inconvenience is

The Cabins at Disney's Fort Wilderness Resort
Floor Plan ~504 Square Feet

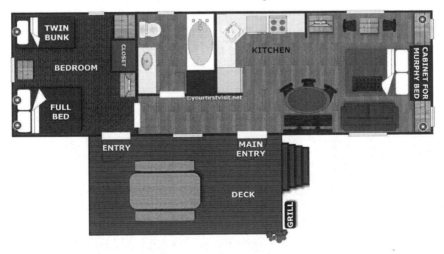

one, and thin kid appeal another). As a result, the phrase "traditional moderate" started being used for all the moderates except the Cabins.

The Cabins are one of two lodging options at Disney's Fort Wilderness Campground and Resort—the other being campsites. Fort Wilderness is one of America's great campgrounds, and the Cabins share in all the wonderful recreational activities available in the rest of this resort. The Cabins are each small, standalone buildings, looking on the outside like a rustic cabin, and on the inside like a nice small wood-paneled mobile home. If driving—and you should have a car to stay in these—you park right in front. Each cabin also has an outdoor barbecue grill and a big deck with picnic table.

As you walk in, you'll find first the full kitchen, then a small dining table and small living room. A near-full-sized bed folds down from a wall in the living room, so this space sleeps two—typically the parents. Further back is a full bath. It's not divided, and is a bit short on hot water, so it doesn't well suit the six people that these cabins can sleep. Beyond this is the back bedroom, with a tight-fitting full bed on one side and a pair of bunk beds on the other.

The Cabins are not the least expensive way to get a Disney room for six—a family suite at All-Star Music is that. But they are the least expensive way to get moderate-level fittings and fixtures for six, and are by far the least expensive way to get a full kitchen.

The challenge, though, is some crowding, especially around the bath, thin kid appeal—unless your kids love campgrounds—and great inconvenience. If you don't have a car, it takes two transport acts to get off Fort Wilderness and to a park—the first bus gets you to another bus stop or boat dock, from which you go to your final destination. We couldn't imagine staying here if you don't have a car.

Fort Wilderness has some family-friendly table service dining—the storied Hoop-Dee-Doo Revue and Mickey's Backyard Barbecue. There's also Trails End restaurant, with great value for money. Plus you have that kitchen. But there's not much in the way of counter service, and to get to these table service venues from the Cabins, you need to take a bus.

The resort has two pools. One is dull but within walking distance of the Cabins; the other, the main pool, was themed in 2009 but remains the weakest among the moderates. This pool is farther (a bus trip for most), and is in the same Meadows area as where you'll find many of Fort Wilderness's other amenities. At the Settlement end of Fort Wilderness, you'll find (via bus...you can't drive to these) the beach, marina, boat docks (with boat service both to the Magic Kingdom, and also to the nearby Wilderness Lodge and Contemporary resorts), and the dining noted above.

If you need the lowest-priced kitchen you can find, need to sleep six, and have a car, the Cabins are great options. Otherwise, not so much.

The Cabins have no extra price options for views and such. They are $368/night on weekdays and $407/night on Fridays and Saturdays during the 2016 Fall season. 2016 peak prices for these rooms are $568/night, and prices bottom out at $348/night.

Deluxe Resort Reviews

DISNEY'S POLYNESIAN VILLAGE RESORT

Disney's Polynesian Village Resort ("Poly"), a monorail resort, is themed around the Pacific islands of Polynesia. Theming at the Polynesian is pervasive and detailed, but more subtle than that of the jaw-dropping Wilderness Lodge and Animal Kingdom Lodge. Lush landscaping, lovely beaches, flaming torches, and exotically styled and named "longhouses" (where you find the rooms) create a delightful impression. In the Great Ceremonial House ("GCH") near the entrance to the resort are dining, shops, guest services, and, on the second floor, access to the resort monorail with service to the Magic Kingdom, the other monorail resorts, and the Transportation and Ticket Center (TTC). Disney Vacation Club Villas opened for booking in the lagoon and east side of the resort in 2015. The recently refurbed main Nanea Volcano Pool is just outside the GCH. (The smaller East Pool closed for refurb in July 2015 with the expectation that it will reopen part way through 2016.)

With travel to the Magic Kingdom available via both monorail and boat, and many rooms at the Polynesian within easy walking distance

Disney's Polynesian Village Resort
Floor Plan   ~ 415 Square Feet

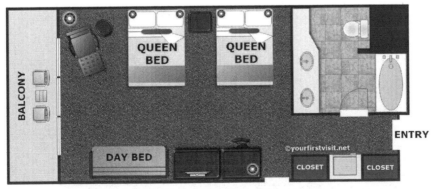

of the TTC and its Epcot monorail, the Polynesian is the most convenient Disney World resort. Transportation to the other parks and Disney Springs is via buses, typically shared with one or two other Magic Kingdom area resorts.

Construction has been ongoing at the Polynesian since 2013, but the most material parts are complete. The last major project is a refurb to the small East Pool, expected to extend into 2016. Until it is complete, avoid pool-facing rooms at the Hawaii, Samoa, Niue, Raratonga, and Tokelau longhouses. Check our sites and TIKIMANPAGES.COM for updates.

All standard rooms at the Poly were refurbished in 2013, and sleep five on two queens and a sofa that flips into a twin. Rooms are about 415 square feet, among the largest at Disney World. Besides the two queens and couch, you'll find an easy chair and ottoman, a desk with a small rolling table underneath, desk chair, mini-fridge, TV/dresser combo, two closets, and a coffeemaker. The spacious bath includes two sinks and a hair dryer, but is not divided, making it a little less family friendly than you'll find in more recently built hotels (the Polynesian was built in the early 70s). Second-floor standard rooms don't have balconies; other floors have patios or balconies. Polynesian DVC offerings available for rent to the general public include Bungalows and Studios. Studios are most comparable to standard Poly rooms, and sleep five on a queen, fold-out couch, and flip-down 72" x 30" Murphy bed. All studios have balconies. All standard rooms and studios are accessed from interior corridors. Like the other deluxe resorts, you can also reserve concierge-supported rooms (Disney calls these "club" rooms) and suites.

The Poly has three table service restaurants and one quick service option. Dining is in GCH, except for the Luau which has its own building at the northwest edge of the resort. 'Ohana is a great family restaurant that features well-loved character breakfasts with Mickey, Lilo, and Stitch. Kona Café has an uninspired setting, but terrific and under-appreciated food. The Luau fills any need you may have for a Polynesian-themed dinner show. The quick service location is Capt. Cook's, too small for the resort but convenient to the pool. More great dining is just a monorail ride away at the Grand Floridian and Contemporary. There's a bar outside of 'Ohana, and downstairs you'll find the most distinctive resort bar on property, Trader Sam's.

Amenities available at the resort include beaches, nightly movies, campfires, jogging trails, playgrounds, boat rental, bike rental, fishing, a volleyball court, and an arcade. Poly guests can use the spa and health club Senses on the Poly side of the Grand Floridian. The beaches are a popular spot for watching the fireworks for the Magic Kingdom across the Seven Seas lagoon. The Poly is one of only three Disney deluxe resorts (the Wilderness and Animal Kingdom Lodges are the others) that are not convention hotels.

At the Poly you can pay extra for views. Standard view five-person rooms are $528/night on weekdays and $592/night on Fridays and Saturdays during the 2016 Fall season. 2016 peak prices for these rooms are $793 and prices bottom out at $508/night.

DISNEY'S GRAND FLORIDIAN RESORT & SPA

Disney's Grand Floridian Resort & Spa ("GF"), a monorail resort inspired by the Hotel Del Coronado in San Diego, is a lovely mix of gorgeous landscaping, white Victorian shapes and details, and red roofs. It visually enchants adults but does nothing in particular for kids. At opening, it supplanted Disney's Contemporary Resort as Disney World's flagship— and most expensive—hotel, leading some Contemporary Cast Members to refer to GF as the "red roof inn". (Remind yourself of this if GF ever seems too stuffy or self-satisfied, although many of the most self-satisfied will migrate to the new Four Seasons, the first five star resort to be located in Disney World.) There are three basic areas at GF: the main building, the outer buildings, and the Disney Vacation Club Villas. The main building has most dining, all shops, guest services, some suites, and several types of "club" rooms (Disney-speak for concierge rooms). The five outer buildings have more club rooms, more suites, all standard rooms, and some smaller but high-ceilinged "dormer" rooms. The Villas are at the southern edge of the resort grounds. From the second floor of the main building, GF guests can access the resort monorail with service to the Magic Kingdom, the other monorail resorts, and the

Disney's Grand Floridian Resort & Spa Floor Plan ~440 Square Feet

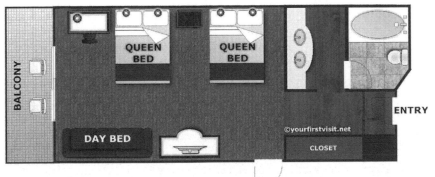

Transportation and Ticket Center (TTC). The uninteresting but large main pool is in a beautifully landscaped area between the main building and the outer buildings, and the smaller but more fun Beach Pool is between the main building and the Villas.

Transportation to the Magic Kingdom is by the resort monorail or a boat shared with the Polynesian. Transportation to Epcot is via the Epcot monorail at TTC, accessible by the resort monorail. Transportation to the other parks and Disney Springs is via buses, typically shared with one or two other Magic Kingdom area resorts. Transportation convenience is above average among the deluxes for a Magic Kingdom focused trip, but not as good as sister monorail resorts the Contemporary and Polynesian.

Adults generally love the exterior and grounds of GF, while reactions to interior decorating choices are mixed, with some finding them stuffy. Kids often don't get the theme—a hotel themed as a hotel?—or it fails to delight them.

Guest rooms at the Grand Floridian were refurbished in 2014, losing much of their former Victorian fussiness. All standard rooms at GF sleep five on two queens and a sofa that flips into a twin bed. Standard rooms are about 440 square feet—larger than the typical rooms at any other Disney-owned hotel. Besides the two queens and couch, you'll find an easy chair, a desk with a small rolling table underneath, a desk chair, mini-fridge, TV, dresser, closet (with robes!), and a coffee-maker. The spacious divided bath includes two sinks and a hair dryer, and a toilet and tub in a separate room. Rooms in the nearby Villas are also available for rent to the general public. Of the four room types at the Villas, studios are most comparable to standard GF rooms. They sleep five in a smaller overall space, but one with a better bath, on a queen, fold-out couch, and flip-down 72" long murphy bed. All rooms are accessed from interior corridors, and all rooms have balconies or patios.

The Grand Floridian has the best adult dining of any Disney resort, some attractive kid dining, and easy access to other great options at the other monorail resorts. GF has five table service restaurants and one quick service option. Two are on the second floor of the main building. Victoria and Albert's is by far the best and most expensive restaurant at Disney World. Kids under ten are not allowed, and jackets are required. Citricos is a seafood-focused establishment with inspired modern fare. "Resort casual" is the appropriate dress. On the first floor is 1900 Park Fare, with character meals at breakfast and dinner—Mary Poppins and others in the morning, and Cinderella and her family in the evening. Also on the first floor is the unpretentious and unambitious Grand Floridian Café—with no dress code, no characters, and no fancy dining, it's usually the easiest to book, but also the least interesting for kids or adults. The fifth table service restaurant, Narcoossee's, fronts the Seven Seas Lagoon near the boat dock, specializes in seafood, and has a resort casual dress code. The quick service option is in the main building but only accessible from outside, and is one of the best quick service options among the deluxes. There's a bar on the second floor of the main building, and another at each pool.

The Grand Floridian has an extensive set of amenities, including beaches, nightly movies, campfires, jogging trails, playgrounds, a pirate cruise, boat rental, fishing, a great spa and fitness center, hot tubs, a volleyball court, and an arcade.

At the Grand Floridian you can pay extra for views. Standard view (Outer Building Garden View) five-person rooms are $663/night on weekdays and $702/night on Fridays and Saturdays during the 2016 Fall season. 2016 peak prices for these rooms are $886 and prices bottom out at $640/night.

DISNEY'S WILDERNESS LODGE

Disney's Wilderness Lodge ("WL"), near the Magic Kingdom, is inspired by the great U.S. National Park Lodges, and celebrates them and the mountain West. Its astonishing theming begins with its jaw-dropping lobby and continues with extensive detail everywhere in the resort. Nearby is the Disney Vacation Club Villas at the Wilderness Lodge, also available to all for rent. Guest services, a shop, and most dining are accessed from the lobby. Most rooms are in two wings off the lobby that enclose a mountain-stream-themed courtyard that ends in the delightful main pool. A smaller pool between the WL and the Villas will close for refurb in late October 2015 and remain closed through 2016.

Disney's Wilderness Lodge   ~340 Square Feet
Floor Plan from yourfirstvisit.net

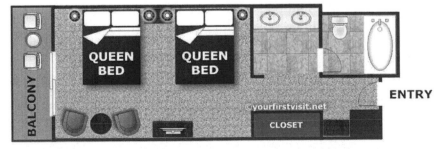

This refurb will also affect other areas southeast of the main Lodge and northeast of the Villas, with an additional smaller impact northwest of the Lodge. Those with courtyard-view rooms at the Lodge and woods view rooms at the Villas should avoid impact from the refurb.

The Wilderness Lodge is on Bay Lake near the Magic Kingdom, which is a ten-minute boat ride away. Boats also connect the Wilderness Lodge with the nearby Contemporary Resort and Fort Wilderness, giving easy access to the great dining options at those resorts. The other theme parks, water parks, and Disney Springs are accessed via shared buses that can take a while. The Wilderness Lodge is well located for a Magic Kingdom-focused trip.

The exterior architecture, lobby, detailing, and pools make the Wilderness Lodge an astonishingly kid-appealing resort. Adults enjoy it as well, although they might find its rooms smaller than expected.

Standard guest rooms at WL, with about 340 square feet, are tied with those at Disney's Animal Kingdom Lodge as the smallest deluxe rooms on property (they are also the least expensive such rooms). No five-person rooms are available except in the Villas—standard rooms sleep four on two queens. You'll also find a table and two chairs, mini-fridge, TV, dresser, closet, and a coffee-maker. The divided bath includes two sinks and a hair dryer, and a toilet and tub in a separate room. Of the three room types at the Villas, studios are most comparable to standard WL rooms. They sleep five in a slightly larger space, on a queen, a fold-out couch, and a fold-down smaller bed that's 32 inches by 75 inches. These five-person studio rooms are great choices for five-person families looking for Wilderness Lodge kid appeal who can fit in their beds. Rooms have balconies or patios, and are accessed from

Jim's Gems
by Jim Korkis

Artist Duane Pasco carved the two 55-foot-tall totem poles for the lobby of the Wilderness Lodge. These totem poles measure 3-feet wide at the top and 5-feet wide at the bottom, and each is constructed of two 27-foot sections spliced together. The goal in designing the totem poles was to use legend and lore common among the many tribes of the Northwest Coast, but not necessarily specific to any one tribe. One pole tells the story of the eagle and the other tells the story of the raven, two animal icons familiar in many Native American stories.

interior corridors. Like the other deluxe resorts, you can also reserve concierge-supported rooms ("club" rooms) and suites, and WL also has larger "deluxe rooms" that sleep six.

There are two table service restaurants at WL. Artist Point has a resort casual dress code, and offers a Pacific Northwest inspired menu. Whispering Canyon Café provides raucous fun and family-friendly dining. There are no character meals here, but these and other kid and adult-appealing meals are available at the Contemporary and Fort Wilderness—each just a boat ride away. WL has one of the better counter service options among the deluxes, and the best bar of the Magic Kingdom resorts. There's another bar at the pool.

Amenities include nightly movies, campfires, jogging trails, fishing, a spa/fitness center, hot tubs, volleyball, and arcades. The beach, playground, and boat rental will be closed for refurb in 2016. More water sports and a pirate cruise are at the nearby Contemporary. WL is one of three deluxe resorts (the Polynesian and Animal Kingdom Lodge are the others) that are not convention hotels.

At the Wilderness Lodge you can pay extra for views. Refurbs will disturb views on the southeast façade of the main lodge and the Bay Lake side of the Villas beginning in late October 2015. Courtyard views in the main lodge are the safest bet, and woods views in the Villas. Standard view rooms are $367/night on weekdays and $407/night on Fridays and Saturdays during the 2016 Fall season. 2016 peak prices for these rooms are $580 and prices bottom out at $325/night.

DISNEY'S CONTEMPORARY RESORT

Disney's Contemporary Resort ("Contemporary"), a monorail resort, is essentially un-themed but still iconic, and, on first impression, visually striking. The massive concrete A-frame with monorails passing through the middle is stunning at first view. However, the spare masses and geometric landscaping quickly fade from notice, and there's not much interesting detail earning a second glance. There are three basic areas at the Contemporary—the main Tower, which is what most people mean when they think of it; the South Garden Wing, low-rise rooms mostly without balconies; and Bay Lake Tower, the Disney Vacation Club offering. Found in the main Tower are dining, shops, guest services, and, from a dedicated escalator and elevator on the fourth floor, access to the resort monorail with service to the Magic Kingdom, the other monorail resorts, and the Transportation and Ticket Center (TTC). The dull but large main pool is outside the Tower, and there's a second dull and somewhat smaller pool between the main pool and Bay Lake. The

Contemporary is the only Disney resort from which you can walk to and from the Magic Kingdom. With travel to the Magic Kingdom available via both monorail and walking, the Contemporary is, by far, the most convenient Disney World resort for trips focused solely on that park.

Transportation to Epcot is via the Epcot monorail at TTC, accessible by the resort monorail. Transportation to the other parks and Disney Springs is via buses, typically shared with one or two other Magic Kingdom area resorts. There's also boat service among the three Bay Lake resorts—the Contemporary, Wilderness Lodge, and Fort Wilderness.

The Contemporary has nothing of the visual kid appeal of the Polynesian or the Wilderness or Animal Kingdom Lodges, but it does make a strong first impression, and some kids continue to be fascinated by the monorail running through the middle.

Standard rooms at the Contemporary were refurbished in 2013 and sleep five on two queens and a sofa that flips into a twin bed. Most rooms are about 400 square feet, among the largest at Disney World. Besides the two queens and couch, you'll find a very large L-shaped desk that is too large to fit gracefully where it is placed, with a small rolling table underneath, a desk chair, mini-fridge, TV, two closets, and a coffee-maker. Clothes storage drawers are in the corner of the desk area, making them a little less usable than those in rooms with more central storage. The spacious bath includes two sinks and a hair dryer, but is not divided, making it less family friendly than you'll find in more recently built hotels (the Contemporary was built in the early 70s). Views from the higher main Tower rooms of the Magic Kingdom or Bay Lake are marvelous, and, because it is Disney World's only high-rise hotel, guests in Tower rooms will also find it the most compact Disney hotel to navigate. All Tower rooms have balconies. Garden Wing rooms have similar size and furnishings to Tower rooms, but are much more spread out, and without the views—or balconies—of the Tower rooms. They are also much less expensive. Of the four room types in the Disney Vacation Club at Bay Lake Tower, studios are most comparable to Tower rooms, but sleep only four in a cramped space with a queen and fold-out couch. All rooms are accessed from interior corridors. Like the other deluxe resorts, you can also reserve concierge-supported Tower rooms ("club" rooms) and suites in both the Tower and the Garden Wing.

The Contemporary has three table service restaurants and one quick service option. All dining is in the Tower. The first floor Wave of American Flavors focuses on locally grown and organic offerings. Chef Mickey's on the fourth floor offers a wildly popular buffet attended by Mickey, Minnie, Donald, Goofy, and Pluto. The top-floor California Grill was revamped in 2013, and offers fine modern American and sushi dining

Disney's Contemporary Resort
Floor Plan   ~394 Square Feet

BALCONY

QUEEN BED

QUEEN BED

©yourfirstvisit.net

ENTRY

DAY BED

CLOSET

with a great view of the Magic Kingdom, especially if you are there during the fireworks. The quick service location is the fourth-floor Contempo Café. More great dining is just a monorail ride away at the Grand Floridian and Polynesian, and a boat ride away at the Wilderness Lodge and Fort Wilderness. There's a weak-looking and mis-placed bar on the fourth floor, a fine setting for a bar at the California Grill, and a pool bar.

The fourth floor of the Contemporary is the center of much of its action, and elevators there can be quite crowded. Guests headed from there to the first floor should consider the escalators.

The Contemporary has as broad a set of amenities as you will find at a Disney resort. They include beaches, nightly movies, campfires, jogging trails, playgrounds, boat rental, bike rental, parasailing, waterskiing, wakeboarding, tubing, tennis, fishing, a spa and fitness center, hot tubs, a Pirate cruise, a volleyball court, and an arcade.

At the Contemporary, you can pay extra for views. Standard (Bay Lake) view five-person main tower rooms are $620/night on weekdays and $705/night on Fridays and Saturdays during the 2016 Fall season. 2016 peak prices for these rooms are $810 and prices bottom out at $610/night.

DISNEY'S BEACH CLUB RESORT

Disney's Beach Club Resort ("BC"), an Epcot resort, is themed to recollect images of Victorian seaside cottages and hotels from Stone Harbor and other Cape May, New Jersey, settings. The exterior architecture is particularly charming, and of high appeal to adults. Kids don't much get its theming until they see the Stormalong Bay pool and its associated beaches and playgrounds. After that, that's all they see... The Beach

Club occupies half of an enormous, long-corridored building, with sister resort The Yacht Club taking up the other half. Nearby you'll find the DVC Beach Club Villas. In the center of the enormous building are kitchens and other back-of the house areas, then on either side the table service restaurants of the two resorts, then the guest service areas (one for each) and shops. Near Crescent Lake you'll find Stormalong Bay pool, shared with the Yacht Club—actually three separate pools, each with its own focus: a sand-bottomed shallow pool delightful for little ones; a pool perfect for drifting or tubing; and a pool for swimming. The larger of two fun water slides accessed from a shipwreck (!) on a Crescent Lake beach splashes down at one end of this pool. Some call Stormalong Bay a "mini water park". That's a stretch, yet does capture the difference between it and every other Disney World pool except those at the Four Seasons. There's two smaller pools at BC—the better one back by the Villas—and another at the very far end of the Yacht Club.

The Beach Club is near the back entrance to Epcot, the International Gateway. For Epcot, walk or take a boat. For most BC rooms, the boats are a long walk away, so walking is often the better choice. Hollywood Studios is best accessed by boat, and the other theme parks, water parks, and Disney Springs via shared buses that can take a while. The Beach Club is wonderfully located for trips centered on Epcot, and a favorite of many returning family visitors. It's not so well located for a Magic Kingdom focused trip.

Adults generally love the architecture and convenience to Epcot of BC, while kids often don't get the theme—a hotel themed as a cottage?—but just don't care after they see the pool.

Disney's Beach Club Resort
Floor Plan   ~381 Square Feet

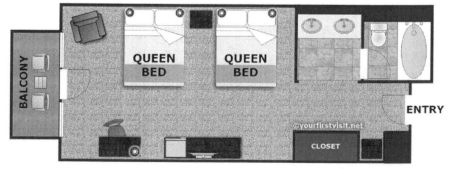

Guest rooms at the BC completed a much-needed refurbishment in 2015. Most standard rooms at BC sleep five on two queens and a daybed (some rooms omit the daybed— the floor plan shows such a room). Standard rooms are about 380 square feet—in the middle of the deluxe range, but well-appointed and proportioned. Five-person rooms have beside the beds a desk with a small rolling table underneath, a desk chair, mini-fridge, TV, dresser, closet, and a coffee-maker. The divided bath includes two sinks and a hair dryer, and a toilet and tub in a separate room. Four-person rooms have the same size, omit the daybed, but add an easy chair. Rooms in the nearby Villas are also available for rent to the general public. Of the three room types at the Villas, studios are most comparable to standard BC rooms. They sleep four in a smaller overall space, on a queen and fold-out couch. (A fold-down fifth sleeping spot is expected to be added in a refurb that at press time had not yet commenced.) All rooms are accessed from interior corridors. Most BC standard rooms have small balconies or patios that seat two, but many BC rooms have tiny balconies with barely room to stand. This choice adds interest and grace to the façade, but impedes livability. Like the other deluxe resorts, you can also reserve concierge-supported rooms (Disney call these "club" rooms) and suites.

BC has two table service restaurants. The Cape May Café offers a character breakfast with Goofy, and other characters like Minnie, Chip and Dale, but not Mickey. In the evening, Cape May converts to a no-character "clambake" buffet. Seafood can be good from a buffet— but it can't be great. By the pool is the glorious Beaches and Cream ice cream and burger-focused establishment, with not remotely enough seats. There's no real counter service here, just a few options in the back of the gift shop. You can walk to sister resort the Yacht Club or the nearby Epcot resort the BoardWalk Inn, but you won't find any counter service at either, nor any kid-appealing table service restaurants. Dining in Epcot is also an option, but may be impractical for families without hopper tickets. There's an indoor bar and another at the pool.

Among them, the three Epcot resorts—the Beach and Yacht Clubs, and BoardWalk Inn—provide within walking distance access to almost any amenity, including beaches, nightly movies, campfires, jogging trails, playgrounds, a pirate cruise, boat rental, fishing, a spa/fitness center, tennis, hot tubs, volleyball, a business center, and arcades.

At the Beach Club you can pay extra for views. Standard view rooms are $450/night on weekdays and $519/night on Fridays and Saturdays during the 2016 Fall season. 2016 peak prices for these rooms are $695 and prices bottom out at $400/night.

DISNEY'S ANIMAL KINGDOM LODGE

Disney's Animal Kingdom Lodge ("AKL"), near the Animal Kingdom theme park, shares with the Wilderness Lodge astonishingly detailed theming and a jaw-dropping lobby, based in its case on African park lodges. It is also near-surrounded with parklands (Disney calls them "savannas") displaying animals. These animals are visible from savanna-view rooms and also from multiple public viewing areas. On several upper floors of the main building (Jambo House) you'll also find Disney Vacation Club spaces, the Jambo House Villas, and, a long walk or short bus ride away, even more DVC Villas at Kidani Village, all available for rent. Guest services and a shop are accessed from the main AKL Jambo lobby. Dining is at a lower level. (Kidani has another lobby, shop, and restaurant.) Most Jambo rooms are in two long-corridored semi-circular wings off the lobby that enclose animal savannas. The main pool is as good as any Disney-owned pool except Stormalong Bay at the Yacht and Beach Clubs. A slightly smaller but still wonderful pool serves Kidani.

The Animal Kingdom Lodge is at the far southwest corner of Walt Disney World. Uniquely among the deluxes, all transport to the theme parks, water parks, and Disney Springs is via buses shared with Kidani. Included in this is the Animal Kingdom park—you can't walk there. AKL thus is not particularly well located.

The animals, exterior architecture, lobby, detailing, and pools make AKL an astonishingly kid-appealing resort. Adults enjoy it as well, although they might find its rooms smaller than expected.

Standard guest rooms at AKL, with about 340 square feet, are tied with those at Disney's Wilderness Lodge as the smallest deluxe rooms on property (standard view rooms also are—for a Disney deluxe—inexpensive). Most first-time visitors ought not to pay for views, as they won't be in their rooms enough, but they absolutely should pay for

Disney's Animal Kingdom Lodge ~340 Square Feet

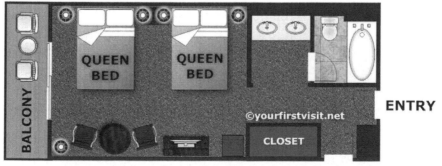

savanna views at AKL. No five-person rooms are available—standard rooms sleep four on two queens. You'll also find a table and two chairs, mini-fridge, TV, dresser, closet, and a coffee-maker. The divided bath includes two sinks and a hair dryer, and a toilet and tub in a separate room. Of the four room types at the Disney Vacation Club Jambo and Kidani Villas, studios are most comparable to standard AKL rooms. They sleep four in a slightly larger space, on a queen and a fold-out couch. Jambo studios are the better choice than Kidani studios, even though smaller, as the Jambo building is much better themed, and dining is much more convenient. Rooms have balconies, and are accessed from interior corridors. Like the other deluxe resorts, you can also reserve concierge-supported rooms ("club" rooms) and suites.

There are two table service restaurants at in the main Jambo building, and another at Kidani. In Jambo, Jiko nears the top of many "best Disney dining" lists, has a resort casual dress code, and offers an eclectic African-inspired menu. Next-door Boma is more family friendly, with a wide-ranging buffet. At Kidani, the underappreciated gem Sanaa has an African/Indian inspired menu. AKL also has one of the better counter service options among the deluxes, and one of Disney World's best bars. There's another bar at each pool. Unlike the other deluxes, there's no easy access to more dining at another hotel.

Amenities include nightly movies, campfires, jogging trails, playgrounds, a spa/fitness center, hot tubs, and arcades. AKL is alone among the Disney deluxe resorts in not being on water, having no beach, and offering no easy access to water sports. AKL is one of three deluxe resorts (the Polynesian and Wilderness Lodge are the others) that are not convention hotels.

At the Animal Kingdom Lodge, you should pay extra for savanna views. Savanna view rooms are $526/night on weekdays and $604/night on Fridays and Saturdays during the 2016 Fall season. 2016 peak prices for these rooms are $735 and prices bottom out at $495/night. These prices are typically around $150–$200/night more than standard view rooms.

DISNEY'S YACHT CLUB RESORT

Disney's Yacht Club Resort ("YC"), an Epcot resort, is themed to resemble a formal New England yacht club. The dull gray exterior does little to accomplish this, but there are some nautical decorative elements in the public areas and rooms. Neither kids nor adults much get its theming. Kids, though, are delighted by Stormalong Bay pool and its associated beaches and playgrounds. The Yacht Club occupies half of an enormous long-corridored building, with sister resort The Beach Club—warmer, more charming, and more inviting—taking up the other half. In the center of the enormous building are kitchens and other back-of the house areas, then on either side the table service restaurants of the two resorts, then the guest service areas (one for each) and shops. Near Crescent Lake you'll find Stormalong Bay pool, shared with the Beach Club—actually three separate pools, each with its own focus: a sand-bottomed shallow pool delightful for little ones; a pool perfect for drifting or tubing; and a pool for swimming. The larger of two fun water slides accessed from a shipwreck (!) on a beach splashes down at one end of this pool. Some call Stormalong Bay a "mini water park". That's a stretch, yet does capture the difference between it and every other Disney World pool except those at the Four Seasons. There's one smaller pool at the far west end of YC, and two smaller ones near the east end of BC.

The Yacht Club is near the back entrance to Epcot, the International Gateway. You can walk or take a boat to Epcot. Hollywood Studios is accessed by a long walk or by boat, and the other theme parks, water parks, and Disney Springs via shared buses that can take a while. The Yacht Club is well located for trips centered on Epcot, but not so well located for a Magic Kingdom focused trip.

All of Disney's marketing material stresses the "formality" of the Yacht Club and the "fun" of the Beach Club. Both points are overstated, but result in families self-selecting into the prettier Beach Club, and conventioneers (both hotels are convention hotels) into the duller Yacht Club. This is fine—the Beach Club is the better family choice on any relevant measure except balconies: all YC rooms have large balconies, while BC rooms have either small or almost uselessly tiny ones.

Guest rooms at the YC are expected to be refurbed in 2016. Most standard rooms at YC sleep five on two queens and a daybed (some

Disney's Yacht Club Resort
Floor Plan   ~381 Square Feet

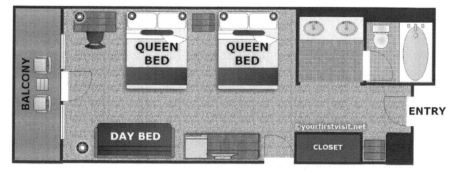

rooms omit the daybed and sleep four). Standard rooms are about 380 square feet—in the middle of the deluxe range, but well-appointed and proportioned. Five-person rooms currently have, beside the beds, a desk with a small rolling table underneath, a desk chair, mini-fridge, TV, dresser, closet, and a coffee-maker. The divided bath includes two sinks and a hair dryer, and a toilet and tub in a separate room. Four-person rooms have the same size, omit the daybed, but add an easy chair. All rooms are accessed from interior corridors. Like the other deluxe resorts, you can also reserve concierge-supported rooms (Disney call these "club" rooms) and suites.

YC has two table service restaurants. The Yachtsman Steak House is a top-notch venue with steaks as good as any Disney restaurant. It has a resort casual dress code. The other table service restaurant, Captain's Grille, is tied with the Grand Floridian Café for being the most uninteresting resort restaurant on property. There's no counter service at all. You can walk to the nearby Beach Club and find a character breakfast at Cape May Café, great burger and ice cream dining at Beaches and Cream, and very weak counter service. The nearby BoardWalk Inn has neither meaningful counter service nor any kid-appealing table service restaurants. Dining in Epcot is also an option, but may be impractical for families without hopper tickets. There's a bar inside and another at the pool.

Among them, the three Epcot resorts—the Beach and Yacht Clubs, and BoardWalk Inn—provide within walking distance access to almost any amenity, including beaches, nightly movies, campfires, jogging trails, playgrounds, a pirate cruise, boat rental, fishing, a spa/fitness center, tennis, hot tubs, volleyball, a business center, and arcades.

At the Yacht Club you can pay extra for views. Standard view rooms are $450/night on weekdays and $519/night on Fridays and Saturdays during the 2016 Fall season. 2016 peak prices for these rooms are $695 and prices bottom out at $400/night.

DISNEY'S BOARDWALK INN

Disney's BoardWalk Inn ("BWI"), an Epcot resort, has a split visual personality. One part of it, facing Crescent Lake, is themed to recall Atlantic coast boardwalk vacation settings. The rest—including the areas with the most rooms—is themed to recall a quieter and more peaceful Colonial-revival style resort with garden courtyards. The BoardWalk Inn is Disney's smallest deluxe resort, but some corridors are as long as those at sister Epcot resorts the Yacht and Beach Clubs. Cutting across the courtyard can save much walking. Connected through the lobby of the BoardWalk Inn is the enormous Disney Vacation Club property

Disney's BoardWalk Villas, also available to all for rent. Guest services and a small shop are in the lobby, and more shopping is downstairs on the BoardWalk. Dining is a little weird—there's next to none "in" the BoardWalk Inn, but several restaurants are accessible just outside on the Boardwalk. In the Villas area you'll find the fun amusement-park themed main pool and a second smaller pool. A third pool, also small, is in an internal courtyard of the Inn.

The BoardWalk Inn is near the back entrance to Epcot, the International Gateway, and is as near Epcot as is the Beach Club, and nearer to Disney's Hollywood Studios. You can walk to either park from it, though most take the boat to the Studios. The other theme parks, water parks, and Disney Springs are reached via shared buses that can take a while. The BoardWalk Inn is well located for trips centered on Epcot and the Studios, but not so well located for a Magic Kingdom-focused trip.

From its interior courtyards, the BoardWalk Inn is the loveliest and most compact of the Epcot resorts, and is highly popular with honeymooners. Kids don't get its theme, and the main pool, while fine, isn't at the standard of the pool at the Beach Club, making the Beach Club a better choice for most families. But adults love it, and the resulting demand means BWI is typically a little more expensive than the Beach Club.

Standard guest rooms at BWI, with about 370 square feet, are similar to those in the Yacht Club and Beach Club, mid-sized among the deluxes but well-proportioned and appointed, sleeping four on two queens or five with an added couch. Rooms also have a desk with a small rolling table underneath, a desk chair, mini-fridge, TV, dresser, closet, and a coffee-maker. The divided bath includes two sinks and a hair dryer, and a toilet and

Disney's BoardWalk Inn
Floor Plan   ~370 Square Feet

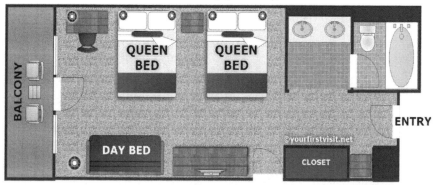

Jim's Gems
by Jim Korkis

The BoardWalk Inn and Villas includes a 190,000-gallon pool themed to resemble the carnival-type atmosphere of one of the most popular of the Coney Island amusement parks: Luna Park. It lasted from 1903 to 1944 and was built and operated by Frederic Thompson and Elmer "Skip" Dundy, who outfitted it with a multitude of towers and spires lit at night by 122,000 electric lights (when electricity was still a novelty). At the resort, the proprietor of the On the Boardwalk Thimbles & Threads shop is "F. Thompson" and inside the resort's main lobby is Dundy's Sundries—Serving the Boardwalk since 1902.

tub in a separate room. Four-person rooms have the same size, omit the couch, but add an easy chair. Of the four room types at the Villas, studios are most comparable to standard BWI rooms. Refurbed in 2015, they sleep five in a similar space on a queen, a fold-out couch, and a fifth fold-down sleeping spot, but can be quite a hike. Rooms have balconies or patios, and are accessed from interior corridors. Like the other deluxe resorts, you can also reserve concierge-supported rooms (Disney call these "club" rooms) and suites, and BW also has larger "deluxe rooms" that sleep six, and Garden Cottages best suited to couples.

The BoardWalk Inn itself has next to no dining, but several restaurants with zero kid appeal are right outside on the BoardWalk itself. These include the sports-bar style ESPN Club; the new Italian restaurant Trattoria al Forno; high-end, expensive seafood at the Flying Fish Café; and the brew pub Big River Grille. There are no character meals, nor any real counter service. More table service dining is at the Yacht and Beach Clubs, and dining in Epcot is an option, but may be impractical for families without hopper tickets. There's a great bar inside and another at the pool.

Among them, the three Epcot resorts—the Beach and Yacht Clubs, and BoardWalk Inn—provide within walking distance access to almost any amenity, including beaches, nightly movies, campfires, jogging trails, playgrounds, a pirate cruise, boat rental, fishing, a spa/fitness center, tennis, hot tubs, volleyball, a business center, and arcades.

At the BoardWalk Inn you can pay extra for views. Standard view rooms are $472/night on weekdays and $510/night on Fridays and Saturdays during the 2016 Fall season. 2016 peak prices for these rooms are $730 and prices bottom out at $459/night.

DISNEY'S OLD KEY WEST RESORT

Disney's Old Key West Resort ("OKW") is a Disney Vacation Club Resort, but unlike those discussed so far it is not paired with a deluxe resort, but rather stands on its own. Like all the other DVC offerings, its accommodations are available to Disney Vacation Club members, to others who have rented points from them, and to anyone using cash just like at any other Disney World resort. Except for dining and convenience, its offerings and amenities are comparable to those at Disney deluxe resorts, which is why we discuss it here.

OKW is themed to recall Key West, which it does a bit here and there. But with dozens of three-story buildings winding among water and fairways, it mostly comes across as a pastel-colored example of a vacation condominium community. Neither kids nor adults much get its theming, and there is little to visually signal you are in Disney World.

Old Key West's two- and three-story accommodations buildings—most of which have no elevators—are scattered across a large expanse, with the central services (dining, shops, check-in, and the main pool) located near the entry to the resort, far from most accommodations buildings. The main pool has a great slide and sandcastle theme, and is fun, but a hike for most guests. Three other pools with fewer amenities serve those who don't wish to walk, drive, take a bus, or get a taxi to the main pool.

OKW is located just south of POFQ and is identified in Disney

Disney's Old Key West Resort Studio Floor Plan ~390 Square Feet

PATIO

QUEEN BED

QUEEN BED

CLOSET

BEDROOM

ENTRY

©yourfirstvisit.net

way-finding material as a Disney Springs Area Resort. Often derided for being isolated, it's actually not that far from Epcot, Disney's Hollywood Studios, and Magic Kingdom. Rather, what makes it inconvenient is the five bus stops needed to serve its sprawl, the bus backtracking that comes from dead-end roads, and the walking distances within it. All transportation to the theme parks and water parks is via bus; there's also a boat to Disney Springs, so don't miss your stop. A car is handy here. We wouldn't stay at OKW without one.

Of the four types of accommodations available at OKW, its studios are most comparable to standard rooms at the deluxe resorts, so they are the focus here. All Disney studios are distinguished from deluxe standard rooms by having a microwave and toaster in addition to the standard coffeemaker and mini-fridge found in both studios and deluxe rooms. Most are also different by having a queen bed and a fold-out couch. Old Key West studios are unique in offering two queens, rather than a queen and sleeper sofa. A sofa creates a more flexible studio; two queens, more comfortable sleeping. OKW studios are about 380 square feet—larger than most other studios—sleep four and have, beside the beds and kitchenette appliances, a table and chairs, TV, dresser, and closet. The bath is not divided, but with a second sink available in the nearby kitchenette the room functions as though it were. Studios here also come with a large patio or balcony.

Larger spaces are also available at OKW. One Bedroom Villas hold five in about twice the space of a studio and Two Bedroom Villas hold nine in about three times the space of a studio. These One and Two Bedroom Villas are among the largest and the most home-like of the DVC offerings. Grand Villas at OKW hold 12 in about five times the space of a studio.

First-timers are often surprised by how thin the dining is at OKW. However, everyone staying here either has a kitchenette, as in the studios, or has the full kitchen that the other OKW accommodations come with. The gift shop is also well-stocked with food. OKW has only one table service restaurant, Olivia's. Much loved among families who return to Old Key West year after year, Olivia's is bright, colorful, and fun, and worth a visit from those staying at OKW—but is by no means destination dining. There's a small counter service venue outside that also serves as the grill for the main pool, and a small bar next to it. Dining in Disney Springs is also an option, but the boats there are slower and less frequent than ideal.

OKW offers most amenities, including nightly movies, campfires, jogging trails, playgrounds, bike rentals, fishing, a spa/fitness center, tennis, basketball, hot tubs, volleyball, and an arcade.

Because of the layout of the accommodations buildings, almost all OKW spaces have nice views, and there are no extra charge options for views or preferred areas. OKW and Saratoga Springs are usually the lowest priced DVC options (other than some not-recommended standard view and "value" studios at the Animal Kingdom Lodge). Studios at OKW are $403/night during the 2016 Fall season. 2016 peak prices for these rooms are $550 and prices bottom out at $368/night.

DISNEY'S SARATOGA SPRINGS RESORT & SPA

Disney's Saratoga Springs Resort & Spa ("SS") is a Disney Vacation Club Resort, but, like Old Key West, it is not paired with a deluxe resort—it stands on its own. As with all the other DVC offerings, its accommodations are available to Disney Vacation Club members, to others who have rented points from them, and to anyone using cash just like at any other Disney World resort. Except for dining and convenience, its offerings and amenities are comparable to those at Disney deluxe resorts, which is why we discuss it here.

Saratoga Springs is themed to recall the vacation, spa, and horse country around Saratoga Springs, New York, and it does do this a bit here and there. But with large three-story buildings winding among water and fairways, it mostly feels like a golf condominium development. You really could be anywhere.

Saratoga Spring's almost 20 accommodations buildings (all with elevators) are scattered in several named areas across a large expanse, with the main services—dining, shops, check-in, and the main pool—located near the center of the resort, and distant from many accommodations buildings. Uniquely, Saratoga Springs has two full-service pools with slides, bars, food and such: the High Rock Spring pool in the central Springs area, and the Paddock pool in the Paddock area. Another pool, the Grandstand pool, has no slide but is otherwise sound, and two smaller pools with few amenities are in the Treehouse and Congress Park areas.

SS is located just east of OKW and is identified in Disney way-finding material as a Disney Springs Area Resort. Often derided for being remote, it's actually not that far from Epcot, Disney's Hollywood Studios, and Magic Kingdom, but is the most isolated resort after the Animal Kingdom Lodge. What makes it particularly inconvenient is the walks to the central services and the five bus stops needed to serve its sprawl (plus two more at the Treehouse Villas—don't even ask). All transportation to the theme parks and water parks is via bus; there's also a boat and a walking path to Disney Springs. A car is handy here—we wouldn't stay at SS without one.

Of the four types of accommodations available at SS, its studios are most comparable to standard rooms at the deluxe resorts, so they are the focus here. All Disney studios are distinguished from deluxe standard rooms by having a microwave and toaster in addition to the standard coffeemaker and mini-fridge found in both studios and deluxe rooms. Most are also different by having a queen bed and a fold-out couch. SS studios are much like most other Disney World studios, except at about 355 square feet are a little smaller. They sleep four and have, beside the bed, sofa bed and kitchenette appliances, a table and chairs, TV, dresser, and a closet. The divided bath has a sink and closet in one part, and toilet and tub in their own room. Studios also come with a patio or balcony.

Disney's Saratoga Springs Resort & Spa Studio Floor Plan ~355 Square Feet

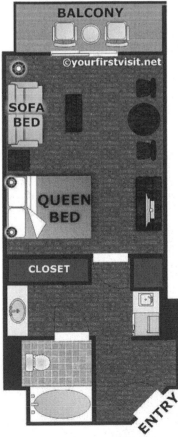

Larger spaces are also available at SS. One Bedroom Villas hold four in about twice the space of a studio and Two Bedroom Villas hold eight in three times the space of a studio. Grand Villas at SS hold 12 in about five times the space of a studio. These are among the smaller of these room types at Disney World, so another DVC venue will be a better choice for most. A unique additional offering at SS is the Treehouse Villas—woefully isolated, with their own buses that go only to Saratoga Springs itself, but a great three-bedroom option for a group of nine with a car or two.

First-timers are often surprised by how thin the dining is at SS. However, everyone staying here either has a kitchenette, as in the studios, or has the full kitchen that the other SS accommodations come with. The gift shop is also well-stocked with food. SS has only one table service restaurant, The Turf Club. Much loved among golfers and romantic for couples, it's less interesting for kids. There's a small counter service venue in the gift shop so that you can apply mustard directly to your stuffed Mickey rather than waiting to stain it by chance, and several of the pools have substantial bar and grill menus. Dining in Disney Springs is also an option, but the boats there are slower and less frequent than ideal, and the walking path is a hike from everywhere except the Congress Park area.

SS offers most amenities, including nightly movies, campfires, jogging trails, playgrounds, bike rentals, fishing, a wonderful spa/fitness center, tennis, basketball, hot tubs, and an arcade. It's also the only Disney resort with a pro shop and golf course start, underneath the Turf Club.

Because of the layout of the accommodations buildings, almost all SS spaces have nice views, and there are no extra charge options for views or preferred areas. Saratoga Springs and OKW are usually the lowest priced DVC options (other than some not-recommended standard view and "value" studios at the Animal Kingdom Lodge). SS studios are $403/night during the 2016 Fall season. 2016 peak prices for these rooms are $550 and prices bottom out at $368/night.

Other Disney World Lodging Options

Besides the Disney-owned value, moderate and deluxe resorts, there are other options as well—none of which we particularly recommend:

- The Disney-owned multi-room spaces at the Disney Vacation club resorts.
- The Disney-owned Campsites at Fort Wilderness.
- The on-property, non-Disney-owned hotels: the Swan, Dolphin, Shades of Green, Four Seasons, and the hotels of the Disney Springs Resort Area.
- Everything else—the offsite hotels and vacation homes.

The positives and negatives of these choices vary, so we'll comment briefly on each.

MULTI-ROOM VILLAS AT
DISNEY VACATION CLUB RESORTS

The Disney Vacation Club ("DVC") Resorts at Walt Disney World are time-shares with rooms that can also be booked via cash reservations, just like any other Disney World resort hotel room.

Except for the studios, which we've already discussed in the "Deluxe Resorts" section, above, what's distinct about the accommodations in these DVC resorts is the extra space and large kitchens—neither of which will be used much during a first visit.

These villas can also be reserved (usually at a huge cost saving) by privately renting "points" from Disney Vacation Club members.

For most first-time family visitors, the Disney Vacation Club Resorts are worth considering only under a few circumstances:

- Large families, especially those aimed at a deluxe property, who are not willing to bet on actually getting connecting rooms. (You can request connecting rooms at WDW, but getting them is not guaranteed.) Villas which can sleep 8, 9, and 12 people are available.
- Smaller families looking to spread out into a One or Two-Bedroom Villa, despite the higher price.
- Families aimed at a deluxe hotel, but who can only pull it off through the cost savings of renting DVC points.
- Families who have targeted a resort with which a DVC property is paired, find it is sold out, but can get into the DVC resort.
- People who already are DVC owners.

All of the DVC resorts except Saratoga Springs and Old Key West are paired with a deluxe resort and mostly share the pros and cons of that resort in terms of convenience, kid appeal, dining, amenities, and such.

There are, however, some real variances across the DVC resorts in the livability of their rooms.

Studios add to the routine amenities of a deluxe room a microwave and toaster, and generally sleep four in a queen and a fold out-sofa. Old Key West Studios have two queens. Studios in the Villas at the Wilderness Lodge ("VWL"), the Polynesian, the BoardWalk Villas, and the Villas at the Grand Floridian ("VGF") (and, when their refurb is complete, the Beach Club Villas) sleep five—the third sleeping spot is a short fold-down murphy bed that's 72ish inches long and sleeps shorter than that. Studios in Bay Lake Tower at Disney's Contemporary ("BLT") sleep four, but we think the room is too cramped when the fold-out couch is opened. All Studios except those at the Polynesian have one bath. Polynesian Studios have one full bath, and a second bath space with sink and shower.

One Bedroom Villas sleep four or five, depending on the resort. They have a king bed bedroom that sleeps two and also a combined full kitchen, dining, and living space that typically sleeps two on a fold-out couch. Old Key West, Bay Lake Tower, and the Villas at the Animal Kingdom Lodge (at Jambo House and Kidani Village, "VAKL") add a third sleeping spot to this area with a fold-out chair; at the Villas at the Grand Floridian, this space gets a third spot from a fold-down murphy bed. All One Bedroom Villas except those at Kidani Village and Bay Lake Tower have a single large divided bath; at those two, there's a small bath in the living/dining/kitchen area and another larger one in the king bedroom.

Disney's Saratoga Springs Resort & Spa
Two Bedroom Villa Floor Plan ~1075 Square Feet

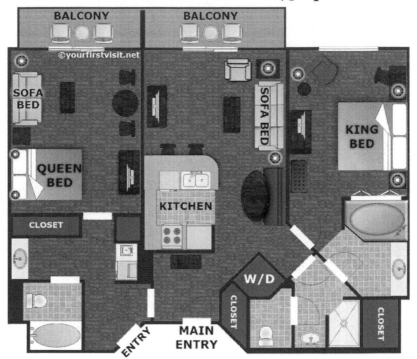

Two Bedroom Villas come in two flavors:

- One type simply combines a Studio and a One Bedroom through a connecting door, and is known as a "lock-off". These lock-off Two Bedroom Villas combine the capacity and merits of the spaces that make them up. Most sleep eight, but those that combine five-person spaces will sleep nine (OKW, BLT, VAKL, VWL) or, at the Villas at the Grand Floridian, ten.

- A second type, designed as a Two Bedroom Villa from the start, is called in the jargon a "dedicated" villa, sleeps eight or nine, and will have minor variations in the second bedroom compared to a Studio, losing the kitchenette, swapping the fold- out couch of the Studio for another queen, and getting another closet instead of an exit to the corridor. At the Grand Floridian, such villas also lose the fold-down bed in the second bedroom and sleep nine.

Two Bedroom Villas don't really have the living or dining space to support the eight or nine people they will hold—a problem particularly acute at the Beach Club Villas, Saratoga Springs, Villas at the Wilderness Lodge, and BoardWalk Villas. See the floor plan, above—a Saratoga

The Villas at Disney's Grand Floridian Resort and Spa
Two-Bedroom "Lockoff" Villa   ~1232 Square feet

Springs example. In this space that sleeps eight, note the seats for four in the living area and three at the dining table.

Chairs can be moved around to add seats in these smaller spaces, but larger groups will find the Two Bedroom Villas at Old Key West, the Villas at Disney's Grand Floridian, Kidani Village, and Bay Lake Tower much more livable. See the Grand Floridian floor plan, above.

Bungalows at the Polynesian are unlike any other DVC two-bedroom spaces, but are too expensive for you to even think about.

Grand Villas, available at all the DVC resorts except the Villas at the Wilderness Lodge, the Beach Club Villas, and the Polynesian Villas and Bungalows, sleep 12 in a king room, two rooms with two queens each, and some sofa beds. They have twice the living/dining/kitchen space of Two Bedroom Villas, and sometimes—at Jambo House, VGF, and most of the BoardWalk Grand Villas—even more.

There's more variation among the Grand Villas than in any other DVC accommodations, so for more on these huge spaces that can go for more than $2,000 a night, see YOURFIRSTVISIT.NET.

CAMPSITES AT FORT WILDERNESS

Fort Wilderness offers three lodging options—Cabins, group campsites, and individual campsites.

The Cabins were discussed earlier in this chapter, among the Moderates. You'll also find there an overview of the dining, extensive amenities, and inconvenience of Fort Wilderness. Neither of us has enough friends to have rented a group campsite, but they are particularly appropriate for scouts and other youth groups. The individual campsites can be booked for ten people and come in four basic types:

- "Tent or Pop-Up Campsites"
- "Full Hook-Up Campsites"
- "Preferred Campsites", and
- "Premium Campsites"

The key distinction is that Premium Campsites are designed for very large RVs, and have no tent pad. So tent campers, and campers with both an RV and a tent, should avoid them. Full Hook-Up sites have both a large RV spot and also a small tent pad. Tent campers are allowed in the Full Hook-Up campsites, but will find themselves in a sea of rumbling RVs should they choose one. Preferred sites have the same configuration as Full Hook-Up sites, but are closer to Magic Kingdom transportation and Fort Wilderness dining.

Anyone planning for tents at Fort Wilderness should keep three points in mind, all related to the commonly intense weather—heat and storms—in Orlando:

- Bring extra flys to serve as sun shades and rain protection. Your tent, ideally, will have a full coverage fly and a mesh inner body.
- Since the tent pads are sand, few traditional stakes will hold in weather. See the Fort Wilderness review on YOURFIRSTVISIT.NET for suggested alternative stakes. If you can walk comfortably around your site, you don't have enough guy lines out.
- All Fort Wilderness sites, including the Tent or Pop-Up sites, have power. So bring extensions cords and multiple fans.

The Campsites at Disney's Fort Wilderness Resort, while wonderful for returning visitors who like to camp or own an RV, are not recommended for typical first-time family visitors to Walt Disney World. The wilderness and backwoodsy theming of this resort, while charming, is so subtle that it will fly over the heads of most kids. Mickey and other Disney themes are almost entirely absent.

Also, the Campsites at Disney's Fort Wilderness Resort are remarkably inconvenient compared to the other Walt Disney World resorts. While often thought of as out of the way, the resort is actually located just across Bay Lake and Seven Seas Lagoon from the Magic Kingdom. Its inconvenience comes not from its location, but rather from the internal bus system that the sprawling Fort Wilderness Resort uses.

To get to any theme park, two transportation actions are required: an internal bus to the appropriate transfer point, and then an external bus or boat to the park itself. This can easily add half an hour or more to daily transportation times—adding up to seven or eight extra hours wasted on internal bus trips over the course of an eight-night visit.

Moreover, simply moving around the seven-hundred acre resort—getting to the pool, the shops, the playgrounds—can be a chore. Even if you have a car, you are discouraged from using it in the campground itself, both officially and by the lack of parking spaces where you might want to go.

OTHER ON-PROPERTY HOTELS

There are two groups of resorts operated by third parties on Disney property.

First, there's a group of four that are comparable to the Disney deluxe resorts in room size, quality, amenities, and location. These are Shades of Green, the Swan, the Dolphin, and the Four Seasons. Full reviews follow, but here's the key points:

- **Shades of Green** is an inexpensive deluxe-level resort near the Polynesian for U.S. service members, career military retirees, other eligible guests, and their families and sponsored friends. Shades guests are eligible for EMH.
- **The Swan and Dolphin** are deluxe hotels near the Epcot resorts—a little closer to Hollywood Studios than Epcot, compared to the other Epcot resorts. The Swan and Dolphin, at press time, are the only non-Disney resorts where FastPass+ is available at 60 days rather than 30 days. Both resorts are very competitively priced, but suffer from a daily $23 resort fee, in addition to $18 per day for parking.
- **The Four Seasons Resort Orlando** opened in 2014 as the first five-star resort at Walt Disney World. It has the largest standard rooms on property, great dining for adults, a character breakfast a couple of times a week with Goofy, and the best pool complex at Walt Disney World. At press time, Four Seasons did not participate in any Disney hotel perks, including EMH.

Second, there's a group of half a dozen or so hotels in the Disney Springs Resort Area. While their prices may initially seem attractive, high resort and parking fees typically push the price up by $30 or more per night. The Disney Springs Resort Area isn't convenient to anything but shopping, and these hotels have their own, often disappointing, park transportation. Opinions of these hotels vary and change, but none but the Hilton has a track record of strong reviews.

None of these non-Disney hotels participate in the Disney Dining Plan, in Disney's Magical Express, or in MagicBands. At press time, among them, only guests at the Swan or Dolphin are able to book FastPass+ 60 days ahead of arrival. All others can only book 30 days ahead.

- Guests at Shades of Green, the Swan, and the Dolphin, get to participate in the Extra Magic Hours program. No other non-Disney owned hotels besides these three offer the Extra Magic Hours program. (The Hilton's participation in EMH ends at the beginning of 2016.)
- Guests at the Swan and Dolphin use the Disney transportation system for travel to the theme parks.

THE DISNEY WORLD SWAN AND DOLPHIN

The Disney World Swan and Disney World Dolphin ("Swan and Dolphin") are paired, connected Starwood convention resorts that share all amenities and have easy access to Epcot and Disney's Hollywood Studios. The two resorts have unusual exterior decorations—off-putting to some and delightful to others—and lovely but un-themed interiors. The larger Dolphin has more amenities just an elevator ride away, but offers full beds in its standard rooms. The smaller Swan is more of a walk to some amenities, but has queen beds in its newly refurbed standard rooms.

The Swan and Dolphin are not owned by Disney, but even so share in the most valuable perk available to guests staying at a Disney-owned resort: they can book FastPass+ at 60 days. Swan and Dolphin guests also are eligible to attend Extra Magic Hours, and the two hotels are fully integrated into the same transportation system that serves Disney's own Epcot resorts—the Yacht Club, Beach Club, and BoardWalk Inn. Guests here don't get free parking at their hotel (but do at the parks), can't use the Dining Plan, and can't use Disney's Magical Express.

The Swan is a long mid-rise building with a curved roof that has enormous statues of swans on top. The Dolphin is larger and taller, rising to a pyramid flanked by enormous statues of a curious nondescript fish. Each hotel has its own amenities which guests at either can use, and the two are connected centrally by a covered walkway, and are connected at the side by a sweep of pool after pool after beach after pool that collectively are the third best pool complex at Disney World.

Walt Disney World Dolphin
Floor Plan ~ 360 Square Feet

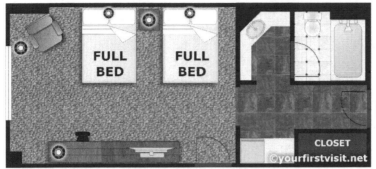

The Swan and Dolphin are just beyond the BoardWalk Villas and Yacht Club. Guests can use either Disney boats or a walking path to get to Disney's Hollywood Studios and Epcot. The other parks and Disney Springs are served by shared buses which can take awhile. This location makes them a fine choice for a visit centered on Epcot, but not so much for a trip focused especially on the Magic Kingdom—as most first visits are.

Standard rooms at the Swan were refurbed in 2015, and a refurb of Dolphin rooms has been announced, but the completion date remains uncertain. At press time, Swan rooms offer two queen beds and a divided bath with two sinks, and the slightly larger (360 vs. 340 square feet) Dolphin rooms (shown above) offer two full beds and a divided bath with a single sink. The queens and extra sink make Swan rooms better for most families.

Other amenities are similar. These rooms have beside the beds and bath a dresser, desk, mini-fridge, TV, closet, and a coffee-maker. All rooms are accessed from interior corridors, and only some have balconies. As is typical of convention hotels, many suites are also available.

The Swan and Dolphin have great adult dining at Kimonos, Shula's Steak House, and Todd English's bluezoo, and some OK kid dining including a character meal at Garden Grove. Casual dining is much better than that at Disney's Epcot resorts. More dining is easily accessible in the Disney hotels, along the nearby BoardWalk, and, for those with hoppers, in Epcot itself.

Amenities at the Swan and Dolphin are comparable to those at Disney deluxe resorts, missing only water sports. Besides the great pool complex, they include playgrounds, spas, fitness centers, tennis, hot tubs, and arcades.

The lack of Disney theming and relative inconvenience to the Magic Kingdom makes us less than keen on the Swan and Dolphin for first-time visitors, and the masses of conventioneers can make them even less fun. (Disney's Epcot resorts are all convention hotels as well, but at a much smaller scale.) But the Swan in particular can be a great choice for a later, more Epcot-focused trip. Dining is better than at Disney's Epcot resorts, the pools are better than those at the BoardWalk Inn (though not as good as those shared by the Yacht and Beach Club), and standard rooms prices are typically lower than what you'd pay for Disney Epcot resort standard rooms.

Prices at the Swan and Dolphin are less transparent than those at the Disney resorts, and sometimes obscure that fact that unlike at the Disney-owned hotels you pay a required resort fee and also have to pay for parking if you have a car. But even with these extra costs, rooms are usually a good bit less than the Disney-owned Epcot resorts, and are often available at a discount.

SHADES OF GREEN

Shades of Green Resort ("Shades") is a military-owned Armed Forces Recreation Center in the heart of Walt Disney World. The resort overall is un-themed and bland—it could be anywhere—but eligible guests who stay here will find some of the nicest rooms at Disney World at very low prices—prices here vary by rate/rank, but generally are competitive most of the year with Disney's least expensive resorts. Eligibility is complicated—see Steve Bell's MILITARYDISNEYTIPS.COM for the full

---

Jim's Gems
by Jim Korkis

Architect Michael Graves' concept for the Walt Disney World Dolphin resort was a tropical island formed by a sudden underwater volcano and earthquake. When the island emerged from under the sea, it lifted dolphins out of the water, and these are the nautical dolphins on the roof. A mountain thrust upward to the sky is the reason for the banana leaves painted along the side of the building to suggest a tropical jungle. The waves of water from this event splashed up onto the Walt Disney World Swan, which is why the waves are painted on the side of that adjacent hotel.

scoop—but its rooms can be booked by eligible "sponsors" who are currently serving or career retired, or the spouses of such folk, plus a host of other classes detailed on Steve's site. (Veterans who are not career retired can stay in September and January.) Sponsors can book a room for themselves as well as 2–5 additional rooms (depending on the time of year and whether a spouse is involved) for their family and friends at the same low rates.

As Shades is not owned by Disney, its guests don't have access to most of the perks that those staying in Disney-owned resorts receive. They do have the opportunity to attend Extra Magic Hours, but don't get free parking at the hotel ($5/day) or the parks ($20/day), can't use the Dining Plan, can't use Disney's Magical Express, and, most importantly, can't book FastPass+ at 60 days. Shades guests book FastPass+ at 30 days.

Shades has a large wood and stone lobby building where guest services, the bus stop, and most dining are located. Guest rooms are in two wings off the lobby. The Palm wing is newer, prettier, and closer to parking. The less attractive Magnolia Wing is closer to the two pools at the resort, one near the lobby and another at the far end of the Magnolia wing that has a kids play area, water slides, and easy access to a sports bar and grill.

Shades is nestled between two golf courses in the Magic Kingdom area, across the street from Disney's Polynesian Village Resort. Park transport is via its own bus system that is not as good as the buses serving the Disney-owned resorts. Buses commonly start too late, run too infrequently, and don't directly serve the Magic Kingdom or Epcot, instead dropping guests headed to those parks off at the Transportation and Ticket Center. Many Shades guests walk to the Polynesian to take

Shades of Green Resort
Floor Plan ~480 Square Feet

advantage of its transportation—it's about half a mile from the lobby at Shades to the Poly's monorail stop.

Standard rooms at Shades sleep five on two queens and a couch that converts into a single bed. These rooms are about 480 square feet—larger than those in any Disney-owned resort. Rooms have beside the beds and couch a large table with two chairs, mini-fridge, TV, dresser, closet, and a coffee-maker. The divided bath includes two sinks and a hair dryer, and a toilet and tub in a separate room. All rooms are accessed from interior corridors, and all have large balconies. A few suites are also available.

Shades has multiple dining options, none of them particularly fun, distinctive or memorable compared to Disney alternatives, but all providing good value for the money. Additional dining is easily accessible at the Polynesian, and from the monorail stop there at other resorts.

Amenities at Shades are thin compared to those at the more expensive Disney-owned resorts, but include playgrounds, a spa, a fitness center, tennis, hot tubs, a family computer center, and an arcade.

You won't find a better room for the money anywhere else at Disney World, but the combination of bland theming, not-so-convenient transport, and 30 day FastPass+ makes us hesitant to recommend it for first-time visitors. Many eligible first-timers will be better served by staying at a Disney-owned resort using Disney's Armed Forces Salute discount, which at press time is expected to be renewed for 2016.

Prices at Shades are based on rank/rate. At press time, standard rooms range from $95/night to $131/night. Unlike the Disney resorts, Shades prices don't vary over the course of the year. Discounts are often available. For more on these and everything Shades or military, see MILITARYDISNEYTIPS.COM.

FOUR SEASONS RESORT

The Four Seasons Resort Orlando at Walt Disney World Resort ("Four Seasons") opened in 2014 as Walt Disney World's first five star resort. Lovely but essentially un-themed (it could be anywhere), the 17-story hotel has elements of Spanish Colonial Revival architecture, with inadvertent references to the Tower of Terror. Four Seasons has the nicest standard rooms on property, the best pool complex at Disney World, and fine dining for adults (and a bit of playful dining for kids). But transportation, theming, and FastPass+ issues make it hard for us to recommend it for first-timers.

Four Seasons is not owned by Disney, and its guests don't have access to the perks that those staying in Disney-owned resorts receive. For example, they aren't eligible for Extra Magic Hours, don't get free parking at the hotel or the parks, can't use the Dining Plan, can't use Disney's Magical Express, and, most importantly, can't book FastPass+ at 60 days. Four Seasons guests book FastPass+ at 30 days.

Four Seasons is a mid-sized high rise with guest services on the lower floors and rooms and suites on the upper floors. One of its long sides overlooks its parking lots, and the other has distant vistas of the Magic Kingdom and Epcot, and near views of its wonderful pool complex—the best at Disney World—which includes an adult-only pool, large lazy river pool, pool slide complex, and family pool.

Four Seasons is deep in the Golden Oak residential area, between Fort Wilderness and Port Orleans Riverside. Park transport is via its own motor coach system that is more comfortable but less convenient than the buses serving the Disney-owned resorts. Coaches run too infrequently, and (as of Dave's last stay) begin their schedules too late and end too early.

There's two flavors of standard rooms at Four Seasons, identical except on their bed side, where one offers two full beds and an easy chair, and the other a king bed and a couch that converts into a queen sized bed that is, by far, the most comfortable sofa bed Dave's ever slept on. (The floor plan is of the king bed variant.) All but the shortest and most slender of families seeking one room should choose the king/sleeper sofa floor plan over the full beds. The most common layout pairs one of each of these room types with connecting doors and a deep entry alcove that can also be closed off at the corridor end—making for an easy, albeit expensive, set-up for families seeking more than one room's worth of space or beds.

Four Seasons Resort Orlando
Standard King Bed Room ~500 Square Feet

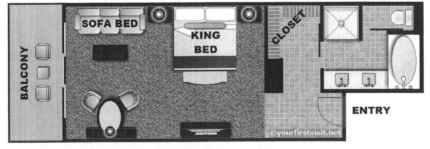

These standard rooms are about 500 square feet—the largest on property—and have beside the beds and chair or couch, a large table with two chairs that can serve as a desk as well, TV, dresser, enormous closet with more drawers, and a coffee-maker/mini-fridge set up all ready for you to order in a full bar. The overly open bath includes two sinks, a hair dryer, a tub and a separate shower, and a toilet in a separate glass-walled room. All rooms are accessed from interior corridors, and all have large balconies. Suites of all flavors are also available, including a nine-bedroom option going for more than $10,000 a night—add taxes and tips, and pretty soon you are talking about real money.

Four Seasons has multiple dining options, including Capa, a distinctive rooftop Spanish steakhouse with distant views of the Magic Kingdom and Epcot fireworks; Ravello, a more casual lower level Italian option; character meals with Goofy certain mornings; and other poolside and casual options. Unlike at the Disney deluxe resorts (except the Animal Kingdom Lodge), there's no easily accessible nearby hotels offering additional dining venues.

Four Seasons offers all the amenities you'll find at any other Disney World hotel except for beaches and water sports. You won't find a more relaxing, delightful, or peaceful resort anywhere else at Disney World, but the combination of bland theming, not-so-convenient transport, and 30 day FastPass+ makes us hesitant to recommend it for first-time visitors. Most first-timers who could afford Four Seasons will be better served by staying at one of the monorail resorts (Contemporary, Grand Floridian, or Polynesian), and saving Four Seasons for a return trip when relaxing at the hotel is as important a priority as is visiting the parks.

Future pricing at Four Seasons is not so easy to uncover as it is at the Disney-owned resorts, but the least expensive rooms at Four Seasons are easily competitive with the Disney monorail resorts, especially if your dates are flexible.

OFF-PROPERTY HOTELS AND VACATION HOMES

An off-site stay may remain attractive due to significantly lower prices, especially when considering the cost for a family of five to stay on property. While it's theoretically possible for a family of five to stay in the Murphy bed rooms at Caribbean Beach or Riverside, we're still talking about five people sharing a single bathroom and 314 square feet of total space. Disney's idea of a value-priced family suite at Art of Animation starts at $327 per night and skyrockets up to $522/night over the holidays.

However, staying off-site presents another set of costs and challenges. First, any scheduled shuttle transportation from most off-site resorts can be as weak as one bus in the morning and one bus at night. These times are often rigid and inconvenient, whether the bus arrives after park opening or departs long before the night-time entertainment or the park closes. Miss the bus and it's an expensive cab ride. Off-site guests often rent cars, but that reduces convenience and increases costs. Parking at the theme parks is $20 per day (due only *once* per day, if you keep your receipt), in addition to potential parking costs back at the hotel. Second, resort fees that typically cost $15-$20 per night are another concern. For some families, the price discount may be too much to overlook this trip, and there's nothing wrong with that. But be sure to consider all the costs associated with a stay that may not be included in the initial price.

There are literally thousands of off-site hotels, motels, campgrounds, vacation homes, condos, etc., in and around Orlando. Target your search to the Highway 192/West Irlo Bronson Highway and/or the Disney Springs Resort Area to narrow your search to convenient locations. The value of honing in on these two areas is simple: from almost any place in Walt Disney World, you can find directional signage to 192, and directional signage to Disney Springs.

Walt Disney World is much more complicated than many first-time visitors imagine, and your first few days of finding your way around will be made simpler by this signage.

- The street address of hotels on 192 will include either "Highway 192" and/or the words "Irlo Bronson Highway".
- The street address of hotels in the Disney Springs Resort Area will include "Hotel Plaza Boulevard".

It's possible to find multiple-bedroom vacation homes available for short-term rentals in the Orlando area for a fraction of the price you'd pay to stay in some of the deluxe large family options at Walt Disney World, even counting your rental car costs. Airbnb is also becoming more accepted in Orlando.

First-time visitors benefit most from staying on property at a Disney owned and operated resort. While more expensive than their off-site counterparts, it's hard to put a price on the convenience and peace of mind that an on-site stay in a Disney resort offers.

How to Spend Your Time

This chapter:

- Provides example, pre-made itineraries for guests arriving on a Saturday and planning to spend nine days in Orlando.
- Presents introductions to touring each of the major theme parks, with reviews and insight into every single theme park attraction.
- Follows with Cheat Sheets that cover everything you need to bring with you to the theme parks. These include what to expect at park open, detailed touring plans including when you can expect to arrive and depart each attraction, FastPass+ priority so you know which experiences will save you the most time, and advice on how to see the night-time spectaculars with the least hassle. Color copies of the newest versions of these Cheat Sheets are available at WWW.EASYWDW.COM/EASY-GUIDE.

We open with a discussion of one of Disney's newest innovations, FastPass+, and how it has transformed the theme park experience in positive and negative ways. Maximizing FastPass+ is an important strategic advantage and we'll cover the best methods to save you hours in line every day.

Next, we focus on itinerary planning, including:

- Deciding how many days to visit each park.
- Picking the best park to visit each day based on crowds and entertainment offerings.
- Creating a daily touring plan that blends easy morning touring, strategically chosen FastPass+ experiences, and the best dining choices.

Example itineraries are provided to give you an idea about how best to plan your vacation in its entirety. Modifications can easily be made depending on where you want to go and what you want to do.

This is the lengthiest chapter because the theme parks are what a Walt Disney World vacation is all about. Plan to digest it over several sessions.

FastPass+ at Walt Disney World

Disney's digital FastPass+ system replaced legacy paper FASTPASS in early 2014. More attractions than ever before offer FastPass+, including night-time spectaculars like IllumiNations at Epcot and character meet and greets like Anna and Elsa at Magic Kingdom.

Each attraction has one or two entrances. At attractions that do not offer FastPass+, there is a single line called the "standby queue". Here, guests simply get in line and wait their turn. At FastPass+ enabled attractions, there are two separate lines—the standby queue and the FastPass+ return queue.

At attractions with both types of entrances, guests with a FastPass+ can experience an attraction with priority boarding. Attractions like Tower of Terror and Toy Story Mania admit as many as seven FastPass+ riders for every one standby rider. Thus, those with FastPass+ wait much less than those in standby lines, and push up standby waits because they receive priority boarding, even if they arrive long after a standby rider.

Disney bills FastPass+ as an "easy way to reserve some of your must-do fun before you leave home". Indeed, all guests with tickets may book three FastPass+ experiences either 60 days in advance (guests staying in Disney-owned hotels or the Swan or Dolphin) or up to 30 days in advance (all other guests). This is one of the most positive features of the program—guests may schedule headlining attractions like Toy Story Mania, Test Track, Soarin', Space Mountain, and the Princess Fairytale Hall Meet and Greets from the comfort of their home long before they arrive in Orlando, or even the day of a visit to the theme park from their smartphone or in-park kiosk. But there are two major negatives:

1. Guests must select a specific one-hour window on a specific day. Based on the ride reviews that follow, you may decide that the group wants to meet Ariel at Ariel's Grotto in Magic Kingdom. But you'll need to pick a specific date and time—August 27 from 2:15pm–3:15pm, for example. (The rest of this chapter helps with all these choices—which days, which rides, which FastPass+, and which times.)

2. Some attractions distribute a very limited number of FastPass+ opportunities, making booking 30–60 days in advance necessary.

Later in this chapter, we'll discuss the importance of choosing which theme park to visit based on crowds and entertainment. This goes hand in hand with Chapter 7, which discusses restaurant reservations, some of which must be booked a whopping six months in advance. Combined with the FastPass+ priority discussion next, picking attractions and theme parks is easy, but being forced to select specific hour-long windows for each ride can feel like too much micro-managing and reduce spontaneity.

There is no such thing as legacy FASTPASS inside the theme parks anymore, which—for those who have visited before—means no more paper FASTPASS tickets. Legacy FASTPASS tickets were generally distributed at each attraction that offered it, necessitating backtracking and long walks to collect FASTPASSes over the course of the day. The good news is that FastPass+ eliminates the need to visit each attraction for which you'd like a FastPass+. Gone are the days of sending Dad to Splash Mountain with everyone's park tickets while the rest of the group rides Buzz Lightyear's Space Ranger Spin 20 minutes away.

The introductions to each theme park below, along with the Cheat Sheets, include a list of the attractions that offer FastPass+. Attractions are ranked based on how much time and hassle using FastPass+ will save. For example, Toy Story Mania is the top priority at Hollywood Studios because using FastPass+ there at 5pm will save 60 or more minutes in line. Muppet Vision 3D is ranked near the bottom because using FastPass+ won't save any time since everyone that shows up for the next show will be admitted. There are a few other considerations also taken into account. For example, the queue for Tomorrowland Speedway at Magic Kingdom is outdoors and exhaust from the cars permeates through the entire area. Speedway is prioritized over several other attractions because it will not only save 20 or more minutes in line, but also bypass much of the stench.

Because FastPass+ experiences can be booked in advance, the new program adds certainty to your schedules and also makes arriving late at a theme park much easier than with the legacy FASTPASS system. Prior to FastPass+, Toy Story Mania legacy FASTPASSes would typically be gone before 11am, with return times well into the evening by 9:45am most days. This meant guests needed to arrive early to secure FASTPASSes with an unknown return time, or find themselves in a 75+ minute standby line at some point later in the day. Now you can leave home knowing you have Toy Story Mania booked in the afternoon, and no longer need to arrive at the park early to assure you can enjoy it.

Unfortunately, Disney has instituted a tiering system at Epcot and Hollywood Studios, which means guests at those parks can initially reserve only one high priority attraction in advance. At Epcot, guests choose between Soarin' and Test Track, among two other lesser choices. At Hollywood Studios, the major decision is between Toy Story Mania and Rock 'n' Roller Coaster, where guests can only initially choose one. Riding both Soarin' and Test Track in one day is easy if you head to one right at park open and then use FastPass+ for the other later in the day. But riding both over the course of one day with a late arrival will be more difficult since both attractions ordinarily see 60–100 minute waits over the course of the day. It's possible that these attractions will be available to book as a fourth FastPass+ selection at a kiosk in the afternoon, but it's unlikely on busier days and return times will be severely limited.

Choosing the Best FastPass+ Time Slots

When considering when to schedule your FastPass+ experiences, there are two main schools of thought. The first is to schedule FastPass+ beginning right at park opening, with the goal of scheduling a 4th FastPass+ at the in-park kiosks as early as possible. To book a 4th FastPass+, you must use the initial three or the window on the third must pass. So if you book Space Mountain for 9–10am, Buzz Lightyear's Space Ranger Spin for 10–11am, and Peter Pan's Flight for 11am–12pm, you would be eligible to schedule a 4th FastPass+ immediately after you use the 3rd or any time after 12pm should you not use the Peter Pan FastPass+.

The benefit here is that each additional FastPass+ selection is based on availability, and availability is better earlier in the day when fewer people have had the opportunity to select additional FastPass+. The downside is that on busier days, there may be very little availability for the priority attractions even at 11am, particularly at Epcot and Hollywood Studios where there are only two or three attractions most people are interested in booking.

Another downside is that using FastPass+ earlier in the day when standby waits are shorter will save less time than using the same FastPass+ later. For example, a Space Mountain FastPass+ used at 9:30am might save 15 minutes in line. A Space Mountain FastPass+ used at 12:30pm might save 60 or more minutes in line because afternoon crowds are so much heavier.

The second school of thought is to schedule FastPass+ in the late morning and afternoon when it will save the most time and take advantage of short standby waits at most attractions in the early morning. Our advice is to begin scheduling FastPass+ as early as 10:30am at a high priority attraction like Soarin' or Seven Dwarfs Mine Train. While availability for a 4th FastPass+ will be worse later in the afternoon, it's likely that the same attractions that were available at 11:30am will be available at 1:30pm.

If you're planning to schedule your first FastPass+ for 9–10am, plan to use it as close to 10am as possible to save the most time and take advantage of short standby waits elsewhere before then.

Also note that scheduling a night-time spectacular in advance inhibits your ability to make additional FastPass+ selections at the in-park kiosks earlier in the day. For example, if you select IllumiNations, Mission: SPACE, and Spaceship Earth as your initial three selections, you won't be able to select a 4th FastPass+ choice because you won't use your third selection until the very end of the night. IllumiNations, the first Fantasmic!, Main Street Electrical Parade, and Wishes are rarely available as a 4th selection. So there are some tradeoffs should you wish to take advantage of the reserved FastPass+ viewing areas at the night-time entertainment.

Finally, keep in mind that FastPass+ does not operate during morning or evening Extra Magic Hours. That's mostly good news for those visiting during the extra time because it means FastPass+ returners won't bog down standby queues unnecessarily, in effect leveling the playing field for all on-site guests in attendance.

Designing Your Own Walt Disney World Itinerary

The art of itinerary design has three parts: dividing your time among the parks, picking the best days to visit each park, and shaping what you do each day to minimize time spent waiting in line.

ALLOCATING YOUR TIME AMONG THE PARKS

Chapter 3 covered in-depth how to divide your time depending on party size, makeup, and length of vacation. As a refresher, most guests will spend the most time at Magic Kingdom, with Epcot being a close second except for those traveling with the youngest children. Most guests spend about a day each at Hollywood Studios and Animal Kingdom, though guests spending just a few days at Disney World may not have time for all four parks.

PICKING THE BEST DAYS TO VISIT THE PARKS

There are several factors that contribute to the decision on which theme park to visit each day, including expected crowds and nighttime entertainment. Daily advice is available at EASYWDW.COM/EASY-GUIDE beginning about six and a half months ahead of a given date. For each day of your visit, you'll find overall crowd levels, recommended parks, night-time entertainment, and a daily explanation of what to expect.

In general, the longer a theme park is open and the more nightly entertainment it offers, the busier it will be. This is especially true at

Magic Kingdom, which can see wildly different operating hours and entertainment offerings, particularly during Mickey's Party Season from early September through the third week in December. It's not uncommon for Magic Kingdom to be open to regular tickets only from 9am–7pm and offer no evening fireworks or parades three or four days per week, while the other days it's open as late as 1am with fireworks and two night-time parades. The days with longer hours are significantly more crowded because people equate longer hours with more bang for their buck. This isn't necessarily true. While a longer day does offer more time in the park, it also brings with it longer lines, increased congestion in common areas, and a more stressful overall experience. With two days at Magic Kingdom, most guests will want to visit on one less crowded day to hammer out the priority attractions and also visit on a day that they can enjoy the nighttime entertainment.

- Animal Kingdom is typically least busy on Sundays and Tuesdays. It's busiest on Mondays, Thursdays, and Saturdays, particularly on days with morning Extra Magic Hours.

- Epcot is generally least busy on Mondays, Wednesdays, and Fridays. Weekends are usually good too, with the exception of the last week in September through mid-November during the Food and Wine Festival, when Friday nights, Saturdays, and Sundays are extremely crowded. It's busiest on Tuesdays and Thursdays.

- Mondays, Wednesdays, and Saturdays are usually best for Hollywood Studios. Sundays and Fridays typically see higher attendance. The exception is Star Wars Weekends from mid-May through mid-June, when Fridays, Saturdays, and Sundays are some of the busiest days of the year.

- Magic Kingdom is typically least busy on Tuesdays and Thursdays and busiest on Saturdays and Mondays.

One reason why Magic Kingdom tends to be busiest on weekends and Mondays, and the other theme parks less crowded on those days, is the number of people that arrive over the weekend and head to the Most Magical Place on Earth first thing. We recommend putting off Magic Kingdom for a Tuesday, not only because it's less crowded and more enjoyable, but also because seeing it first might spoil the very different experiences at the other theme parks. While much of Magic Kingdom is an exercise in excitement and sensory overload, Epcot in particular takes more time and thought to discover its richness. This isn't to say the other theme parks are "bad", but it can be difficult to get young kids excited about an educational boat ride about horticulture after experiencing the 50-foot plunge on Splash Mountain the day before.

But there are exceptions to these general guidelines, which is where the daily crowd calendars and recommended parks come into play. Be sure to check out your dates as soon as possible. Once you've sorted out which parks you will visit on which days, begin entering the details in the planning sheet, on the facing page. (There's room in it for dining as well, which is coming in Chapter 7.)

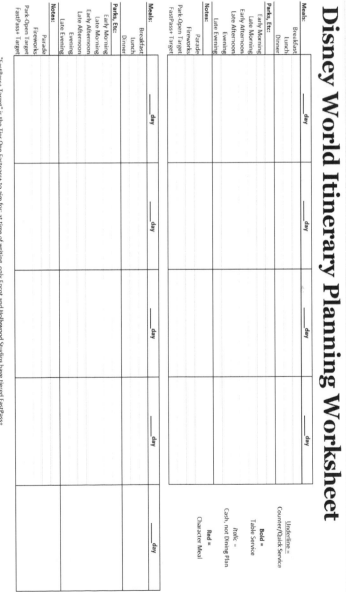

Disney World Itinerary Planning Worksheet

Underline = Counter/Quick Service

Bold = Table Service

Italic = Cash, not Dining Plan

Red = Character Meal

	____day	____day	____day	____day
Meals:				
Breakfast				
Lunch				
Dinner				
Parks, Etc:				
Early Morning				
Late Morning				
Early Afternoon				
Late Afternoon				
Evening				
Late Evening				
Notes:				
Parade				
Fireworks				
Park Open Target				
FastPass+ Target				

"FastPass+ Target" is the Tier One Fastpass+ to aim for; at time of writing, only Epcot and Hollywood Studios have tiered FastPass+

DESIGNING YOUR PARK APPROACH FOR EACH DAY
··

After you've divided your days among the parks, and picked days to visit each park, your final step is designing your approach for each day. There are two easy ways to go about this:

1. Model your visit around the daily agendas you'll find linked to from the itineraries on YOURFIRSTVISIT.NET/ITINERARIES. We give two examples of these itineraries after the worksheet.

2. Use the park overviews and ride reviews that come just after the example itineraries, to tailor the easyWDW Cheat Sheets to a trip that's perfectly adapted to your group and the length of your trip!

Example Itineraries for Disney World

If you have chosen to do an eight-night, nine-day trip with a Saturday arrival, and your kids are at least 8 years old and 48 inches tall, then you'll find an itinerary for dates within the next six or so months (they are released as Disney releases its operating calendar) at YOURFIRST-VISIT.NET/ITINERARIES. Scan down the dates at that link and click to the itinerary suggested for that date—taking special note of words like "but see this for required changes...".

When you do so, you'll find an itinerary like one of the two examples that follow, and with it links to daily touring plans based on that itinerary and a tailored To-Do List with suggested FastPass+. While the examples below will give you an idea about what we're looking at, they do change based on different weekly schedules. The list at YOURFIRSTVISIT. NET/ITINERARIES will be updated with itineraries for each specific week.

EXAMPLE ITINERARY: TYPICAL HIGHER-CROWD WEEKS

Disney World FastPass+ High Crowd Itinerary from yourfirstvisit.net

	Saturday	Sunday	Monday	Tuesday
Meals:				
Breakfast	*Travel*	*Hotel Room**	*Hotel Room**	*Hotel Room**
Lunch	*Travel*	Backlot Express	Sunshine Seasons	Hotel or Hollywood Studios Counter
Dinner	7p Akershus or San Angel Inn	Hotel Counter	Hotel or Epcot Counter	**7p 50's Prime Time Cafe**
Parks, Etc:				
Early Morning	Travel	At Hollywood Studios by 8.15a	At Epcot by 8.15a	Off
Late Morning	Travel	Hollywood Studios	Epcot	Off
Early Afternoon	Check In/Epcot ASAP	Hollywood Studios	Epcot	*Hollywood Studios by 2p or so*
Late Afternoon	Epcot	Hollywood Studios	Epcot	Hollywood Studios
Evening	Epcot	Off	(Optional) Epcot	Hollywood Studios
Late Evening				
Notes:				
Parade				
Fireworks	Illuminations	N/A	Illuminations	Fantasmic
Park-Open Target	N/A	Rock 'N Roller Coaster	Test Track	N/A
FastPass+ Target	Illuminations	Toy Story Midway Mania	Soarin	Fantasmic

Legend:
- Underline = Counter/Quick Service
- **Bold** = Table Service
- *Italic* = Cash, not Dining Plan
- Red = Character Meal

	Wednesday	Thursday	Friday	Saturday	Sunday
Meals:					
Breakfast	*Hotel Room**	*Hotel Room**	*Hotel Room**	*Hotel Room**	*Hotel Room**
Lunch	TBD Cinderella's Royal Table**	Flame Tree Barbecue	**Chef Mickey's 11a**	7p Crystal Palace	Travel
Dinner	**6.15p Hoop-Dee-Doo Revue****	Yak and Yeti	*Magic Kingdom or Hotel Counter*		Travel
Parks, Etc:					
Early Morning	Magic Kingdom by 8.15a	Off	Magic Kingdom by 8.15a	Magic Kingdom by 8.15a	Animal Kingdom by 8.15a
Late Morning	Magic Kingdom	Off	Magic Kingdom	Magic Kingdom	Animal Kingdom
Early Afternoon	Magic Kingdom	Animal Kingdom by noon	Magic Kingdom	Off	Off
Late Afternoon	Magic Kingdom	Animal Kingdom	Magic Kingdom	Magic Kingdom by 6p	Off
Evening	Hoop-Dee-Doo Revue	Animal Kingdom	Off	Magic Kingdom	Travel
Late Evening					Travel
Notes:					
Parade	Afternoon Parade			Evening Parade	
Fireworks		N/A		Wishes	
Park-Open Target	Peter Pan	Kali River Rapids	Space Mountain	Big Thunder Mountain	Expedition Everest
FastPass+ Target	Seven Dwarfs Mine Train		Enchanted Tales with Belle	Splash Mountain	Kilimanjaro Safaris

*Cereal, fruit, juice etc. in room   **Two Table Service credits

Version 9/14; thanks to Josh of easyWDW.com for help and permission to use his findings...but errors are mine alone

EXAMPLE ITINERARY: TYPICAL LOWER-CROWD WEEKS

Disney World FastPass+ Lower-Crowd Itinerary v2 from yourfirstvisit.net

This does not work for all dates!! See yourfirstvisit.net/itineraries

Legend:
- Underline = Counter/Quick Service
- **Bold** = Table Service
- *Italic* = Cash, not Dining Plan
- Red = Character Meal

	Saturday	Sunday	Monday	Tuesday
Meals:				
Breakfast	*Travel*	*Hotel Room* *	*Hotel Room* *	*Hotel Room* *
Lunch	*Travel*	Backlot Express	Sunshine Seasons	Flame Tree Barbecue
Dinner	**7p Akershus or San Angel Inn**	**6p 50s Prime Time Café**	Hotel or Epcot Counter	Yak and Yeti
Parks, Etc:				
Early Morning	Travel	Off	At Epcot by 8.15a	Off
Late Morning	Travel	Off	Epcot	Off
Early Afternoon	Check In/At Epcot ASAP	At Hollywood Studios by noon	Epcot	At Animal Kingdom by noon
Late Afternoon	Epcot	Hollywood Studios	Epcot	Animal Kingdom
Evening	Epcot	Hollywood Studios	(Optional) Epcot	
Late Evening				
Notes:				
Parade				
Fireworks	Illuminations			
Park-Open Target	n/a	n/a	Test Track	n/a
FastPass+ Target	Illuminations	Toy Story Midway Mania	Soarin	Expedition Everest

	Wednesday	Thursday	Friday	Saturday	Sunday
Meals:					
Breakfast	*Hotel Room* *	*Hotel Room* *	*Hotel Room* *	*Hotel Room* *	*Hotel Room* *
Lunch	**Chef Mickey's 11a**	Hotel Counter	**TBD Cinderella's Royal Table** **	Magic Kingdom or Hotel Counter	*Travel*
Dinner	Magic Kingdom or Hotel Counter	Hollywood Studios Counter	**6.15p Hoop-Dee-Doo Revue** **	**6p Crystal Palace**	*Travel*
Parks, Etc:					
Early Morning	Off	Off	At Magic Kingdom by 8.15a	At Magic Kingdom by 8.15a	At Animal Kingdom by 8.15a
Late Morning	Off	Off	Magic Kingdom	Magic Kingdom	Animal Kingdom
Early Afternoon	At Magic Kingdom by noon	At Hollywood Studios by noon	Magic Kingdom	Off	*Travel*
Late Afternoon	Magic Kingdom	Hollywood Studios		Off	*Travel*
Evening	Magic Kingdom	Hollywood Studios	Hoop Dee Doo Revue	Magic Kingdom	*Travel*
Late Evening				Magic Kingdom	
Notes:					
Parade			Afternoon Parade	Evening Parade	
Fireworks		Fantasmic		Wishes	
Park-Open Target	n/a	n/a	Peter Pan	Big Thunder Mountain	Kilimanjaro or Everest
FastPass+ Target	Space Mountain	Rock 'n' Roller Coaster	Seven Dwarfs Mine Train	Splash Mountain	Festival of the Lion King

*Cereal, fruit, juice etc. in room   **Two Table Service credits

"FastPass+ Target" is the Tier One Fastpass+ to aim for; at time of writing, only Epcot and Hollywood Studios have tiered FastPass+

Version 5/14; thanks to Josh of easyWDW.com for help and permission to build on his findings...but conclusions are mostly mine, and errors are mine alone

Disney's Animal Kingdom

Disney's newest major theme park is also its easiest to tour. Each of the headliner attractions (except the over-hyped Kali River Rapids) enjoys healthy capacity and relatively short peak waits. On the downside, the park's circular layout may require backtracking to visit all the rides and shows. The Animal Kingdom Cheat Sheet at the end of this chapter minimizes walking and waits as much as possible.

Until the new evening show Rivers of Light opens, with FastPass+, a late arrival at Animal Kingdom can be just as effective as an early arrival. Animal Kingdom tends to empty by 4pm, leaving waits at the major attractions short from then until close. This may be tempered somewhat by the fact that Animal Kingdom often closes by 5 or 6pm. Still, Expedition Everest, Kali River Rapids, and the DinoLand attractions all see reduced waits in these periods, to the point where ride vehicles often leave partially empty because there aren't enough people around to fill a vehicle. After the evening show opens, we expect higher crowds in the park in the late afternoons and early evenings.

FASTPASS+ AT ANIMAL KINGDOM

After Rivers of Light opens, ten attractions at Animal Kingdom will offer FastPass+, from among which you can pre-book three. On hot days, FastPass+ is best used at Kali River Rapids in the afternoon when waits are longest and temperatures highest. For guests that need to meet Mickey, The Adventurers Outpost Meet and Greet has a limited capacity and is another priority. The best uses on cooler days without Mickey are at Kilimanjaro Safaris and Expedition Everest.

FastPass+ Priority

1. Kali River Rapids (when highs are 80+ degrees)
2. Adventurers Outpost Mickey and Minnie Meet
3. Kilimanjaro Safaris
4. Expedition Everest
5. Rivers of Light*
6. Kali River Rapids (when highs are less than 80 degrees)
7. DINOSAUR
8. Primeval Whirl
9. Festival of the Lion King
10. Finding Nemo the Musical
11. It's Tough to Be a Bug

*More information on Rivers of Light, the nighttime spectacular expected to open in Spring 2016, is available in the "Discovery Island" section, below. The preliminary FastPass+ ranking for the show is based on how FastPass+ works at other nighttime extravaganzas. It should be easy enough to see Rivers of Light without using FastPass+. And using it on the show means little or no ability to select 4th and subsequent FastPass+ experiences because you won't have an opportunity to use it until near the end of the night

ARRIVING AT ANIMAL KINGDOM

Arriving 45 minutes before open puts you in the best position to enjoy the shortest waits possible first thing in the morning as well as have an opportunity to re-ride Expedition Everest, DINOSAUR, Kali River Rapids, or other attractions a second time in the standby line before considerable waits begin to develop. Believe it or not, a 9am arrival is actually "late" and thousands of guests will already be in line at Kilimanjaro Safaris and Expedition Everest before you even scan your ticket.

Almost all guests arrive by Disney bus or their own transportation. Guests parking early can easily walk to the main entrance. Guests arriving later and parking farther out have the option of walking or taking a tram. Those arriving via Disney bus will be dropped off just a minute or two walk away from the main entrance.

Bag check precedes the ticket windows. Ticket windows generally have nonexistent lines because it's rare that a group begins their vacation at Animal Kingdom. Guest Services is located on the far left both inside and outside the main entrance. Stroller and wheelchair rentals are located on the right just inside the main entrance.

Rainforest Café sits on the left with an entrance/exit both inside and outside the park. Theme park admission is thus not required to dine at the restaurant, which is only convenient as you enter or exit the park.

THE OASIS

Unlike the entry into any other Disney theme park, The Oasis is completely devoid of shops, restaurants, and loud stimuli. Instead, the area works to transition visitors into the lush, tropical, animal-filled surroundings that set the tone for the rest of the park. Expansive animal habitats display iguanas, anteaters, macaws, ducks, and a variety of other animals amidst rushing waterfalls, dense vegetation, and a burgeoning canopy. Guests arriving prior to park opening will want to breeze through the Oasis with plans to return either in the afternoon or on the way out. Time spent here at open will only result in thousands of people passing you and filling the queues for the major attractions, in turn pushing up wait times. With an afternoon arrival, plan to slowly meander around the winding pathways, taking in the various exhibits for 15 to 30 minutes.

DISCOVERY ISLAND

After The Oasis, guests cross a bridge to Discovery Island, the central hub for the entire park. Discovery Island circles the 14-story hand-carved Tree of Life, the park's central icon and an easy marker for guests trying to make their way back to the main drag from one of the peripheral lands. DinoLand and Asia are off to the right, in addition to the Adventurer's Outpost Mickey and Minnie meet and greet, It's Tough to Be a Bug 4D show, and Flame Tree Barbecue, the park's best quick service. Off to the left is Pizzafari, another quick service option—much less interesting than Flame Tree, but air-conditioned. Past Pizzafari is the park's Starbucks location, followed by Africa, one of the three major lands. (Camp Minnie-Mickey closed in 2013.)

Discovery Island is where you'll find the bulk of the shopping opportunities, with Island Mercantile and Disney Outfitters supplying the widest selection. Virtually anything you would find in any of the smaller stores can be found here. Plan to return in the afternoon for some air-conditioned perusing when few people are shopping and the waits at the attractions are longer. Like the major stores at the other theme parks, Island Mercantile and Disney Outfitters remain open for at least 30 minutes after close, allowing for last-minute impulse buys.

Adventurers Outpost

RANKING Don't miss for those that want to meet Mickey and Minnie together; skippable otherwise. **EMH** No. **FP+** Yes. High priority for guests wanting to meet the characters. **TYPE** Meet-and-greet. **REQUIREMENTS** None.

WHAT TO EXPECT Guests line up outside the winding queue before entering a small air-conditioned room prior to the meet and greet. Mickey and Minnie greet together in their safari outfits with a fun adventurer's background. This is the only regular meet-and-greet where both Mickey and Minnie greet and take pictures together. **SCARY FACTOR** None.

WHEN TO GO Before 9:45am, one hour before close, or with FastPass+.
EXPECT TO WAIT Peak afternoon waits are typically 25 to 40 minutes.
LENGTH About two minutes of signing, mingling, and picture taking.

It's Tough to Be a Bug

RANKING Minor attraction. **EMH** Morning. **FP+** Yes. Low priority. **TYPE** 4D Show. **REQUIREMENTS** None.

WHAT TO EXPECT The theater is dark, loud, and there are a number of effects that "add" to the experience. Otherwise, It's Tough to Be a Bug is a fun 3D theater show (in-theater special effects make it "4D") based on *It's a Bugs Life* that most guests enjoy. **SCARY FACTOR (WITH MINOR SPOILERS)** Low for those 12 and older, but it may frighten younger kids. Animatronic spiders, termites, beetles, hornets, and more make appearances; several effects add to the anxiety: smoke, a "sting" from the back of the seat, insects dropping from the ceiling, and the sensation that bugs are running under your feet. If you're scared of bugs, this show may not be for you. At the same time, all of the bugs are "cartoony" like in the movie and not particularly realistic.

WHEN TO GO Afternoon when waits have peaked elsewhere. **EXPECT TO WAIT** Only as long as it takes for the next show to start. **LENGTH** 8 minutes. **WHERE TO SIT** Target the back few rows and let guests fill about half the row before entering. With apprehensive kids, instead sit at the end of a row for an easy exit.

Rivers of Light

Expected to debut sometime in Spring 2016, Rivers of Light is an all-new nighttime spectacular set on Discovery River between Expedition Everest on the Asia side and Discovery Island on the Flame Tree Barbecue side. The show will marry state-of-the-art projection technology, water screens, floating lanterns, and live Cirque-du-Soleil-style acrobatics, into a show that is certain to provide more than a few surprises. The majority of the seating area is on the Expedition Everest side. Rivers of Light will assuredly offer FastPass+, and potentially available will be lunch/dinner packages that include seating in a reserved section.

Rivers of Light (and other expected after-dark enhancements that include a nighttime version of Kilimanjaro Safaris and a projection show on the Tree of Life) should significantly change Animal Kingdom's landscape. Add the Avatar expansion expected to open in 2017 and you have a park that will likely be open until at least 9pm in the summer with nighttime entertainment and attractions that will keep guests in the Park later.

Most guests planning visits after Rivers of Light debuts will likely want to see the show, which should be scheduled nightly shortly after dusk and likely right around Park close. Overall demand and the number of seats remains to be seen, but based on similar Disney offerings at other parks, it will likely be necessary to secure seats about an hour in advance. Those skipping the show will likely be able to enjoy short waits at the major attractions around show time because the nighttime spectaculars pull so many people away. Stay tuned to EASYWDW.COM and YOURFIRSTVISIT.NET in the coming months for updates.

AFRICA

Home to Kilimanjaro Safaris, Festival of the Lion King, Pangani Forest Exploration Trail, and the Wildlife Express Train to Rafiki's Planet Watch, Africa is Animal Kingdom's largest, and arguably most immersive, land. Guests enter through Harambe, a rural African marketplace surrounded by buildings inspired by the ones Disney Imagineers saw during their travels across the continent. You'll see everything from a fortress reminiscent of Zanzibar to thatched huts built by the Zulu in South Africa.

Tusker House Restaurant (a Mickey-hosted character meal), Harambe Popcorn, Dawa Bar, and Tamu Tamu Refreshments are the first buildings guests see as they cross the bridge over to Africa. Farther back, Mombasa Marketplace is the large store on the right, offering authentic African crafts, Animal Kingdom merchandise, and African wines. Kusafiri Bakery is on the left, primarily serving baked treats and beverages. The entrance to Kilimanjaro Safaris is straight back with the entrance to Pangani Forest Exploration Trail around to the right near the Wildlife Express Train station. Harambe Market is the area's principal, open-air quick-service venue. Here, you'll find a nice variety of African wines and soft drinks, in addition to tasty entrees like the ground beef kabob flatbread, sausage fried in curried corn batter, and spice-rubbed Karubi-style ribs, with an African milk tart for dessert. The area is most pleasant in cool weather, as there is little to protect guests in line from the elements, and all seating is outdoors.

Festival of the Lion King

RANKING Major attraction. **EMH** No. **FP+** Yes. Low priority. FastPass+ users enter the theater before standby if they arrive 20+ minutes early and have their choice of seats. **TYPE** Musical theater show. **REQUIREMENTS** None.

WHAT TO EXPECT Lion King reopened in a new theater on June 1, 2014, though few things changed from its original run in Camp Minnie-Mickey. The show reprises songs and characters from the movie and features acrobatics, Animatronics, singing, dancing, fire, theater, and the most elaborate costumes and sets you'll find at Disney World. With more than 50 performers, there is almost too much to take in. **SCARY FACTOR** Low, the theater is dark and sometimes loud, but there is little to frighten youngsters.

WHEN TO GO First and last shows are least crowded. **EXPECT TO WAIT** Arrive 10 to 20 minutes early. **LENGTH** 30 minutes. **WHERE TO SIT** The section you choose isn't as important as the row you select. Higher than the eighth row provides a better view of the various floats and sets.

Jim's Gems
by Jim Korkis

Festival of the Lion King was meant to be a temporary show at the park when it first opened April 22, 1998, but became so popular that it continues to be performed. The impressive floats that serve as intriguing set pieces are actually recycled from The Lion King Celebration parade that ran at Disneyland from 1994–1997. They were modified and updated for Walt Disney World. The changes include removing Simba's sweetheart, Nala, and Mufasa's face in an overhead spinning sun design from the Lion float. While the Disneyland parade featured six floats, only four floats are used in the beloved musical show.

Kilimanjaro Safaris

RANKING Don't miss. **EMH** Morning. **FP+** Yes. High priority. **TYPE** Safari ride. **REQUIREMENTS** None.

WHAT TO EXPECT Riders board a 32-passenger open-air safari truck and take a mildly bumpy, fully narrated trip through the 100-acre Harambe Wildlife Reserve. It's basically a simulated, shortened safari through life-like savannas populated with rare animals, including black and white rhinoceroses, cheetahs, flamingos, lions, giraffes, warthogs, zebras, wildebeests, ostriches, crocodiles, antelopes, and more. The animals aren't always "out" and your viewing may be limited by the time of day and simple luck of the draw. Disney is expected to add a nighttime version of the Safaris sometime in 2016, most likely in the spring around the time Rivers of Light opens. Expect Disney to use artificial lighting and other effects to make the savanna appear to be under perpetual sunset. **SCARY FACTOR** None. **CAN WE HANDLE IT?** Mild jostling. If you have back or neck problems, request a front row where it's less bumpy.

WHEN TO GO Immediately after park open, in the final hour of operation, or with FastPass+. Safaris closes before dusk. Check for the "last safari" time—you need to be in line before this time to ride. **EXPECT TO WAIT** 35 to 70 minutes in the afternoon. **LENGTH** 20 minutes. **WHERE TO SIT** Those sitting on the ends of the rows have the most unobstructed views. Otherwise, the driver's side seems to offer the best view overall.

Pangani Forest Exploration Trail

RANKING Minor attraction. **EMH** Morning. **FP+** No. **TYPE** Self-guided walking tour, zoo exhibit. **REQUIREMENTS** None.

WHAT TO EXPECT Visitors walk along the path and enter various enclosures and exhibits that show off the animals in their native habitats. Expect to see hippopotamuses, meerkats, naked mole rats, gorillas, okapi (the only known relative of the giraffe), and an extensive number of rare African bird species. **SCARY FACTOR** Zero.

WHEN TO GO Last hour of operation, which may be earlier than park close. Kilimanjaro Safaris spits out thousands of guests an hour right at the doors to Pangani, causing crowding from 9:30am to 4pm along the narrow paths. The gorillas are also out more consistently in the late afternoon. Closes shortly before dusk. **EXPECT TO WAIT** No waits. **LENGTH** Pangani Trail is a little less than a half mile long. Most visitors spend about 30 minutes moving through the trail and the various exhibits.

Rafiki's Planet Watch

RANKING Fun but skippable. **EMH** No. **FP+** No. **TYPE** Zoological exhibits and interactive experiences. **REQUIREMENTS** None.

WHAT TO EXPECT Rafiki's Planet Watch is a collection of nicely air-conditioned diversions from long waits in the hot sun. You'll find a variety of exhibits that you'll need to take some time with if you want to get anything out of them. There are no rides, thrills, or excitement at Planet Watch—just educational exhibits. Here's what's available:

- *Affection Section*, a petting zoo. The animals here are mostly species that are endangered or otherwise at risk.
- *Sounds of the Rainforest*, a five-minute auditory exhibit narrated by Grandmother Willow from *Pocahontas*.
- *Conservation Station*, the main building at Rafiki's Planet Watch housing the majority of the live and hands-on exhibits. Veterinarians and wildlife experts will answer questions and give insight into how the Animal Kingdom operates. You can view live-camera feeds of backstage areas where the animals are kept, as well as a variety of other exhibits featuring a wealth of information on conservation efforts around the globe. Exhibits and activities can change on a daily basis because the area is actually used for live preparation and animal surgeries, so you never know what you'll see.
- *Character Meet and Greets*: Rafiki and friends are often on hand to meet guests to short lines.

SCARY FACTOR Minimal. There is a snake or two and the mornings may feature intensive veterinary procedures on the wildlife, but both can be avoided.

WHEN TO GO Between 11am and 3pm when crowds and temperatures peak elsewhere. There are no waits and the main building offers plentiful air conditioning. Closes shortly before dusk. **EXPECT TO WAIT** Riders must board the Wildlife Express in the back right corner of Africa. Expect to wait up to ten minutes to board the train and another seven minutes to ride over. **LENGTH** As little or as long as you want. Most guests spend about 30 minutes.

Wildlife Express Train

RANKING Fun but skippable. **EMH** No. **FP+** No. **TYPE** Slow-moving transportation. **REQUIREMENTS** None.

WHAT TO EXPECT Guests wait at the station for the slow-moving, open-air train that arrives every eight-or-so minutes. All guests seated on the train sit facing the sights as it slowly travels through backstage areas where riders have an opportunity to see where the elephants sleep, among other things. This is the only way to travel to and from Rafiki's Planet Watch. **SCARY FACTOR** Zero.

WHEN TO GO Between 11am and 3pm when crowds and temperatures peak elsewhere is best. Begins operation 30 minutes after regular park open and closes shortly before dusk. **EXPECT TO WAIT** Between two and ten minutes. **LENGTH** The trip lasts about seven minutes.

ASIA
....

Home to perhaps Disney's best roller coaster, in addition to a white water rafting ride, jungle trek, and the underrated Flights of Wonder, Asia has a lot to offer underneath its dense vegetation and gorgeously detailed theming. Asia is accessible via Discovery Island, a path from Africa, or DinoLand. Guests arriving from Africa or Discovery Island will first happen upon Flights of Wonder, which is located in a nondescript theater on the left. Continuing on, Yak & Yeti Restaurant and quick service are located on the left. Both serve very good Pan-Asian fare, though the quick service arm only offers outdoor seating that is uncomfortable in the summer heat and rain. Just past Yak & Yeti on the left is the walkway to Kali River Rapids and Maharajah Jungle Trek. Free lockers are available near Kali River Rapids to keep belongings dry while enjoying the ride. Continue ahead and Expedition Everest is unmistakable in the distance. The ride entrance is again on the left. Passing Everest will take you to The Theater in the Wild, home of *Finding Nemo–The Musical*, and then on to the rest of DinoLand.

Shopping is thin through Asia, though you don't want to miss the clever Yak & Yeti-themed merchandise to the right of the quick service, or all the Expedition Everest-themed merchandise at the attraction's exit.

Expedition Everest

RANKING Don't miss. **EMH** Morning. **FP+** Yes. High priority. **TYPE** Roller coaster. **REQUIREMENTS** 44" or taller.

WHAT TO EXPECT Interesting artifacts in the queue create the back story of a mysterious beast that resides in the sacred mountains. Riders board (two per row) a train that traverses high speed twists, turns, and drops before a final confrontation with the Yeti. **SCARY FACTOR** Medium-High. Guests plummet down an 80-foot drop at speeds up to 50 miles per hour in the dark, but it could be worse. **CAN WE HANDLE IT?** If you enjoyed Rock 'n' Roller Coaster, or any other "big coaster", you shouldn't have a problem. It is more intense than Space Mountain, but not so intense that the younger crowd won't be jumping up and down begging to ride. Some motion sickness risk, but no loops or inversions. Little jostling or jerkiness.

WHEN TO GO At park open, in the final hour of operation, or with FastPass+. **EXPECT TO WAIT** 25 to 50 minutes in the afternoon. **LENGTH** 3 minutes. **WHERE TO SIT** The first row provides the best view, but the last provides the wildest ride. There really isn't a bad seat on the train. **SINGLE RIDER LINE**: Yes, to the right of standby entrance. Waits are typically under ten minutes.

Flights of Wonder

RANKING Minor attraction. **EMH** No. **FP+** No. **TYPE** Stage show. **REQUIREMENTS** None.

WHAT TO EXPECT Guests enter a covered outdoor theater and find seats on bleacher-style benches without backs. A skilled trainer introduces viewers to over 20 species of birds, including a Great Horned Owl, Harris Hawk, and bald eagle. Tour Group Leader Guana Joe (or Jane) and his intense fear of birds provides comic relief throughout the show that includes several incredible tricks. We think it's under-rated. **SCARY FACTOR** Low for anyone without ornithophobia.

WHEN TO GO One of the last two shows will minimize crowds without wasting precious morning touring time. Otherwise, whenever it's convenient. **EXPECT TO WAIT** Arrive ten minutes early. **LENGTH** 30 minutes. **WHERE TO SIT** At least half way back in the center section is best, though there isn't a bad seat in the house.

Kali River Rapids

RANKING Major attraction. **EMH** Morning. **FP+** Yes. High priority when temperatures are 80+. **TYPE** Flume ride. **REQUIREMENTS** 38" or taller.

WHAT TO EXPECT Expect to get drenched on Kali, which follows a story about the destruction caused by illegal forestry. Riders board large rafts that seat 12 people in a circle around the outside perimeter of the raft. Your raft will be pulled up a 90 foot hill and then be released to freely but briefly float down the rapids, passing through geysers, waterfalls, and beautiful tropical jungles before plummeting down a 30-foot waterfall. The drop isn't fast or particularly thrilling, but it is still fun. Our opinion is that it's not worth the wait or the possible discomfort of wet socks and clothes. Complimentary lockers are located across from the entrance. Put everything you don't want getting wet inside before riding. **SCARY FACTOR** The ride starts off with a 90 foot uphill ascent, but there are no steep drops.

WHEN TO GO When it's hot, visit before 10am or in the last hour of operation. **EXPECT TO WAIT** 35 to 70 minutes in the afternoon when it's hot; 15 to 20 minutes when temperatures are under 70. **LENGTH** 5 minutes total, 2 of which are spent on the initial lift. **WHERE TO SIT** Anywhere.

Maharajah Jungle Trek

RANKING Minor attraction. **EMH** No. **FP+** No. **TYPE** Self-guided walking tour, zoo exhibit. **REQUIREMENTS** None.

WHAT TO EXPECT Maharajah Jungle Trek does not suffer from several of the problems that plague the Pangani Trail—the trail is wider, there is more room to view the animals, and the walkways aren't as crowded. This makes Maharajah more pleasant in the afternoon. Otherwise, like Pangani, Maharajah is a trail that takes visitors through several zoo-like exhibits and enclosures. You'll see Bengal tigers, the world's largest Komodo dragon, Malayan tapirs, Blackbuck and Elds deer, and hundreds of exotic birds. Bats are located in a separate house that's easy to skip if you prefer. **SCARY FACTOR** None.

WHEN TO GO Much of the Trek is shaded and cooler than other areas in the Animal Kingdom, which makes it a good choice during the afternoon heat when attraction lines elsewhere are longest. Closes shortly before dusk. **EXPECT TO WAIT** No waits. **LENGTH** Maharajah is a little longer than a third of a mile and most visitors spend about 20 minutes walking through it.

DINOLAND USA

By far the least appreciated land in any domestic Disney theme park, DinoLand follows the story of the Dino Institute and their Time Rover Tours. The fictitious backstory is that, in 1947, researchers found dinosaur fossils in Diggs County and "Dino fever" took hold of the area, bringing in thousands of tourists. A local entrepreneurial couple, Chester and Hester, took advantage of the influx by building Chester and Hester's Dino-Rama, a collection of cheap carnival games, gaudy colors, and off-the-shelf rides.

Indeed, much of DinoLand is themed to a cheap carnival built on top of a parking lot—on purpose. Whether it works is another debate, but the Imagineers that designed the park would tell you it took more time and energy to make the parking lot look old and decrepit than it did to install much of the vegetation around the park.

Guests walking from Asia will first see The Theater in the Wild on their left. This houses one of Disney's most elaborate stage shows, *Finding Nemo–The Musical*. In the center of DinoLand sits Primeval Whirl and TriceraTop Spin. TriceraTop Spin is a spinner similar to Dumbo and The Magic Carpets of Aladdin, while Primeval Whirl is an off-the-shelf wild-mouse-style coaster. Farther back to the left of Restaurantosaurus is DINOSAUR, the land's major attraction and a fun dark ride that transports lucky riders back to the end of the late Cretaceous period. Restaurantosaurus itself is a burger-and-nugget quick service option with fun theming, plentiful air conditioning, and refillable fountain beverages.

Chester & Hester's Dinosaur Treasures shop is located near TriceraTop Spin's exit. There's nothing here that isn't available elsewhere. Another small store is located at DINOSAUR's exit. Here, you'll find some fun dinosaur-themed merchandise.

DINOSAUR

RANKING Don't miss. **EMH** Morning. **FP+** Yes. Medium priority. **TYPE** Dark ride. **REQUIREMENTS** 40" or taller.

WHAT TO EXPECT DINOSAUR is located in the Dino Institute, an elaborately themed queue area with authentic dinosaur fossils. After you move through the queue, you will be taken to watch a short video where the storyline is explained. Once the pre-show concludes, you will move to the next area where you board a 12-person (three rows with four people in each row) Time Rover vehicle. Once strapped in, you will embark on your wild ride through time and space. **SCARY FACTOR** High. DINOSAUR is one dark, loud, bumpy ride. Although there are no drops more than a few feet and the vehicles don't move particularly fast, this may still prove to be the scariest ride at Animal Kingdom. **CAN WE HANDLE IT?** Besides being scary and bumpy, DINOSAUR is rough on those with even moderate motion sickness.

WHEN TO GO Before 10:30am or two hours before park close. **EXPECT TO WAIT** 25 to 40 minutes in the afternoon. **LENGTH** 4 minutes. **WHERE TO SIT** Put apprehensive kids in the middle seats. The front row affords the best view.

Finding Nemo the Musical

RANKING Major attraction. **EMH** No. **FP+** Yes. Low priority. **TYPE** Musical theater show. **REQUIREMENTS** None.

WHAT TO EXPECT Featuring the *Finding Nemo* characters, the show is housed in an air-conditioned theater with fairly comfortable bench seats with backs. Tony Award-winner Robert Lopez and his wife Kristen Anderson-Lopez (now of "Let It Go" fame) penned 16 original songs for the show, and Michael Curry, who helped design the wildly successful *Lion King* Broadway show, served as lead designer. The actors and puppeteers wear costumes and are just as much a part of the show as the puppets themselves. Don't be put off by this being "just a puppet show" because it's much, much more than that. **SCARY FACTOR** Low. Nemo gets into some trouble with a shark puppet, but that's about it.

WHEN TO GO First and last shows are least crowded. **EXPECT TO WAIT** You'll want to be lined up about 20 minutes before it begins. **LENGTH** 40 minutes. **WHERE TO SIT** Plan to sit at least half way up in the middle seating section. Sitting any closer may result in a cropped view of the stage that requires a lot of head turning to see the action. FastPass+ users who arrive 20+ minutes early file into the theater before standby guests.

Primeval Whirl

RANKING Fun but skippable. **EMH** Morning. **FP+** Yes. Medium priority. **TYPE** Wild mouse coaster. **REQUIREMENTS** 48" or taller.

WHAT TO EXPECT Riders board four-person spinning ride vehicles reminiscent of Mad Tea Party. The vehicles travel up a steep incline before being unleashed on the track that features no serious drops or g-forces. It is a herky-jerky ride with the occasional neck-snapping stop. **SCARY FACTOR** Medium. While technically less intense than other coasters, the spinning can be disconcerting and it "feels" like you're higher up than you are. **CAN WE HANDLE IT?** The ride can be incredibly hard on necks and backs. Anyone with pain should skip the ride.

WHEN TO GO Before 10:30am or two hours before park close. **EXPECT TO WAIT** 15 to 30 minutes in the afternoon. **LENGTH** 3 minutes. **WHERE TO SIT** The common advice is to evenly distribute weight on each side of the vehicle for less spinning. Or conversely, stick two heavier people on one side and two lighter people on the other for more spinning. Does it have an effect? Probably not, but it might make you feel better.

The Boneyard

RANKING Fun for kids, skippable for everyone else. **EMH** No. **FP+** No. **TYPE** Playground. **REQUIREMENTS** None.

WHAT TO EXPECT The Boneyard is an elaborately themed playground aimed at young kids and has several stories of sand pits, swings, and things to climb on. **SCARY FACTOR** None.

WHEN TO GO Visit with youngsters when the bigger kids are riding Primeval Whirl and DINOSAUR. Otherwise, visit in the late morning or afternoon when waits elsewhere peak. The Boneyard does get hot, so save it for the end of the day during the summer. **EXPECT TO WAIT** Very rarely any wait. **LENGTH** As long as it takes to pry Junior away.

TriceraTop Spin

RANKING Fun diversion, especially with kids. **EMH** Morning. **FP+** No. **TYPE** Spinning ride. **REQUIREMENTS** None.

WHAT TO EXPECT Riders enter four-person dinosaur-themed vehicles with two rows of two people. Each row has a joystick that can slightly alter the way the vehicle moves: either up and down or back and forth. The ride vehicles slowly move around the base of the ride in a circle. **SCARY FACTOR** Minimal. Although the ride does move up, down, and side to side, it's geared towards young children and it shouldn't frighten anyone.

WHEN TO GO Before 11am or about two hours before park close. **EXPECT TO WAIT** Peak waits of 10 to 15 minutes are common. It's a walk-on, early and late. **LENGTH** 90 seconds. **WHERE TO SIT** Your choice, though young kids will be asked to sit on the inside so they won't accidentally fall out. Riders in the front can reach behind and use the joystick in the back row if there's nobody back there.

Epcot

Epcot is Walt Disney World's second most popular theme park and a quintessential part of any theme park vacation. Most guests with older kids will want to prioritize a second day here over a second day at Animal Kingdom or Hollywood Studios due to Epcot's vast size and the time it takes to experience many of its attractions. Epcot is unlike any other theme park, and many of its attractions take time and a little effort to enjoy.

Epcot consists of two very different pieces– Future World and World Showcase. Future World is where you'll currently find the headlining rides like Soarin' and Test Track, in addition to the bulk of the secondary attractions. It's the area located just inside the main entrance and consumes the north half of the park. World Showcase is home to most of the dining and shopping experiences, in addition to the emphasis on the cultures of the world that the park is so famous for providing.

Future World almost always operates from 9am (rarely, it opens at 8am) through regular park close, although the Imagination Pavilion, Energy Pavilion, both Innoventions buildings, and all the attractions inside them typically close at 7pm. World Showcase currently operates from 11am through park close, though Akershus Royal Banquet Hall in Norway serves breakfast beginning at 8am and the bakery in France usually begins operating at regular park open.

Likely in the spring of 2016, two attractions will open in Epcot's Norway: Frozen Ever After, a re-do of the old Maelstrom ride, and a Frozen meet and greet. We think it likely that these will open at 9am rather than 11am. If so, they will likely change morning crowd patterns at Epcot, attracting more younger kids to the park and shifting some families away from focusing on Soarin' to prioritizing the Frozen attractions. EASYWDW.COM and YOURFIRSTVISIT.NET will provide updates on how to tour Epcot when these attractions are open.

FASTPASS+ PRIORITY

FastPass+ at Epcot is divided into two tiers. In Tier 1 are Soarin', Test Track, Illuminations, and Living with the Land. Guests may initially select only one Tier 1 experience. Soarin' is the top priority because it's more convenient to ride it in the afternoon with FastPass+. We expect that Disney will add both Frozen attractions to Tier 1 after they open.

Tier 1 (choose one)

1. Frozen Ever After*
2. Frozen Meet-and-Greet**
3. Soarin'
4. Test Track
5. Illuminations
6. Living with the Land

*Frozen Ever After is the Frozen-inspired attraction that is expected to open in the Norway Pavilion in World Showcase sometime in Spring 2016, most likely around May. For guests traveling before the ride opens, Soarin' makes the most sense as your Tier 1 FastPass+ selection. For those visiting after it opens, it's likely that it will be the most sought after Tier 1 FastPass+ experience and have afternoon waits that exceed Soarin' and Test Track.

**A Frozen Meet and Greet is expected to open next to Frozen Ever After at the same time. Anna and Elsa currently meet at Princess Fairytale Hall in Magic Kingdom with peak waits in the 70- to 120-minute range. Those waits should translate over to Epcot, where Anna and Elsa saw waits that peaked around four hours when they briefly met at Epcot in 2013. Fortunately, the hourly capacity should be higher in their new location, which will help cut down on wait times

Tier 2 (choose two)

1. Spaceship Earth
2. Mission: SPACE Orange

3. Character Spot
4. Mission: SPACE Green
5. Turtle Talk with Crush
6. The Seas with Nemo and Friends
7. Journey into Imagination with Figment
8. Captain EO

Note: Mission: SPACE does not require you to select Orange or Green when booking the experience, but guests planning on using it for the Orange side will want to prioritize it higher than those planning the Green side.

ARRIVING AT EPCOT

Guests aiming to take advantage of shorter morning waits should arrive at the main entrance at least 45 minutes before open, or at the International Gateway at least 30 minutes before open.

Most guests arrive at the main entrance via Disney bus or their own automobile. Guests staying at the Beach Club, Yacht Club, BoardWalk Inn, Swan, and Dolphin have the option of walking from their resort or taking the boat to the International Gateway entrance in the World Showcase between the United Kingdom and France Pavilions. Guests transferring from Magic Kingdom or the Magic Kingdom parking lot (Transportation and Ticket Center) arrive at the main entrance via the monorail.

Guest Services outside the main entrance is on the far right, while Guest Services inside is on the far left past Spaceship Earth. Wheelchair and ECV rental are on the left just inside the entrance. At the International Gateway, Guest Services is located next to the ticket booths on the left outside bag check. Wheelchairs and EVCs are available for rental inside on the left.

FUTURE WORLD EAST

Future World East is where you'll find three of Future World's four top priority attractions: Test Track, Sum of All Thrills, and Mission: SPACE. Most guests visiting only for one day will want to start on this side, and guests spending two or more days will also want to plan a morning starting with Test Track or a late arrival with Test Track as a FastPass+ selection.

Bypass Spaceship Earth, the park's icon, first thing in the morning. The iconic structure that looks like a giant golf ball enjoys lower peak waits than the headliners and sees shorter waits after 6pm. Many uninformed guests ride Spaceship Earth first thing, putting them at a great disadvantage as they won't arrive at Test Track until at least 9:30am, when waits will already be hitting 30+ minutes.

Dining choices are slim—Electric Umbrella is really it, and it serves a limited menu featuring Disney's standard burgers, chicken nuggets, and sandwiches. The Vegetarian Flatbread is an unlikely standout. Various stands serve snacks, including pretzels, churros, and beer.

Mouse Gear is the largest store in Epcot, offering the widest assortment of theme park merchandise outside of World of Disney at Disney Springs.

Ellen's Energy Adventure

RANKING Minor attraction. **EMH** No. **FP+** No. **TYPE** Dark ride. **REQUIRE-MENTS** None.

WHAT TO EXPECT A 45-minute experience about energy begins when riders are seated in what looks like a conventional theater where they will be shown the first of several films featuring Ellen DeGeneres and Bill Nye. After that, your section of the theater will break away from the other ride vehicles and you will slowly be taken through a variety of Animatronic scenes and films. With limited time at the park, this is the easiest attraction to skip due to its long duration and outdated Animatronics. **SCARY FACTOR** Low. Some young children may find Animatronic dinosaurs startling.

WHEN TO GO In the afternoon, or with a shorter child while the rest of the group rides the thrill rides. Usually closes at 7pm. **EXPECT TO WAIT** Less than ten minutes. **LENGTH** 45 minutes, with no way to exit in the middle. **WHERE TO SIT** Around the fourth row, which makes it easier to see the films.

Innoventions East (excluding Sum of All Thrills)

RANKING Afternoon diversion. **EMH** No. **FP+** No. **TYPE** Exhibits and interactive experiences. **REQUIREMENTS** None.

Jim's Gems
by Jim Korkis

At 165 feet in diameter, Spaceship Earth is the largest geodesic sphere in the world. It is covered with 954 triangular panels of alucobond (anodized aluminum on both sides heat-bonded with a polyethylene core in the center) and is supported fifteen feet off the ground by six steel legs driven deep into the Florida bedrock. The Imagineers created an unseen gutter about mid-point on the sphere to collect rain water and channel it through the structure and its supporting legs to underground drains. In that way, the rain water does not cascade down the side of Spaceship Earth onto the guests below.

WHAT TO EXPECT Mostly a collection of interactive experiences; each exhibit will take 15–30 minutes to complete. **SCARY FACTOR** Low. *Storm Struck* is a 4D film that simulates a storm in a small theater, but nothing else is frightening. *Note*: VISION House and Test the Limits Lab are closed.

WHEN TO GO In the afternoon. Usually closes at 7pm. **EXPECT TO WAIT** Just a few minutes for the next experience to begin. **LENGTH** Varies—generally about 20 minutes for each experience. Some families spend hours, others skip entirely.

Mission: SPACE

RANKING Major attraction. **EMH** Morning, Evening. **FP+** Yes. High priority for Orange (intense), lower priority for Green (less intense). **TYPE** Simulator. **REQUIREMENTS** Must be 44" tall to ride. Mission: SPACE has more warnings than any other ride at Disney World, and is the only ride where you will be handed a card with all of the various warnings on it. Consider skipping if you have suffered motion sickness on any other ride, or are claustrophobic.

WHAT TO EXPECT Mission: SPACE is a space flight simulator, where riders board small four-person capsules that are intended to mimic the inside of a space shuttle. There are two versions of this ride: the Orange Team features a spinning takeoff with G-forces up to 2.5, and is much more thrilling and much more risky for those with physical or motion sickness issues. The Green Team is identical to the Orange Team ride in every way except there is no spinning takeoff, and thus, no G-forces to worry about. After the initial takeoff, the rest of the ride is rather tame with only slight movements by the simulator while you watch a small screen in front of you. On the Orange Team, the intense aspects last for about 15 seconds at takeoff and again for a short amount of time when the spacecraft travels through an asteroid field. **SCARY FACTOR** Medium. The ride itself is not particularly scary, but there are some iffy moments. Mission: SPACE does induce anxiety due to negative hype over people getting sick from the spinning. **CAN WE HANDLE IT?** Apprehensive riders should begin with the Green Team.

WHEN TO GO Before 10:30am, after 7pm, or with FastPass+. **EXPECT TO WAIT** Orange Team peak waits are in the 25–45 minute range, while Green Team waits are usually 15–20 minutes. **LENGTH** 5 minutes. **WHERE TO SIT** Experience is the same from any of the four seats.

Spaceship Earth

RANKING Don't miss. **EMH** Morning, Evening. **FP+** Yes. High Tier 2 priority. **TYPE** Dark ride. **REQUIREMENTS** None.

WHAT TO EXPECT Spaceship Earth is a slow moving, dark omnimover ride that takes guests as high as 16 stories inside Epcot's famous geodesic sphere. Visitors ride past more than 20 Animatronic displays featuring scenes from the past 40,000 years that depict how communication techniques have changed with time. A classic. **SCARY FACTOR** Low. The ride is dark, but there are no startling elements.

WHEN TO GO After 6pm or with FastPass+. **EXPECT TO WAIT** Peak waits of 30 minutes are common. Expect to wait less than 10 minutes after 6pm. **LENGTH** 15 minutes. **WHERE TO SIT** Each row seats two to three people. The view from the left is arguably better.

Sum of All Thrills

RANKING Minor attraction. **EMH** No. **FP+** No. **TYPE** Simulator. **REQUIREMENTS** 48" or taller to ride and 54" or taller to add inversions.

WHAT TO EXPECT Guests design and, via simulation, ride their own rides. Guests first watch a short pre-show video introducing the importance of science. Next is the interactive design stage where riders design the intensity and ride elements, choosing from among a bobsled for a tame ride, or a roller coaster or fighter jet for the most intense experience. Finally, riders board a Kuka Arm simulator and experience their creation. **SCARY FACTOR** Medium. Riders choose how intense their ride is. **CAN WE HANDLE IT?** Probably. The wary can design a slower ride without inversions. Check the example ride vehicle first if claustrophobia is a concern.

WHEN TO GO Immediately after Test Track in the morning or after 6pm. Usually closes at 7pm. **EXPECT TO WAIT** 20–30 minutes in the afternoon. **LENGTH** 20 minutes total with about 90 seconds in the simulator. **WHERE TO SIT** In one of the two seats right next to each other.

Test Track

RANKING Don't miss. **EMH** Morning, Evening. **FP+** Yes. Second highest Future World Tier 1 priority behind Soarin'. Test Track is more convenient to get to in the morning and offers a single rider line. **TYPE** Dark/thrill ride. **REQUIREMENTS** 40" or taller.

WHAT TO EXPECT After a 2012 renovation, riders are to imagine themselves to be "inside" a computer simulation of a car being tested. Guests first design their own prototype automobile at a kiosk. The design process takes about three minutes and riders choose what they want their automobile to look like and whether they want to favor capability, efficiency, responsiveness, or power. In a surprise to many, this design step does not affect the ride in any way. Riders then board six-person vehicles with two rows of three seats each and embark on their journey with several sharp turns and increases and decreases in speed before launching outside at speeds up to 65 miles per hour. **SINGLE RIDER**: Test Track offers a single-rider line with the entrance to the left of standby. Waits are usually shorter than standby or FastPass+ because single riders don't go through the design process and the seating arrangement creates more openings.

SCARY FACTOR Low. Test Track is just a little more intense than normal driving.

WHEN TO GO Immediately after park opening, in the final hour of operation, or with FastPass+. **EXPECT TO WAIT** 60 to 100 minutes in the afternoon. **LENGTH** 5 minutes. **WHERE TO SIT** Request the front row for the best view.

FUTURE WORLD WEST

Three large pavilions make up the bulk of Future World West. Soarin' on the lower level of the Land Pavilion is its headlining attraction and a top morning priority. Most other attractions can safely be saved for the afternoon or early evening. Prior to its 2013 refurbishment, Character Spot was a top priority. Now that it has doubled its capacity, afternoon waits usually hover between 20 and 40 minutes.

Starbucks is located in the old Fountain View Café building to the right of the fountain. Club Cool, situated behind it, offers free samples of Coca-Cola products from around the world. Sunshine Seasons is arguably the best quick service in any theme park. You'll find it in between Soarin' and Living with the Land in the Land Pavilion. Coral Reef and Garden Grill are the two table service restaurants. Coral Reef receives mixed reviews, but the view of The Seas aquarium is intriguing. Garden Grill is a fun family-style character meal hosted by farmers Mickey, Pluto, Chip, and Dale inside the Land Pavilion.

Retail is light, with small stores and kiosks popping up at most attraction exits.

Captain EO

RANKING Skippable, though the air-conditioned theater is comfortable. **EMH** Evening. **FP+** Yes. Lowest priority. **TYPE** 4D show. **REQUIREMENTS** None.

WHAT TO EXPECT An eight-minute documentary hosted by George Lucas and Francis Ford Coppola precedes the loud 17-minute 3D show. 4D effects are slim, but the theater briefly shakes. The show's plot is both nonsensical and difficult to follow, but *Thriller*-era Michael Jackson has some interest for some. **SCARY FACTOR** EO is dark with aliens, danger, and several unrealistic torture scenes that last a few seconds. It shouldn't upset anyone over the age of ten, but apprehensive youngsters may want to sit it out.

WHEN TO GO For most: never. For the rest: in the afternoon or early evening when waits elsewhere are long. EO usually closes at 7pm. **EXPECT TO WAIT** Only as long as it takes for the next show to start. **LENGTH** 8-minute pre-show, 17-minute show. **WHERE TO SIT** In the middle at least half way from the screen.

Character Spot

RANKING Don't miss for those who wish to meet the characters; skippable for others. **EMH** Evening. **FP+** Yes. High Tier 2 priority. **TYPE** Meet and greet. **REQUIREMENTS** None.

WHAT TO EXPECT Guests line up indoors with televisions playing old cartoon clips. Guests then meet Mickey, Minnie, and Goofy individually in their classic outfits. **SCARY FACTOR** None.

WHEN TO GO As late in the evening as possible—ideally after 7pm. Waits are also short before 10:15am **EXPECT TO WAIT** Peak waits are typically 40 minutes. **LENGTH** About five minutes of signing, mingling, and picture taking.

Circle of Life

RANKING Skippable. **EMH** Evening. **FP+** No. **TYPE** Film. **REQUIREMENTS** None.

WHAT TO EXPECT *Circle of Life* is a film starring the *Lion King's* Timon, Pumba, and Simba that focuses on environmental responsibility, and, with no apparent irony, on why building mega-resorts can be bad for the environment. The film features both cartoon and live-action scenes. **SCARY FACTOR** None.

WHEN TO GO Afternoon or early evening. It usually closes at 7pm. **EXPECT TO WAIT** Only as long as it takes for the next show to start. **LENGTH** 15 minutes. **WHERE TO SIT** Near the back for a quick exit.

Innoventions West

Virtually all of Innoventions West closed in late April 2015. What remains is a bank of Sony Playstation 3 consoles with a variety of sports and Disney games that are free to play. The Disney Visa Meet and Greet is also here. Cardholders have an opportunity to meet one or two characters with relatively short lines from 1–7pm daily. Get in line at your convenience if you have your card with you.

Journey into Imagination with Figment

RANKING Minor attraction. **EMH** Evening. **FP+** Yes. Low priority. **TYPE** Dark ride. **REQUIREMENTS** None.

WHAT TO EXPECT Narrated by Dr. Nigel Channing with frequent interruptions by Figment the purple dragon, Journey takes riders slowly through a variety of rooms, each designed to stimulate the senses. **SCARY FACTOR** Low. This will only startle the young that are extremely prone to attraction anxiety.

WHEN TO GO In the afternoon or with a shorter child while the rest of the group rides the thrill rides. Usually closes at 7pm. **EXPECT TO WAIT** Peak waits of 20 to 30 minutes are common. **LENGTH** 5 minutes. **WHERE TO SIT** Any row is fine.

Living with the Land

RANKING Minor attraction. **EMH** Morning, Evening. **FP+** Yes. Lowest Tier 1 priority. **TYPE** Slow boat ride. **REQUIREMENTS** None.

WHAT TO EXPECT Living with the Land is a meandering, educational boat ride about crop cultivation. It's more fun than it sounds! **SCARY FACTOR** Low, unless you have a fear of genetically modified organisms.

WHEN TO GO By 10:30am or after 5pm is best. Usually closes at 7pm. **EXPECT TO WAIT** Less than ten minutes in most scenarios. **LENGTH** 15 minutes. **WHERE TO SIT** Request the first row for the best view.

Soarin'

RANKING Don't miss. **EMH** Morning, Evening. **FP+** Yes. Highest Future World Tier 1 priority. **TYPE** Simulator. **REQUIREMENTS** Must be 40" tall to ride.

WHAT TO EXPECT Riders are led into a large room with an 80-foot-tall concave movie screen and three ride vehicles, each of which has three rows. Once all riders are seated, the vehicles are lifted into the air so that each row is above the row below it. A series of scenes are projected onto the screen and the ride vehicles move with the scenes to simulate a hang-gliding flight. Disney is working on expanding capacity by adding a third theater, in addition to changing the theme from "Soarin' Over California" to "Soarin' Around the World", complete with a totally new digital film and projection system. Expect the new version to debut in later 2016. **SCARY FACTOR** Minimal. The ride takes visitors 40 feet in the air, which may be frightening for those intensely scared of heights. Motion sickness is much less of a problem than "hang glider" might imply. The ride is gentle and there are no significant drops or sharp turns.

WHEN TO GO Immediately after park open, in the final hour of operation, or with FastPass+. **EXPECT TO WAIT** Peak waits of 60–100 minutes are common. **LENGTH** 5 minutes. **WHERE TO SIT** The best seats are in the front row of the middle vehicle because other people's feet won't be dangling in front of your face. This is one of the rare rides where your request will actually make a major difference in how much you enjoy the attraction. Strongly consider requesting the first row.

The Seas with Nemo and Friends

RANKING Minor attraction. **EMH** Evening. **FP+** Yes. Low priority. **TYPE** Dark ride. **REQUIREMENTS** None.

WHAT TO EXPECT Nemo & Friends is a slow "clam-mobile" ride through a long *Finding Nemo* themed tunnel. The neatest part of the attraction is when the characters from *Finding Nemo* are shown swimming with real fish inside of the 5.7 million gallon salt-water tank. The ride lets visitors out at The Seas Pavilion, which is full of hands-on activities and places to view the 6,000+ underwater animals that live within one of the largest undersea environments in the world. **SCARY FACTOR** Low. There is a friendly shark Animatronic and it's dark, but that's about it.

WHEN TO GO Before 11am or after 7pm. **EXPECT TO WAIT** Peak waits of 10–20 minutes are common. Expect to wait less than five minutes before 10:30am and after 7pm. **LENGTH** 5 minutes. **WHERE TO SIT** Each clam-mobile seats three across a single row.

Turtle Talk with Crush

RANKING Don't miss for those with young kids, major attraction for everyone else. **EMH** Evening. **FP+** Yes. Medium priority. There are no reserved seats, but FastPass+ guarantees admittance to the next show. **TYPE** Interactive show. **REQUIREMENTS** None.

WHAT TO EXPECT Turtle Talk is a live, interactive show featuring Crush, the turtle from *Finding Nemo*. The theater is small and the kids are asked to sit up front. Crush moves, chats, and fields audience questions in real time, and every show is unique and drop-dead cute. **SCARY FACTOR** Zero.

WHEN TO GO Shows usually begin at 9:40am and run until 8:40pm. Visit before 10:30am or after 7pm. **EXPECT TO WAIT** Up to 30 minutes in the afternoon, but usually just as long as it takes for the next show to begin. **LENGTH** 15 minutes. **WHERE TO SIT** Kids should sit on the floor up front. Adults file into the bleacher-style seating in back.

WORLD SHOWCASE

World Showcase is a collection of 11 individual pavilions, each themed to a country from around the world. The emphasis is undoubtedly on eating, drinking, and shopping, but each pavilion offers authentic entertainment and shows. In Mexico, you'll find a meandering boat ride similar to it's a small world, often with short waits. Disney closed Maelstrom on October 5, 2014, with the expectation that a ride based on *Frozen* will replace it sometime in early 2016.

Frozen Ever After, the new ride expected to open in the Norway Pavilion in May 2016, is set to dramatically shift how crowds flow into and around Epcot. It's likely that Disney will open the ride, which is expected to have an hourly capacity below 1,000 riders per hour, at 9am to help ease waits. That's a departure from how most of World Showcase operates with its current 11am open for all other attractions. If and when that happens, it will likely cause the majority of guests at rope drop to head straight back to Norway, before doubling back to Future World for Test Track or another priority.

In this scenario, the bad news is that waits at Test Track will be longer after the Frozen ride due to the number of people that head straight to Test Track because they're more interested in thrills than Olaf. The good news is that it should increase the ability to select Soarin' or Test Track as a 4th or subsequent FastPass+ selection on the day-of because so many guests are securing Frozen in advance instead. The opening may also help pull even more people away from Soarin' and The Land Pavilion in Future World West because Frozen is all the way on the other side.

One thing is almost for certain – demand will far outstrip supply for Frozen Ever After and peak waits will be extremely high. When it opens, consider making it your first stop, use FastPass+, or get in line right before IllumiNations starts in the evening to reduce waits as much as possible.

Historically, many kids have been bored with the lack of rides, so Disney has installed a variety of interactive experiences designed to engage them. The most popular is Agent P's World Showcase Adventure themed to the popular *Phineas and Ferb* television show. Guests have an opportunity to pick up a handset from several pavilions and embark on a kind of scavenger hunt throughout World Showcase. Kids also have the opportunity to sit down with Cast Members in each pavilion and decorate Duffy or Agent P drawings. Even if you're not interested in the Frozen ride after it opens, moving up to World Showcase as close to 11am as possible guarantees low crowds at the various stores, exhibits, entertainment, and food outlets.

IllumiNations

IllumiNations is the park's nighttime spectacular, scheduled every night, almost always at regular park close, and lasting for about 15 minutes. It takes place on World Showcase Lagoon with viewing available from around World Showcase. Detailed advice on where to see the show is in the Epcot Cheat Sheet at the end of the chapter.

RANKING Don't miss. **EMH** No. **FP+** Yes. Low Tier 1 priority. The Fast-Pass+ viewing location is at the base of World Showcase across from the United States Pavilion in an area called Showcase Plaza. It's a low priority because the show is easy enough to see outside the viewing area and using FastPass+ at Soarin' or Test Track will save more time. Note that the view is excellent and using FP+ eliminates much of the wait required for one of the prime viewing locations. Those skipping Test Track and Soarin' or planning to arrive late for dinner and the show may find use in selecting it. **TYPE** Fireworks show. **REQUIREMENTS** None.

WHAT TO EXPECT Guests begin to fill in along the railing as far as two hours in advance, but most guests will find satisfying viewing locations as few as 15 minutes before show time. The action takes place on World Showcase Lagoon as fireworks explode above a massive rotating globe. **SCARY FACTOR** Low. The fireworks are occasionally loud, particularly at the end. **TYPICAL SCHEDULE**: Begins at regular park close. **LENGTH** 15 minutes.

Our World Showcase reviews begin in Mexico and run clockwise around World Showcase Lagoon.

Mexico Pavilion

Framed by a giant Mesoamerican pyramid, Mexico is home to a boat ride, two sit-down restaurants, a quick service outlet, a tequila bar, a margarita stand, a Donald Duck meet and greet, and a live mariachi band. Most of what Mexico offers is located inside the dark, air-conditioned pyramid that acts as a cool respite from the heat. Grab a margarita and enjoy the heritage exhibits, stores, ambiance, and music.

Minor attraction: Gran Fiesta Tour is a relaxing, slow-moving boat ride through the world of *The Three Caballeros*. The ride lasts about seven minutes and follows Jose Carioca and Panchito as they hunt down Donald before a big gig. Waits are under five minutes most of the time. On busier days, visit before 12:30pm or after 7pm.

Norway Pavilion

Themed to a Viking-era village, Norway features a replica of the 14th century Akershus Fortress, originally built to protect Oslo from attack. Disney's version is sanitized—you'll find a princess-hosted character meal inside. The richly detailed stave church features a *Frozen* tie-in with artwork and artifacts that show how reality influenced the movie. Kringla Bakeri, the pavilion's quick service, offers excellent, inexpensive treats. At the Puffin's Roost, guests can peruse fun Norway-themed merchandise alongside authentic (and expensive) hand-knit apparel, perfume, and toys.

Frozen Ever After, the boat ride expected to replace Maelstrom sometime around May 2016, and its accompanying Anna and Elsa Meet and Greet, will likely have a major impact on how crowds flow in and out of World Showcase. With the expectation that the ride will operate beginning at 9am, many more guests than ever before will hurry back to the Norway Pavilion and keep the area congested for most of the day. The best plan of attack will likely be using FastPass+ in the afternoon and instead focusing on the Future World attractions first thing in the morning.

China Pavilion

An intricately detailed triple-arched ceremonial gate welcomes visitors to China. Immediately past the gate is a replica of the Temple of Heaven, inside of which guests can view *Reflections of China*, a 15-minute Circle-Vision 360 film that covers the more positive Chinese traditions and culture (as in all World Showcase shows except the American Adventure, no negative aspects of the culture appear). Visit the air-conditioned, standing-room-only theater at your leisure. While you wait for the next film to begin, check out the cultural exhibit through the door on the left. Chinese acrobats perform most days either in the courtyard or inside the Temple of Heaven in the Hall of Prayer for Good Harvests.

Nine Dragons is the pavilion's table service restaurant, serving up traditional and contemporary Chinese food at prices lower than most other restaurants on property. It has a lousy reputation, but the food has improved in recent memory and the portions are large. Lotus Blossom is the quick service arm, serving Panda Express quality fast food at higher prices. It's best skipped. The Joy of Tea stand on the water is a surprisingly good spot to pick up a strong drink or fruity cocktail depending on the group's mood at the time.

Shopping in China is above average at the expansive House of Good Fortune on the left side of the pavilion. You'll find silk robes, traditional fans, tea sets, jewelry, puppets, and more.

Jim's Gems
by Jim Korkis

The Norway Pavilion covers approximately 58,000 square feet and was designed to look like a Norwegian village. It cost $46 million to build and was officially dedicated on June 3, 1988. The village included a detailed Stave church based on the 1212 A.D. Gol Stave Church in Norway, and the exterior of Restaurant Akershus resembled its namesake fortress in Oslo. Four styles of Norwegian architecture were showcased in the pavilion to represent the different areas of the country: Setesdal, Bergen, Oslo, and Alesund. Norway sold the pavilion back to the Disney Company in 1992 and dropped all financial support in 2002.

Germany Pavilion

Featuring a statue of Saint George slaying a dragon, and a clock tower with a glockenspiel that chimes on the hour, the architecture in Germany is interesting and varied. The main attraction is Altenmunster Oktoberfest beer on draft—there are no traditional attractions or entertainment here. Still, take a moment to peruse Karamell-Kuche (Caramel Kitchen), in addition to the stores that offer made-in-Germany toys, cuckoo clocks, beer steins, toys, apparel, and other fun items. As you walk toward Italy, pay special attention to the outdoor model train set on the left.

Biergarten is the table service restaurant, featuring a smorgasbord of traditional German salads, roasted meats, pretzel bread, soups, and more. A traditional oompah band plays intermittently throughout the day inside the restaurant. Lunch is priced well. Sommerfest is the pavilion's quick service, offering a variety of bratwurst, frankfurters, and other traditional German foods. Seating for it is scarce.

Italy Pavilion

The focal point of the Italy Pavilion is the 105-foot-tall functioning replica of St Mark's Campanile, the bell tower that looks out over the World Showcase Lagoon. Also prominently featured is a replica of the Doge's Palace, originally built by the Venetians in the early 14th century. In typical Disney fashion, the Palace is full of fine Italian perfume, handmade masks, soccer jerseys, pasta, and other items Italia. Italy is otherwise mostly restaurants and bars. Best is Via Napoli in the back of the pavilion, serving authentic Neapolitan pizzas. Without a reservation, try Tutto Gusto, the wine bar attached to the Tutto Italia restaurant with hundreds of Italian wines, rare Italian beer on draft, and an appetizer and dessert menu that's hard to beat. Tutto Italia is more formal, but still perfect for families and couples, serving regional Italian fare. A mime and a flag-waving troupe entertain guests most days.

United States Pavilion

The United States Pavilion is mostly housed inside of a single Colonial-style mansion that was built using 110,000 hand-made Georgian clay bricks.

Major attraction: *The American Adventure*, a 30-minute theater show blending film and Animatronics, is the principal attraction. The patriotic show briefly retells the history of America and runs on a set schedule with the next show listed on posters outside the pavilion. The theater seats over a thousand in comfortable air-conditioning, making it a perfect respite from the afternoon heat. The show is often preceded in the afternoon by the Voices of Liberty a cappella group inside the mansion.

Outside, the America Gardens Theater is home to various free concerts throughout the year with space-available seating, including Flower Power, Sounds like Summer, Eat to the Beat, and the Candlelight Processional.

Liberty Inn is the quick service outlet. Recent menu overhauls have brought a New York Strip Steak for about $12 and more interesting salad and entrées like Fried Shrimp with Old Bay Coleslaw and the Red, White, and Blue Salad with Field Greens, Craisins, Pecans, Apples, Blue Cheese, and a Sherry Vinaigrette. Seating is plentiful indoors and outdoors. Fife & Drum Tavern outside serves beer, pretzels, turkey legs, popcorn, and an assortment of other snacks.

Japan Pavilion

The red torii gate and the 85-foot-tall Goju-no-to pagoda welcome guests to the Japan Pavilion. These and other buildings are surrounded by beautiful gardens made up of native Japanese plants, bamboo, and evergreen, maple, and monkey puzzle trees. The large courtyard in the middle of the pavilion makes Japan feel more open, relaxed, and less cluttered than other pavilions. Be sure to cross the bridge leading to the White Heron Castle and check out the koi fish below.

While there are no rides or theater shows in Japan, the pavilion is still rich with entertainment and culture. Enjoy the athletic Taiko drummers outside on the pagoda steps and the cultural exhibits inside the castle. The Mitsukoshi Department Store on the right side of the pavilion is among the best in Disney World, offering more than 50,000 unique products. Kimonos, Samurai swords, Bonsai trees, chopstick sets,

Jim's Gems
by Jim Korkis

To honor the opening of the Magic Kingdom in 1971, Japan's Emperor Hirohito presented to Roy O. Disney a stone Japanese lantern to light the way to success and happiness. For almost ten years, the gift was on display, without any placard, at the Polynesian Village Resort. With the opening of a Japan Pavilion at World Showcase in 1982, the lantern was moved to the right-hand side of the entrance to the pavilion. The deer on the side of the lantern represents the famous Japanese Nara Deer Park adjacent to the Nara Prefecture's Kasuga Shrine, famous for its thousands of lanterns.

calligraphy brushes, toys, and everything in between are available for purchase. Check out the popular Pick-a-Pearl where guests can pick an oyster and discover what's inside. Hundreds of relatively inexpensive food and drink items are available in the final room, in addition to a sake bar with samples available by the glass.

Dining options are even more plentiful. Teppan Edo and Tokyo Dining are two very different table service restaurants. Teppan Edo, a traditional hibachi-grill experience similar to Benihana, is one of the more consistent restaurants on property, offering grilled meat, fish, and vegetables. Tokyo Dining focuses on sushi and tempura in a contemporary setting. Outside, Katsura Grill serves quick service sushi, teriyaki, and other traditional food. Indoor air-conditioned seating is available, in addition to the beautiful outdoor garden setting. Food at Katsura is merely okay, but it's a relaxing location. A sake bar also serving cocktails and beer is located outside across from Mitsukoshi Department Store. Also outside, Kabuki Café serves kaki gori (snow cones) with traditional toppings, in addition to smoothies, beer, and other snacks.

Morocco Pavilion

Morocco is represented by architecture and monuments from three famous Moroccan cities: Casablanca, Fez, and Marrakesh. Koutoubia Minaret, the focal point of the pavilion, is a replica of the 12th century Marrakesh prayer tower. Morocco is the only state-sponsored World Showcase pavilion, and the country played an integral part in the design and construction of the buildings, gardens, and Bab Boujeloud arch. The King of Morocco actually sent his personal craftsmen to construct and lay tile in much of the pavilion, making this one of the most authentic areas in Epcot. Because of the religious significance of many of Morocco's buildings, lights are not shined on the pavilion during IllumiNations.

Morocco is the most-passed-over pavilion, which is unfortunate because there is a lot to see and do, despite it not offering a major show or ride. B'net Houariyat entertains guests with live music and dancing most days on the outdoor stage. We highly recommend taking 20–30 minutes to explore the marketplace, museum, and art gallery. Restaurant Marrakesh is the under-rated Moroccan restaurant in the pavilion, specializing in couscous and anything with a shank. A belly dancer appears inside the restaurant throughout the day. Spice Road Table opened in late 2013, offering small Mediterranean tapas, wines, cocktails, and desserts. It's a beautiful restaurant that overlooks the picturesque lagoon. While reservations are offered, it's virtually never necessary to book one in advance. Tangierine Café is the quick service, featuring shawarma and falafel. While the food is a bit more expensive, portions are large and the food is freshly prepared. It's our favorite World Showcase quick service.

France Pavilion

The replica of the Eiffel Tower is the most recognizable feature of the France Pavilion. The buildings are themed like those found in Paris between 1870 and 1910, otherwise known as La Belle Epoque, or The Beautiful Time. France features a gorgeous courtyard area with a fountain and immaculately maintained gardens.

France's main attraction is an 18-minute film titled *Impressions de France*. Projected onto five large screens, *Impressions* provides a 200-degree panoramic view of France, its people, and its culture. You'll experience many of France's most popular destinations, including the gardens at Versailles, the Eiffel Tower, and the breathtaking French Alps. Unlike the films at China or Canada, you'll be able to sit and relax during the air-conditioned show. In addition, the fun Serveur Amusant comedy/acrobat show is scheduled throughout the afternoon most days.

France is home to two sit-down restaurants, a quick service boulangerie patisserie (bakery), and an ice cream parlor. Les Chefs de France downstairs is themed to a casual Parisian bistro and serves an excellent, relatively inexpensive three-course lunch in addition to a la carte items. Upstairs is the ritzier Monsieur Paul, serving a more expensive dinner-only menu catered toward adults. Les Halles Boulangerie Patisserie, located in the back of the pavilion, serves sandwiches, quiche, salads, desserts, and other French specialties. It's an excellent spot to pick up a snack or a meal. Finally, L'Artisan des Glaces serves freshly prepared sorbet and ice cream with the option of a shot of liquor poured on top.

Shopping includes wine, perfume, and fun French-themed Disney merchandise.

United Kingdom Pavilion

The United Kingdom Pavilion is one of the more architecturally diverse World Showcase pavilions, with the Hampton Court Palace, Anne Hathaway's (William Shakespeare's wife) thatched roof cottage, two castles, and a miniature version of Hyde Park represented. You'll see replicas of the red phone booths England is so famous for, as well as a variety of beautiful garden areas.

The British Revolution, playing hits from The Who, Beatles, Led Zeppelin, and others, is the entertainment here. Several shops carry a range of British goods, including tea, perfume and makeup, apparel, and a lot of Guinness- and Beatles-related merchandise.

Rose & Crown Dining Room is the pavilion's table service restaurant. It's casual, low key, and your best opportunity to watch IllumiNations from a restaurant while you dine. The Pub next door is an excellent spot to grab a pint. Yorkshire County Fish Co. outside serves excellent fast food fish and chips with limited picturesque seating along the lagoon.

Canada Pavilion

Gorgeous Victoria Gardens and a replica of the Canadian Rockies complete with a 30-foot waterfall lead guests into the Canada Pavilion. The Hotel du Canada, modeled after Ottawa's Fairmont Chateau Laurier, is the pavilion's largest and most magnificently detailed building. Canada features a Circle-Vision 360 film similar to *Reflections of China*. The 18-minute *O' Canada!* show is projected onto nine individual screens that surround the theatre. The film is presented in such a way that each screen shows the view looking out in that particular direction, so you feel like you're right in the middle of the shot. While it's standing-room-only, the theater is large and air-conditioned. A 15-minute Canadian Lumberjack show is scheduled daily at the outdoor stage.

Le Cellier is the pavilion's table service restaurant, primarily offering steak. Like Monsieur Paul in France, it's a signature restaurant, which means it will set you back two Dining Plan credits and is more expensive out of pocket than most restaurants.

Shopping is limited to stuffed animals and other toys, along with apparel items and some food and beverages.

Disney's Hollywood Studios

Disney's Hollywood Studios opened as a combined theme park and working production studio under the name Disney-MGM Studios on May 1, 1989. The name changed to Disney's Hollywood Studios in 2008. While several famous shows and movies were filmed or animated on site, it's been more than ten years since any serious studio work has happened here.

It's now "just" a Disney theme park, but several of Hollywood Studios' rides and shows are among the best Walt Disney World has to offer. With a total of five rides and a dozen shows, its repertoire is thin, but what it does offer will satisfy most guests and fill an entire day.

Touring the Studios is more complicated than one might expect due to long lines at the headliners and several lengthy stage shows that run on a limited schedule. The layout is also a bit confusing for first-time visitors. The Cheat Sheet map at the end of the chapter will make traversing the park significantly easier.

WHAT THE FUTURE MAY BRING

On August 15, 2015, Disney announced two major new lands headed for Hollywood Studios: Star Wars Land and Toy Story Land. Star Wars is at least five years off and Toy Story probably won't arrive much sooner. Even so, the additions mean a lot of changes coming over the next few years. Some have already happened, including the closures of The Magic of Disney Animation, Backlot Tour, and American Idol Experience. Many other closures are expected depending on where Star Wars ends up. Most of Echo Lake may close, including Indiana Jones Epic Stunt Spectacular. If Star Wars is headed for the Streets of America, then Lights, Motors, Action! Extreme Stunt Show will likely close. Other expected closures include One Man's Dream and Voyage of the Little Mermaid to make way for Toy Story Land, which is expected to go in behind where Pixar Place and Toy Story Mania currently sit. Rumors continue swirling about the possibility of an unannounced Cars Land addition as well.

Guests visiting in 2016 should experience much of what Hollywood Studios currently offers, though it's impossible to say how quickly Disney will shutter current attractions and when construction walls will begin showing up. Still, it's unlikely that construction should impact most visits. Pay attention to EASYWDW.COM and YOURFIRSTVISIT.NET for updates.

In an attempt to keep attendance steady and offer additional experiences in the meantime, Disney announced that Season of the Force will begin on January 8 and continue through March 20. Included is a weekend fireworks show and the expectation that Star Wars meet and greets and other experiences will be available daily. A Star Wars Launch Bay concept is also expected to open in December 2015, most likely in

Jim's Gems
by Jim Korkis

In building the replica of Grauman's Chinese Theater, the Disney Imagineers used the original blueprints of the original 1927 Meyer and Holler structure in Hollywood for reference, and the façade was built to full scale, rather than the forced perspective of some of the other buildings on Hollywood Boulevard. One of the few adjustments was that the ticket booth directly in front of the original theater was moved to the side for the Disney version so as not to block the entrance. The twenty-two-ton central roof section was constructed separately and hoisted into place by crane as a finishing touch.

the old Animation Building space near Disney Jr. Live on Stage. Here, guests will be able to experience interactive exhibits featuring the past six films in the *Star Wars* saga, in addition to the upcoming *Episode VII – The Force Awakens*. It's unlikely that the Launch Bay will need to be prioritized over key rides, though the meet and greets may be popular.

FASTPASS+ PRIORITY

FastPass+ at the Studios is divided into two tiers. In Tier 1 are Toy Story Midway Mania, Rock 'n' Roller Coaster, Great Movie Ride, Fantasmic!, and Beauty and the Beast: Live on Stage. Guests may initially select only one Tier 1 attraction, which can make it a struggle to visit both Toy Story Mania and Rock 'n' Roller Coaster on a single day without an early arrival. Most guests will want to select Toy Story as their Tier One FastPass+ and ride Rock 'n' Roller Coaster standby early in the morning.

Guests may initially select two of the eight attractions that make up Tier 2. Here's our suggested priority among them—most should pick two of the first four.

Tier 1 (choose one)

1. Toy Story Midway Mania
2. Rock 'n' Roller Coaster
3. Fantasmic!
4. The Great Movie Ride
5. Beauty and the Beast Live on Stage

Tier 2 (choose two)

1. Tower of Terror
2. Voyage of the Little Mermaid
3. Star Tours
4. Frozen Sing-Along
5. Indiana Jones Epic Stunt Spectacular
6. Disney Jr. Live on Stage
7. Lights, Motors, Action! Extreme Stunt Stunt Show
8. Muppet Vision 3D

ARRIVING AT THE STUDIOS

Arriving at least 45 minutes prior to park opening is essential for guests interested in signing up their 4–12 year old for the Jedi Training Academy or riding Toy Story Mania first thing without a significant wait. Arriving closer to regular open will only result in thousands of guests in line in front of you at the priority attractions.

Most guests arrive via Disney bus or their own automobile at one of the Studios' two entrances. The bus stops are just minutes away from the main entrance, while guests driving have the option of walking or taking a tram from the parking lot. Guests staying at the BoardWalk Inn, Yacht Club, Beach Club, Swan, or Dolphin either walk or take the boat that begins service one hour before regular open. Walking or taking the boat both take about 25 minutes, but walking cuts down on the wait for the first boat and allows you to arrive much earlier in the morning.

Guest Services is located on the left inside and outside of the main entrance. The primary MyMagic+ service center is located inside the main entrance on the left. Ticket booths in front of the entrance can handle any purchases or upgrades, usually with non-existent lines. Wheelchair and stroller rental are just inside on the right.

HOLLYWOOD BOULEVARD

Hollywood Boulevard, the Studios' main drag, is similar to Main Street, U.S.A. at Magic Kingdom. The left side consists almost entirely of retail with Mickey's of Hollywood and Keystone Clothiers carrying the widest selection of merchandise in the park. PhotoPass and a couple smaller stores are on the right, followed by Trolley Car Café, the park's sizable Starbucks location. Hollywood Brown Derby, a pricey signature restaurant that costs two credits on the Dining Plan, serves the best food in the park on the right near the end of the Boulevard. To the right of it sits Starring Rolls, the best place for a quick croissant or muffin first thing in the morning or a sandwich or cupcake later in the day. The classic Great Movie Ride stands tall at the end of the street.

Jim's Gems
by Jim Korkis

The Camera Man statue at the end of Hollywood Boulevard was sculpted by Aldo and Andrea Favilli (father and son). At the feet of the camera man are a director's megaphone and an open script that includes the names of people who inspired Andrea. The statue was commissioned by the late Roy E. Disney and and was installed in Burbank, California ("the heart of Hollywood"), in 1991. A replica of the Burbank statue was later placed in Disney's Hollywood Studios in 1995 with a plaque that states: "Movies are a medium of expression like a symphony orchestra...or a painter's brush on canvas." — Walt Disney

Great Movie Ride

RANKING Major attraction. **EMH** Morning, Evening. **FP+** Yes. Low Tier 1 priority. **TYPE** Dark ride. **REQUIREMENTS** None.

WHAT TO EXPECT Housed inside of a full-size replica of the famous Grauman's Chinese Theater, Movie Ride's preshow area features movie memorabilia and a large room with a giant movie screen that plays short clips from popular older movies. Riders board 70-person slow-moving vehicles, and a live narrator helps move the story along as you travel through famous movie scenes recreated with the help of Animatronic characters. Turner Classic Movies took over sponsorship of the attraction in early 2015. Changes are slim for the most part, though there are updates to the clips that play before and after the ride, in addition to sections of pre-recorded information on-ride. Movies represented include *Alien, Casablanca, Fantasia, Mary Poppins, Raiders of the Lost Ark*, the *Public Enemy*, and the *Wizard of Oz*. **SCARY FACTOR** Moderate for the very young, low for everyone else. The *Alien* scene is ominous and the *Indiana Jones* section has snakes and skeletons.

WHEN TO GO After 5pm or with FastPass+. **EXPECT TO WAIT** Peak afternoon waits of 30 minutes are common. **LENGTH** 25 minutes. **WHERE TO SIT** Rows seat six and the view is best on either the far left or right sides. Request the middle section of the vehicle for the best syncing between the visuals and audio.

ECHO LAKE
....

Star Tours is the standout in this land, which is also home to Indiana Jones Epic Stunt Spectacular, Frozen Sing Along, and Jedi Training Academy, in addition to several eateries. 50's Prime Time Café, with its comfort food and fun atmosphere, is Dave's favorite Studios restaurant. Hollywood & Vine next door is a Disney Jr character buffet for breakfast and lunch that is a lot of fun with kids of the appropriate age. Dinner has historically had no visiting characters, but Disney has been adding characters to dinner for seasonal promotions. Backlot Express is the quick service, with Disney staples like chicken nuggets, hamburgers, hot dogs, and sandwiches. The food at Backlot isn't great, but there's nicely themed air-conditioned seating inside. Min & Bill's Dockside Diner on Echo Lake serves hot dogs, turkey legs, and booze, and is an excellent stop for those in a hurry. Tatooine Traders sits adjacent to Star Tours and is the best location for *Star Wars* merchandise. *Indiana Jones* merchandise is available at the show's exit and to the right of 50's Prime Time.

A Note on Jedi Training Academy: Kids between the ages of 4 and 12 can participate in this show held next to Star Tours that trains them in the arts of the Jedi. Because slots are severely limited in number, sign up your kids first thing. To sign up for a slot, bring the participating child to the building across from Indiana Jones and in front of Star Tours, immediately after the park opens. Ask for an afternoon show to not interfere with morning touring. If they can't accommodate, let others sign up first, and then sign up for a show after 12pm.

Otherwise, with no high priority attractions, Echo Lake is best saved for the late morning or afternoon, particularly with a FastPass+ for Star Tours.

Frozen Sing-Along

RANKING A must for fans of Frozen, surprisingly enjoyable for everyone else. **EMH** No. **FP+** Yes. FastPass+ guarantees the user a seat at a specific show, but there is no reserved section for FastPass+ users. Because all guests are allowed into the theater about 15 minutes before show time, FP+ users need to arrive at least 20 minutes before the show starts to see any advantage, which is usually early enough that there would be plenty of availability in standby. In other words, using FP+ here is only beneficial if you plan to arrive about five minutes before show time and don't care where you sit—only that you'll be able to. **TYPE** Stage show. **REQUIREMENTS** Nothing more than your patience.

WHAT TO EXPECT Guests enter a comfortable, air-conditioned theater for an engaging stage show featuring Anna, Elsa, and the newly-appointed "Royal Historians" of Arendelle. Anna appears briefly at the beginning and Elsa joins her for a powerful number at the end of the show, but the bulk of the time is spent enjoying the genuinely funny banter between the historians with a crowd that intermittently bursts out into song. **SCARY FACTOR** Only your neighbor's singing voice.

WHEN TO GO Those not interested in Rock 'n' Roller Coaster, Tower of Terror, and the other thrill rides may want to take advantage of low crowds for the first show, which typically starts at 9:30am. Otherwise, plan to see an afternoon show when waits and crowds have peaked elsewhere. **EXPECT TO WAIT** Arrive 20–30 minutes before show time. **LENGTH** 25 minutes. **WHERE TO SIT** In the middle section about halfway up.

Indiana Jones Epic Stunt Spectacular Show

RANKING Major attraction. **EMH** No. **FP+** Yes. Low priority. **TYPE** Show. **REQUIREMENTS** None.

WHAT TO EXPECT A large theater seats about 2,000 people on bleacher-style seating. In the show, actors perform a series of stunts that mirror those from the movie *Raiders of the Lost Ark*, and the director explains how they are executed so they are safe and seem real. You'll see large explosions, sword fights, car chases, gun battles, and a number of other exciting stunts. **SCARY FACTOR** Low. While there are some thrilling moments on stage, the audience is never in any danger, real or imagined.

WHEN TO GO The first show of the day, usually around 11:15am, is the least crowded. The last show of the day is the second best bet. **EXPECT TO WAIT** Arrive at least 20 minutes early. **LENGTH** 30 minutes. **WHERE TO SIT** At least half way up, in the center section.

Star Tours

RANKING Major attraction. **EMH** Morning, Evening. **FP+** Yes. Moderate priority. **TYPE** Motion simulator show. **REQUIREMENTS** 40" or taller.

WHAT TO EXPECT Riders sit in a large 40-person simulator themed like the inside of a StarSpeeder 1000 spaceship. A 3D movie plays in the front and the ride vehicle tilts, bumps, vibrates, sways, etc., so it feels like you're actually inside of the StarSpeeder making the journey that you see in front of you. Disney advertises that the attraction has "more than 50 story combinations" because there are four scenes during the ride, each of which has a few different character or destination possibilities. For example, you might visit Chewbacca's home planet of Kashyyyk or the icy planet of Hoth after being directed by Yoda, Admiral Ackbar, or Princess Leia. Star Wars fans may wish to ride two or three times over the course of the day to see as many of the scenes as possible. In addition, Disney is expected to add new scenes from *Episode VII: The Force Awakens* in late 2015. **SCARY FACTOR** Low. There is a moderate amount of danger involved, but it isn't realistic enough to be scary. **CAN WE HANDLE IT?** The biggest problems are motion sickness and the jerkiness of the ride. Avoid if similar attractions have caused problems.

WHEN TO GO After the priority attractions, in the last two hours of operation, or with FastPass+. **EXPECT TO WAIT** 20–40 minute afternoon waits are common. **LENGTH** 5 minutes. **WHERE TO SIT** Views are similar from most seats. You'll experience the most motion in the far left or right seat in the back row.

STREETS OF AMERICA

Three shows and a playground situate themselves along the Streets of America, the farthest land from the main entrance. None of them build long waits, making the Streets a perfect afternoon destination. Retail is light, with a store specializing in Muppet merchandise sitting across from Muppet Vision 3D's exit.

Dining is more plentiful with Mama Melrose's Ristorante Italiano serving as the Italian-inspired table service restaurant. Pizzas here are significantly better than Pizza Planet next door for not much more money, but the restaurant's pricier fare is inconsistent. Studio Catering Co. is our favorite Studios quick service, serving above average sandwiches, salads, and wraps. High Octane Refreshments next door serves the best mixed drinks and offers the best beer menu of the bars in the park. Finally, Toy Story Pizza Planet is the land's primary quick service, serving up standard Disney pizza that runs about $10 for a personal size pie. It does not resemble Pizza Planet from the film *Toy Story* in any way.

Honey, I Shrunk the Kids Movie Set Adventure

RANKING Great for kids, skippable for everyone else. **EMH** Morning. **FP+** No. **TYPE** Playground. **REQUIREMENTS** None.

WHAT TO EXPECT Movie Set Adventure is a playground with a soft surface geared towards kids older than three. It features oversized objects since you've been shrunk down to the size of an ant, so you'll naturally run into a 52-foot-long water hose, 40-foot-tall bumblebees, 30-foot-tall blades of grass, and a bunch of slides and other objects to play on. **SCARY FACTOR** None.

WHEN TO GO After 11am. Closes before dusk. **EXPECT TO WAIT** Very rarely any wait. **LENGTH** As long as it takes to pry Junior away.

Lights, Motors, Action! Extreme Stunt Show

RANKING Major attraction. **EMH** No. **FP+** Yes. Low priority. **TYPE** Show. **REQUIREMENTS** None.

WHAT TO EXPECT Lights, Motors, Action is a stunt show spectacular featuring more than 40 vehicles. You'll see furious car chases and jet ski escapes, among other stunts that include fireballs, high-speed jumps, and five-story falls. All the while, the director teaches the audience about how the stunts are safely executed, filmed, and edited. The seating section is largely uncovered and gets extremely hot when temperaturs are high. Consider skipping in the summer. **SCARY FACTOR** Low. There are some thrill elements, but the audience is never in any danger.

WHEN TO GO There are usually only two shows scheduled: one around 1:20pm and one around 4:30pm. The 1:20pm show is usually easier to fit into an itinerary. **EXPECT TO WAIT** Arrive at least 15 minutes early. **LENGTH** 35 minutes. **WHERE TO SIT** At least half way up in the center section.

Muppet Vision 3D

RANKING Don't miss. **EMH** Morning, Evening. **FP+** Yes. Low priority. **TYPE** 4D show. **REQUIREMENTS** None.

WHAT TO EXPECT A 12-minute pre-show video in a room full of Muppet gags welcomes viewers. The theater is large, air-conditioned, and comfortable. The 4D film follows the Muppets as they prepare for a show and features a live-action Sweetums character at the end. **SCARY FACTOR** Low. At times the show is loud.

WHEN TO GO Afternoon when crowds have peaked elsewhere. **EXPECT TO WAIT** Only as long as it takes for the next show to start. **LENGTH**

12-minute pre-show, 17-minute show. **WHERE TO SIT** Let guests stream in and fill about half of a row at least half way back from the front before entering in order to sit in the middle.

COMMISSARY LANE

Located behind the Great Movie Ride, Commissary Lane is home to just ABC Commissary and Sci-Fi Dine-In. ABC Commissary is a decent quick service with an improved menu and plentiful air-conditioned seating, but choices are limited to a handful of options. Sci-Fi, with its fun drive-in theater theme, is Josh's favorite Studios restaurant, serving reliably good sandwich and burger fare. The more expensive options at Sci-Fi are over-priced given the quality, and best skipped by those paying cash.

PIXAR PLACE

By far the most congested area in the park, Pixar Place is home to the Studios' most popular attraction: Toy Story Midway Mania! With a severely limited capacity, and with few other things to occupy the time of little kids, Toy Story Mania reliably has the longest waits of any WDW attraction. Expect peak waits in the 60–120 minute range. It is the highest priority ride at the park and must be ridden either first thing in the morning, with FastPass+, or right before close in order to avoid a long wait.

Toy Story Midway Mania!

RANKING Don't miss. **EMH** Morning, Evening. **FP+** Yes. Highest Tier 1 priority. **TYPE** Interactive 3D shooting game. **REQUIREMENTS** None.

WHAT TO EXPECT Riders enter slow-moving vehicles and shoot targets to score points with toy guns attached to the front of the ride vehicle. Toy Story Mania is in 3D (with required 3D glasses) and also includes 4D elements. There are five midway style games to play during the ride, none of which are violent. It's a lot more fun to experience than to read about! **SCARY FACTOR** Mild spinning should not upset even the most prone to motion sickness.

WHEN TO GO Immediately after the park opens, in the last 30 minutes of operation, or with FastPass+. **EXPECT TO WAIT** Afternoon peak waits are 60–120+ minutes. Disney is expanding Midway Mania by adding another track that's expected to open sometime in late 2016. The increased capacity should help ease waits and increase FastPass+ availability, but Toy Story will likely continue to see the longest average and peak waits in the park. **LENGTH** 5 minutes. **WHERE TO SIT** Pairs of riders sit next to each other and compete with the pair facing the opposite direction in the same vehicle.

MICKEY AVENUE
....

Mickey Avenue is the corridor that connects Pixar Place with the Animation Courtyard behind Great Movie Ride, now home to just one attraction: Walt Disney: One Man's Dream.

Walt Disney: One Man's Dream

RANKING Minor attraction. **EMH** Morning, Evening. **FP+** No. **TYPE** Walk-through exhibit with an optional film. **REQUIREMENTS** None.

WHAT TO EXPECT A sincere, interesting look at the man behind the Walt Disney Company, featuring memorabilia and artifacts from Walt Disney's life and models of Disney park attractions from around the world. The optional 15-minute film at the end is highly recommended. **SCARY FACTOR** None.

WHEN TO GO See it when waits are long at other rides, or you simply are nearby. **EXPECT TO WAIT** No waits. **LENGTH** As long as you like—most guests spend about 30 minutes, including the film.

ANIMATION COURTYARD
....

Here you'll find the large Animation Building (The Magic of Disney Animation and the Animation Academy closed in July 2015) and several character meet-and-greets including Sofia the First and Doc McStuffins. Voyage of the Little Mermaid, an enchanting stage show featuring a live Ariel, is arguably the land's best attraction. Disney Jr. Live on Stage, aimed specifically at preschoolers, is a favorite of most of them. There are no dining options here, but two shops are located on the Voyage of the Little Mermaid side, including one that's almost entirely princess merchandise.

Disney Jr Live on Stage

RANKING Don't miss for young kids, skippable for everyone else. **EMH** No. **FP+** Yes. Low priority. **TYPE** Musical stage show. **REQUIREMENTS** None.

WHAT TO EXPECT Features characters from *Mickey Mouse Clubhouse, Handy Manny, Little Einsteins,* and *Jake and the Never Land Pirates* in a fun musical stage show. There is no conventional seating in the theater except for in the very back where there are several benches. Parents and kids are expected to sit on the floor throughout the show—at least until the singing, dancing, and clapping start. There is a lot of audience participation throughout, and little ones really get into it. **SCARY FACTOR** None.

WHEN TO GO Try to see one of the first two or last two shows. **EXPECT TO WAIT** Arrive at least 15 minutes early. **LENGTH** 22 minutes. **WHERE TO SIT** With seating on the floor, there isn't an outstanding place to sit.

Voyage of the Little Mermaid

RANKING Major attraction. **EMH** Evening. **FP+** Yes. Moderate priority. **TYPE** Musical stage show. **REQUIREMENTS** None.

WHAT TO EXPECT A mixture of puppets, Animatronics, and live actors tell the story of the Little Mermaid inside of a comfortable, relatively small theater. **SCARY FACTOR** Medium for young kids. Ursula, the wicked octopus, may frighten young children. She is 12-feet tall, 10-feet wide, and accompanied by loud effects and darkness. You might want to prepare youngsters by reminding them that she can't leave the stage.

WHEN TO GO The first two or last two shows of the day are least crowded. **EXPECT TO WAIT** Up to 30 minutes in the afternoon. **LENGTH** 15 minutes. **WHERE TO SIT** Let half of a row file in first to be in the center. Sit at least half way back for a full view of the stage.

SUNSET BOULEVARD

Here, you'll find two of Hollywood Studios' best rides: Rock 'n' Roller Coaster and Tower of Terror. The entrance to the Hollywood Hills Theater, where the night-time spectacular Fantasmic! takes place, is located on the right before Tower of Terror. Nearby *Beauty and the Beast* is an excellent stage show that has been running longer than any other WDW show.

Sunset Boulevard is primarily lined with retail on the left and right sides of the street before arriving at the attractions. On the right is a store offering *Frozen*-inspired merchandise, followed by a store offering Planet Hollywood merchandise, and then a store selling mostly apparel and higher-end watches and purses. On the left is Sweet Spells, offering freshly baked treats similar to those found at Main Street Confectionery at Magic Kingdom, in addition to other packaged edibles. Further up is Reel Vogue, which usually sells *Nightmare Before Christmas* merchandise, in addition to *Star Wars* stuff, "Made with Magic" items like the Sorcerer Mickey Wand, and generic character merchandise. At the exit to Rock 'n' Roller Coaster is a store selling a smorgasbord of rock 'n' roll-inspired merchandise. The shop at the exit to Tower of Terror features over a hundred items themed to the attraction, including Hollywood Tower Hotel robes and bells.

Sunset Ranch Market is an outdoor collection of six individual stands serving all kinds of food—barbecue, burgers, sandwiches, turkey legs, salads, ice cream, fruit, snacks, and more. The common seating area is outdoors. Hollywood Hills Theater offers snacks and drinks, in addition to a few heartier items like hot dogs for about 90 minutes before Fantasmic! starts.

Beauty and the Beast Live on Stage

RANKING Major attraction. **EMH** No. **FP+** Yes. Low priority. **TYPE** Stage show. **REQUIREMENTS** None.

WHAT TO EXPECT This 25-minute Broadway-style musical features characters, music, and scenes from *Beauty and the Beast*. The sets are elaborate, the costumes are first-rate, and the acting is excellent. **SCARY FACTOR** None.

WHEN TO GO The first show of the day, usually around 11:45am, is the least crowded. The last show of the day is the second best bet. **EXPECT TO WAIT** Arrive at least 20 minutes early. **LENGTH** 30 minutes. **WHERE TO SIT** At least half way up in the center section.

Fantasmic!

RANKING Don't miss. **EMH** No. A show may be scheduled to start during or after evening EMH begins, but anyone is welcome to attend. **FP+** Yes, low priority in most situations. There is dedicated FastPass+ seating near the center, but getting a good seat within the section requires an early arrival. And choosing Fantasmic! in advance means you won't be able to schedule a 4th FP+ at an in-park kiosk because the show is so late and you won't have an opportunity to use your Fantasmic! FastPass+ until the end of the night. **TYPE** Fireworks and live action show. **REQUIREMENTS** None.

WHAT TO EXPECT The theater seats about 9,000 people on bleacher seating without backs. Mickey is the star of the show as he appears on stage with over 50 live performers as film sequences featuring many best-loved Disney moments and characters, plus Pocahontas, play on screens made of water, fireworks shoot overhead, and fire and magic potions abound. **SCARY FACTOR** Moderate for the young. Mickey is in a considerable amount of danger with a 40-foot-tall dragon and all the villains. Sit near the back with anxious toddlers for a quick escape if it gets to be too much.

TYPICAL SCHEDULE: Presented once or twice per evening almost every evening of the year. Show times vary, depending on when it gets dark, and may be as early as 7pm or as late as 10.30 pm. The second show, if scheduled, will be less crowded. **LENGTH** 30 minutes. **WHERE TO SIT**: Arrive at least 45 minutes early for the first show. Arriving 20 minutes early is sufficient for the second show. Sit at least half way up, as close to the center as possible.

Rock 'n' Roller Coaster

RANKING Don't miss. **EMH** Morning, Evening. **FP+** Yes. High Tier 1 priority. **TYPE** Roller coaster. **REQUIREMENTS** 44" or taller.

WHAT TO EXPECT An Aerosmith video pre-show explains why you are about to drive really fast. Next you board a limousine-themed roller coaster vehicle that seats 24 people in rows of two. The vehicle will then propel out of the gate with the force of a supersonic jet. **SCARY FACTOR** With max speeds over 60 miles per hour, three inversions, and multiple corkscrews, this is arguably Disney's most intense roller coaster. The dark setting may actually ease fears as the track is never fully visible to riders. **CAN WE HANDLE IT?** The initial launch is the most intense part—the rest of the ride is relatively tame compared to any major coaster at Six Flags or Universal. Anyone that made it through Everest or Space Mountain should be fine.

WHEN TO GO First thing or immediately after Toy Story Mania, in the final hour of operation, or with FastPass+. Rock 'n' Roller Coaster offers a single-rider line, but because it's impossible to know how many people are ahead of you in it before you actually get to the indoor pre-show area, it's not recommended. **EXPECT TO WAIT** 50 to 100 minutes in the afternoon. **LENGTH** 90 seconds. **WHERE TO SIT** Request the front row for the best view, the middle if you're apprehensive, or the back to see all the twists and turns.

Twilight Zone Tower of Terror

RANKING Don't miss. **EMH** Morning, Evening. **FP+** Yes. Highest Tier 2 priority. **TYPE** Elevator drop. **REQUIREMENTS** 40" or taller.

WHAT TO EXPECT A pre-show video in the dilapidated hotel's library explains the circumstances surrounding your unfortunate visit. After a tense five- to ten-minute wait in the boiler room, you board your elevator, which will embark on an eerie journey through the hotel. Anyone going down? **SCARY FACTOR** High. The most obviously frightening ride at Disney World, and one of few that puts an emphasis on fear. There are no particularly scary images or scenes, but Disney does an excellent job of building tension up to the final drop, which begins at 170 feet above ground at a speed faster than gravity would naturally pull. **CAN WE HANDLE IT?** Motion sickness can be an issue, but otherwise walk the nervous past the ride exit and note that almost everyone leaves with a smile on their faces."

WHEN TO GO Immediately after Toy Story Mania and/or Rock 'n' Roller Coaster, in the final hour of operation, or with FastPass+. **EXPECT TO WAIT** 50–100 minutes in the afternoon. **LENGTH** 5 minutes. **WHERE TO SIT** All seats are good, but the view from the front row is the least obscured.

The Magic Kingdom

The original Walt Disney World theme park and the most popular theme park in the world, Magic Kingdom offers more attractions, entertainment, and atmosphere than any of the other theme parks. Its offerings are varied, from elaborate stage shows to classic dark rides to roller coasters. Magic Kingdom is best toured over two or more days, but guests with limited time still have the opportunity to visit the highlights and take in the fabulous nighttime entertainment.

FASTPASS+ PRIORITY

There are far more FastPass+ opportunities at Magic Kingdom than at any of the other theme parks, making the decision on which to pick difficult. Consider picking three high-priority attractions in a Land that you don't plan to visit until the afternoon or evening. For example, if you plan to start your day with The Magic Carpets of Aladdin, Jungle Cruise, Big Thunder Mountain, and Splash Mountain, then you may want to use FastPass+ in the afternoon in Fantasyland at Peter Pan's Flight, Anna/Elsa, and the Mine Train, or in Tomorrowland at Space Mountain, Tomorrowland Speedway, and Buzz Lightyear.

FastPass+ Priority

1. Anna and Elsa at Princess Fairytale Hall
2. Seven Dwarfs Mine Train
3. Peter Pan's Flight
4. Space Mountain
5. Splash Mountain (when high temperatures are 80+ degrees)
6. Cinderella and Rapunzel at Princess Fairytale Hall
7. Enchanted Tales with Belle
8. Big Thunder Mountain Railroad
9. Ariel at Ariel's Grotto
10. Buzz Lightyear's Space Ranger Spin
11. Tomorrowland Speedway
12. Jungle Cruise
13. Haunted Mansion

Jim's Gems

by Jim Korkis

Cinderella Castle is 189-feet high and made of concrete, steel, cement, gypsum plaster, plastic shingles, and fiberglass over a six-hundred-ton framework of steel. No actual bricks were used in the construction, but the illusion of them reinforces the forced perspective design. These "bricks" are of different sizes, larger at the bottom and progressively smaller toward the top, giving the impression that the castle is taller than it actually is. In addition, Main Street, U.S.A. rises about six feet from Town Square to the castle, which also makes the castle seem taller, and farther away as well.

14. Splash Mountain (when high temps are less than 80 degrees)
15. Pirates of the Caribbean
16. The Many Adventures of Winnie the Pooh
17. Mickey at Town Square Theater
18. Barnstormer
19. Disney Festival of Fantasy Parade (doesn't save any time and the location is in the sun, but there are a limited amount available)
20. Main Street Electrical Parade (prioritize first/only parade; second parade on the same night sees light crowds)
21. Wishes
22. it's a small world
23. Tinker Belle at Town Square Theater
24. Dumbo the Flying Elephant
25. Under the Sea Journey of the Little Mermaid
26. Magic Carpets of Aladdin
27. Mad Tea Party
28. Monsters Inc. Laugh Floor
29. Mickey's PhilharMagic

ARRIVING AT MAGIC KINGDOM

Magic Kingdom's parking lot is located at the Transportation and Ticket Center (TTC) across Seven Seas Lagoon. Guests arriving via their own automobile or buses from off-site resorts (including Shades of Green and the Four Seasons) will need to transfer from the TTC to Magic Kingdom via the resort monorail, express monorail, or ferry boat. The express monorail is the fastest because it's a direct route that takes about three minutes. There are also more monorails on the express beam, so a fresh monorail car arrives every three to five minutes. The resort monorail is often less crowded, but the trip takes about 20 minutes with stops at the Polynesian and Grand Floridian resorts first. The five-minute ferry ride is scenic and less cramped because there's more room to spread out. Our preference is the ferry, though the express monorail is often a few minutes faster. Guests traveling from Epcot will also transfer at the Transportation and Ticket Center.

Most guests arrive here from Disney resorts and the Swan and Dolphin via Disney buses, which pick-up and drop-off just a couple minutes walk from the main entrance. Guests from the Contemporary have the option of walking about ten minutes or taking the resort monorail. Guests at the Polynesian and Grand Floridian may take the resort monorail or watercraft. Guests at the Wilderness Lodge and Ft. Wilderness may take a bus or watercraft. Watercraft trips are usually slower, but more scenic.

Guest services is located on the far right outside the entrance and on the left at City Hall inside the entrance. Lines are often shorter inside at City Hall. Wheelchair and ECV rentals are located on the right just inside the entrance. Stroller rental is located underneath the train station.

If you don't have lunch reservations at Be Our Guest, and wish for them, try to book as soon as possible for the lunch window of your touring plan. Using the My Disney Experience app to do so while waiting for the park to open is simplest.

MAIN STREET, U.S.A.

Main Street, U.S.A. is themed to a small town at the turn of the 20th century. The train station works to block the view of what's inside as guests pass underneath. Once through, the magnificent Cinderella Castle shines in the distance. To the right in Town Square Theater is a Magician Mickey Mouse meet and greet, and the only location where Mickey may talk to guests. Tinker Bell meets separately in the same building. Next door is the below-average Tony's Town Square restaurant themed to *Lady and the Tramp*. Here you'll find Italian food that's generally done better at Olive Garden.

On the left is package pickup and Guest Services. Inside the fire station, guests can sign up to play the interactive Sorcerers of the Magic Kingdom game. Five playing cards per person may be picked up daily. Next to it is Harmony Barber Shop with surprisingly reasonable prices. Stop in for a fun first haircut or some "pixie dust" for a lot less money than the Bibbidi Bobbidi Boutique in Fantasyland. Also on the left, the Emporium stretches for much of Main Street, offering just about every piece of theme park merchandise from toys and plush to Mickey Crocs.

On the right, The Chapeau offers a wide selection of hats, and Main Street Confectionery is your best spot for handmade treats and cupcakes. Further up on the right is Main Street Bakery, which now hosts the park's Starbucks. Past that is Main Street Cinema, Uptown Jewelers, and Crystal Arts, all offering upscale items like Dooney and Bourke bags and Ray-Ban sunglasses. Uptown Jewelers is also home to the Pandora store that offers theme park-exclusive charms.

At the end of Main Street on the left is Casey's Corner, serving hot dogs with interesting toppings like barbecue pork and coleslaw or a Polish sausage with stone-ground mustard and grilled onions. Farther on the left is Crystal Palace, which hosts a Winnie the Pooh and friends buffet for all three meals. On the right is Plaza Ice Cream Parlor, which is a great spot for a sundae in the afternoon. To the right of it is The Plaza Restaurant, serving the most inexpensive table service sandwich fare on property.

Mickey Mouse at Town Square Theater

RANKING Don't miss for little kids who need to meet Mickey; skippable for others. **EMH** No. **FP+** Yes. Medium priority for guests wanting to meet Mickey. **TYPE** Character meet-and-greet. **REQUIREMENTS** None.

WHAT TO EXPECT Magician Mickey greets guests inside Town Square Theater. At press time, this is the only location where he speaks. The inter-action is unique and often times enchanting as kids and adults alike discuss sports, Magic Kingdom rides, birthday buttons, etc. Note that occasionally there are technical difficulties and Mickey will be his traditional silent self. **SCARY FACTOR** None.

WHEN TO GO First two or last two hours of operation, during a parade, or with FastPass+. Skip first thing in the morning for higher priorities. **EXPECT TO WAIT** 35–50 minutes in the afternoon. **LENGTH** 3–4 minutes of chatting, signing, mingling, and picture taking.

Tinker Bell at Town Square Theater

RANKING The only place to normally meet Tink. **EMH** No. **FP+** Yes, low priority. **TYPE** Character meet-and-greet. **REQUIREMENTS** A willingness to be shrunk down to fairy size.

WHAT TO EXPECT Tinker Bell meets alone in a location that doesn't make a lot of thematic sense, but she does feature a nice backdrop and it is air-conditioned. **SCARY FACTOR** None.

WHEN TO GO In the first two or last two hours of operation or with FP+. **EXPECT TO WAIT** 10–20 minutes in the afternoon. **LENGTH** About a minute of one-on-one time.

Jim's Gems
by Jim Korkis

The hitching posts on Main Street, U.S.A., were the contribution of Art Director Emile Kuri, who won an Academy Award for his work on the Disney feature film 20,000 Leagues Under the Sea (1954). Part of the filming was done at an authentic 1840 mansion and the owner was especially pleased with the care Kuri had taken of the house. In appreciation, he gifted Kuri with an original vintage hitching post from the property. Kuri later used that antique to create a mold for Main Street's posts.

The Walt Disney World Railroad

RANKING Minor attraction. **EMH** No. **FP+** No. **TYPE** Steam train tour around the outer perimeter of the park, with additional stops in Frontierland near Splash Mountain and Fantasyland near Barnstormer. **REQUIREMENTS** None.

WHAT TO EXPECT The Disney World Railroad is a relaxing way to see parts of the Magic Kingdom that you might miss by simply walking around in a hurry. Some very minor vignettes are only visible from the train (and the steamboat). You board at any of the three stations and ride for as long as you like around the 1.5 mile track. If you are traveling between areas near two of the stops, the train is a nice break from walking. The strollers Disney rents at the park are not allowed on the train. You will need to remove your belongings, name card, and have your receipt handy to pick up a new stroller at your final destination. Skippable for those on shorter visits. **SCARY FACTOR** None.

WHEN TO GO Anytime attraction. See it when waits are long at other rides, or when you want to use it as transport to save walking. The train stops operating prior to Wishes in the evening and does not usually resume service. **EXPECT TO WAIT** Only for the next train—7–10 minutes. **LENGTH** A full circle around the Magic Kingdom takes about 20 minutes. **WHERE TO SIT** Views are best from the side where you board.

ADVENTURELAND

Split into two distinct areas—the Arabian Village and Caribbean Plaza—Adventureland is distinctively adventure-y. In the Arabian section, you'll find most of the attractions—Tiki Room, Jungle Cruise, Magic Carpets of Aladdin, and Swiss Family Treehouse—as well as the cult favorite Citrus Swirl, a blend of frozen orange juice and vanilla ice cream, at Sunshine Tree Terrace. The Skipper Canteen restaurant, themed to the nearby Jungle Cruise attraction, is expected to open in late 2015 in the old Adventureland Veranda space to the right of Sunshine Tree Terrace. Expect an immersive atmosphere, plenty of surprises, and an enchanting overall experience, though food quality and pricing remain to be seen. If Be Our Guest Restaurant in Fantasyland is any indication, reservations here will be a hot commodity and should be prioritized for those interested.

Agrabah Bazaar is the primary, smallish store offering wares perfect for adventurers. A store sponsored by Sunglass Hut is across from Swiss Family Robinson Treehouse, offering sunglasses that mostly cost hundreds of dollars. To the right of the Pirates entrance is the signup building for the fun Pirate's Adventure Treasures of the Seven Seas interactive game. It includes a high-quality map that sends players around Adventureland unlocking secrets and setting off surprises. Visit in the afternoon as a fun diversion when waits peak elsewhere.

Arabian Village opens up to Caribbean Plaza on the Frontierland side, hosting the Pirates of the Caribbean attraction with an expansive store at its exit offering everything pirate. Tortuga Tavern is the land's quick service, often only open from 11am–3pm and serving taco and nacho fare across from Pirates. It's a nice way to mix up the usual burgers and nuggets found elsewhere. Aloha Island behind The Magic Carpets of Aladdin, which recently relocated from its spot now occupied by Sunshine Tree Terrace, serves the popular Dole Whip, a frozen pineapple-flavored treat.

Enchanted Tiki Room

RANKING Minor attraction. **EMH** Evening. **FP+** No. **TYPE** Audio-Animatronics show. **REQUIREMENTS** None.

WHAT TO EXPECT A groundbreaking attraction when it originally opened at Disneyland in the early 60s, the Enchanted Tiki Room entertains with singing Animatronic birds. Today it feels quaint—kids don't enjoy it a lot, and while adults are charmed, it's not a priority. Many Disney fans love it because of its history, but it's ultimately skippable for those immune to nostalgia. **SCARY FACTOR** Not much—just a bit of thunder and lightning.

WHEN TO GO Anytime attraction. See it when waits are long at other rides, or you need to get out of the weather. **EXPECT TO WAIT** 10–15 minutes for the next show. **LENGTH** 10 minutes. **WHERE TO SIT** Sit in the last row, towards the center.

Jungle Cruise

RANKING Don't miss. **EMH** No. **FP+** Yes. Medium priority. **TYPE** Comedy disguised as a river cruise. **REQUIREMENTS** None.

WHAT TO EXPECT This boat ride takes you through areas themed as several of the world's great rivers, inhabited by Audio-Animatronic people and animals. Your (human) skipper guides the tour, making corny jokes and telling silly puns along the way. The effects are dated, but the skipper can make the ride so much fun that it's not to be missed. **SCARY FACTOR** Low. There is a short section in dark ruins, but that's it.

WHEN TO GO First two or last two hours of operation, or with FastPass+. **EXPECT TO WAIT** 35–70 minutes in the afternoon. **LENGTH** 10 minutes. **WHERE TO SIT** Anywhere along the edge of the boat—avoid the interior seats.

Magic Carpets of Aladdin

RANKING Skippable but fun. **EMH** Evening. **FP+** Yes. Low priority. **TYPE** Spinning ride. **REQUIREMENTS** None.

WHAT TO EXPECT This slow-loading, low capacity ride raises four-person magic-carpet themed vehicles and then spins riders in the air over Adventureland. You can control how high you go. The ride is fun and offers some spectacular views, but most guests won't want to spend more than a few minutes waiting. **SCARY FACTOR** Low. **CAN WE HANDLE IT?** Motion sickness is rarely an issue. A camel may spit water in your general direction.

WHEN TO GO Anytime attraction. See it when waits are long at other rides, or you simply are nearby. **EXPECT TO WAIT** 10–20 minutes in the afternoon. **LENGTH** 2 minutes. **WHERE TO SIT** Cast Members will assign your group a carpet—the experience is the same from all. The front seat controls height, the back seat tilt.

Pirates of the Caribbean

RANKING Don't miss. **EMH** Evening. **FP+** Yes. Low priority. **TYPE** Boat ride through pirate-themed Audio-Animatronics and settings. **REQUIREMENTS** None.

WHAT TO EXPECT One of the most famous rides at the park, Pirates sends riders floating through a Disneyfied version of a town ransacked by pirates. In a reversal of what usually happens, the Jack Sparrow films were based on the ride, and Jack and others from the films are present in many scenes. **SCARY FACTOR** This is a lighthearted, playful ride, yet one with lots of skeletons and implied violence. Skip it if Haunted Mansion was too much. **CAN WE HANDLE IT?** There's a mild drop towards the beginning of a few feet that may result in a bit of water splashing over the first row, but that's it.

WHEN TO GO In the first two or last two hours of the day is best. **EXPECT TO WAIT** 15–40 minutes in the afternoon. **LENGTH** 10 minutes. **WHERE TO SIT** All seats have a similar experience. The front row has slightly better views, and a better chance of getting a little wet.

Swiss Family Treehouse

RANKING Skippable but fun. **EMH** Evening. **FP+** No. **TYPE** Self-guided walking tour. **REQUIREMENTS** There are a lot of stairs up and down.

WHAT TO EXPECT The Treehouse replicates the living conditions from the popular film that few probably remember. While interesting, the attraction is not particularly compelling and guests visiting over one day usually have higher priorities. **SCARY FACTOR** Low. **CAN WE HANDLE IT?** The top of the tree is high; the stairs all the way up and down can be tough on cranky knees or hips.

WHEN TO GO Anytime attraction. See it when waits are long at other rides, or you simply are nearby. **EXPECT TO WAIT** No wait to 5 minutes in the afternoon. **LENGTH** 10 minutes or so.

FRONTIERLAND
••

Home to Big Thunder Mountain, Splash Mountain, and one of the park's most popular quick services, most guests will spend a considerable amount of time here. Fortunately, both rides enjoy hefty capacities that make it possible to visit them in the second hour of operation. You'll also find two anytime attractions: the comfortable serenading of bears in Country Bear Jamboree, and Tom Sawyer Island, where adventures await.

Pecos Bill is the principal quick service, now offering a menu featuring beef, chicken, or vegetable burritos, rice bowls, and fajitas. Additionally, more expensive items are available beginning at 4pm. Diamond Horseshoe once offered a lively evening show and table service fare, but its current iteration is rarely open and serves below-average sandwiches and salads. Golden Oak Outpost is located at the Pecos' side exit, serving waffle fries with toppings like pulled pork and coleslaw or brown gravy and white cheddar, in addition to sweet potato nuggets and beverages. Westward Ho alongside the river serves snacks, in addition to corn dogs. Two to three carts also position themselves along the river across from Diamond Horseshoe, serving turkey legs, churros, and pretzels. Lines are usually shorter at similar stands around the corner in Liberty Square.

Of course, you'll find several merchandise opportunities here, too. Splash Mountain's exit offers some attraction-branded merchandise, in addition to several shops between Pecos Bill and Diamond Horseshoe that offer everything from freshly baked treats to limited-edition pins.

Big Thunder Mountain Railroad

RANKING Don't miss. **EMH** Evening. **FP+** Yes. High priority. **TYPE** Runaway train-themed roller coaster. **REQUIREMENTS** 40" or taller.

WHAT TO EXPECT Prospective miners board trains consisting of three cars, each with five rows that seat two to three people. With top speeds under 30 miles per hour, Big Thunder is not an intense experience, but the theming is first rate. **SCARY FACTOR** Minimal for a roller coaster—there are two scenes inside caves that are loud and dark, but anyone that made it through any other Disney coaster will be just fine. **CAN WE HANDLE IT?** Some motion sickness issues for the highly susceptible, and jostling.

WHEN TO GO First 2 or last 2 hours of operation, or with FastPass+. **EXPECT TO WAIT** 40–60 minutes in the afternoon. **LENGTH** 4 minutes. **WHERE TO SIT** The back provides the wildest experience. Sit up front for a tamer ride.

Country Bear Jamboree

RANKING Minor attraction. **EMH** Evening. **FP+** No. **TYPE** Audio-Animatronics show. **REQUIREMENTS** None.

WHAT TO EXPECT A musical review and show with country-and-western songs performed by Animatronic bears. Wildly popular when it opened, it is now attended largely by roots/country music fans, diehard Disney fans, and visitors looking for a bit of a rest and some air conditioning. The characters are fun but the jokes are hokey, and the songs, while fun to those with wide musical tastes, aren't everyone's favorite. Skippable for many on shorter visits. **SCARY FACTOR** None. **CAN WE HANDLE IT?** The music is more bluegrass/western than modern country.

WHEN TO GO Anytime attraction. See it when waits are long at other rides, or you need to get out of the weather. **EXPECT TO WAIT** 10–15 minutes for the next show. **LENGTH** 15 minutes. **WHERE TO SIT** Sit in the middle row, toward the center. Wait for 25 people or so to enter a row first, and follow them.

Splash Mountain

RANKING Don't miss. **EMH** No (surprisingly). **FP+** Yes. High priority on hot days, medium on cool days. **TYPE** Mostly a gentle log ride, with fewer thrills than you'd guess from outside. **REQUIREMENTS** 40" or taller.

WHAT TO EXPECT Splash Mountain is the ride that most showcases all of the best of Disney. You float past brilliantly executed scenes based on the Br'er Rabbit character from Disney's (unavailable) *Song of the South*. And here and there—especially towards the end—there's some thrilling drops. **SCARY FACTOR** The very visible final drop, from 52 feet up and at 40 miles per hour at a 45-degree angle, is greatly misleading. Most of this ride is gentle floating through darling settings. But besides the final drop, there are several much shorter drops. **CAN WE HANDLE IT?** You may get wet—especially if you sit in the front, but possibly from any seat. The visible final drop scares many off who would absolutely love this ride. Trust us and give it a chance.

WHEN TO GO First two or last two hours of operation, or with FastPass+. **EXPECT TO WAIT** 15–90+ minutes in the afternoon (the longer waits on crowded hot days, the shorter on cold low-crowd days). **LENGTH** 12 minutes. **WHERE TO SIT** The front seat has the best view, but is most likely to get wet. Those seated on the left side of the log enjoy the best views of the Animatronics.

Tom Sawyer Island

RANKING Minor attraction. **EMH** No. **FP+** No. **TYPE** Self-guided walking tour and playground. **REQUIREMENTS** None.

WHAT TO EXPECT Tom Sawyer Island is only accessible via motorized rafts that board near the entrance to Big Thunder Mountain Railroad. Once on the island, visitors can explore numerous areas themed to Tom Sawyer and Huck Finn—caves, a mine, two bridges, a working water wheel, and Fort

Langhorn, a play area. Benches are plentiful and the Island is a terrific spot to take a break. Skippable for those without kids, or on a short visit. **SCARY FACTOR** None.

WHEN TO GO Anytime attraction. See it when waits are long at other rides, or you simply are nearby. Afternoons tend to be best, but note that it closes before dusk. **EXPECT TO WAIT** 5–15 minutes to get raft transport in the afternoon. **LENGTH** Allow 30–45 minutes+ including time spent waiting for the rafts, more if your kids really need to run around.

The Walt Disney World Railroad

See the "Main Street" entry on the railroad, which stops in Frontierland near the exit to Splash Mountain.

LIBERTY SQUARE

To the left of Cinderella Castle, Liberty Square offers the fewest attractions and eateries of any land, but what is offered is all above average in terms of quality. Hall of Presidents is a perfect way to spend a hot afternoon, while Haunted Mansion is quintessential Disney.

Columbia Harbour House across from Haunted Mansion is our favorite quick service, offering a delicious fried shrimp platter, in addition to salads, unique sandwiches, grilled salmon, and excellent soups. Sleepy Hollow Refreshments serves excellent waffle sandwiches from 11am–5pm, as well as funnel cakes, waffles, and other ice cream treats. Liberty Tree Tavern is one of our favorite table service restaurants for lunch, when it offers a reasonably priced a la carte menu. The dinner buffet no longer features characters and it's expensive out of pocket.

Across from Hall of Presidents is Ye Olde Christmas Shoppe, which offers primarily Christmas-related merchandise. Memento Mori near Haunted Mansion's exit offers the full line of Haunted Mansion merchandise, along with kitchen-related items.

Hall of Presidents

RANKING Minor attraction. **EMH** No. **FP+** No. **TYPE** Audio-Animatronics show. **REQUIREMENTS** None.

WHAT TO EXPECT A theater show featuring film clips and animatronics of all of the U.S. Presidents. The show is patriotic and expounds on the hardships and triumphs of the United States through the years. The theater is air-conditioned, comfortable, and seats over 700 people, which makes it a nice and easy attraction to enjoy in the afternoon heat. Enjoyed most by adults and patriotic Americans, dull for most kids. Skippable for those on shorter visits. **SCARY FACTOR** None, other than it's full of politicians.

WHEN TO GO Anytime attraction. See it when waits are long at other rides, or you need to get out of the weather. **EXPECT TO WAIT** Arrive either at 20 or 50 minutes past the hour and your wait should be just ten minutes. **LENGTH** 25 minutes. **WHERE TO SIT** In the middle row, toward the center.

The Haunted Mansion

RANKING Don't miss. **EMH** Evening. **FP+** Yes. Medium priority. **TYPE** Light-hearted, slow-moving ride through a haunted house and its grave-yard. **REQUIREMENTS** None.

WHAT TO EXPECT One of the most famous rides at the park, the Haunted Mansion is one of Disney's best and most enduring attractions. Intended to be a fun and goofy ride, not a frightening experience, you won't see anything truly gruesome or disgusting. This is a must-ride for almost all guests. **SCARY FACTOR** Haunted Mansion is much more spooky than it is scary, but a lot of kids are going to be apprehensive about entering the foreboding building. Rest assured that it's a lot of fun. **CAN WE HANDLE IT?** Yes, those brave enough to enter enjoy the experience.

WHEN TO GO First two or last two hours of operation, or with FastPass+. **EXPECT TO WAIT** 20–50 minutes in the afternoon, longer if the Hall of Presidents and Liberty Square Riverboat have just let out guests, as they do every thirty minutes. **LENGTH** 10 minutes. **WHERE TO SIT** Each Doom Buggy seats two to three. Sit apprehensive youngsters (or dads) in the middle.

The Liberty Square Riverboat

RANKING Minor attraction. **EMH** No. **FP+** No. **TYPE** Steamboat tour around the Rivers of America. **REQUIREMENTS** None.

WHAT TO EXPECT The Liberty Square Riverboat is a stately three-tiered paddle-wheel boat that slowly circles Tom Sawyer Island and offers fantastic views of Splash Mountain, Big Thunder Mountain Railroad, and several other popular attractions. Some minor vignettes otherwise visible only from the Walt Disney World Railroad also appear. The voice of Mark Twain narrates the journey. Skippable for those on short visits. **SCARY FACTOR** None.

WHEN TO GO Anytime attraction. See it when waits are long at other rides, or you need to get out of the weather. **EXPECT TO WAIT** Arrive either at 20 or 50 minutes past the hour and your wait should be just ten minutes. **LENGTH** 17 minutes. **WHERE TO SIT** Bow and stern locations where you can easily see both riverbanks are best. Otherwise sit on the port side. (That's left when facing the bow—the end without the paddlewheel.)

FANTASYLAND
....
With the longest list of attractions, this is where most guests will spend the majority of their time. Fortunately, most attractions enjoy short durations and healthy capacities, making it relatively easy to bang out the majority of rides in under an hour first thing in the morning or when crowds ease in the late evening. Mickey's PhilharMagic is an outstanding 3D anytime attraction, and Enchanted Tales with Belle is an afternoon FastPass+ priority.

Be Our Guest Restaurant is the park's newest restaurant, serving quick service breakfast and lunch, in addition to table service dinner. Reservations are usually required for any of these meals and can be made up to 180 days in advance. We like breakfast for those that can secure a reservation close to 8am with a 9am park open. Diners will be able to enter the park early, when fewer people are around, for pictures and also beat the rush to a priority attraction like Seven Dwarfs Mine Train so long as they exit the restaurant by 8:45am. Later breakfasts are not recommended because they take up precious morning touring time. Lunch is mostly soups, salads, and sandwiches, in addition to quiches and braised pork, and all available for under $15 each. Dinner is more of a typical table service experience with a menu featuring steaks, salmon, chicken, lamb, and a vegetarian ratatouille, with cupcakes and cream puffs for dessert, just like at lunch. More information is available in Chapter 7—Where to Eat.

Pinocchio Village Haus is the primary dinnertime quick service, located to the left of the entrance to New Fantasyland. The flatbread pizzas and salads are above average and there's plentiful air-conditioned seating in addition to outdoor patio seating. Gaston's Tavern between Be Our Guest and Journey of the Little Mermaid serves pork shanks, cinnamon rolls, and snacks. The pork is surprisingly tender and a nice alternative to the more-difficult-to-eat-than-you-might-expect turkey legs. Indoor seating is minimal, but the theming is exquisite throughout. Friar's Nook, located across from the entrance to Seven Dwarfs Mine Train, serves several hearty macaroni-and-cheese dishes with a variety of toppings, including pot roast. Storybook Treats is Fantasyland's version of the Plaza Ice Cream Parlor, serving decadent sundaes and other ice-cream treats. Cheshire Café serves snacks, drinks, and cake cups next to Mad Tea Party, while Prince Eric's Village Market serves drinks, lemonades, sno-cones, and snacks across from the Journey of the Little Mermaid ride in New Fantasyland. Finally, Big Top Souvenirs across from Dumbo is yet another spot to find freshly made treats, including caramel corn, candied apples, and fudge, in addition to the frozen Goofy's Glacier drinks.

Shopping is plentiful in and around Fantasyland. Castle Couture to the left of Mickey's PhilharMagic is one of the best spots for princess merchandise. Across the way is Sir Mickey's, primarily offering toys and apparel. Two great stores are located back in New Fantasyland: Bonjour Gifts, to the right of Gaston's Tavern, offers unique glassware, goblets, and other upscale items, and Big Top Souvenirs offers toys and apparel.

Ariel's Grotto

RANKING Don't miss for little kids who need to meet Ariel; skippable for others. **EMH** Morning, Evening. **FP+** Yes. High priority for guests wanting to meet Ariel. **TYPE** Character meet and greet. **REQUIREMENTS** None.

WHAT TO EXPECT After winding through a line themed to undersea rockwork, meet Ariel in her picturesque grotto. **SCARY FACTOR** None.

WHEN TO GO First or last hour of operation, or with FastPass+. **EXPECT TO WAIT** 25–45 minutes in the afternoon. **LENGTH** About a minute with everyone's favorite undersea princess.

The Barnstormer

RANKING Minor attraction. **EMH** Morning, Evening. **FP+** Yes. Low priority. **TYPE** Roller coaster. **REQUIREMENTS** 35" or taller.

WHAT TO EXPECT This slow-loading, low-capacity ride with some light theming around Goofy's stunt plane is the tamest coaster at Disney World, and best thought of as a "starter" roller coaster. Fun, swoopy, and brief, its features are fully visible, so there's no surprises. Great fun for little kids, but skippable for others. **SCARY FACTOR** Low. Mild speeds and heights. **CAN WE HANDLE IT?** If your kids decide after it begins that they aren't ready for coasters, it will be over within seconds. Ride vehicles are low to the ground with just enough room for two average-size adults to sit side by side.

WHEN TO GO First two or last two hours of operation, or with FastPass+. **EXPECT TO WAIT** 25–40 minutes in the afternoon. **LENGTH** Less than 1 minute. **WHERE TO SIT** The front seat has the best view, but no seats are bad.

Dumbo the Flying Elephant

RANKING Minor attraction. **EMH** Morning, Evening. **FP+** Yes. Low priority. **TYPE** Spinning ride. **REQUIREMENTS** None.

WHAT TO EXPECT Charming Dumbos with two riders side by side rise from their delightfully decorated base and slowly spin. Riders control how high or low their Dumbo flies. A favorite of little kids, but skippable for adults. Those not using FastPass+ have the option to wait in an air-conditioned play area instead of the typical queue. **SCARY FACTOR** Low. The mild heights may trouble the most severely acrophobic. **CAN WE HANDLE IT?** Spinning is too slow to affect motion sickness. Little kids can't ride alone.

WHEN TO GO First two or last two hours of operation, or with FastPass+. **EXPECT TO WAIT** 30–50 minutes in the afternoon. **LENGTH** Less than 2 minutes. **WHERE TO SIT** All seats are good.

Enchanted Tales with Belle

RANKING Major attraction. **EMH** Morning, Evening. **FP+** Yes. High priority. **TYPE** Combined walk-through tour, Audio-Animatronic show, interactive show, and character photo op. **REQUIREMENTS** None.

WHAT TO EXPECT This experience starts as a tour of Maurice's cottage, magically shifts to the Beast's Mansion where audience volunteers are recruited by Madame Wardrobe for a show, moves to the Beast's Library where under Lumiere's direction the volunteers act the show out for Belle, and ends with the show volunteers getting a chance to meet and have pictures with Belle. Only show volunteers get photos by default, so if your kids aren't picked for a part, have them volunteer at the last "anybody else?" casting call. Drop dead cute, it's Disney at its best. **SCARY FACTOR** None.

WHEN TO GO During the afternoon parade, in the final hour of operation, or with FastPass+. **EXPECT TO WAIT** 20–40 minutes in the afternoon. **LENGTH** 25 minutes.

it's a small world

RANKING Minor attraction. **EMH** Morning, Evening. **FP+** Yes. Low priority. **TYPE** Boat ride. **REQUIREMENTS** None.

WHAT TO EXPECT Boats seating 20 or so float past miniatures of singing children from around the world, colorfully attired and accompanied by toys and representations of their cultures. A world-famous tour-de-force of design, song writing, and artistic unity. **SCARY FACTOR** None.

WHEN TO GO Before 11am, in the final two hours of operation, or with FastPass+. **EXPECT TO WAIT** 20–35 minutes in the afternoon. **LENGTH** 11 minutes. **WHERE TO SIT** Seats at the sides of the boat have the best view.

Mad Tea Party

RANKING Minor attraction. **EMH** Morning, Evening. **FP+** Yes. Low priority. **TYPE** Spinning ride. **REQUIREMENTS** None.

WHAT TO EXPECT Spinning tea cups lightly themed to *Alice in Wonderland* delight kids, annoy most adults. Skippable for those on shorter visits. **SCARY FACTOR** None. **CAN WE HANDLE IT?** There's three simultaneous spins: the whole ride, a group of cups, and individual cups. Don't ride if you are subject to motion sickness.

WHEN TO GO Anytime attraction. See it when waits are long at other rides, or you simply are nearby. **EXPECT TO WAIT** 5–15 minutes in the afternoon. **LENGTH** 90 seconds. **WHERE TO SIT** In a different cup than your children, who will wish to spin much more than you do.

The Many Adventures of Winnie the Pooh

RANKING Minor attraction. **EMH** Morning, Evening. **FP+** Yes. Low priority. **TYPE** Dark ride. **REQUIREMENTS** None.

WHAT TO EXPECT Four-person "honey pots" make their way through multiple, richly-detailed Winnie the Pooh-themed scenes featuring Pooh, Eeyore, Piglet, Owl, Tigger, and others. **SCARY FACTOR** Low—a briefly blustery day where the ride vehicle tips up and down slightly for a few seconds.

WHEN TO GO First two or last two hours of operation, or with FastPass+. **EXPECT TO WAIT** 30–40 minutes in the afternoon. **LENGTH** 3 minutes. **WHERE TO SIT** All seats are good.

Mickey's PhilharMagic

RANKING Don't miss. **EMH** Morning, Evening. **FP+** Yes. Lowest priority. **TYPE** 4D show. **REQUIREMENTS** None.

WHAT TO EXPECT This 3D film (supplemented by in-theater effects—hence 4D) tells the tale of Donald getting in trouble, with Mickey ultimately to the rescue. Interwoven between are some of the best bits from some of Disney's most popular films: *Peter Pan*, *Aladdin*, *Little Mermaid*, *Lion King*, and more. It's a must-see because of its fun and diabolically creative celebration of some of Disney's best-loved animation. **SCARY FACTOR** Low. 3D effects and typical cartoon mayhem spook some little ones. Take off their 3D glasses if this happens.

WHEN TO GO Anytime attraction. See it when waits are long at other rides, or you simply are nearby. **EXPECT TO WAIT** Up to 15 minutes for the next show. **LENGTH** 12 minutes. **WHERE TO SIT** Sit in a middle row, towards the center. Wait for 25 people or so to enter a row first, and follow them.

Peter Pan's Flight

RANKING Don't miss. **EMH** Morning, Evening. **FP+** Yes. High priority. **TYPE** Dark ride. **REQUIREMENTS** None.

WHAT TO EXPECT Pirate ships seating 2–3 people fly through scenes from *Peter Pan*. Kids love it, but teens and adults are mixed. For some, the flight over London instantly makes it among their favorite rides at Disney World; others find it pedestrian, a little dull—especially the middle section—and overrated. It's a "Don't miss" so that you can discover for yourself where you stand. **SCARY FACTOR** Dark, but not scary.

WHEN TO GO At park open, in the final hour of operation, or with FastPass+. **EXPECT TO WAIT** 50–70+ minutes in the afternoon. **LENGTH** 3 minutes. **WHERE TO SIT** All seats are good.

Pete's Silly Sideshow: Goofy and Donald

RANKING Don't miss for little kids who need to meet Goofy or Donald; skippable for others. **EMH** No. **FP+** No. **TYPE** Character meet and greet. **REQUIREMENTS** None.

WHAT TO EXPECT Goofy and Donald in elaborate circus costumes greet guests in a tent at Pete's Silly Sideshow. Minnie and Daisy greet in the same tent, but their line is separate. **SCARY FACTOR** None.

WHEN TO GO Anytime attraction. See it when waits are long at other rides, or you simply are nearby. **EXPECT TO WAIT** 10–20 minutes in the afternoon. **LENGTH** About a minute with each character individually.

Pete's Silly Sideshow: Minnie and Daisy

RANKING Don't-miss for little kids who need to meet Minnie or Daisy; skippable for others. **EMH** No. **FP+** No. **TYPE** Character meet and greet. **REQUIREMENTS** None.

WHAT TO EXPECT Minnie and Daisy in elaborate circus costumes greet guests in a tent at Pete's Silly Sideshow. Goofy and Donald greet in the same tent, but their line is separate. **SCARY FACTOR** None.

WHEN TO GO Anytime attraction. See it when waits are long at other rides, or you simply are nearby. **EXPECT TO WAIT** 20–30 minutes in the afternoon. **LENGTH** About a minute with each character individually.

Prince Charming Regal Carrousel

RANKING Minor attraction. **EMH** Morning, Evening. **FP+** No. **TYPE** Slowly spinning carousel. **REQUIREMENTS** None.

WHAT TO EXPECT As stately and lovely a carousel as you will ever see, the essence of this ride is obvious from simply looking at it. Ride it if you have kids that wish to; just watch it otherwise. **SCARY FACTOR** None, other than getting the spelling right (two r's in carrousel). **CAN WE HANDLE IT?** Spins too slowly to bother most.

WHEN TO GO Anytime attraction. See it when waits are long at other rides, or you are nearby. **EXPECT TO WAIT** 5–10 minutes in the afternoon. **LENGTH** 2 minutes. **WHERE TO SIT** Along the outside for the best photo opportunities.

Princess Fairytale Hall: Anna and Elsa

RANKING Must-do for guests who require a picture with Anna and Elsa; skippable for others. **EMH** Morning, Evening. **FP+** Yes. High priority for those who want to greet these characters. **TYPE** Character meet and greet. **REQUIREMENTS** None.

WHAT TO EXPECT There is one line to meet Anna and Elsa, but they take pictures and sign autographs separately. Cinderella and Rapunzel greet in the same building, but their line (and FastPass+) is entirely separate. **SCARY FACTOR** None.

WHEN TO GO Immediately at park open, or with FastPass+. The characters meet through 30 minutes before park close. **EXPECT TO WAIT** Waits of 45 minutes or more materialize immediately after park open and often peak at 75–120 minutes. **LENGTH** 3–5 minutes of signing, mingling, and picture taking.

Princess Fairytale Hall: Cinderella and Rapunzel

RANKING Don't miss for those who need to meet Cinderella and Rapunzel; skippable for others. **EMH** Morning, Evening. **FP+** Yes. High priority for those who want to greet these characters. **TYPE** Character meet and greet. **REQUIREMENTS** None.

WHAT TO EXPECT Cinderella and Rapunzel greet guests in Princess Fairytale Hall. Anna and Elsa greet in the same building, but their line (and FastPass+) is entirely separate. **SCARY FACTOR** None.

WHEN TO GO At park open, in the final hour of operation, or with Fast-Pass+. **EXPECT TO WAIT** 30–60 minutes in the afternoon. **LENGTH** 3–5 minutes of signing, mingling, and picture taking.

Seven Dwarfs Mine Train

RANKING Don't miss. **EMH** Morning, Evening. **FP+** Yes. High priority. **TYPE** Combined roller coaster and dark ride. **REQUIREMENTS** 38" or taller.

WHAT TO EXPECT This ride combines the swoops and curves of a moderate roller coaster with richly detailed scenes from *Snow White*, focusing especially on the Dwarfs. The vehicles are small and seating may be uncomfortable for guests over six feet tall. **SCARY FACTOR** Low—the roller coaster parts are mild and the dark scenes brief. **CAN WE HANDLE IT?** A new ride system (cars that swing side to side) increases the impressions of speed and make the ride more comfortable for those with motion sickness. However, it will add side-to-side jostling to typical coaster back-and-forth jostling, making the ride rough on those with back and neck issues.

WHEN TO GO Immediately at park open, in the final hour of operation, or with FastPass+. **EXPECT TO WAIT** 50–90+ minutes in the afternoon. **LENGTH** 3 minutes. **WHERE TO SIT** The front row provides the best views while the back row offers the wildest ride.

Under the Sea ~ Journey of the Little Mermaid

RANKING Major attraction. **EMH** Morning, Evening. **FP+** Yes. Low priority. **TYPE** Dark ride. **REQUIREMENTS** None.

WHAT TO EXPECT Two-to three person "clamshells" take you under the sea into a fairly literal re-telling of the *Little Mermaid*. There's much color and movement, and the party scene is particularly well-done, but those who are not Little Mermaid fans may find it dull. If just one Little Mermaid attraction is enough for you, see the one at Disney's Hollywood Studios instead. **SCARY FACTOR** Low. It has its moments shrouded in darkness, but it's not in any way scary.

WHEN TO GO First two or last two hours of operation, or with FastPass+. **EXPECT TO WAIT** 30–40 minutes in the afternoon. **LENGTH** 5 minutes. **WHERE TO SIT** All seats are good.

The Walt Disney World Railroad

See the "Main Street" entry on the railroad for more details. The Fantasyland stop is near the entrance to The Barnstormer.

TOMORROWLAND
....

One of the most popular lands, and the one located just off the Hub to the right, Tomorrowland is home to several of Magic Kingdom's most popular attractions, including the venerable Space Mountain and Buzz Lightyear's Space Ranger Spin. Several anytime attractions are also situated here, including the Carousel of Progress, Tomorrowland PeopleMover, and Monsters Inc. Laugh Floor.

Tomorrowland has no table service restaurants, but Cosmic Ray's Starlight Café is one of Magic Kingdom's most popular quick services. Offering rotisserie chicken, ribs (after 4pm), burgers, sandwiches, hot dogs, chicken nuggets, and salads, you'll find a wider selection of food here than at most other quick service locations. Tomorrowland Terrace is another major quick service, located closer to the Plaza Restaurant on Main Street than the rest of Tomorrowland, but it's only open when Magic Kingdom is crowded. If it is open, the menu consists of a burger, chicken sandwich, chili cheese dog, lobster roll, and chicken nuggets. Lunching Pad is located underneath Astro Orbiter in the center of Tomorrowland, serving a couple of forgettable hot dogs, in addition to sweet cream-cheese pretzels, and frozen beverages. Also near Astro Orbiter, Cool Ship serves beverages and snacks. Rounding out the choices is Auntie Gravity's Galactic Goodies, serving smoothies, snacks, and ice cream treats.

Mickey's StarTraders and Merchant of Venus near Stitch's Great Escape are the two primary stores, though most everything sold here is available elsewhere. There are small shops at the exits to Buzz Lightyear and Space Mountain as well.

Astro Orbiter

RANKING Skippable but fun. **EMH** Morning, Evening. **FP+** No. **TYPE** Spinning ride. **REQUIREMENTS** None.

WHAT TO EXPECT This slow-loading, low capacity ride spins riders high over Tomorrowland. Twelve "rocket ships" load from an elevated platform (two to a vehicle), raise up, and spin. You can control how high you go. Views are nice, and being high is bit of a thrill, but not worth long waits. **SCARY FACTOR** Medium. This is the most intense spinner attraction at WDW, with the high altitude and rocket ships that slant inward. **CAN WE HANDLE IT?** Put a parent with each kid to help with any fears about height. Those with severe fear of heights should sit this out. Motion sickness is rarely an issue. Note that the seating situation is different than other spinner rides. Riders sit one in front of the other with their legs spread out to the sides. Two adults may want to split up as parties of one for a more comfortable ride. The brief elevator ride before and after the ride is packed full and cramped.

WHEN TO GO At park open or in the final hour of operation. **EXPECT TO WAIT** 20–40 minutes in the afternoon. **LENGTH** 2 minutes. **WHERE TO SIT** Seat adults in back with the kids up front.

Buzz Lightyear's Space Ranger Spin

RANKING Don't miss. **EMH** Morning, Evening. **FP+** Yes. Medium priority. **TYPE** Dark ride shooting gallery. **REQUIREMENTS** None.

WHAT TO EXPECT In this slow-moving ride, prospective space rangers protect the universe by turning their ride vehicle and shooting an "ion cannon" at targets as they traverse a series of *Toy Story*-themed spaces. Vehicles hold more than two, but have only two cannons. Scores are tallied, so you compete with your ride-mate. The simple concept—being inside a *Toy Story*-themed video game—delights almost everyone. **SCARY FACTOR** None. **CAN WE HANDLE IT?** A joystick controls much of the spinning. Keep youngsters away to enjoy a ride with less motion.

WHEN TO GO First two or last two hours of operation, or with FastPass+. **EXPECT TO WAIT** 25–80 minutes in the afternoon. **LENGTH** 5 minutes. **WHERE TO SIT** All vehicles and seats give the same experience.

Monsters Inc. Laugh Floor

RANKING Minor attraction. **EMH** Evening (usually first hour only). **FP+** Yes. Low priority. **TYPE** Interactive show. **REQUIREMENTS** None.

WHAT TO EXPECT Mike Wazowski, the one-eyed green monster from *Monsters Inc.*, puts on a comedy show to collect laughs from the audience to power Monstropolis. Cool technology allows the monsters to directly interact with the audience. The laughs typically are weak—though often fun for kids. Turtle Talk with Crush at Epcot uses similar technology much, much better. Those on shorter visits may elect to skip. **SCARY FACTOR** None, if your kids have seen the movies. **CAN WE HANDLE IT?** Avoid if you already have had enough Billy Crystal in your life.

WHEN TO GO Anytime attraction. See it when waits are long at other rides, or you need to get out of the weather. **EXPECT TO WAIT** 10–20 minutes in the afternoon. **LENGTH** 10 minutes. **WHERE TO SIT** As in most shows, the center of the theater seating, midway back, give the best views.

Space Mountain

RANKING Don't miss. **EMH** Morning, Evening. **FP+** Yes. High priority. **TYPE** Roller coaster in the dark. **REQUIREMENTS** 44" or taller.

WHAT TO EXPECT In one of the park's most popular rides, small three-person rockets, coupled together in flights of two, blast into the darkness of space and traverse sharp curves and minor dips past planets, stars, moons, and meteors, before returning to the launch facility. **SCARY FACTOR** Moderate. Because the ride is in the dark, speed seems much higher than it is, and everything that happens is unexpected. This scares some. But otherwise it's a very mild coaster. **CAN WE HANDLE IT?** Motion sickness typically is not an issue, but the ride's jerkiness can aggravate back/neck/shoulder pain.

WHEN TO GO At park open, in the final hour of operation, or with Fast-Pass+. **EXPECT TO WAIT** 45–120+ minutes in the afternoon. **LENGTH** 3 minutes. **WHERE TO SIT** The six seats in each coupled-together ride vehicle are single file. Front seats are the most fun. If you are concerned a kid might panic, sit behind them so you can comfort them by touch. The third and fourth seats are the least jerky.

Stitch's Great Escape!

RANKING Skippable. **EMH** Morning, Evening. **FP+** No. **TYPE** Audio-Animatronics show. **REQUIREMENTS** 40" or taller.

WHAT TO EXPECT Stitch's Great Escape replaces a prior show that was great, but far too scary to be in the Magic Kingdom—or perhaps anywhere at Disney World. However, Stitch's Great Escape replaced only one of the many scary elements of the old show, added the annoyances of Stitch—Animatronic belching, anyone? —and now scares kids and bores adults. **SCARY FACTOR** High. Guests are trapped in separated individual seats while scary things happen around them, often in the dark. This attraction has the highest potential to scare kids tall enough for it of any Disney World attraction, and because of the seat design, parents can't comfort kids until the end of the "show". **CAN WE HANDLE IT?** Don't go if your kids have been scared by anything else at Disney World.

WHEN TO GO Anytime attraction. See it when waits are long at other rides, or you need to get out of the weather. **EXPECT TO WAIT** 5–10 minutes in the afternoon. **LENGTH** 10 minutes. **WHERE TO SIT** On a different ride.

Tomorrowland Speedway

RANKING For little kids: don't miss. For everyone else: skippable. **EMH** Morning, Evening. **FP+** Yes. High priority only if you have little kids. **TYPE** Slow, go-cart-style ride on a highly constrained track. **REQUIREMENTS** 32" or taller to ride, 54" or taller to drive.

WHAT TO EXPECT An opportunity for kids to drive or ride along a speedway-themed track in a small two-seater car, at speeds of less than 8 mph along a guide rail that prevents getting out of their lane. Go-cart-style rides can be fun for adults, but this isn't. Young kids tall enough to drive love it, and waits can be long. **SCARY FACTOR** A reminder that Junior is turning 16 far too soon. **CAN WE HANDLE IT?** Both the queue and the ride reek of exhaust and are largely unprotected from the sun. Getting rear-ended by a gleeful 6 year old is common, which can be rough on your back and neck.

WHEN TO GO At park open, in the final hour of operation, or with FastPass+. **EXPECT TO WAIT** 20–40 minutes in the afternoon. **LENGTH** 5 minutes. **WHERE TO SIT** All vehicles give the same experience. If the kids are tall enough (54"+), let them drive. Then keep whining at them, "Are we there yet?"

Tomorrowland Transit Authority PeopleMover

RANKING Minor attraction. **EMH** Morning, Evening. **FP+** No. **TYPE** Tour above and through Tomorrowland. **REQUIREMENTS** None.

WHAT TO EXPECT This slow-moving elevated attraction sends four-person magnetically powered vehicles around Tomorrowland and through parts of several rides, providing a bit of a tour of the land's attractions, and a rest for weary feet. Skippable for those on short visits. **SCARY FACTOR** None.

WHEN TO GO Anytime attraction. See it when waits are long at other rides, or you need to get out of the weather. **EXPECT TO WAIT** No wait to 10 minutes in the afternoon. **LENGTH** 10 minutes. **WHERE TO SIT** All vehicles and seats give the same experience.

Walt Disney's Carousel of Progress

RANKING Minor attraction. **EMH** Morning, Evening. **FP+** No. **TYPE** Audio-Animatronics show. **REQUIREMENTS** None.

WHAT TO EXPECT The theater-style seating area rotates through four charming scenes of American family life, highlighting changes in home technology from the turn of the last century until the mid-90s. Designed for, and an enormous hit at, the New York World's Fair of 64/65, the ride suffers from the lack of a recent update and is dull for many kids. Many diehard Disney fans love it—and it's the only ride in the park that Walt Disney touched. Unlike most theater shows, leaving midway through is not allowed due to the theater's movement. **SCARY FACTOR** None.

WHEN TO GO Anytime attraction. See it when waits are long at other rides, or you need to get out of the weather. **EXPECT TO WAIT** 5–10 minutes in the afternoon. **LENGTH** 20 minutes. **WHERE TO SIT** As in most shows, the center of the theater seating, midway back, give the best views.

PARADES, FIREWORKS, AND SHOWS

Afternoon Festival of Fantasy Parade

RANKING Don't miss. **EMH** No. **FP+** Yes. Low priority. **TYPE** Parade. **REQUIREMENTS** None.

WHAT TO EXPECT Featuring astonishing floats, a great mix of characters, and wonderful walking entertainers, this parade (which debuted in early 2014) is a don't miss. **SCARY FACTOR** None.

TYPICAL SCHEDULE: Begins at 3pm most days of the year. Unusual events, e.g., tapings of shows on Main Street, may result in different times. The busiest days of the year often see two parades: one around noon, the other at 3pm or 3:30pm. Heavy rain may lead to the parade being scaled back, or even cancelled. **LENGTH** 15 minutes once it arrives.

WHERE TO SEE IT: The parade begins in Frontierland to the left of Splash Mountain, takes a turn near Hall of Presidents, and continues down Main Street, exiting in between the Firehouse and Emporium. People begin staking out spots on Main Street more than an hour before showtime, but most days of the year there are great spots still available in Frontierland just 15–30 minutes before the parade. The height of the floats means that even little kids don't need to be right in front, but the great entertainers and walking characters will be hard for them to see from farther back. Plan to see it across from Pecos Bill where crowds are lighter and you can be on your way sooner. The FastPass+ viewing area is in Town Square near the entrance around the flag pole. While a nice view, it is directly in the sun with virtually no shade or protection from the elements and doesn't benefit from the view of Cinderella Castle, like the previous location. Because the parade takes about 20 minutes to arrive, you'll end up waiting just as long, if not longer, than you would seeing it in Frontierland.

Evening Main Street Electrical Parade

RANKING Major entertainment. **EMH** No. A parade may be scheduled at the beginning of an evening EMH, but everyone is welcome to stay and watch. **FP+** Yes, low priority now that the location has moved to Town Square away from Cinderella Castle. **TYPE** Parade. **REQUIREMENTS** None.

WHAT TO EXPECT Disney's World's current evening parade has been around in some form for decades. Some view it as a worthy classic, others as an offering that was dated more than a decade ago. **SCARY FACTOR** While the repetitive music and some of the floats may seem like they're straight out of a Stanley Kubrick movie, the parade isn't overtly scary.

TYPICAL SCHEDULE: Runs twice most nights during busier weeks, and as rarely as 2–3 nights a week during quieter weeks and during periods when the park frequently closes for evening parties. Heavy rain may lead to the parade being scaled back, or even cancelled. **LENGTH** 15 minutes once it arrives.

WHERE TO SEE IT: The parade begins on Main Street between the Emporium and the Firehouse, and exits to the left of Splash Mountain. If you are seeing the parade before Wishes, pick your spot based on where you want to view Wishes from. Otherwise, pick a spot in Frontierland 15–45 minutes before the parade, depending on how crowded the park is. Floats are low compared to the afternoon parade, so getting your kids at the front pays off. On nights with two parades, the second parade is much less crowded.

Evening Castle Show: Celebrate the Magic

RANKING Don't miss. **EMH** No. **FP+** No, but the show is visible from the Wishes viewing area described below. **TYPE** Projection show. **REQUIRE-MENTS** None.

WHAT TO EXPECT Astonishing visual projections transform Cinderella Castle in many fun and breathtaking ways. Hard to describe in words, it's one of Disney World's best offerings. **SCARY FACTOR** None.

TYPICAL SCHEDULE: Runs twice most nights during busier weeks, and as rarely as 2–3 nights a week during quieter weeks and during periods when the park frequently closes for evening parties. When both Wishes and the evening parade are on, Celebrate the Magic most commonly has a show prior to Wishes with the potential for a second after. **LENGTH** 10 minutes.

WHERE TO SEE IT: The show is best seen from near the castle. The Wishes FastPass+ location is one of the best spots, as are other locations on Main Street no further back than Casey's Corner.

Wishes: Evening Fireworks

RANKING Don't miss. **EMH** No. **FP+** Yes, low priority, The viewing locations are in front of Casey's Corner and Plaza Restaurant on either side of Main Street. Guests may select which side they prefer. If you're exiting the park immediately after the show, choose the Tomorrowland/Plaza Restaurant side and exit through the Main Street bypass directly behind the viewing area to avoid the Main Street crowds. **TYPE** Fireworks show. **REQUIREMENTS** None.

WHAT TO EXPECT A great fireworks display, lightly tied to a narrated story, with some affecting music. **SCARY FACTOR** Too loud for some little kids.

TYPICAL SCHEDULE: Runs almost every night most of the year, but as few as 3 nights a week during the early-September to mid-December period when the park frequently closes at 7pm for evening parties. Wishes may begin as early as 8pm or as late as 10pm. The Electrical Parade is usually scheduled one hour before Wishes, with Celebrate the Magic beginning 15 minutes before Wishes. Thunderstorms with lightning will delay the show. **LENGTH** 15 minutes.

WHERE TO SEE IT: Wishes was designed to be seen on Main Street in front of Cinderella Castle, but the fireworks are visible from parts of Adventure-land, Fantasyland, Liberty Square, and Tomorrowland. We like to see the show from around Casey's Corner, which is far enough back that crowding is less of a concern and the fireworks are centered above the Castle. The FP+ viewing areas provide a decent view, but don't have much advantage over regular viewing areas elsewhere and aren't necessarily recommended, particularly when it inhibits your ability to acquire 4th and subsequent FP+.

The Cheat Sheets

The Cheat Sheets that follow are designed to break down all of our touring advice and principles into an easy guide that can be brought along to the theme parks. Print out the newest versions in color at EASYWDW.COM/EASY-GUIDE.

Each Cheat Sheet covers one park, and includes:

- Coded maps
- Touring overviews
- General FastPass+ priorities
- Daily touring plans that include specific FastPass+ suggestions

The maps are shaded based on the best time to visit the various attractions:

- The dark gray attractions are your top morning priorities, or best saved for the very end of the day or FastPass+.
- Medium gray attractions are best visited in the first/second hour of operation, or in the last two hours the park is open. They're a lower priority than the dark attractions because waits build slower and peak lower.
- Light gray attractions are designated "anytime", which is another way of saying they're best saved for the afternoon when waits at the higher priority attractions are longer. Most shows are designated "light gray" because you want to save them for the afternoon or evening when waits are longer at the major attractions.

Attractions that offer FastPass+ are followed by a +. FastPass+ kiosks are noted with the FP+ symbol. Also included are bathrooms, quick services, restaurants, and the larger stores.

Several touring plans are included with each Cheat Sheet. You may need to make changes based on the previous reviews (which is why we offer them), particularly with kids too short or too easily scared to experience certain attractions. For example, you may want to avoid roller coasters, character meets (at press time, no rides include both), or motion simulators, etc. Once you've picked your plan, it's easiest to simply cross off attractions the group isn't interested in experiencing. That will only result in shorter waits at the next attraction. Also consider substituting attractions coded the same. For example, you may want to substitute a second ride on Great Movie Ride over Star Tours because motion simulators may prove problematic.

Animal Kingdom Cheat Sheet

PARK MAP

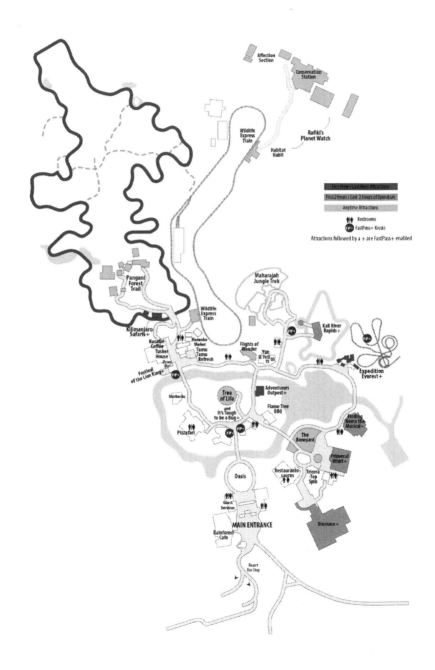

TOURING AT ANIMAL KINGDOM

GENERAL TOURING PHILOSOPHY Until Rivers of Light open, touring Animal Kingdom is fairly straightforward. We like to begin at Kilimanjaro Safaris in the upper left-hand corner and then work right through Asia and then DinoLand. You'll find short to non-existent waits through lunch if you follow the touring plan below, in addition to minimizing walking. After lunch, relax and visit the low-key attractions and stage shows when temperatures and humidity peak. Depending on crowds, plan to arrive 10–20 minutes early for Finding Nemo the Musical and Festival of the Lion King. Flights of Wonder is a charming, funny, and informative show that should not be skipped. More so than any other theme park, Animal Kingdom empties out by 4:15pm because there's no nighttime entertainment to keep guests at the park. Stay through close and you'll find low crowds in the last 60–120 minutes of operation. We expect operating hours and crowd patterns to change after Rivers of Light opens, with more people spending late afternoon and early evening in the park while waiting to see the new show. Updated advice will be available on EASYWDW.COM and YOURFIRSTVISIT.NET.

CHARACTERS Mickey and Minnie in Adventurers Outpost are the only priority and they are FastPass+ enabled. Meet them in the first 30 minutes or last hour of operation or use FastPass+. Russell and Dug next to It's Tough to Be a Bug are the second highest priority.

ROPE DROP Animal Kingdom usually begins letting guests inside the park 30 minutes prior to open with only The Oasis section immediately accessible. Guests are held in front of the Tree of Life until closer to ten minutes before official open. Once the rope drops, guests are walked in large groups toward Africa, Asia, and DinoLand. Arrive 45 minutes prior to open and position yourself on the left side of the ropes for Africa and Kilimanjaro Safaris or to the right for Asia and Expedition Everest or DinoLand for Primeval Whirl and DINOSAUR.

FASTPASS+ AT ANIMAL KINGDOM

FASTPASS+ PRIORITY It's relatively easy to tour Animal Kingdom without FastPass+ if you tour efficiently in the first or last two hours of operation. Doing so will give you an opportunity to use FastPass+ elsewhere. Here, FastPass+ is best used at Kali River Rapids in the afternoon when waits are longest and temperatures highest. The Adventurers Outpost Meet and Greet has a limited capacity and is another priority. A third use is best at Kilimanjaro Safaris or Expedition Everest. Consider acquiring a 4th or 5th FastPass+ selection to one or both of the shows in the afternoon.

1. Kali River Rapids (when highs are 80+ degrees)
2. Adventurers Outpost Mickey and Minnie Meet
3. Kilimanjaro Safaris
4. Expedition Everest
5. Rivers of Light*
6. Kali River Rapids (when highs are less than 80 degrees)
7. DINOSAUR
8. Primeval Whirl
9. Festival of the Lion King
10. Finding Nemo the Musical
11. It's Tough To Be A Bug

*River of Light is expected to open in Spring 2016. When it does, it should be possible to see the show relatively hassle-free without using FastPass+. However, FastPass+ will guarantee a seat for the show for late arrivers and the seating area will likely be front and center, potentially making it a good choice for those skipping most attractions with height requirements or with no desire to re-ride attractions.

4TH FASTPASS+ SELECTION AVAILABILITY Attractions 6–11 above should have plenty of availability around 1pm. Attractions 1–5 will have limited or no availability.

FASTPASS+ KIOSKS Add or change FastPass+ at the following locations:

- *Disney Outfitters*—On the right just after crossing the bridge into Discovery Island
- *Island Mercantile*—On the left just after crossing the bridge into Discovery Island
- *Kali River Rapids*—Next to the entrance
- *Harambe Breezeway*—Next to Tusker House and on the walkway into New Harambe

MORNING TOURING PLAN WITH FASTPASS+

Use FastPass+ at Adventurers Outpost Mickey/Minnie Meet 10:30–11:30am (meet around 11am), Kali River Rapids 11:30am to 12:30pm (ride around 12:15pm), and for the third your choice, though Expedition Everest at 12:30pm would make a lot of sense.

1. Ride Kilimanjaro Safaris: 8:55–9:25am.
2. Ride Expedition Everest: 9:40–9:55am.
3. Ride DINOSAUR: 10:05–10:25am.
4. Ride Primeval Whirl: 10:30–10:45am.

5. Ride TriceraTop Spin: 10:47–11:00am.

6. Meet Mickey and Minnie at Adventurers Outpost with Fast-Pass+: 11:05–11:20am.

7. Have lunch. Flame Tree Barbecue and Yak & Yeti are nearby, very good, and a little different. Pizzafari and Restaurantosaurus offer ample air-conditioned seating. Tusker House is a character meal in Africa with a variety of options.

8. Ride Kali River Rapids with FastPass+: 12:15–12:30pm.

9. Then follow the Afternoon Plan, below.

MORNING TOURING PLAN WITHOUT FASTPASS+

1. Ride Kilimanjaro Safaris: 8:55– 9:25am.

2. Ride Kali River Rapids or Meet Mickey at Adventurers Outpost: 9:35–9:50am.

3. Ride Expedition Everest: 9:55–10:15am.

4. Ride DINOSAUR: 10:25–10:55am.

5. Ride Primeval Whirl: 11:00–11:20am.

6. Ride TriceraTop Spin: 11:22–11:35am.

7. Have lunch. Restaurantosaurus and Flame Tree Barbecue are nearby.

8. Then follow the Afternoon Plan, below.

AFTERNOON TOURING PLAN

12:30PM–3:30PM Take it easy. Do It's Tough to Be a Bug, Wilderness Explorers, Maharajah Jungle Trek, Flights of Wonder, Finding Nemo the Musical, Festival of the Lion King, Rafiki's Planet Watch, and Boneyard.

3:30PM–CLOSE While Animal Kingdom no longer offers a daytime parade, the park continues to empty as early as 3pm with no nighttime entertainment to keep people sticking around and few people park hopping. Visit DinoLand with two hours to close and Asia in the final hour of operation to find far shorter waits than the afternoon.

LATE ARRIVAL ALTERNATIVE (WITH 6PM OR LATER CLOSE)

Arrive between 10:30–11am. Schedule FP+ at Expedition Everest (12:30–1:30pm), Adventurers Outpost Mickey and Minnie Meet (1:30–2:30pm), and Kali River Rapids (2:30pm–3:30pm).

1. Visit Oasis Exhibits until 11:00am.

2. See It's Tough to Be a Bug on Discovery Island: 11:15–11:30am.

3. See Finding Nemo the Musical: 11:40am–12:45pm (12pm start).

4. Ride Expedition Everest in Asia with FastPass+: 12:50–1:05pm.

5. Have lunch. Yak & Yeti and Flame Tree Barbecue are closest.

6. Meet Mickey and Minnie at Adventurers Outpost with Fast-Pass+: 2:00–2:15pm.

7. Walk Maharajah Jungle Trek: 2:20–2:45pm.

8. Ride Kali River Rapids with FastPass+: 2:50–3:15pm.

9. Grab a snack—carts and kiosks are available on the walk to Africa: 3:20–3:35pm.

10. See Festival of the Lion King in Africa: 3:40–4:30pm (4pm start).

11. Ride Kilimanjaro Safaris: 4:35–5:10pm.

12. Ride Primeval Whirl in DinoLand: 5:25–5:40pm.

13. Ride DINOSAUR: 5:50–6:10pm.

14. Return to Asia for Expedition Everest or a skipped attraction with a 7pm or later close.

With a 5pm close, arrive at 10am and start with DINOSAUR and Primeval Whirl before moving to It's Tough to Be a Bug and Finding Nemo the Musical. With a later close, you can push back your arrival by an hour or spend more time re-riding attractions in DinoLand with two hours to close and Asia with one hour to close.

TYPICAL ANIMAL KINGDOM WAIT TIMES IN MINUTES

Low Crowds, 5pm Close

	9:30am	10am	11am	12pm	1pm	2pm	3pm	4pm	5pm	6pm
DINOSAUR	10	10	10	15	15	15	10	10	5	5
Expedition Everest	10	10	15	15	20	20	20	15	10	5
It's Tough to Be a Bug	5	5	5	5	5	5	5	5	5	5
Kali River Rapids (hot)	10	10	20	25	30	30	20	15	15	10
Kali River Rapids (cool)	5	5	10	10	10	10	15	10	5	5
Kilimanjaro Safaris	10	15	20	30	20	20	15	10	10	5
Primeval Whirl	10	10	10	15	15	10	10	10	5	5
TriceraTop Spin	5	5	5	5	5	5	5	5	5	5

Moderate Crowds, 6pm Close

	9:30am	10am	11am	12pm	1pm	2pm	3pm	4pm	5pm	6pm
DINOSAUR	10	10	20	30	30	30	30	20	10	10
Expedition Everest	10	20	25	30	35	30	25	20	10	5
It's Tough to Be a Bug	5	5	5	10	10	10	10	5	5	5
Kali River Rapids (hot)	10	15	30	40	50	60	50	40	30	20
Kali River Rapids (cool)	5	10	15	20	20	20	15	15	10	5
Kilimanjaro Safaris	20	30	40	50	40	30	30	20	10	5
Primeval Whirl	10	10	15	20	20	20	15	10	5	5
TriceraTop Spin	5	10	10	15	15	15	15	10	5	5

Heavy Crowds, 8pm Close

	9:30am	10am	11am	12pm	1pm	2pm	3pm	4pm	5pm	6pm	7pm	8pm
DINOSAUR	10	20	40	50	50	40	40	30	30	20	20	10
Expedition Everest	30	45	45	50	60	60	45	40	35	35	25	10
It's Tough to Be a Bug	5	5	10	10	15	15	15	15	10	10	5	5
Kali River Rapids (hot)	10	20	40	70	80	90	90	90	70	50	30	10
Kali River Rapids (cool)	5	5	15	15	20	30	30	30	30	20	20	5
Kilimanjaro Safaris	15	60	70	70	70	70	60	50	40	30	15	10
Primeval Whirl	10	20	30	35	30	30	30	20	20	10	10	5
TriceraTop Spin	5	5	15	25	25	20	10	10	10	5	5	5

Epcot Cheat Sheet

PARK MAP

TOURING AT EPCOT
. . . .

GENERAL TOURING PHILOSOPHY Because of its massive size and the long length of many of its attractions, Epcot is best experienced over two days. Until the Frozen attractions open in (likely) the spring, there are exactly two morning priorities: Soarin' and Test Track. Because they are about ten minutes away from each other and each takes about 20 minutes to experience even with a minimal initial wait, it's best to focus on one or the other over two separate mornings. This way, you significantly cut down on the amount of walking necessary and you won't run into waits longer than a few minutes all day. On your Test Track day, visit Future World East and the World Showcase Pavilions from Mexico through the U.S. On your Soarin' day, hit Future World West and the Pavilions from Canada through Japan. After they open, the Frozen attractions will be the highest priority for many, and likely will shift crowd patterns. Updated touring advice will be available on our sites, but Epcot will still be quite doable in two days if you arrive well before open and judiciously use FastPass+.

With just one day, things currently are a bit more complicated, and will become even more so after the Frozen attractions open. There are a few ways to make it work. First, Test Track has a single rider line with actual waits that are often shorter than standby or even FastPass+. However, your group won't ride together and you won't have an opportunity to design a car in the regular preshow. You can enter the single rider line later in the day and find waits of 10–15 minutes. Second, you could use FastPass+ at Soarin' or Test Track to minimize afternoon waits. Third, if you're planning to skip IllumiNations, you could visit either Soarin' or Test Track in the morning and then the other right before close. Waits will be relatively short at the end of the night and you won't be wasting valuable touring time since the park is closed. As long as you're in line before official park close, you'll ride, regardless of the posted wait.

Until the Frozen Ever After ride opens in the Norway Pavilion sometime around May 2016, there will be no World Showcase attractions that typically see long lines. You may otherwise need to wait a few minutes for the next show to begin in China, France, and Canada. They are all worth seeing. You generally get out of World Showcase what you put in—spend some time exploring and you'll get much more out of it than someone that simply walks past the Pavilions. Updated advice for one day visits to Epcot after the Frozen attractions open will be posted on our sites YOURFIRSTVISIT.NET and EASYWDW.COM.

CHARACTERS The Princesses in World Showcase can see substantial waits. Mickey, Minnie and Goofy at Character Spot can also see 20–40 minute waits. It's best to do Character Spot near park close to avoid long waits or use FastPass+. If you're skipping Soarin' and Test Track in the morning, visit Character Spot right after park open. Most other characters will have 5–15 minute waits. Random characters may also appear. Check in between the Canada and United Kingdom Pavilions and to the left of Liberty Inn in the United States in the afternoon.

ROPE DROP Epcot has two entrances and guests are ordinarily allowed to enter the park from either entrance 30 minutes prior to official open, though only Spaceship Earth will be operating this early. Guests entering from both entrances are held near the Fountain of Nations in Future World until closer to ten minutes before official open, when the ropes are dropped and cast members walk guests toward Test Track and Soarin'. Plan to arrive by 8:15am (7:15am with an 8am open), and after the park opens, position yourself at the ropes as close to Soarin' or Test Track as possible to reduce morning waits.

FASTPASS+ AT EPCOT

FASTPASS+ PRIORITY FastPass+ at Epcot is divided into two tiers. Guests may initially select only one Tier 1 experience. Until the Frozen rides open, we recommend Soarin' because its location makes it more convenient to visit in the afternoon with FastPass+, and Test Track offers a single rider line that reduces waits. For those visiting after the Frozen offerings open, it's likely that they will be the most sought after Tier 1 FastPass+ experience, and have afternoon waits that exceed those at Soarin' and Test Track.

There are eight options for Tier 2, and you may initially select two of them. Most guests will want to initially select two of the top four choices.

Tier One (choose one)

1. Frozen Ever After
2. Frozen Meet-and-Greet
3. Soarin'
4. Test Track
5. IllumiNations
6. Living with the Land

Tier Two (choose two)

1. Spaceship Earth
2. Mission: SPACE Orange

3. Character Spot
4. Mission: SPACE Green
5. Turtle Talk with Crush
6. Journey into Imagination with Figment
7. The Seas with Nemo and Friends
8. Captain EO (temporarily closed for 3D movie promos)

4TH FASTPASS+ SELECTION AVAILABILITY Test Track and Soarin' will most likely be unavailable by 12pm or have limited availability with return times late in the evening. IllumiNations is also unlikely to be available, though you can run into availability due to cancellations. Living with the Land and low priority Tier 2 attractions like The Seas and Journey into Imagination may have availability, but it's easier to head to the attraction at a recommended time of day and wait a few minutes rather than hunt down a kiosk and wait there for a FastPass+ that won't save you much time. Options are better when crowds are lower, but Soarin' and Test Track openings remain limited by noon.

FASTPASS+ KIOSKS Add or change FastPass+ at the following locations:
- Future World West breezeway across from Character Spot
- Future World East breezeway outside Mouse Gear and across from Electric Umbrella
- International Gateway in between UK and France Pavilions near entrance/exit
- Innoventions West

TWO DAY TOURING PLAN

Two Day Plan, Morning Day 1
Use FastPass+ at Soarin' (10:30–11:30am) and your choice of two Tier 2 Attractions.

1. Ride Soarin': 9:00–9:25am.
2. Ride Living with the Land: 9:30–9:45am.
3. Ride The Seas with Nemo and Friends at The Seas: 9:55–10:05am.
4. See Turtle Talk with Crush and look around The Seas: 10:10–10:40am.
5. Ride Soarin' again with FastPass+: 10:50–11:15am.
6. Have lunch at Sunshine Seasons in the Land, or in World Showcase.

Two Day Plan, Afternoon and Evening Day 1

You have a lot of options depending on what you want to do and where you plan to have dinner. You won't find any waits at the attractions in the Imagination Pavilion if you'd like to do those now. Consider heading up to World Showcase beginning with the Canada Pavilion. Even though there aren't waits at the attractions in Canada, France, etc., touring the area in low crowds means you'll have an easier time perusing the shops and fewer people in front of you at the various acts. Consider returning to Future World around 5pm. You'll be exiting World Showcase when crowds peak there and returning to Future World where waits will be short for everything other than Soarin' and Test Track.

Two Day Plan, Morning Day 2

Use FastPass+ at Test Track (9:30–10:30am), Spaceship Earth (10:30–11:30am), and a third attraction.
1.   Ride Test Track: 8:55–9:20am.
2.   Ride Sum of All Thrills in Innoventions East: 9:25–9:45am.
3.   Ride Mission: SPACE: 9:50–10:10am.
4.   Ride Test Track with FastPass+: 10:15–10:35am.
5.   Ride Spaceship Earth with FastPass+: 10:40–11:00am.

Two-Day Plan, Late Morning and Afternoon Day 2

You have some options depending on what you plan to do in World Showcase and whether you're heading back to Future World. Now would be a fine time to visit Ellen's Energy Adventure or anything in Innoventions East other than Sum of All Thrills. But those are lengthy attractions that could be kept for a 5pm return. Consider heading up to World Showcase beginning with the Gran Fiesta Tour in the Mexico Pavilion. You can stay in World Showcase or take the boat in Germany back to Future World around 5pm when crowds thin. Standby waits will be short for anything other than Test Track, which has the single rider line, and Soarin'.

TWO DAY LATE ARRIVAL TOURING PLAN

A late arrival is relatively straightforward over two days by using FastPass+ at the priority attractions on one side of the park each day. Future World crowds thin after 5pm as most people move to World Showcase for shopping, dinner, and IllumiNations. Most nights, Captain EO/Disney Movie Preview, Journey into Imagination, Innoventions East, Living with the Land, and Circle of Life close at 7pm.

Two Day Late Arrival Plan, Day 1
Use FastPass+ at Spaceship Earth (10:30–11:30am), Character Spot (11:30am–12:30pm), Test Track (5:00–6:00pm).
1. Arrive between 10:30 and 11:00am.
2. Ride Spaceship Earth with FastPass+: 11:00–11:20am.
3. Visit Character Spot with FastPass+: 11:30–11:45am.
4. Ride Gran Fiesta Tour: 12:00–12:15pm.
5. Have lunch. There are lots of options in World Showcase.
6. Explore Mexico through Italy and take boat in Germany or walk back to Future World by 5:00pm.
7. Ride Test Track with FastPass+: 5:15–5:45pm.
8. Ride Ellen's Energy Adventure or explore Innoventions East: 5:50–6:40pm.
9. Ride Sum of All Thrills: 6:45–7:15pm.
10. Ride Mission: SPACE with FastPass+: 7:20–7:45pm.
11. Have dinner. Electric Umbrella is nearby in Future World, or head to World Showcase.
12. See IllumiNations or get in line for Test Track at 8:55pm.

Two Day Late Arrival Plan, Day 2
Use FastPass+ at Turtle Talk with Crush (11:00am–12:00pm) and Soarin' (1:00–2:00pm), and a third of your choice.
1. Arrive between 10:30 and 11:00am.
2. Ride The Seas with Nemo and Friends: 11:10–11:25am.
3. See Turtle Talk with Crush with FastPass+ and look around Seas Pavilion: 11:25am–12:00pm.
4. Have lunch at Sunshine Seasons: 12:15–1:15pm.
5. Ride Soarin' with FastPass+: 1:20–1:45pm.
6. Ride Living with the Land: 1:50–2:15pm.
7. Ride Journey into Imagination with Figment: 2:20–2:40pm.
8. See Captain EO/Disney Movie Preview: 2:50–3:20pm.
9. Tour World Showcase from Canada to the United States.
10. Enjoy dinner in World Showcase or back in Future World.
11. See IllumiNations or get in line for Soarin' at 8:55pm.

ONE DAY TOURING PLAN WITH FASTPASS+
Use FastPass+ at the following attractions: Character Spot: 11:00am–12:00pm, Soarin': 12:00–1:00pm, and Spaceship Earth: 1:00– 2:00pm.

Morning and Early Afternoon Plan
1. Ride Test Track: 8:55–9:20am.
2. Ride Sum of All Thrills: 9:25–9:45am.
3. Ride Mission: SPACE Green or Orange: 9:50–10:10am.
4. Ride The Seas with Nemo and Friends: 10:25–10:35am.
5. See Turtle Talk with Crush: 10:35–11:00am.
6. Visit Character Spot with FastPass+: 11:05–11:20am.
7. Ride Living with the Land: 11:30–11:50am.
8. Have lunch at Sunshine Seasons: 11:55am–12:45pm.
9. Ride Soarin' with FastPass+: 12:50–1:15pm.
10. Ride Spaceship Earth with FastPass+: 1:25–1:45pm.
11. Ride Journey into Imagination with Figment: 1:55–2:10pm.
12. See Captain EO/Disney Movie Preview: 2:15–2:45pm.

Later Afternoon and Evening Plan
Visit World Showcase beginning with Canada.

ILLUMINATIONS
IllumiNations is the nightly entertainment at Epcot, scheduled at 9pm most nights. For the best spots, arrive 30 to 45 minutes before the start of the show. The problem you may run into when looking for a spot is that certain sections are roped off for private parties that have spent big bucks to get a prime spot on the water. So you may need a backup plan.

Best Spots
1. Base of the World Showcase directly across from the United States Pavilion. This "front of house" view is elevated with a direct view of the globe and fireworks. Parts of this area are reserved for FastPass+.
2. The next best spot is the bridge connecting the UK and France. It can't be reserved and the IllumiNations cruisers will stop below you, enjoying a similar view.
3. The Italy Isola, or raised section across from Italy. Parts can be reserved, but the viewing location behind the seated guests is almost as good.

4. The stretch from Mexico to Norway is good. Areas closer to Norway have fewer people.

5. Other options: there's limited space outside Tokyo Dining on the second level in Japan. Limited viewing is available along Canada into the UK. There are areas to the right of the UK downstairs that are good locations, but they may be reserved for private events.

6. Rose & Crown has patio seating and a reserved platform for those dining inside prior to the show. La Hacienda de San Angel also has indoor viewing, but only some of the tables face the windows. It isn't a great choice if you're looking for a guaranteed view. Consider a meal that begins after 7:45pm.

After IllumiNations, hang out for 20–45 minutes and let others exit in front of you.

TYPICAL EPCOT WAIT TIMES IN MINUTES

Low Crowds

	9:30am	10am	11am	12pm	1pm	2pm	3pm	4pm	5pm	6pm	7pm	8pm
Ellen's Energy Adventure	5	5	5	5	5	5	5	5	5	5	n/a	n/a
Gran Fiesta Tour	n/a	n/a	5	5	5	5	5	5	5	5	5	5
Journey into Imagination	5	5	5	10	10	5	5	5	5	5	n/a	n/a
Living with the Land	5	5	5	5	5	5	5	5	5	5	n/a	n/a
Mission: SPACE (Green)	5	5	10	10	10	10	10	10	10	10	5	5
Mission: SPACE (Orange)	10	10	15	20	15	15	15	15	15	15	10	10
Seas with Nemo	5	5	10	10	10	10	10	5	5	5	5	5
Soarin'	20	30	45	50	60	60	50	50	40	40	30	30
Spaceship Earth	5	10	20	20	15	10	10	10	5	5	5	5
Sum of All Thrills	5	10	15	20	20	20	20	20	20	10	n/a	n/a
Test Track	20	30	50	60	50	40	40	40	40	40	30	20

Moderate Crowds

	9:30am	10am	11am	12pm	1pm	2pm	3pm	4pm	5pm	6pm	7pm	8pm
Ellen's Energy Adventure	5	5	5	5	5	5	5	5	5	5	n/a	n/a
Gran Fiesta Tour	n/a	n/a	5	5	5	5	5	5	5	5	5	5
Journey into Imagination	5	10	15	20	20	20	20	15	15	10	n/a	n/a
Living with the Land	5	10	20	20	20	20	15	10	10	5	n/a	n/a
Mission: SPACE (Green)	5	15	20	20	20	20	20	20	20	15	10	5
Mission: SPACE (Orange)	10	25	30	30	40	30	30	30	30	20	20	10
Seas with Nemo	5	10	20	20	20	20	15	10	10	10	5	5
Soarin'	50	60	70	70	70	60	60	60	50	40	30	30
Spaceship Earth	10	25	30	30	25	20	20	20	15	10	5	5
Sum of All Thrills	5	15	25	25	30	25	25	20	20	10	n/a	n/a
Test Track	30	60	70	70	70	70	60	60	60	60	40	20

Heavy Crowds

	9:30am	10am	11am	12pm	1pm	2pm	3pm	4pm	5pm	6pm	7pm	8pm
Ellen's Energy Adventure	5	5	5	5	5	5	5	5	5	5	n/a	n/a
Gran Fiesta Tour	n/a	n/a	5	10	15	20	15	15	15	15	10	10
Journey into Imagination	5	10	25	30	30	30	30	30	20	20	n/a	n/a
Living with the Land	5	10	20	30	30	30	20	20	15	10	n/a	n/a
Mission: SPACE (Green)	5	20	40	50	60	50	50	45	40	30	20	10
Mission: SPACE (Orange)	10	25	50	60	75	70	60	60	50	40	30	15
Seas with Nemo	5	15	30	30	20	20	15	15	10	10	10	5
Soarin'	90	100	120	100	100	100	100	95	90	80	60	60
Spaceship Earth	20	40	45	50	50	30	30	25	20	15	10	5
Sum of All Thrills	5	25	30	40	40	40	30	30	30	30	n/a	n/a
Test Track	70	90	100	100	100	100	100	90	80	70	60	50

Hollywood Studios Cheat Sheet

PARK MAP

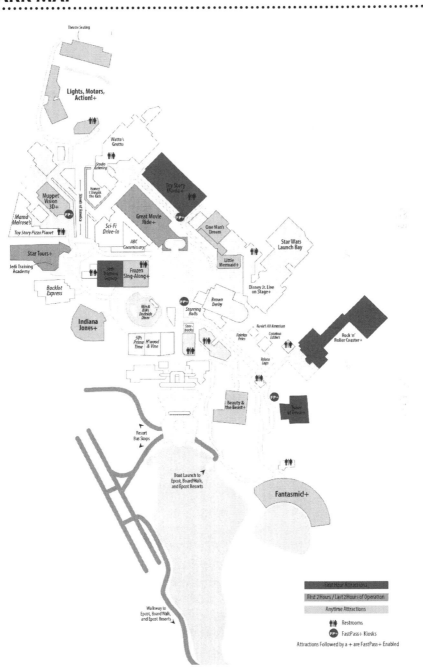

TOURING AT DISNEY'S HOLLYWOOD STUDIOS

GENERAL TOURING PHILOSOPHY Toy Story Mania is the highest priority and should be most guests' first stop. It's also the top FastPass+ priority. Rock 'n' Roller Coaster and Tower of Terror are the other two ride priorities. Star Tours and Great Movie Ride are the only other rides that often have posted waits longer than 15 minutes. A typical problem is trying to see all the scheduled shows, which take 40–60 minutes to experience. With one day, you may need to prioritize several of the lengthy attractions that appeal to your group while skipping others— there just isn't enough time.

CHARACTERS The Toy Story characters across from Toy Story Mania see 30–50 minute afternoon waits and usually begin appearing at 9am. Doc McStuffins, Sofia the First, Mickey, and other Disney Jr characters meet in Animation Courtyard outside Disney Jr. Live on Stage usually beginning at 9:30am and continuing intermittently through the early evening. Waits are typically 15 to 30 minutes. Classic characters like Goofy, Donald, Daisy, Stitch, and Pluto greet in front of Great Movie Ride from open through the early afternoon. Visit before 10am to minimize waits.

JEDI TRAINING ACADEMY Kids between the ages of 4 and 12 have the opportunity to participate in this show held next to Star Tours. You must bring the participating child to the old Sounds Dangerous building across from Indiana Jones Epic Stunt Spectacular immediately after the park opens to guarantee a slot. There are usually 12–15 shows scheduled throughout the day. Ask for a show in the afternoon so it doesn't interfere with morning touring. If they can't accommodate, let others sign up first and then sign up for a show after 12pm. Kids participating in the show are required to return to the sign-up location 30 minutes before the show to practice.

ROPE DROP Hollywood Studios may be the most essential rope drop due to how fast Toy Story Mania wait times skyrocket. If you're not among the first 200–300 people to reach the attraction, you can expect to wait 25–40+ minutes at Toy Story Mania even if you hurry straight there. Guests are ordinarily allowed inside the park 30 minutes prior to official open with three sets of internal ropes set up around the park. One rope is located near 50's Prime Time Café and Jedi Training Academy and Star Tours. Another is right before the turn onto Sunset Boulevard for Rock 'n' Roller Coaster and Tower of Terror. A third is located near the Min & Bill's boat on Echo Lake well in front of The Great Movie Ride at the end of Hollywood Boulevard. 15 minutes prior to official open, the ropes will be dropped and guests will be walked to the priority attraction of their choice. Arrive at least 45 minutes before official open and position yourself as close as possible to the internal rope nearest where you're headed.

FASTPASS+ AT HOLLYWOOD STUDIOS

FASTPASS+ PRIORITY Guests may initially select one Tier One attraction, which makes it a struggle for those arriving late to ride both Toy Story Mania and Rock 'n' Roller Coaster. Most guests want to select Toy Story Mania and ride Rock 'n' Roller Coaster standby early in the morning. Rock 'n' Roller Coaster offers a single rider line, though waits are usually in the 15–30 minute range due to the way the vehicles are loaded, and it's impossible to gauge how many people are in line until the final loading area. Select Great Movie Ride as a 4th FP+ or ride after 6pm to minimize waits.

Tier 1 (choose one)

1. Toy Story Midway Mania
2. Rock 'n' Roller Coaster
3. Fantasmic!—1st Show. Only use FP+ for the 2nd Fantasmic! if you can get it as a 4th FP+.
4. The Great Movie Ride
5. Beauty and the Beast Live on Stage

Tier 2 (choose two)

1. Tower of Terror
2. Voyage of the Little Mermaid
3. Star Tours
4. Frozen Sing-Along
5. Indiana Jones Epic Stunt Spectacular
6. Disney Jr. Live on Stage
7. Lights, Motors, Action! Extreme Stunt Show
8. Muppet Vision 3D

With average peak waits of 60+ minutes, Tower of Terror FastPass+ is a no-brainer if you want to ride it. A second Tier 2 selection may be less obvious. FastPass+ is largely useless at the shows, as users must arrive early to enjoy any benefit and with the chance that the reserved seats will be worse than standby. Voyage of the Little Mermaid wins out due to its small theater and the likelihood that guests arriving in the afternoon will have to wait through at least one complete show before entering the theater, resulting in actual waits of 15–30 minutes. FastPass+ allows you to walk right in to the specified show even as it nears being full, with less lead time. Star Tours enjoys a healthy capacity with plentiful FastPass+ availability and is usually available as a 4th FP+, but it would save you 20+ minutes in the heart of the afternoon. The Frozen Sing-Along is prioritized over the other shows because it's least likely to be available as a 4th FP+ and shows are most likely to be full, making FastPass+ more useful.

4TH FASTPASS+ SELECTION AVAILABILITY Toy Story Mania, Rock 'n' Roller Coaster, Tower of Terror, and Frozen Sing-Along will either have extremely limited or no availability come 12pm. The first Fantasmic! may or may not be available, but by selecting it early you won't be able to use FastPass+ elsewhere until after the show in the late evening. Using a 4th FP+ at Great Movie Ride or Star Tours makes the most sense, but standby waits are reliably short before 10:30am or after 6:30pm most days anyway.

FASTPASS+ KIOSKS Add or change FastPass+ at the following locations:

- Main tip board near the end of Hollywood Boulevard
- To the right of the entrance to Muppet Vision 3D
- Tower of Terror's old FASTPASS machines to the left of the attraction entrance
- Toy Story Midway Mania's old FASTPASS machines to the right of the attraction entrance

TOURING PLAN

Morning Plan
Use FastPass+ at Tower of Terror (9:00–10:00am), Toy Story Midway Mania (10:000–11:00am), Frozen Sing-Along or Star Tours (11:05–11:20am for the Sing-Along, 11:00am-12:00pm for Star Tours).

1. Ride Toy Story Midway Mania: 9:00–9:20am.
2. Ride Rock 'n' Roller Coaster: 9:30–9:50am.
3. Ride Tower of Terror with FastPass+: 9:52–10:10am.
4. See Voyage of the Little Mermaid: 10:20–10:40am (10:25am show).
5. Ride Toy Story Midway Mania with FastPass+: 10:45–11:05am.
6. See the Frozen Sing-Along with FastPass+: 11:15am–12:00pm (11:30am show).
7. Visit the Muppet Vision FastPass+ kiosk and select The Great Movie Ride for after lunch..
8. Have lunch: Studios Catering Co., Backlot Express, and ABC

Commissary are nearby. Sci-Fi Dine-In and 50's Prime Time are nearby inexpensive table service restaurants.

9. Ride Great Movie Ride with FastPass+: 12:30–1:00pm.

10. Visit the main tip board FastPass+ kiosk and schedule Star Tours for a convenient time or plan to return in the last two hours of operation when standby waits are low.

Alternative: If you'd only like to ride Toy Story once and prefer to ride Rock 'n' Roller Coaster and Tower of Terror multiple times, head to the thrill rides first and rely on FP+ at Toy Story Mania later in the day. Single rider at Rock 'n' Roller Coaster is best from 9:30–11:30am.

Afternoon and Evening Plan

It's time for the Studios' scheduled stage shows and high capacity attractions like Beauty and the Beast, One Man's Dream, and Muppet Vision 3D. For good seats at Beauty and the Beast, Frozen Sing-Along, and Indiana Jones, arrive 15–25 minutes before show time—earlier results in better seats. For Disney Jr. Live on Stage, Jedi Training Academy, and Lights, Motors, Action! Stunt Show, arriving 5–15 minutes early will suffice. Visit desired characters in the last 60–90 minutes that they're scheduled to appear.

CHARACTER-CENTRIC TOURING PLAN

Morning Plan

Use FP+ at Toy Story Midway Mania (10:00–11:00am), Frozen Sing-Along (11:05–11:20am), and Disney Jr. Live on Stage (1:10–1:25pm).

1. If desired, sign the kids ages 4–12 up for Jedi Training Academy. If you're not doing this, you may be able to ride Toy Story Midway Mania standby with a short wait before meeting the characters. Long waits may develop if you sign kids up for Jedi Training.

2. Visit Toy Story Characters: 9:05–9:15am.

3. Visit Sofia the First/Jake the Pirate in Animation Courtyard: 9:20–9:45am.

4. Meet characters in front of the Great Movie Ride building: 9:45–10:15am.

5. See Voyage of the Little Mermaid: 10:20–10:40am (10:25am show).

6. Ride Toy Story Midway Mania with FastPass+: 10:45–11:05am.

7. See the Frozen Sing-Along with FastPass+: 11:15am–12:00pm (11:30am show).

8. Have lunch. Studio Catering Company and Pizza Planet are closest.

9. See Disney Jr. Live on Stage with FastPass+: 1:00–1:45pm.

10. Get Great Movie Ride FastPass+ at the tip board FP+ kiosk for later in the day or return in the last two hours of operation when waits are short.

Afternoon Plan

Same as the "Afternoon and Evening Plan", above.

LATE-ARRIVAL TOURING WITH FASTPASS+

Use FastPass+ at Toy Story Mania or Rock 'n' Roller Coaster and for two of the attractions from Tier 2 that you would like to experience. Most people will want to select Tower of Terror and Little Mermaid or Star Tours. Visit the anytime attractions in the afternoon when crowds are heaviest, prioritizing the shows that run on a set schedule. Visit characters in the last 60–90 minutes they're scheduled to appear. End the evening with Fantasmic! or visit Rock 'n' Roller Coaster, Tower of Terror, and Toy Story Mania (in that order) in the final 90 minutes when waits are shorter. Disney will allow guests to enter the line and ride any operating attraction right up until official park close regardless of posted wait time. Posted waits at the end of the night are usually exaggerated.

EVENING ENTERTAINMENT: FANTASMIC!

Hollywood Studios' nighttime spectacular is scheduled at least once almost every night. During busier times, a second show is scheduled 90 minutes after the start of the first, and the most crowded days of the year can see three shows. Shows can start as early as 6:30pm or as late as 10pm. If two shows are scheduled, the second will virtually always be less crowded, especially if it begins at 9pm or later, due to the number of families that opt for the earlier show. If you're headed to the first or only Fantasmic!, plan to arrive 45–75 minutes early to secure good seats together. For the second show, an arrival 15–30 minutes early should suffice. Seating is bleacher-style, uncomfortable, and without backs. The best seats are at least half-way up in the middle section. Any closer and you risk getting wet and won't be able to see what's happening on the water. The Fantasmic! Dining Package, a fixed price meal at Hollywood Brown Derby, Hollywood & Vine, or Mama Melrose, guarantees a seat for the show and a three-course meal. Its reserved seats are front and center. Arrive at least 20 minutes early. FastPass+ has a reserved section next to the Dining Package section. Because it's in Tier 1, most guests will want to use their pre-scheduled selection on Toy Story Midway Mania or Rock 'n' Roller Coaster and either see the second Fantasmic! or check to see if the show is available as a 4th FP+ selection.

TYPICAL HOLLYWOOD STUDIOS WAIT TIMES IN MINUTES

Low Crowds, 7pm Close

	9:30am	10am	11am	12pm	1pm	2pm	3pm	4pm	5pm	6pm	7pm
Great Movie Ride	5	10	20	15	10	10	10	10	10	5	5
Muppet Vision 3D	5	5	5	5	5	5	5	5	5	5	5
Rock 'n' Roller Coaster	20	30	40	40	40	40	30	30	30	30	20
Star Tours	5	10	10	20	20	10	10	10	10	5	5
Tower of Terror	10	20	30	30	30	30	30	30	30	20	10
Toy Story Midway Mania	45	50	60	60	60	60	60	60	50	40	20
Voyage of the Little Mermaid	10	10	10	10	10	10	10	10	10	10	10

Moderate Crowds, 9pm Close

	9:30am	10am	11am	12pm	1pm	2pm	3pm	4pm	5pm	6pm	7pm	8pm	9pm
Great Movie Ride	10	20	25	20	15	15	15	10	15	20	15	5	5
Muppet Vision 3D	5	5	5	5	5	5	5	5	5	5	5	5	5
Rock 'n' Roller Coaster	30	50	60	70	70	60	60	60	60	40	30	30	20
Star Tours	5	10	20	30	30	20	20	20	10	10	5	5	5
Tower of Terror	20	30	40	50	50	50	40	40	30	30	20	20	10
Toy Story Midway Mania	60	70	70	80	70	70	70	70	60	60	60	30	20
Voyage of the Little Mermaid	10	10	20	20	20	20	20	20	20	20	10	10	10

Heavy Crowds, 9pm Close

	9:30am	10am	11am	12pm	1pm	2pm	3pm	4pm	5pm	6pm	7pm	8pm	9pm
Great Movie Ride	15	20	25	30	30	25	20	20	20	20	20	15	5
Muppet Vision 3D	5	5	5	5	5	5	5	5	5	5	5	5	5
Rock 'n' Roller Coaster	45	60	80	80	80	75	70	70	60	50	50	40	20
Star Tours	10	20	30	40	40	40	30	30	30	30	20	10	10
Tower of Terror	30	40	60	70	80	80	70	60	50	40	40	30	20
Toy Story Midway Mania	70	90	100	100	100	90	90	80	70	70	60	50	30
Voyage of the Little Mermaid	10	20	20	20	20	20	20	20	20	20	10	10	10

Magic Kingdom Cheat Sheet

PARK MAP

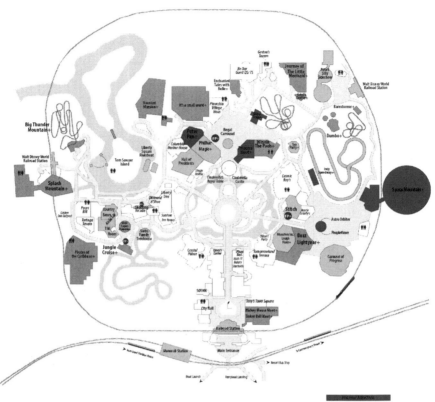

First Hour Attractions
First 2 Hours / Last 2 Hours of Operation
Anytime Attractions

👫 Restrooms

FP+ FastPass+ Kiosks

Attractions followed by a + are FastPass+ enabled.

TOURING AT MAGIC KINGDOM

GENERAL TOURING PHILOSOPHY With 60+ attractions, Magic Kingdom is best toured over two or more days. The best plans compartmentalize the park by visiting two or three Lands each day. Visit the character and attraction priorities in one Land before moving on to the next. Have lunch and then head back to the same Lands visiting the "anytime attractions". This minimizes both waiting and walking. One-day touring will require more walking. You can still accomplish a lot by touring intelligently, but some attractions will need to be skipped.

CHARACTERS Unlike the other three parks, there are characters that need to be prioritized ahead of the priority attractions. Visit Anna/Elsa, Merida, or Cinderella/Rapunzel first thing in the morning, in the last hour of their appearance, or use FastPass+ to avoid 30–75+ minute waits.

ROPE DROP Magic Kingdom opens its ticketing gates 60 minutes before official park open. Guests are held just inside the entrance in the courtyard in front of the train station. The opening show, featuring Mickey and the gang arriving via steam train, begins about 13 minutes prior to park open and lasts about six minutes. The best viewing area is front and center, but this puts you at a disadvantage entering the park as everyone off to the sides will enter before you. To minimize morning waits, move to the far left or right of the courtyard in front of one of the entrances. At the conclusion of the show, the park is opened and Cast Members walk guests slowly up Main Street and through the Castle. Break off from this group as early as possible. If you're headed to Adventureland or Frontierland, make a left after passing Casey's Corner. If you're headed to Tomorrowland, take a right after passing Plaza Ice Cream Parlor. If you're headed to Mine Train, veer right of Cinderella Castle toward Mad Tea Party and take a left at Mad Tea Party toward the Mine Train's entrance across from Winnie the Pooh.

FASTPASS+ AT MAGIC KINGDOM

FASTPASS+ PRIORITY There are far more FastPass+ opportunities at Magic Kingdom than any of the other theme parks, making the decision on which to pick difficult. Consider picking three high priority attractions in a Land that you don't plan to visit until the afternoon or evening. For example, if you plan to start your day with The Magic Carpets of Aladdin, Jungle Cruise, Big Thunder Mountain, and Splash Mountain, then you may want to use FastPass+ in the afternoon in Fantasyland at Peter Pan's Flight, Anna/Elsa, and the Mine Train, or in Tomorrowland at Space Mountain, Tomorrowland Speedway, and Buzz Lightyear.

1. Anna and Elsa at Princess Fairytale Hall
2. Seven Dwarfs Mine Train
3. Peter Pan's Flight
4. Space Mountain
5. Splash Mountain (when high temperatures are 80+ degrees)
6. Cinderella and Rapunzel at Princess Fairytale Hall
7. Enchanted Tales with Belle
8. Big Thunder Mountain Railroad
9. Ariel at Ariel's Grotto
10. Buzz Lightyear's Space Ranger Spin
11. Tomorrowland Speedway
12. Jungle Cruise
13. Haunted Mansion
14. Splash Mountain (when high temperatures are less than 80 degrees)
15. Pirates of the Caribbean
16. The Many Adventures of Winnie the Pooh
17. Mickey at Town Square Theater
18. Barnstormer
19. Disney Festival of Fantasy Parade (doesn't save any time and the location is in the sun, but there are a limited amount available)
20. Main Street Electrical Parade (prioritize first/only parade; second parade on the same night sees light crowds)
21. Wishes
22. "it's a small world"
23. Tinker Bell at Town Square Theater
24. Dumbo th Flying Elephant
25. Under the Sea ~ Journey of the Little Mermaid
26. Magic Carpets of Aladdin
27. Mad Tea Party
28. Monsters Inc. Laugh Floor
29. Mickey's PhilharMagic

4TH FASTPASS+ SELECTION AVAILABILITY Unlike the other parks, Magic Kingdom has plenty of FP+ enabled attractions and 20 or more will still have availability even around 2pm. Schedule a high priority attraction with limited availability for after a break or schedule several lower priority experiences back-to-back if you plan to stay in the park.

Check easywdw.com/waits or the My Disney Experience app to verify wait times are long enough to make searching out a kiosk and booking a FP+ worthwhile.

FASTPASS+ KIOSKS Add or change FastPass+ at the following locations:

- *Adventureland*—Jungle Cruise's old FASTPASS machines to the left of the entrance
- *Adventureland*—Breezeway to the right of Diamond Horseshoe across from Swiss Treehouse
- *Fantasyland*—To the right of Mickey's PhilharMagic
- *Tomorrowland*—To the left of Stitch's Great Escape entrance

TWO DAY TOURING PLAN

Two-Day Plan, Morning Day 1

Use FastPass+ at Mine Train (12:00–1:00pm), Enchanted Tales with Belle (1:00–2:00pm), and Anna and Elsa at Fairytale Hall or an alternate (2:00–3:00pm).

1. Ride Space Mountain: 9:00–9:20am.
2. Ride Buzz Lightyear's Space Ranger Spin: 9:25–9:35am.
3. Ride Astro Orbiter: 9:37–9:55am.
4. Ride Tomorrowland Speedway: 10:00–10:20am.
5. Ride The Many Adventures of Winnie the Pooh: 10:25–10:40am.
6. Ride Dumbo: 10:45–11:00am.
7. Ride The Barnstormer: 11:03–11:20am.
8. Ride Journey of the Little Mermaid: 11:25–11:45am.
9. Have lunch. Be Our Guest and Pinocchio Village Haus are closest.
10. Ride Seven Dwarfs Mine Train with FastPass+: 12:45–1:00pm.
11. Visit Enchanted Tales with Belle with FastPass+: 1:00–1:30pm.
12. See Mickey's PhilharMagic and/or ride Prince Regal Royal Carrousel: 1:35–2:00pm.
13. Visit Anna and Elsa at Princess Fairytale Hall with FastPass+: 2:00–2:15pm.
14. Visit Fantasyland FastPass+ kiosk to schedule a 4th FastPass+ for after the parade.
15. See Festival of Fantasy Parade in Frontierland: 2:30–3:15pm.

Two Day Plan, Afternoon and Evening Day 1

Consider an afternoon break or visit the anytime attractions in Fantasyland and Tomorrowland like Mickey's PhilharMagic, Prince Regal Carrousel, Monsters Inc. Laugh Floor, Tomorrowland PeopleMover, Carousel of Progress, and Stitch's Great Escape.

Two-Day Plan, Morning Day 2

Use FastPass+ at Peter Pan's Flight (10:00–11:00am), Jungle Cruise (11am–12pm), and Pirates of the Caribbean (12:00–1pm).

1. Ride Big Thunder Mountain Railroad: 9:10–9:20am. Ride again if desired.
2. Ride Splash Mountain: 9:23–9:45am.
3. Ride Haunted Mansion: 9:55–10:15am.
4. Ride "it's a small world": 10:17–10:40am.
5. Ride Peter Pan's Flight with FastPass+: 10:42–10:55am.
6. Ride Jungle Cruise with FastPass+: 11:05–11:25am.
7. Have lunch. Tortuga Tavern and Pecos Bill are closest. Columbia Harbour House, Liberty Tree Tavern, and Casey's Corner are relatively close.
8. Ride Pirates of the Caribbean with FastPass+: 12:30–12:50pm.
9. Visit the Adventureland Breezeway FastPass+ kiosk to select a 4th experience.

Two Day Plan, Afternoon and Evening Day 2

Consider an afternoon break or visit the anytime attractions like Tom Sawyer Island, Hall of Presidents, Liberty Square Riverboat, Country Bear Jamboree, Enchanted Tiki Room, and Swiss Family Treehouse.

CHARACTER-CENTRIC TWO DAY TOURING PLAN

Two Day Character-Centric Plan, Morning Day 1

Use FastPass+ at Seven Dwarfs Mine Train (11am–12pm) Enchanted Tales with Belle (12:00–1:00pm), and Anna and Elsa at Fairytale Hall (1:00–2:00pm).

1. Meet Mickey in Town Square Theater: 9:00–9:15am.
2. Ride Peter Pan's Flight: 9:18–9:30am.
3. Meet Ariel at Ariel's Grotto: 9:35–9:50am.
4. Ride Journey of the Little Mermaid: 9:52–10:05am.
5. Meet Gaston outside Gaston's Tavern in New Fantasyland: 10:07–10:15am.
6. Meet Daisy and Minnie at Pete's Silly Sideshow: 10:20–10:30am.
7. Meet Donald and Goofy at Pete's Silly Sideshow: 10:31–10:40am.
8. Ride The Barnstormer: 10:42–10:55am.
9. Ride Dumbo the Flying Elephant: 11:00–11:20am.
10. Ride Seven Dwarfs Mine Train with FastPass+: 11:25–11:40am.
11. Have lunch. Be Our Guest Restaurant and Pinocchio Village

Haus are closest. Cosmic Ray's is nearby.

12. Experience Enchanted Tales with Belle with FastPass+: 12:40–1:10pm.

13. Meet Anna and Elsa in Princess Fairytale Hall with FastPass+: 1:15–1:35pm.

4th FastPass+ Selection. Many Adventures of Winnie the Pooh or Tinker Bell are your best choices.

Two Day Character-Centric Plan, Afternoon and Evening Day 1
Consider an afternoon break or visit the anytime attractions in Fantasyland and Tomorrowland like Mickey's PhilharMagic, Prince Regal Carrousel, Monsters Inc. Laugh Floor, Tomorrowland PeopleMover, Carousel of Progress, and Stitch's Great Escape.

Two Day Character-Centric Plan, Morning Day 2
Use FastPass+ at Buzz Lightyear (12:15–1:15pm), Space Mountain (1:15–2:15pm), and Cinderella/Rapunzel (2:15–3:15pm).

1. Meet Merida in Fairytale Garden: 9:00–9:25am.
2. Meet Aladdin and Jasmine at Agrabah Bazaar: 9:30–9:45am.
3. Ride Jungle Cruise: 9:50–10:15am.
4. Ride Big Thunder Mountain Railroad: 10:25–10:45am.
5. Ride Splash Mountain: 10:47–11:15am.
6. Meet Chip 'n' Dale across from Diamond Horseshoe: 11:20–11:35am.
7. Have lunch. Pecos Bill and Tortuga Tavern are closest. Columbia Harbour House and Liberty Tree Tavern are nearby.
8. Ride Buzz Lightyear's Space Ranger Spin with FastPass+: 1:00–1:15pm.
9. Meet Buzz Lightyear at the exit to Space Ranger Spin: 1:17–1:40pm.
10. Ride Space Mountain with FastPass+: 1:45–2:05pm.
11. Meet Rapunzel/Cinderella at Princess Fairytale Hall with FastPass+: 2:15–2:30pm.
12. See Festival of Fantasy Parade in Frontierland or Liberty Square: 2:40–3:20pm.

4th FastPass+ Selection: Town Square Tinker Bell, Tomorrowland Speedway, "it's a small world", or Haunted Mansion are good choices.

Two Day Character-Centric Plan, Afternoon and Evening Day 2:
Consider an afternoon break or visit the anytime attractions like Tom Sawyer Island, Hall of Presidents, Liberty Square Riverboat, Country Bear Jamboree, Enchanted Tiki Room, and Swiss Family Treehouse.

Visit it's a small world, Haunted Mansion, and any other skipped attractions as late in the evening as possible. Check Times Guide for missed characters (Tiana in particular) and visit them in the last hour they're scheduled to appear.

ONE DAY TOURING PLAN

One Day Plan, Morning and Afternoon:

Use FastPass+ at Seven Dwarfs Mine Train (9:00–10:00am), Jungle Cruise (10:00–11:00am), and Pirates of the Caribbean (11:00am–12:00pm).

1. Ride Peter Pan's Flight: 9:00–9:10am.
2. Ride The Many Adventures of Winnie the Pooh: 9:15–9:25am.
3. Ride Seven Dwarfs Mine Train with FastPass+: 9:27–9:40am.
4. Ride Big Thunder Mountain Railroad: 9:55–10:15am.
5. Ride Splash Mountain 10:17–10:40am.
6. Ride Pirates of the Caribbean: 10:50–11:20am.
7. Ride Jungle Cruise with FastPass+: 11:22–11:45am.
8. Ride Space Mountain with FastPass+: 12:00–12:20pm.
9. Visit Stitch's Great Escape FastPass+ kiosk and select Buzz Lightyear that includes 1:15pm.
10. Have lunch. Cosmic Ray's is nearby.
11. Ride Buzz Lightyear with FastPass+: 1:15–1:30pm.
12. Visit Stitch's Great Escape FastPass+ kiosk and select Haunted Mansion that includes 2:15pm.
13. Ride Tomorrowland PeopleMover or see Monsters Inc. Laugh Floor: 1:35–2:00pm.
14. Ride Haunted Mansion with FastPass+: 2:15-2:35pm.
15. Visit the Fantasyland FastPass+ kiosk and select "it's a small world" that includes 3:30pm.
16. See the Festival of Fantasy Parade from Liberty Square or Frontierland: 2:40-3:15pm.
17. Ride "it's a small world" with FastPass+: 3:30-3:50pm.
18. Visit the Fantasyland FastPass+ kiosk and select an attraction.
19. See Mickey's PhilharMagic: 4:00–4:30pm.
20. Ride Prince Regal Royal Carrousel: 4:32–4:45pm.
21. Have dinner. Pinocchio Village Haus is closest. Be Our Guest Restaurant would be perfect if you've snagged reservations.

One Day Plan, Evening

Your evening depends greatly on when Magic Kingdom closes, when Wishes is scheduled, and ultimately how long you want to stay. Visit attractions marked anytime on the map until about 30 minutes before Wishes, then move to Main Street to see the show. Return to Liberty Square or Frontierland for the Electrical Parade, keeping in mind the second Parade (when offered) is far less crowded. Return to Tomorrowland with two hours to close and Fantasyland in the last hour to find much shorter waits than in the afternoon, ending the day with Peter Pan's Flight and Mine Train if desired.

LATE ARRIVAL

Crowds only diminish most nights after 9pm as families invariably leave early with small children. The later it gets, the lower wait times will be, particularly if close is 11pm or later. Use FastPass+ when you arrive when wait times are longest. Visit the light gray anytime attractions until two to three hours before close. Then move on to the medium gray attractions like Buzz Lightyear and Big Thunder Mountain and finish the night with the highest priority attractions like Peter Pan's Flight, Mine Train, and Space Mountain.

EVENING ENTERTAINMENT AND EXIT

MAIN STREET ELECTRICAL PARADE The Electrical Parade is scheduled on between 3 and 7 nights per week, usually between 7pm and 11pm. It begins on Main Street and exits to the left of Splash Mountain. The best viewing locations are near Pecos Bill and outside Hall of Presidents in Liberty Square. Two Parades are often scheduled with the second beginning two hours after the first. If this is the case, see the later Parade as it will be far less crowded. Arrive 20–30 minutes early if there's one Parade or 10–15 minutes early for the second Parade. The FastPass+ viewing location is around the Flag Pole in Town Square on Main Street for both the Electrical Parade and Festival of Fantasy. It provides a decent view, but the viewing area is directly in the sun and the parades are easy enough to see without FastPass+ in most situations.

CELEBRATE THE MAGIC AND WISHES The Castle Projection Show usually begins 15 minutes before Wishes. Position yourself on Main Street just in front of Casey's Corner for the best view of the show, which is almost immediately followed by Wishes Fireworks. Arrive 30 minutes before Wishes is scheduled to start. The Wishes FastPass+ viewing areas are on both sides of Main Street in gated areas. Seeing

Wishes with FP+ is not recommended due to how crowded the area becomes. Most guests can see it just as easily, or potentially even more easily, from a non-reserved location. If you're exiting after the show, try to use the Main Street bypass in between Plaza Restaurant and Tomorrowland Terrace.

EXIT Consider getting in line for Mine Train, Peter Pan's Flight, or another attraction with a few minutes until close. Main Street stores will remain open for about an hour after park close. Linger a bit while others exit in front of you. The Express Monorail is the fastest way to the Transportation and Ticket Center (parking lot) unless the line is significantly backed up. The ferry is often a more comfortable ride with more room to spread out, particularly up the stairs on the second level.

TYPICAL MAGIC KINGDOM WAIT TIMES IN MINUTES

Low Crowds, 8pm Close

	9:30am	10am	11am	12pm	1pm	2pm	3pm	4pm	5pm	6pm	7pm	8pm
Ariel's Grotto	10	15	30	30	30	30	30	30	30	20	15	10
Astro Orbiter	10	15	20	30	30	30	30	20	20	20	15	10
Barnstormer	5	5	10	20	20	20	15	15	15	10	10	5
Big Thunder Mountain	10	20	25	45	40	40	40	40	30	20	15	10
Buzz Lightyear Spin	5	10	20	30	40	40	30	30	25	20	15	10
Dumbo	10	15	15	20	30	25	20	20	20	15	10	5
Enchanted Tales w/Belle	15	20	30	40	30	30	30	30	30	20	15	10
Haunted Mansion	10	20	20	30	40	30	30	30	25	20	10	5
it's a small world	5	10	15	20	25	25	25	20	20	20	15	5
Jungle Cruise	10	20	25	40	50	40	30	30	30	30	20	10
Mad Tea Party	5	5	5	10	10	10	10	10	5	5	5	5
Magic Carpets of Aladdin	5	10	15	20	20	20	20	20	20	15	10	5
Many Adventures of Pooh	10	15	20	25	30	30	30	25	20	15	10	5
Monsters Inc. Laugh Floor	10	10	10	10	10	10	10	10	10	10	10	10
Peter Pan's Flight	30	45	50	60	70	60	60	60	50	40	30	15
Pirates of the Caribbean	5	10	20	30	35	30	30	30	20	20	15	5
Prince Regal Carrousel	5	5	5	5	5	5	5	5	5	5	5	5
Princess Fairytale Anna/Elsa	70	80	80	90	90	90	80	70	70	60	60	40
Prin. F. Cinderella/Rapunzel	20	30	40	40	45	40	30	30	30	30	20	15
Seven Dwarfs Mine Train	60	60	70	80	80	80	70	60	60	50	50	40
Space Mountain	10	15	30	40	50	50	40	40	35	25	20	15
Splash Mountain (hot)	10	20	25	35	45	40	35	30	30	25	15	10
Splash Mountain (cold)	5	5	10	15	20	20	20	15	10	10	5	5
Stitch's Great Escape	5	5	5	5	5	5	5	5	5	5	5	5
Swiss Family Treehouse	0	0	0	0	0	0	0	0	0	0	0	0
Tomorrowland Speedway	10	20	25	30	30	30	20	20	20	20	15	10
Tomorrowland PeopleMover	0	0	0	0	0	0	0	0	0	0	0	0
Town Square Mickey	20	25	30	30	35	30	20	30	25	20	15	10
Under the Sea-Little Mermaid	20	20	20	30	30	30	20	20	20	20	10	10

Moderate Crowds, 10pm Close

	9:30am	10am	11am	12pm	1pm	2pm	3pm	4pm	5pm	6pm	7pm	8pm	9pm	10pm	11pm
Ariel's Grotto	10	15	35	30	45	45	40	40	40	40	30	20	20	10	5
Astro Orbiter	10	20	20	30	40	30	30	30	30	20	20	20	20	15	10
Barnstormer	5	10	20	20	30	20	20	20	20	20	15	15	15	10	5
Big Thunder Mountain	10	20	30	40	50	50	40	40	40	40	35	30	20	15	10
Buzz Lightyear Spin	5	15	30	30	40	40	30	40	40	40	30	30	20	15	10
Dumbo	10	15	25	30	30	30	30	30	25	20	15	15	15	10	5
Enchanted Tales w/Belle	20	30	40	40	40	40	40	40	40	30	30	30	20	20	10
Haunted Mansion	10	20	30	35	40	35	30	30	30	30	25	20	15	10	10
it's a small world	10	15	20	25	30	35	25	20	20	20	20	15	10	10	10
Jungle Cruise	10	20	35	45	50	50	40	40	40	40	35	30	25	20	10
Mad Tea Party	5	5	10	15	15	15	15	15	10	10	10	10	5	5	5
Magic Carpets of Aladdin	5	10	15	20	20	20	20	20	15	10	5	10	5	5	5
Many Adventures of Pooh	10	20	30	30	35	30	30	30	30	30	20	20	15	10	5
Monsters Inc. Laugh Floor	10	10	10	10	10	10	10	10	10	10	10	10	10	10	10
Peter Pan's Flight	45	60	60	70	70	80	60	60	60	60	60	60	40	30	20
Pirates of the Caribbean	5	10	30	40	45	40	40	30	30	30	20	20	15	5	5
Prince Regal Carrousel	5	5	5	5	5	5	5	5	5	5	5	5	5	5	5
Princess Fairytale Anna/Elsa	70	30	30	30	30	30	80	70	70	70	70	60	50	40	40
Prin. F. Cinderella/Rapunzel	20	40	50	60	50	50	50	40	40	40	40	30	20	30	20
Seven Dwarfs Mine Train	60	70	80	90	80	80	80	70	70	70	60	60	40	40	30
Space Mountain	10	35	50	60	70	80	60	60	60	60	50	45	40	30	10
Splash Mountain (hot)	15	25	50	60	60	60	50	60	60	60	50	40	30	15	10
Splash Mountain (cold)	5	10	15	25	25	20	20	20	20	20	15	10	5	5	5
Stitch's Great Escape	5	5	5	5	5	5	5	5	5	5	5	5	5	5	5
Swiss Family Treehouse	0	0	0	0	0	0	0	0	0	0	0	0	0	0	0
Tomorrowland Speedway	10	20	25	40	40	30	30	30	30	30	20	15	15	10	10
Tomorrowland PeopleMover	0	0	0	0	0	0	0	0	0	0	0	0	0	0	0
Town Square Mickey	20	25	30	30	35	30	20	30	25	20	15	15	15	15	10
Under the Sea-Little Mermaid	20	20	25	30	40	30	30	30	30	20	20	20	10	10	5

Heavy Crowds, Midnight Close

	9:30am	10am	11am	12pm	1pm	2pm	3pm	4pm	5pm	6pm	7pm	8pm	9pm	10pm	11pm	12pm
Ariel's Grotto	10	20	40	50	50	60	50	50	50	40	35	25	20	15	10	5
Astro Orbiter	10	20	30	30	40	40	40	30	30	30	30	25	20	15	10	10
Barnstormer	5	10	25	30	40	40	35	35	30	30	30	20	20	10	5	5
Big Thunder Mountain	15	25	40	45	60	70	60	60	60	50	50	40	40	25	20	10
Buzz Lightyear Spin	10	15	40	45	60	60	45	45	45	45	40	30	35	15	10	10
Dumbo	10	15	30	40	50	50	50	50	50	45	30	25	15	10	5	5
Enchanted Tales w/Belle	20	30	40	50	40	40	40	40	40	30	30	30	20	20	20	10
Haunted Mansion	10	20	30	40	45	40	40	30	30	30	25	15	15	10	10	5
it's a small world	10	15	20	30	40	40	30	30	25	25	20	15	15	10	5	5
Jungle Cruise	10	20	40	50	60	50	50	40	40	40	35	30	25	15	15	10
Mad Tea Party	5	5	10	20	25	25	20	20	15	15	15	10	10	5	5	5
Magic Carpets of Aladdin	10	15	20	30	30	25	25	20	20	20	15	15	10	10	5	5
Many Adventures of Pooh	20	30	30	40	50	45	45	40	40	35	30	30	25	20	15	10
Monsters Inc. Laugh Floor	10	10	10	20	20	20	20	10	10	10	10	10	10	10	10	10
Peter Pan's Flight	45	60	70	80	90	90	80	80	70	70	70	70	60	50	35	25
Pirates of the Caribbean	5	10	35	45	55	60	50	50	40	40	35	25	20	15	15	10
Prince Regal Carrousel	5	5	5	5	5	5	5	5	5	5	5	5	5	5	5	5
Princess Fairytale Anna/Elsa	70	90	90	120	100	100	90	80	80	80	80	70	60	50	40	40
Prin. F. Cinderella/Rapunzel	30	40	50	60	60	60	60	50	50	50	40	40	40	30	20	20
Seven Dwarfs Mine Train	70	90	90	90	100	100	90	90	80	80	80	80	70	60	50	40
Space Mountain	20	40	60	70	80	90	80	80	80	70	70	70	60	40	30	15
Splash Mountain (hot)	15	30	50	70	70	80	70	70	60	60	50	40	60	25	20	15
Splash Mountain (cold)	5	15	25	30	30	30	30	30	30	30	25	10	10	5	5	5
Stitch's Great Escape	5	5	5	10	10	10	10	10	10	10	10	5	5	5	5	5
Swiss Family Treehouse	0	0	0	0	0	0	0	0	0	0	0	0	0	0	0	0
Tomorrowland Speedway	10	20	30	40	50	40	40	30	30	30	30	25	20	15	10	5
Tomorrowland PeopleMover	0	0	5	5	5	5	5	5	5	5	5	5	5	0	0	0
Town Square Mickey	20	30	30	40	50	50	30	45	40	30	30	25	20	20	20	10
Under the Sea-Little Mermaid	20	20	30	30	40	40	40	40	30	30	30	20	20	10	10	10

Party Night, 7pm Close

	9:30am	10am	11am	12pm	1pm	2pm	3pm	4pm	5pm	6pm	7pm
Ariel's Grotto	10	15	30	30	30	30	30	30	30	20	10
Astro Orbiter	10	15	20	30	30	30	30	20	20	20	15
Barnstormer	5	5	10	20	20	20	15	15	15	10	10
Big Thunder Mountain	10	20	25	35	45	40	40	40	30	20	15
Buzz Lightyear Spin	5	10	20	30	40	40	30	30	25	20	10
Dumbo	10	15	15	20	30	25	20	20	20	15	10
Enchanted Tales w/Belle	15	20	30	40	30	30	30	30	30	20	20
Haunted Mansion	10	20	20	30	40	30	30	30	25	20	10
it's a small world	5	10	15	20	25	25	20	20	20	15	10
Jungle Cruise	10	20	25	40	50	40	30	30	30	30	20
Mad Tea Party	5	5	5	10	10	10	10	10	5	5	5
Magic Carpets of Aladdin	5	10	15	20	20	20	20	20	20	15	5
Many Adventures of Pooh	10	15	20	25	30	30	30	30	20	15	10
Monsters Inc. Laugh Floor	10	10	10	10	10	10	10	10	10	10	10
Peter Pan's Flight	30	45	50	60	70	60	60	60	50	40	20
Pirates of the Caribbean	5	10	20	30	35	30	30	30	20	15	10
Prince Regal Carrousel	5	5	5	5	5	5	5	5	5	5	5
Princess Fairytale Anna/Elsa	70	80	80	90	90	90	80	70	70	60	60
Prin. F. Cinderella/Rapunzel	20	30	40	40	45	40	30	30	30	30	20
Seven Dwarfs Mine Train	60	60	70	80	80	80	70	60	60	50	50
Space Mountain	10	15	30	40	50	50	40	40	35	25	10
Splash Mountain (hot)	10	20	25	35	45	40	35	30	30	25	10
Splash Mountain (cold)	5	5	10	15	20	20	20	15	10	10	5
Stitch's Great Escape	5	5	5	5	5	5	5	5	5	5	5
Swiss Family Treehouse	0	0	0	0	0	0	0	0	0	0	0
Tomorrowland Speedway	10	20	25	30	30	30	20	20	20	20	10
Tomorrowland PeopleMover	0	0	0	0	0	0	0	0	0	0	0
Town Square Mickey	20	25	30	30	35	30	20	30	25	20	10
Under the Sea-Little Mermaid	20	20	20	30	30	30	20	20	20	20	20

Where to Eat

First-time family visitors to Walt Disney World need to know three things about dining:

1. Several dining venues are among the most memorable and delightful experiences Walt Disney Word has to offer. Options range from dining in the banquet hall inside Cinderella Castle with the Disney Princesses to sharing sushi and filet mignon on the 15th floor of the Contemporary to joining Mickey and the Gang for lunch in an exotic African marketplace.

2. Table service reservations open 180 days in advance, and availability at the most sought-after restaurants is gobbled up almost immediately. A list of the hardest restaurants to reserve follows later.

3. Disney World dining is expensive. Expect to pay 25–40% more on-property than you would for comparable meals off-property, whether we're talking about a fast food hamburger at Cosmic Ray's or a 28-ounce Porterhouse at Yachtsman Steakhouse. In effect, most of the upcharge is a convenience fee, but the Disney restaurants offer a reliably consistent experience, many times in unique settings.

The rest of this chapter:

- Offers suggestions on where to eat
- Explains how to reserve meals at Disney World—and why starting to do so 180 days before your visit is crucial
- Introduces and compares the various Disney Dining Plans
- Shares some thoughts on saving money

The chapter ends with overviews of dining at the parks and brief reviews of all the Disney World table service dining options.

Where to Eat at Walt Disney World

Service, food quality, and atmosphere vary immensely among the Disney World restaurants, even those inside the same park with similar price points. The information and reviews that follow will help identify restaurants that are the perfect fit for your group's budget and preferences. Disney World dining locations come in several shapes and sizes:

QUICK OR COUNTER SERVICE Basically a fancy name for fast food, quick service locations don't accept reservations and food is usually ordered at a register and then available for pickup several minutes later. (Be Our Guest is the one exception. It accepts and sometimes requires a reservation for quick service breakfast and lunch.) Quick service is usually cheaper and faster than table service. Menus, food quality, and atmosphere vary wildly among the various options, making your choices more important than you might expect.

TABLE SERVICE These venues are typical restaurant experiences, where a host will seat your party and a server will take your order and deliver the food to the table. Most require reservations, particularly for dinner. Prices range from $12 sandwiches at The Plaza Restaurant in Magic Kingdom to $185+ for a seven-course meal at Victoria & Albert's. Buffets are generally lumped into this category, even when guests typically serve themselves.

DINNER SHOWS Spirit of Aloha at the Polynesian and Hoop-Dee-Doo Revue at Fort Wilderness offer all-you-care-to-enjoy family-style dining accompanied by two-hour shows. Mickey's Backyard Barbecue, also located at Ft. Wilderness, is an all-you-care-to-enjoy buffet amidst fun line dancing and live music.

FAVORITE FAMILY DINING

In addition to the food, the most fun and best-loved family dining contains some or all of the following:

- A fun setting
- Some kind of show and/or interactive play-along elements
- Visits by Disney characters like Mickey, Tigger, or the Disney Princesses.

On almost every family's list of the best among these are:

- The Hoop-Dee-Doo Musical Revue, a silly, energetic dinner show with interactive elements and plenty of audience participation at Disney's Fort Wilderness Resort.

- The Princess meals: Cinderella's Royal Table in the Magic Kingdom and Akershus Royal Banquet Hall in Epcot. The first has the better setting, the second is much less expensive.
- Dining with Tigger, Pooh, and friends at the Crystal Palace in the Magic Kingdom.
- Dining with Mickey and friends at Chef Mickey's at Disney's Contemporary Resort and 'Ohana breakfast at Disney's Polynesian Resort.
- Dining in the Beast's Castle at Be Our Guest Restaurant in the Magic Kingdom.
- Various degrees of wait-staff induced silliness at 50's Prime Time Café in Disney's Hollywood Studios and Whispering Canyon Café at Disney's Wilderness Lodge.
- Exotic settings in the local versions of national chain restaurants like the Rainforest Café, in both Disney's Animal Kingdom and Disney Springs, and T-REX in Disney Springs.

SELECTING CHARACTER MEALS

Character meals are table service meals or dinner shows where the group has the opportunity to interact and take pictures with the characters during the dining experience. There are several benefits to these meals. First, they replace the lengthy waits to meet the characters inside the theme parks. At Magic Kingdom, meeting Mickey, Minnie, Goofy, Donald, and Pluto might take 90 or more minutes standing in line, often outdoors and unprotected from the heat and rain. At Chef Mickey's, you can enjoy your ice cream sundae while they all come to you. In addition, several characters don't ordinarily meet outside of character meals, including Piglet, Beast, and Prince Charming.

When deciding on a character meal, first identify which characters you'd like to meet. Then narrow down the potential choices by cost, setting, and convenience via the reviews that follow.

Character meal options include:

Animal Kingdom:
- Tusker House: Mickey, Donald, Daisy, Goofy in safari gear.

Epcot:
- Garden Grill: Mickey, Pluto, Chip, Dale in farming apparel.
- Akershus Royal Banquet Hall: Belle, in her yellow gown, joins diners for a picture before they're seated. Ariel, Aurora, Jasmine, and Snow White usually greet tableside.

Hollywood Studios:

- Hollywood & Vine (breakfast and lunch only): Sofia, Doc McStuffins, Jake, Handy Manny.
- Hollywood & Vine (dinner only): There may be seasonal characters appearing at dinner.

Magic Kingdom:

- Be Our Guest Restaurant (dinner only): While not a "character meal" per se, guests have the opportunity to meet and take pictures with Beast after the meal.
- Cinderella's Royal Table: Pictures with Cinderella before the meal, with Ariel, Aurora, Jasmine, and Snow White usually meeting tableside.
- Crystal Palace: Pooh, Tigger, Eeyore, and Piglet.

Resorts:

- 1900 Park Fare Breakfast at Grand Floridian: Mary Poppins, Alice, the Mad Hatter, Tigger, and Winnie the Pooh.
- 1900 Park Fare Dinner at Grand Floridian: Cinderella and Prince Charming, Lady Tremaine, Anastasia, Drizella, Fairy Godmother.
- Cape May Café at Beach Club Resort (breakfast only): Goofy, Minnie, and Donald in ridiculous beach outfits.
- Chef Mickey's at Contemporary Resort: Mickey, Minnie, Chip, Dale, and Goofy in culinary outfits.
- 'Ohana (breakfast only): Mickey, Pluto, Lilo, Stitch in Hawaiian outfits.
- Mickey's Backyard Barbecue at Fort Wilderness: Mickey, Minnie, and "friends"—typically Goofy, Chip, Dale in cowboy outfits.

For the princesses, we prefer Cinderella's Royal Table, which is also the only opportunity to see inside the beautiful castle. Absurdly expensive? Yes, but it's a special experience that can't be duplicated elsewhere.

For Mickey, we like Garden Grill at Epcot and Tusker House lunch at Animal Kingdom. Both are conveniently located inside the theme parks, making them easy to access while you're visiting those parks. For Mickey at the resorts, Chef Mickey's is a family favorite, as is breakfast at 'Ohana.

DINING FOR COUPLES

For couples looking for the most romantic atmosphere and the best food, we suggest:

- **California Grill**: Located on the 15ᵗʰ floor of the Contemporary Resort, California Grill offers breathtaking views of Magic Kingdom during the evening fireworks, in addition to a great menu focused on fresh ingredients, sushi, and contemporary cocktails.
- **Artist Point**: Nestled inside Wilderness Lodge, this romantic rendezvous is themed to the restaurants found in the great National Park lodges of the west. Buffalo, salmon, and a terrific mushroom soup and berry cobbler are menu mainstays.
- **Victoria & Albert's**: For a truly special occasion; astonishing dining.

WHAT ABOUT EARLY BREAKFAST AT THE PARKS?

Tusker House at Animal Kingdom, Akershus at Epcot, Hollywood & Vine at Hollywood Studios, and Cinderella's Royal Table, Crystal Palace, and Be Our Guest Restaurant at Magic Kingdom all routinely open at 8am for breakfast, which is often a full hour before the rest of the park. Many people recommend these 8am breakfasts because they afford an opportunity to get pictures in the park "when nobody else is around". Unfortunately, and particularly at Magic Kingdom and Hollywood Studios, this is not usually the case because hundreds of other people have the same idea. 8am reservations are also awfully early and awfully expensive. Transportation from the resorts is also dodgier and less consistent so early. With the parks routinely opening at 15 minutes prior to the officially stated time, an 8am reservation either means rushing through the meal and hoping the characters arrive in time for a hasty exit, or wasting precious morning touring time eating. Instead, we recommend a late breakfast or early lunch, which allows you to sleep in an extra hour and hit the priority attractions when crowds are lowest before taking a restful, air-conditioned break with the characters.

The one potential exception is Be Our Guest, which currently serves quick service breakfast wihout characters for $21.99 for adults and $13.99 for kids. It includes choice of entrée, beverage, and a pastry platter for the table to share. If you can secure a reservation no later than 8:15am, you can enjoy the meal and exit the restaurant before 8:45am. This offers a great advantage for those planning to visit Seven Dwarfs Mine Train or Princess Fairytale Hall first thing because diners have the ability to arrive before anyone entering from the main entrance. Doing so also avoids the rush up Main Street.

RECOMMENDED DINING
••

Families using the 9-day itineraries introduced in Chapter 6 will find recommended dining at the top of each day in the graphic of the itinerary. The associated To-Do Lists for these itineraries have instructions on when and how to book the reservable table service meals, in addition to walking you through each step of the planning process. Each of the park "Cheat Sheets" in the previous chapter has recommended counter-service options.

Our recommendations are not set in stone. Families with much younger kids may wish to cut some of the non-character meals and replace them with character meals. Families with teens might want to do the opposite. Substitutions can be based on the graphic below—which ranks the Disney World theme park and resort table service options based on kid and adult appeal—or on the capsule reviews that follow at the end of this chapter.

Guide to Disney World Dining

Bold=Character Meal; <u>Underline</u>=Requires 2 Dining Plan Credits; (paren)=which meal, if ratings differ; *Italic*=Resort Casual Dress Code; CAPS=Location (see key below)

K I D A P P E A L	High	**Chef Mickey's** C, 50's Prime Time Café HS	**Akershus** E, Beaches & Cream BC, Biergarten E, **<u>Cinderella's Royal Table</u>** MK, **Crystal Palace** MK, <u>Hoop-dee-Doo Revue</u> FW, **<u>Mickey's Backyard Barbecue</u>** FW, **'Ohana** P (b), Rainforest Café AK DTD, San Angel Inn E, Sci-Fi Dine-in Theater HS, **Tusker House** AK (b,l), Whispering Canyon Café WL	
	Medium	**Hollywood and Vine*** HS	**Cape May Café** BC (b), Cape May Café BC (d), Coral Reef E, ESPN Club BW, **Garden Grill** E, La Hacienda de San Angel E, Liberty Tree Tavern MK, Mama Melrose's HS, Nine Dragons E, **1900 Park Fare** GF (b,d), 'Ohana P (d), Olivia's OKW, Plaza MK, Restaurant Marrakesh E, Rose & Crown E, Sanaa KAKL, Tony's Town Square MK, Turf Club SS, Tusker House AK (d), Tutto Italia E, Via Napoli E, Yak & Yeti AK	Be Our Guest MK (d), *California Grill* C, Boma AKL, <u>Hollywood Brown Derby</u> HS, Le Cellier E, Teppan Edo E
	Low	<u>Spirit of Aloha Polynesian Luau</u> P	Big River Grille BW, Captain's Grille YC, Grand Floridian Café GF, Kona Café P, Les Chefs de France E, Spice Road Table E	*Artist Point* WI, Monsieur Paul's E, *Citricos* GF, *Flying Fish Café* BW, *Jiko* AKL, *Narcoossee's* GF, Queen Victoria's Room** GF, Tokyo Dining E, Victoria & Albert** GF, The Wave C, *Yachtsman Steakhouse* YC
		Low	Medium	High

ADULT APPEAL

Locations: AK=Animal Kingdom, AKL=Animal Kingdom Lodge, BC=Beach Club, BW=BoardWalk, C=Contemporary, DTD=Downtown Disney, E=Epcot, FW=Fort Wilderness, GF=Grand Floridian, HS=Hollywood Studios, KAKL=Kidani Village at AKL, MK=Magic Kingdom, OKW=Old Key West, SS=Saratoga Springs, WL=Wilderness Lodge, YC=Yacht Club

* Though a character meal, low kid appeal except for fans of Playhouse Disney
** Not on Dining Plan; jacket required; no kids under 10

In the graphic, high adult appeal is based on "date night" criteria: a restaurant having fine dining, fine service, and a lovely setting. High kid appeal means that a restaurant has the elements that make the rest of Disney World a joy for kids—playful action, characters, and a fun setting—and also has a menu suited to picky eaters. By these criteria, it's hard for a restaurant to appeal to both. Be Our Guest in the Magic Kingdom comes closest, and if it had a better kids menu for picky eaters, would be ranked with high appeal for both groups.

Because kids and adults vary, it's best to use the chart and the reviews at the end of this chapter together.

Advance Dining Reservations

Make Advance Dining Reservations (ADRs) beginning 180 days before your first planned table service meal.

The best Disney World dining options have limited capacity and are wildly popular. Because of this, these restaurants can be filled almost as soon as reservations open for them—180 days before the dining date.

One topic that surprises first-time visitors is the importance and fun of dining experiences. Because quality and price vary so much between restaurants in the same vicinity, researching your options and booking the best restaurants far in advance puts you in the best possible position to have a fun, stress-free vacation. Identify your table service dining favorites as soon as possible and then make your ADRs as soon as reservations open.

Note that ADRs are not "reservations" in the traditional sense. With the exception of Victoria & Albert's and the dinner shows, the restaurant does not actually reserve a table. Instead, your party will receive the next available table that opens up. This can lead to the occasional long wait, particularly at the popular buffets that are often overbooked. To help mitigate this, book a meal right after the restaurant starts service or near the end of service when empty tables are more common.

MAKING YOUR RESERVATIONS

Reservations currently open 180 days before the date of dining—online at 6 a.m. and over the phone at 7 a.m. Moreover, if you are staying at a Disney World hotel, once 180 days from your hotel arrival date rolls around, you can make ADRs for not just that day, but also for the first ten days of your visit. You'll sometimes see this referred to as 180+10. Input your arrival date into HTTP://PSCALCULATOR.NET/PSCALC.PHP to identify the first day you can make reservations. As an example, let's say you're visiting from December 1–8 and staying on property at Art of Animation. According to the calculator, the first day you can make reservations is June 4. Not only could you make reservations for December 1, the first day of our hypothetical vacation, but you can also make reservations for up to ten additional days because you're staying at a Disney-owned resort. Off-site guests visiting on the same dates would also be able to make their reservations for December 1 on June 4, but they would need to call or go online again on June 5 to book December 2, June 6 to book December 3, and so forth.

Most table service reservations require prospective diners to put a credit card on file. A $10 per person fee will be assessed if the group does not show up within 15 minutes of the reservation time. To avoid this fee, cancel the reservation no later than the day before. Same-day cancellations will be charged the no-show fee. Note that only one person needs to show up regardless of how many people are on the reservation. So if you have a reservation for six and only three show up, your party will not be assessed any fees. If weather, transportation delays, or something else causes you to miss your reservation, visit Guest Services and explain your case. Disney will likely waive the charge for worthy stories.

The hardest reservations to get, and which you should book as soon as you can, are:

- Be Our Guest Restaurant [Magic Kingdom]
- Cinderella's Royal Table [Magic Kingdom]
- Chef Mickey's [Contemporary Resort]
- 'Ohana [Polynesian Resort]
- Akershus Royal Banquet Hall [Epcot]
- 1900 Park Fare Dinner [Grand Floridian Resort]
- California Grill [Contemporary Resort]
- Crystal Palace [Magic Kingdom]

Typically, over 40 restaurants will have same-day reservations available at some point during the day. It's always best to secure reservations via 407-WDW-Dine, DISNEYWORLD.COM, the My Disney Experience mobile app, or in person at Guest Services or the restaurant itself. It's not uncommon for a restaurant to entirely turn guests away without reservations, particularly at peak dinner times. Make reservations as soon as you know where you want to eat.

The Disney Dining Plan

Disney World dining is expensive. For some guests, it may even be the priciest component of the vacation, eclipsing the cost of lodging and theme park tickets. The three versions of the Disney Dining Plan (Quick Service, Regular, and Deluxe) are a way to prepay some of these dining expenses.

Years ago, when the Regular Dining Plan included appetizer and tip at sit-down restaurants, you could actually save some money by using these plans. These days it's hard for us to recommend them:

- The Quick Service Dining Plan is priced so high that it's only possible to break even or come out ahead if you use the credits solely for lunch and dinner. From there, you'll need to order only the most expensive items to eke out a potential savings of a dollar or two per day.
- At a cost north of $60 per adult per day, the Regular Dining Plan is expensive and saving money with it requires planning only the most expensive meals.
- The Deluxe Dining Plan comes with three quick or table service meals per day at a cost of about $110 per day per adult. Users either spend three or more hours per day eating table service meals or use their credits on faster quick service meals, in turn reducing the value of each credit.

With only a couple of exceptions, we suggest skipping the dining plans. Exceptions include:

- If you take comfort in pre-paying some of your dining expenses as a budgeting tool (even if this means you spend more money), the Quick Service or Regular plans may make sense for you—the cash loss may be worth the budget comfort. It's nice knowing that food is pre-paid and users are free to order whatever entrees and desserts that they like, even if those prices are higher than they're accustomed to paying. As an alternative, consider loading a Disney gift card with the amount of money you plan to pay for meals.
- Pricing on the Regular Plan is advantageous for groups with kids under the age of ten that plan multiple buffets and character meals. The cost of a child buffet at many character meals exceeds their cost of the Regular Dining Plan for that day.

With or without a dining plan, the typical family eating their meals on property should budget $35–$60+ per adult per day, and between $15 and $40/day for the kids—depending on their ages and appetites.

DINING PLAN CREDITS AND WHAT THEY COVER

The Dining Plans are only available to guests staying at Disney owned and operated resorts. All guests on a single reservation (except children under three—not covered on any plan) must opt for the same Dining Plan if you elect to purchase it. There's no such thing as having four people on a room reservation and only three people on the Deluxe Plan. And it isn't possible for one person to purchase Deluxe, while the other chooses Regular. Everyone over the age of nine must pay the adult rate, regardless of how much they plan to eat. And kids 3–9 might be required order from the Kids' Menu if the dining location has one.

Those on the Dining Plan receive a number of credits based on the number of nights they're staying. The Dining Plan and credits are not connected to theme park tickets or anything else—just the number of nights on the reservation. The credits are usable from the check-in day through midnight on the checkout day. Credits can be used in any order on any of these days. On a three-night stay, a guest could conceivably use all their credits on the first day, the last day, or space them out.

Quick service meals generally consist of one entrée or combo meal, one dessert, and one non-alcoholic beverage. Virtually every quick service on property participates in the Dining Plan, and all quick service meals cost one credit.

Table service meals, including one entrée, one dessert, and one non-alcoholic beverage, cost one or two credits. Two credit meals are signature experiences at the most expensive dinner shows, buffets, and restaurants like Hoop-Dee-Doo Revue, Cinderella's Royal Table, and California Grill. The Deluxe Dining Plan credits also include an appetizer, in addition to the entrée, dessert, and non-alcoholic beverage. Snack credits can be used on many small food items. The number and variety of items eligible for snack credits were greatly expanded in the summer of 2015. Examples include candy apples, ice cream bars, pastries, and bottles of water and soda. Look for the Dining Plan symbol on any menu to see what is eligible to be paid for with a snack credit.

Also in the summer of 2015, various quick service substitutions became more easily available—although always ask first, as policies are not set in stone and can vary by restaurant. For example, in some venues a quick service credit can be used instead as three snack credits (you have to get all three snacks at the same time), and when using quick service credits in the normal fashion, various sides can be substituted for desserts, drinks, or both.

The credits don't always cover everything you might want at a meal and no credits cover alcohol (except beer and wine at the dinner shows) or tips. Most guests have some additional dining expenses, in addition to the cost of the Dining Plan.

THE QUICK SERVICE DINING PLAN

The Quick Service Dining Plan includes per person, per night:

- Two quick service meals
- One snack

In addition, each guest receives a refillable mug for use at their resort's quick service, and, if available, pools.

So a family of four staying for five nights would receive ten quick service meals, five snacks, and a refillable mug each. At press time, after-tax pricing is:

- $42.77 per night for those ten and older
- $17.54 per night for kids ages three to nine

Adult quick service entrees are typically $8–$11 in the theme parks. Add a $3 fountain beverage and a $4 carrot cake and your average meal comes to around $17. Eat two of those, in addition to a $4 Mickey Ice Cream Bar, and add about $2.50 for a day's worth of the refillable mug, and you've come out just about even. Kids' Picks generally come in around $7 each. Eat two and add a $3 popsicle and the use of the refillable mug, and you've covered the day's cost.

While technically possible to eke out a savings of a dollar or two per day, those savings evaporate whenever you eat breakfast, when prices are usually lower and dessert isn't included, or whenever someone is forced to order something they ordinarily wouldn't. It also makes it difficult to schedule a table service meal or character buffet since they aren't included on the Plan. You can pay cash for such meals, but if doing so pushes you to using a credit for breakfast—or worse, ending your vacation with unused credits—the Quick Service plan will cost you money.

THE "REGULAR" DINING PLAN

The "Regular" Dining Plan—often known simply as the Disney Dining Plan—includes per person, per night:

- One quick service meal
- One table service meal
- One snack

In addition, each guest receives a refillable mug for the duration of the stay. At press time, after-tax pricing is:

- $61.82 per night for those ten and older
- $20.98 per night for kids ages three to nine

Child pricing is advantageous with a cost just $3.44 more than the Quick Service Plan. With several character buffets priced over $20, it's relatively easy for kids to come out ten dollars or more ahead each day they dine at such a venue. For those older than 9, the price of $20/per day more than the Quick Service is harder to justify. There are meals where you do well—Akershus for dinner, after tax, is over $50. A day for family members older than 9 with a typical counter service lunch, a snack, and Akershus for dinner will cost less under the Dining Plan than cash. Dinner at Crystal Palace approaches this cost, as does Chef Mickey's.

Outside of buffets, it's difficult to find restaurants with average entrée and dessert prices high enough to cover the cost of the Plan. Let's assume you're spending the day at Hollywood Studios and select 50's Prime Time Café for dinner. You select the second most expensive entrée, the $24 pork chop, and the most expensive dessert (Traditional Warm Apple Crisp a la Mode for $7.49) with a $5 milkshake as your beverage. With tax, the meal comes out to $38.87, which is $22.95 away from covering the cost of the Dining Plan with just a quick service meal and snack to go. At the costliest quick service, Fairfax Fare, the most expensive quick service meal you could put together is $24 with tax. That's about $5 higher than average. Even so, add a $4 Mickey Ice Cream Bar as a snack after going out of your way to order the most expensive items at the park. If you had simply ordered the fried chicken instead of the pork chop at 50's Prime Time, and the turkey leg instead of the chicken platter at Fairfax Fare, you would come out $2 behind the cost of one day on the Dining Plan.

The economics of two-credit meals are even worse. Signature restaurant prices generally are about 1.5x the cost of regular restaurants, but cost twice the number of credits, resulting in a lower per-credit value. For example, the most expensive meal you could put together on the Dining Plan at California Grill is a $55 Colorado Lamb Rack, $14 Chocolate Pudding Cake, and $4 Coke. That's $73, or just $36.50 per credit for the most expensive meal at one of the most expensive restaurants on property. To compare, Teppan Edo in the Japan Pavilion at Epcot offers several entrees for $28–$32. Add dessert and a drink and your single credit has a value of about $10 more than California Grill.

THE DELUXE DINING PLAN

The Deluxe Dining Plan includes per person, per day:

- Three meals per day—either quick service or table service. Table service meals include an appetizer where applicable.
- Two snacks

In addition, each guest receives a refillable mug for the duration of the stay. At press time, after-tax pricing is:

- $111.73 per night for adults
- $32.56 per night for kids ages three to nine

On paper, there is a lot of value potential here, particularly for kids under the age of ten. To maximize that value, however, you could be spending more than three hours a day dining—even more if you avoid two-credit meals—and building an itinerary largely around being at specific restaurants at specific times. And let's not forget the actual cost. A family of two adults, a 15-year old, and a 7-year old would cost a whopping $368 per day. For that, Josh and Dave will cook and serve your family of four both lunch and dinner, while intermittently breaking out into song and dance. (A word to the wise though: Josh's specialty is Hot Pockets and Dave's favorite ingredient is Sriracha.)

Saving Money on Dining

Purchasing ingredients and preparing meals where you're staying is the easiest way to slash a food budget. This works best for quick breakfasts in the room. Pack or purchase a dozen bagels or donuts, fruit, cereal and milk, and some protein bars and you can easily eliminate busy breakfasts at the resort food court, in addition to cutting meal time down to a few minutes from 30+.

Unfortunately, Disney doesn't make purchasing these items economical at its resort gift shops, for reasons you might be able to guess. Other than Fort Wilderness and the Disney Vacation Club properties, pickings can be slim and prices are high. On top of that, only Ft. Wilderness cabins and the villas in the DVC resorts have kitchens, making even simple prep work difficult in most situations. If you have a car and the time to shop, we recommend the Speedway stores on property for convenience. One is located across the street from the BoardWalk Inn near Epcot, another after the exit to Magic Kingdom parking, and the third is across the street from the Marketplace section of Disney Springs. For a better selection, visit the Winn-Dixie (and nearby liquor store) at 1957 S Apopka Vineland Rd, in Orlando, or the Publix (and nearby liquor store) at 29 Blake Boulevard, in Kissimmee. The nearest to your hotel will be about a 10–15 minute drive.

Without transportation or the ability to venture out to a supermarket on vacation, consider a grocery delivery service. We like GARDENGROCER. COM and WEGOSHOP.COM. Garden Grocer is the most popular, but you're limited to what you can order based on their web store. We Go Shop will visit whatever area store you specify for whatever specific products you want, but the delivery fee is higher. Both deliver beer and wine. Also consider Amazon Pantry, which will deliver directly to your resort.

Dining Reviews: Introduction

Brief reviews of the table service restaurants in the parks, Disney Springs, and the Disney resorts follow.

First, you'll find reviews of the restaurants inside each theme park, in alphabetical order. Next, you'll find an alphabetized list of the resorts, with reviews of all restaurants located at that resort.

We start with the venue name and location within its area, indicating also whether a meal is a character meal or a dinner show. We then note cuisine, operating hours, and whether or not it is on the Disney Dining Plan (abbreviated as DDP)—note that some DDP meals require two credits and are so indicated. Next, we give typical prices and any available discounts for Disney Vacation Club ("DVC") members, those who have purchased Tables in Wonderland ("TiW") discount cards*, Annual Passholders ("AP"), and holders of Disney Visa cards. We then get into the food and ambiance of the restaurants themselves. This material is necessarily brief—for more, see Josh's EASYWDW.COM. Prices, menus, hours, required credits, discounts etc., are all subject to change.

We also throw some Disney jargon around:

- Signature Restaurant: two credit venues usually aimed at adults—that is, thin on kid appeal, but with finer and more elegant dining. Most have a mild dress code, e.g., on men, pants are preferred, nice shorts are OK, but no tank tops.
- Family Style: food for the entire table is served on platters and shared amongst the table.
- Walk-up: trying to get a seating without having a reservation.

Note also that some venues will require full pre-payment—at press time, Hoop-Dee-Doo, Spirit of Aloha, Mickey's Backyard Barbecue, and Cinderella's Royal Table—and most others will require a credit card so that a no-show fee can be charged. To avoid no-show fees, cancel no later than 11:59pm on the day before the reservation.

*Only Annual Passholders, DVC owners, and Florida residents are eligible to buy the Tables in Wonderland card. Visit TABLESINWONDERLAND.COM for more information on availability and blackout dates. As a bonus, Tables in Wonderland holders receive 20% off their meals at Flame Tree Barbecue, Pizzafari, and Restaurantosaurus.

Dining Reviews: The Theme Parks and Disney Springs

DINING AT DISNEY'S ANIMAL KINGDOM

Disney's Animal Kingdom offers a nice variety of consistently high-quality restaurants and quick services, and we like each for different reasons. The Rainforest Café at the front of the park is much less crowded than the Disney Springs iteration, and offers the same fun atmosphere fueled by Animatronics and a vast menu. Theme park admission is not required to dine there. Tusker House in Africa is a low-key character meal featuring Donald and Mickey for all three meals. The expansive buffet area makes sampling the 30+ items easy, and the characters have more time to spend with guests than at the more crowded resort character meals. Yak & Yeti serves up fantastic Pan-Asian food in a restaurant full of authentic artifacts from India, China, and elsewhere.

Quick service options at Animal Kingdom are above average as well. Pizzafari serves up standard Disney pizza in a colorful, air-conditioned space. Pizza is serviceable, but expect to pay about $10 each for a personal pan. Restaurantosaurus in DinoLand USA is your burger and nugget option. You'll find plenty of air-conditioned seating, in addition to outdoor patio tables. Better is Yak & Yeti Local Food Cafes, which serves up Asian specialties like Teriyaki Beef and Honey Chicken. Unfortunately, all seating is outdoors, and it can be uncomfortably hot and wet in the summer. Harambe Market in the Africa section opened in May 2015 near the entrance to the Wildlife Express train that transports guests to Rafiki's Planet Watch. It adds another open-air quick service option with outdoor seating and a unique menu that includes four entrées and a half dozen South African wines. It's an excellent choice if the weather cooperates, but with all seating outdoors, it can be unpleasant in the rain or heat. Best is Flame Tree Barbecue, where you'll find Disney's best quick service ribs, pork sandwiches, and half chickens. While seating is outdoors, it's better covered with fans overhead. Walk all the way down to the water for expansive views of Asia and Expedition Everest.

Jim's Gems
by Jim Korkis

Flame Tree Barbeque offers good barbeque and a beautiful view of Expedition Everest and Discovery River. However, the counter service eatery was designed to showcase a predator and prey motif. Even the exterior sign has images of a crocodile taking a bite of a fish and an owl hunting rabbits. These motifs are repeated inside with images of snakes eating mice, anteaters slurping up ants, and spiders trapping butterflies. The backs of all the chairs feature predators, while the design on the tabletops depicts their prey. It is all part of the well-known "circle of life".

Rainforest Café

Front of park; theme park admission not required to dine

CUISINE American. **HOURS** 8:30am–park close. **DDP** Yes. **DISCOUNTS** No TiW; DVC: 10% on up to four entrees; AP: 10% on up to four entrees.

PRICES Breakfast: $10–$14. Lunch/Dinner Appetizers: $7–$19. Entrées: $13–$26. Kids: $6–$7.

OVERVIEW Part of a chain of 25+ restaurants around the world, Rainforest Cafe blends an immersive environment with a laundry list menu. Dine on steaks, pastas, salads, burgers, or one of 50+ other items, while Animatronic gorillas pound their chests, birds sing, and thunder booms from the starry night sky. The food won't impress, but it's all serviceable and portions are huge. The restaurant is extremely loud and the atmosphere may startle young children apprehensive about rides like DINOSAUR and Haunted Mansion, although older children love the atmosphere. Because it's located at the front of the park, plan to eat when you're near the entrance/exit.

Tusker House

Character meal, in Africa

CUISINE African-inspired. **DDP** Yes. **DISCOUNTS** 20% TiW.

HOURS AND PRICES *Breakfast* (8–10:55am): $32 adults, $19 kids. *Lunch* (11am–3:30pm; may extend later): $41 adults, $25 kids. *Dinner* (4:30pm–15 minutes before park close): $44 adults, $21 kids. Pricing may vary depending on the season.

OVERVIEW Donald, Daisy, Mickey, and Goofy greet guests tableside inside this vibrant African marketplace. Some of the 30+ items at each meal retain touches of African flair and spice, but Disney is careful to cater to the typical American palate. Character interaction is among the best, with the characters leading parades around the restaurant and playing games with guests.

Yak & Yeti

Asia, between Flights of Wonder and Kali River Rapids

CUISINE Asian. **HOURS** 11am–park close. **DDP** Yes. **DISCOUNTS** No TiW; DVC: 10% on up to four entrees; AP: 10% on up to four entrees.

PRICES Lunch/Dinner Appetizers: $5–$16. Entrées: $17–$26. Kids: $8–$10.

OVERVIEW Located in Asia, this air-conditioned respite is appropriately themed to a rural countryside sanctuary set in the heart of the Himalayan Mountains. The menu is reminiscent of P.F. Chang's and features such favorites as Lettuce Cups, Crispy Honey Chicken, and Sweet-and-Sour Pork, in addition to Kalbi Steak & Shrimp and a Kobe Beef Burger. Portions are large and service is friendly as guests dine amongst hundreds of authentic artifacts from all over Asia. Request a window table upstairs for a great view.

DINING AT EPCOT

Epcot offers an overwhelming number of dining options, predominantly located in World Showcase with national cuisines tied into the respective pavilions. You could very easily visit Epcot every day for a month and dine in a different venue each day. We present reviews of all the table service options below, but our recommended restaurants are Biergarten in Germany, Via Napoli in Italy, Akershus Banquet Hall in Norway, and San Angel Inn in Mexico.

Biergarten is a richly themed buffet restaurant with a cornucopia of authentic German items like beer cheese soup, sauerbraten, spaetzle, veal sausage, mini frankfurters, and a whole lot more. A live oompah band plays intermittently with guests invited up to the dance floor to sing and dance along.

Via Napoli is an authentic Neapolitan pizzeria serving the best pizza (by far) on property. A large mezzo-metro pizza is plenty to feed a family of four for about $11 per person, making it a great value. Stay conservative with a signature pepperoni pie or try something like the Prosciutto e Melone Signature Pie (fontina, mozzarella, prosciutto, and cantaloupe).

Akershus is the part-buffet, part-table service character meal in Norway. While pricey, it's significantly less expensive than Cinderella's Royal Table at the Magic Kingdom, and the price includes a digital picture with Belle in her yellow gown, along with four other princesses meeting tableside. The cold buffet guarantees everyone will have plenty to eat, and the entrees are varied and above average as well.

At San Angel Inn, guests dine underneath perpetual twilight as the boats from the Gran Fiesta Tour next door glide by. Food quality is a bit lower than at our other three picks, but the unique atmosphere can't be replicated elsewhere.

Quick service options at Epcot are even more abundant.

Of the Future World options, Sunshine Seasons near Soarin' in the Land Pavilion receives nearly universal acclaim. Serving freshly grilled pork chops, rotisserie chicken, salmon, salads, sandwiches, Asian entrees, and more, with plentiful air-conditioned seating, it's a great choice for a convenient Future World lunch. Electric Umbrella is your Future World spot for the usual Disney hamburgers and chicken nuggets, in addition to a great vegetarian flatbread.

In World Showcase, you may pick a quick service based on the mood— or location—of the group at the time. We both highly recommend Tangierine Café in Morocco. While the menu of shawarma, falafel, kefta, and tabouleh might initially seem exotic, the typical Mediterranean flavors are more familiar than you might expect. Food is also higher quality and portions are larger than at just about any other quick service. Josh likes the U.K.'s Fish and Chips, particularly when a table overlooking the lagoon is available. Liberty Inn in the U.S. serves a surprisingly good New York Strip Steak for around $12, in addition to the excellent Southwest Chicken Salad and new additions like the Fried Shrimp with Old Bay Coleslaw. With plenty of air-conditioned and outdoor seating, the only thing keeping it from being highly recommended is the fact that it's all American, and it seems like World Showcase should be an opportunity to try something a little different. Dave wishes that Liberty Inn would shift to an all-barbecue theme, highlighting all the different U.S. barbecue variants and their regional fixin's. Sommerfest in Germany is quite good, but the seating section consists of only a handful of tables, and there's rarely anywhere comfortable to sit.

We don't care much for La Cantina de San Angel in Mexico or Lotus Blossom Café in China. La Cantina is expensive and serves lower quality food than just about any other Mexican restaurant, for more money. Panda Express serves better food than Lotus Blossom. Katsura Grill in Japan doesn't live up to its potential, but the udon and chicken cutlet curry are good and the outdoor garden seating area is among the most peaceful you'll find. The sushi largely disappoints. Boulangerie Patisserie in France offers some unique quiche, sandwich, and salad fare, but the ordering process is confusing and the seating section is small, loud, and chaotic.

Overall, visiting Tangierine Café or Sunshine Seasons for lunch and one of our recommended table service restaurants for dinner is your best bet. But most guests are satisfied no matter where they choose to dine.

Akershus Royal Banquet Hall

Princess character meal, in Norway Pavilion

CUISINE Norwegian/American. **DDP** Yes. **DISCOUNTS** 20% TiW.

HOURS AND PRICES *Breakfast* (8–11:10am): $48 adults, $29 kids. *Lunch* (11:45am–3:30pm): $49 adults, $30 kids. *Dinner* (4:55pm–park close): $58 adults, $34 kids.

OVERVIEW Themed to a 14th century Scandinavian castle, Akershus is Epcot's much less expensive version of Cinderella's Royal Table. A picture with Belle begins the adventure and will be available on PhotoPass, and four other princesses meet tableside—usually Ariel, Aurora, Cinderella, and Snow White. For breakfast, guests are brought platters of hot breakfast foods like scrambled eggs, potato casserole, sausage, and bacon. Lunch and dinner feature a set menu of Norwegian and American favorites like Norwegian Meatballs with Lingonberry Sauce, Salmon, and Chicken Breast. All meals include unlimited access to the cold bar, which includes bread, salads, sliced meats, cheeses, fish, and a variety of other chilled foods, including traditional Scandinavian items. Kids' meals include pizza, salmon, pasta, and meatballs. Breakfast is the most consistent and least expensive meal.

Biergarten

Germany Pavilion

CUISINE German. **HOURS** 12pm–park close. **DDP** Yes. **DISCOUNTS** 20% TiW; 10% AP; 10% DVC; 10% Disney Visa.

PRICES Lunch: $28-$32 adults, $16-$18, kids. Dinner: $39–$43 adults, $18–$20 kids.

OVERVIEW Be transported to a quaint Bavarian village in the heart of Oktoberfest at this German buffet that features live oompah music throughout the day. Selections include bratwurst, rotisserie chicken, pork schnitzel, and a variety of seasonal salads. Dessert includes Apple Strudel and Black Forest Cake. The selection and food quality are both outstanding. Service is genuinely friendly and the music is a lot of fun. Tables seat eight and smaller parties will be seated with others. There is no dedicated buffet section for kids, though most will be happy loading up on macaroni and cheese, chicken, pretzel rolls, and dessert. The liters of beer are the best price on property.

Coral Reef

To the right of The Seas with Nemo and Friends

CUISINE American. **HOURS** 11:30am–park close. **DDP** Yes. **DISCOUNTS** 20% TiW.

PRICES Lunch/Dinner Appetizers: $7–$17. Entrées: $19–$33. Kids: $9–$11.

OVERVIEW More than 4,000 creatures, including sharks, rays, and turtles, join diners seated in front of the 5.7 million gallon aquarium glass here at Coral Reef. Food is average table service quality and the menu skews towards fish and beef with the salmon and trout standing out as excellent. Kids love the aquarium view and their menu features fried shrimp, steak, cheesy shells, and a burger. Request a lower-level aquarium view at check-in.

Garden Grill

Character meal, upper floor of the Land Pavilion

CUISINE American. **DDP** Yes. **DISCOUNTS** 20% TiW.

HOURS AND PRICES *Breakfast* (8–10:30am): $32 adults, $19 kids. *Lunch* (11:30am–3pm): $37 adults, $21 kids. *Dinner* (4–8pm): $45 adults, $21 kids.

OVERVIEW Join Chip, Dale, Mickey, and Pluto at this fun restaurant featuring views of the Living with the Land ride below. All three meals are served family-style with the usual assortment of eggs, bacon, and other favorites at breakfast. Lunch and dinner include filet of beef, turkey breast, sustainable fish of the day, vegetables, mashed potatoes, and non-alcoholic beverages (alcohol is available for an additional cost). Kids receive chicken drumsticks, macaroni-and-cheese, broccoli, and sweet potato fries. Dessert is cupcakes for the kids, and bread pudding and a baked pie for adults. Food is quite good, and this is one of the more laid-back character meals, with excellent character interaction.

La Hacienda de San Angel

Mexico Pavilion, outside on the water

CUISINE Mexican. **HOURS** 4pm–park close. **DDP** Yes. **DISCOUNTS** No TiW; 10% DVC.

PRICES Dinner Appetizers: $7–$13. Entrées: $24–$27. Kids: $8–$10.

OVERVIEW This restaurant on the Lagoon features floor-to-ceiling windows with the potential for grand views of World Showcase Lagoon. The limited menu (five entrée choices averaging $26) skews away from typical Tex-Mex and towards grilled and marinated meats and seafood. Parties of two or more should stick to one of the two combination skillets for $59 each; plenty of food for up to three to share. Kids' meals include cheese quesadillas, steak or chicken tacos, and grilled chicken. Food quality and service range from below average to average. The nearby San Angel Inn is more charming.

Le Cellier Steakhouse

Canada Pavilion (look for the walkway down to the O Canada! show)

CUISINE Steak and fish, mostly. **HOURS** 12pm–park close. **DDP** 2 Credits. **DISCOUNTS** 20% TiW.

PRICES Lunch/Dinner Appetizers: $10–$17. Entrées: $28–$50. Kids: $8–$15.

OVERVIEW Now a two-credit signature meal on the Dining Plan, this dark, wine-cellar-themed restaurant that focuses on Canadian beef is an expensive proposition. No steak currently comes in under $49. While cozy, tables are virtually on top of each other, creating a less-than-intimate atmosphere. Food quality is high and service is typically above average, but it's hard to justify these prices. On the plus side, the $10 cheese soup is excellent, the complimentary pretzel bread is out of this world, and the Unibroue beer on draft is world-class. Kids, who are unlikely to be enthralled by the restaurant, can get in on the action with a grilled sirloin steak, seared salmon, and a kids' portion of the cheese soup.

Les Chefs de France

France Pavilion, ground level

CUISINE French. **HOURS** 12pm–park close. **DDP** Yes. **DISCOUNTS** 20% TiW lunch only; 15% DVC lunch only; 10% AP Lunch Monday-Friday

PRICES Lunch/Dinner Appetizers: $7–$15. Lunch Entrées: $15–$30. Dinner Entrées: $19–$35. Kids: $8–$10.

OVERVIEW This family-friendly Parisian café provides a casual atmosphere for guests to sample French cuisine like Quiche Lorraine, Casserole of Burgundian Escargots, and Duck Breast and Leg Confit. Steaks, roasted chicken, and broiled salmon are also available. The charming French service is perhaps a bit too authentic at times, but meals at this busy brasserie are a lot of fun. The three-course lunch for under $30 is an excellent value. The kids' menu may be limiting, with just Chicken Strips, Ground Beef Steak on a Brioche Bun, and Grilled Fish typically available.

Monsieur Paul

France Pavilion, above Les Chefs de France

CUISINE French. **HOURS** 5:30pm–park close. **DDP** 2 credits. **DISCOUNTS** None.

PRICES Dinner Appetizers: $14-$29. Entrées: $38–$43. Kids: $13.

OVERVIEW This upscale gourmet French restaurant replaced Bistro de Paris above Les Chefs de France in December 2012. Couples looking for the most intimate experience inside Epcot should look no further, but the formal atmosphere is not particularly kid friendly. In fact, the restaurant only recently introduced a kids' menu that includes just roasted chicken breast or filet mignon served with mashed potatoes. The very French staff may struggle to communicate in English, but they are among the most attentive property wide. Food impresses in quality and presentation and is not much more expensive than the pricier entrees downstairs.

Nine Dragons

China Pavilion

CUISINE Chinese. **HOURS** 12pm–park close. **DDP** Yes. **DISCOUNTS** 20% TiW; 10% AP Lunch Monday-Friday only; 20% DVC lunch; 10% DVC dinner.

PRICES Lunch/Dinner Appetizers: $4–$12. Entrées: $13–$27. Kids: $8–$10.

OVERVIEW Featuring a beautiful glass mural of two dragons chasing a glowing pearl, rosewood wall panels, and Chinese lantern lighting, Nine Dragons is not your typical neighborhood dive. The menu offers familiar favorites like Kung Pao Chicken ($16) and Honey-Sesame Chicken ($17) along with traditional dishes like the Fragrant Five-Spiced Fish ($22). Kids can get in on the action with interesting items like Pot Stickers, Sweet-and-Sour Chicken, and Ginger Ice Cream. Portions are huge and the kitchen consistently executes food that is less expensive than other restaurants. Service is friendly but tends to be abrupt. While Nine Dragons suffers from a poor reputation, we think it's improved handily in recent memory and don't have any qualms about recommending it, particularly as a last-minute walk-up.

Restaurant Marrakesh

Morocco Pavilion, in the very back

CUISINE Moroccan/Mediterranean. **HOURS** 11:30am–park close. **DDP** Yes. **DISCOUNTS** 20% TiW; 10% AP Lunch Monday–Friday only; 20% DVC.

PRICES Lunch/Dinner Appetizers: $6–$17. Lunch Entrées $15–$28. Dinner Entrées $21–$45. Kids: $8–$10.

OVERVIEW This hard-to-find restaurant in the back of the Morocco Pavilion is unique and under-rated. Themed to an ornate Moroccan palace, stained-glass chandeliers provide the only light for the visiting band and belly dancer that perform throughout the day. Lunch is a better value with the same entrees as dinner at reduced prices, including a three-course chicken kebab lunch under $20. Kids' entrees may disappoint, offering only chicken tenders, a hamburger, or Moroccan-style Pasta. Consider letting adventuresome kids sample some items from one of the adult feast samplers. Rarely busy, this is the easiest walk-up at Epcot and the easiest reservation to snag same-day.

Rose & Crown Dining Room

United Kingdom Pavilion

CUISINE British. **HOURS** 12pm–park close. **DDP** Yes. **DISCOUNTS** 20% TiW.

PRICES Lunch/Dinner Appetizers: $6–$12. Entrées: $15–$31. Kids: $9–$11.

OVERVIEW Situated along World Showcase Lagoon, Rose & Crown provides the only guaranteed IllumiNations viewing from a restaurant. Views are best outside on the patio, but guests seated inside the family-friendly pub, heavy on wooden furniture, will be invited outside shortly before the show. Food quality has fallen in recent years as chefs seem to push out a new menu every couple months. Stick with long-standing favorites like Bangers & Mash, Fish & Chips, and Shepherd's Pie. Kids choose from a menu that includes steak and fish & chips.

Rose & Crown Pub

United Kingdom Pavilion

CUISINE Mostly beer. **HOURS** 12pm–park close. **DDP** No. **DISCOUNTS** 20% TiW.

PRICES Limited food menu with prices ranging from $4–$13.

OVERVIEW Frosted windows protect the privacy of those imbibing inside this cozy pub, which is virtually always hopping. The entrance is separate from the restaurant and reservations are not accepted here. Draft beer includes Bass, Bodington's, Guinness, Stella, and Harp. Scotch flights, mixed drinks like the Pimm's Cup, and wine are other options.

San Angel Inn

Mexico Pavilion, inside the pyramid

CUISINE Mexican. **HOURS** 11:30am–park close. **DDP** Yes. **DISCOUNTS** 20% TiW; 10% AP Lunch Monday–Friday only; 10% DVC.

PRICES Lunch/Dinner Appetizers: $8–$13. Lunch Entrées: $18–$27. Dinner Entrées: $24–$29. Kids: $9–$10.

OVERVIEW San Angel Inn sits inside the Mesoamerican pyramid, and is themed as a Mexican village square at twilight. The evening theming makes the restaurant dark, to the point where reading the menu is nearly impossible without the help of tabletop candles. Like La Hacienda outside, the limited menu focuses on grilled meats rather than burritos and enchiladas. Unfortunately, tables are so close together that diners a table over might as well be on your reservation, eliminating any sense of intimacy. A good family choice as parents will find the setting romantic, and kids will find it fun. Request a table on the water for a delightful view of the Gran Fiesta Tour boats gliding by below. Kids' menu items include beef or chicken tacos, cheese quesadillas, and grilled chicken or tilapia.

Spice Road Table

Morocco Pavilion, along the Lagoon

CUISINE Moroccan/Mediterranean. **HOURS** 11am–park close. **DDP** Yes. **DISCOUNTS** 20% TiW.

PRICES Small Plates: $7–$12. Entrees: $24-30. Kids: $8.

OVERVIEW This water-side eatery offers small-plate Mediterranean specialties like lamb sliders, fried calamari, and harissa chicken rolls. Additional emphasis is placed on mixed drinks, Moroccan wine, and Mediterranean beer. Spice Road accepts reservations, but walk-ups are nearly always available without a wait. Unfortunately, small plates do not translate to good values here, and two or three $8 plates of bland food in limited quantities are unlikely to satisfy most appetites. Entrée options are limited to just five and include items like Mixed Grill Beef and Chicken Skewers and Coriander-crusted Rack of Lamb. Kids can pick from a Beef Slider or Chicken Kebab for $8 each. The view of IllumiNations is mostly blocked by islands and trees. Stop by for drinks and snacks, but crafting a filling meal here will be more expensive than Restaurant Marrakesh in the back of the pavilion.

Teppan Edo

Japan Pavilion, above Mitsukoshi Department Store

CUISINE Japanese steakhouse. **HOURS** 12pm–park close. **DDP** Yes. **DISCOUNTS** No TiW. 10% AP Lunch; 10% DVC Lunch.

PRICES Lunch/Dinner Appetizers: $4–$10. Sushi: $10–$16. Entrées: $18–$32. Kids: $9–$14.

OVERVIEW This Japanese steakhouse seats eight guests around each of the many hibachi grills in one of six contemporary, windowless dining rooms. Parties with fewer than eight will most likely be seated with other parties. Food is prepared at each grill by Japanese chefs who interact with guests and put on a small show while cooking. Steak, chicken, shrimp, swordfish, vegetables, and other entrees are consistently under-seasoned, but the accompanying dips aid flavor. All meals arrive alongside rice and yakisoba. Kids are usually enamored by the friendly chefs as meals are created before their eyes. Service is sweet and attentive. We would rate this restaurant higher if it weren't so similar to the Benihana chain.

Tokyo Dining

Japan Pavilion, above Mitsukoshi Department Store

CUISINE Japanese, mostly tempura and sushi. **HOURS** 12pm–park close. **DDP** Yes. **DISCOUNTS** 20% TiW; 10% AP Lunch; 10% DVC Lunch.

PRICES Lunch/Dinner Appetizers: $3–$12. Individual Sushi: $10–$16. Sushi Samplers: $13–$28. Entrées: $17–$30. Kids: $11–$12.

OVERVIEW Tokyo Dining is a sleek, traditional Japanese restaurant with floor-to-ceiling windows looking out at World Showcase Lagoon on one side. It is much quieter and calmer than sister restaurant Teppan Edo, and, without the hibachi grills, is a more traditional dining experience. The menu focuses on sushi and tempura, with over two dozen selections. Kids enjoy their choice of teriyaki chicken or tempura chicken or shrimp. Service is among the friendliest anywhere. Go for dinner when the menu is the same as lunch.

Tutto Italia

Italy Pavilion, on the left

CUISINE Italian. **HOURS** 11:30am–park close. **DDP** Yes. **DISCOUNTS** 20% TiW; 10% AP Lunch Monday–Friday only; 15% DVC.

PRICES Lunch/Dinner Appetizers: $9–$30. Lunch Entrées: $17–$30. Dinner Entrées: $23–$30. Kids: $10+.

OVERVIEW Featuring murals of ancient Rome amid shimmering chandeliers, Tutto Italia evokes Old World charm inside this traditional, formal Italian restaurant. Your omnipresent server will cater to your every need as you peruse a menu heavy on pasta, prosciutto, and lean protein. Lunch is much less expensive than dinner, with most sandwiches and entrees under $20. Unlike most restaurants that offer "Kids Complete Meals" for $9–$12, Italia offers only a la carte options with $6 appetizers, $10 entrees (pizza, spaghetti, mozzarella sticks, chicken tenders), and $6 desserts. The venue is not unique, but service is splendid with high-quality food and a keen eye for detail.

Via Napoli

Italy Pavilion, in the back

CUISINE Pizza (predominantly). **HOURS** 11:30am–park close. **DDP** Yes. **DISCOUNTS** 20% TiW; 10% AP Lunch Monday-Friday; 15% DVC.

PRICES Lunch/Dinner Appetizers: $8–$26. Salad Entrées: $18–$24. Pasta Entrées: $21–$30. Pizzas: $17–$41. Kids: $10+.

OVERVIEW Themed to a rustic Neapolitan pizzeria, Via Napoli takes its pizza, which is cooked at 900 degrees in one of three wood-fired ovens, very seriously. So seriously that they import their flour and tomatoes from Italy and source water from a secret spring in Pennsylvania that has the same unique properties as water from the homeland. Prices may seem high at first glance, but a $41 specialty mezzo metro pizza is plenty to feed four to five hungry adults, bringing per-person costs lower than most other Disney restaurants. Napoli is loud and service is frequently impersonal, but stick to the big pizzas and you'll leave satisfied for not much more money than quick service.

DINING AT DISNEY'S HOLLYWOOD STUDIOS

Disney's Hollywood Studios runs the food quality gamut more than any of the other theme parks. Our recommendations are Sci-Fi Dine-In Theater and 50's Prime Time Café, both of which offer richly themed atmospheres and relatively inexpensive fare. Dave prefers the comfort food favorites at 50's Prime Time, while Josh gives the nod to Sci-Fi, with its fun mockup of a dine-in theater and inexpensive sandwich and hamburger fare. Much more expensive—and with much finer food—is Hollywood Brown Derby, a signature restaurant (two credits on the Dining Plan) where the servers wear tuxedos and the fancy entrees average $33. Mama Melrose serves relatively inexpensive basic Italian favorites alongside flatbread pizzas that are higher quality than nearby Pizza Planet for only a couple dollars more. Hollywood & Vine is a fun character buffet for breakfast and lunch with kids still at the Disney Junior age, but dinner is too expensive when considering the low quality food and lack of characters most of the year.

Quick service fare has improved at the Studios, but is still lacking compared to the other parks. Best are Studio Catering Co. and Starring

Rolls, both of which serve above-average sandwiches. Starring Rolls sandwiches are served cold, while many of Studio Catering Co.'s are freshly pressed and served warm. Sunset Ranch Market offers the widest selection of food, including barbecue, pizza, hamburgers, and turkey legs, but seating is all outside and the multiple storefronts that make up the market necessitate standing in more than one line if you'd like to order different kinds of food.

We're less enthusiastic about most of the other options. Toy Story Pizza Planet serves up standard Disney pizza in a loud atmosphere, but the setting does not resemble Pizza Planet from the movie, making it disappointing for guests expecting more. Backlot Express is your spot for typical Disney burgers and chicken nuggets, in addition to hot dog and sandwich offerings. It's richly themed with a lot of covered outdoor seating, but the food is decidedly below average. Finally, ABC Commissary offers the most air-conditioned seating and a newly improved menu featuring an Asian salad with chicken and a couscous, quinoa, and arugula salad with salmon, but the steak is nowhere near as good as at Liberty Inn at Epcot. Overall, we recommend Studio Catering Co., Starring Rolls, and Sunset Ranch Market first, with Backlot Express and ABC Commissary as air-conditioned backups for simpler food.

50's Prime Time Café

Echo Lake, near Hollywood & Vine

CUISINE American comfort food. **HOURS** 11am–park close. **DDP** Yes. **DISCOUNTS** 20% TiW.

PRICES Lunch/Dinner Appetizers: $6–$11. Entrees: $14–$24. Kids: $9.

OVERVIEW This nostalgic throwback to a simpler time features a number of period piece knick-knacks as well as televisions that show clips from 1950s-era shows. Themed to Mom's kitchen, your servers will take responsibility for raising you right and dole out punishment as required. The kids are sure to get a kick out of your server chastising Dad for wearing his Mickey Ears to the table. A good sense of humor is needed to enjoy the fried chicken, pot roast, meatloaf, and Mom's other comfort foods. Fried chicken, the fresh fish, and the chicken pot pie are your best bets. Request a table with a TV.

Hollywood Brown Derby

End of Hollywood Boulevard, on the right

CUISINE Contemporary American fine dining. **HOURS** 11:30am–park close. **DDP** 2 credits. **DISCOUNTS** 20% TiW; 10% AP; 10% DVC; 10% Disney Visa.

PRICES Lunch/Dinner Appetizers: $9–$16. Entrees: $29–$49. Kids: $6–$14.

OVERVIEW Serving up the best food at Hollywood Studios, this signature restaurant focuses on Filets of Beef and Blue Lump Crab Spring Rolls rather than burgers and chicken nuggets. This replica of the original Brown Derby retains much of the glitz and glamour of the 1930s original, with white linen tablecloths, tuxedo-clad servers, and an exquisite eye for detail. That is, if it weren't for all the guests wearing cargo shorts, WDW t-shirts, and Goofy hats. Kids are unlikely to connect with the restaurant, but they are more than welcome, with a kids' menu that includes hot dogs, fish sticks, grilled black grouper, and penne pasta.

When the weather is nice, the outdoor patio area works as a walk-up lounge that offers a menu of tapas and drinks, in addition to the full Brown Derby menu. If there's space, it's a great way to indulge on a margarita flight or glass of wine alongside a famous Cobb Salad or innovative sliders. The only discount the lounge accepts is Tables in Wonderland.

Hollywood & Vine

Character meal (breakfast and lunch, only), at Echo Lake near 50's Prime Time Café

CUISINE American. **DDP** Yes. **DISCOUNTS** 20% TiW; 10% AP Breakfast; 10% DVC; 10% Disney Visa.

HOURS AND PRICES *Breakfast* (8–10:55am): $32 adults, $19 kids. *Lunch* (11am–2:25pm): $41 adults, $25 kids. *Dinner* (3:30pm–30 minutes before park close, no characters): $37 adults, $20 kids. Pricing may vary by season.

OVERVIEW Featuring Doc McStuffins, Sofia the First, Jake from *Jake and the Neverland Pirates*, and Handy Manny for Play 'n Dine breakfast and lunch, this character meal is squarely aimed at kids who are invited to join the characters for singing, dancing, and parading throughout the meal. Food is best at breakfast, which includes all the usual suspects like Mickey waffles, bacon, and made-to-order omelets. Lunch and dinner bring specialties like Pastrami Rubbed Porkloin, Beer Braised Boneless Beef Short Ribs, and Lobster & Shrimp Mac n' Cheese that all sound better than they taste. Visit this extremely loud buffet only for breakfast or lunch with kids excited about meeting the characters, as food quality is average at best. The expensive, characterless dinner should be skipped.

Note: The restaurant is home to occasional, seasonal character dinners. Check disneyworld.com or ask when booking if anything special is going on.

Mama Melrose's Ristorante Italiano

Streets of America, across from the exit to Muppet Vision 3D

CUISINE Americanized Italian. **HOURS** 12pm–park close. **DDP** Yes. **DISCOUNTS** 20% TiW.

PRICES Lunch/Dinner Appetizers: $6–$11. Entrees: $13–$35; Kids: $9.

OVERVIEW Mama Melrose herself (not really) serves up Americanized Italian food in this backlot warehouse that's been repurposed (not really) into an eclectic neighborhood eatery. Mama does pizzas ($17 or less), spaghetti ($20), and Chicken alla Parmigiana ($20) better than the more expensive steaks ($33) and Pork Tenderloin ($24). With one menu served all day, Mama is best at dinner. While not as richly themed as Sci-Fi or 50's, Mama's checked curtains, overhead Christmas lights, and old-time photographs of Disney characters create a fun and casual atmosphere. Kids' menu includes cheese pizzas, chicken parmesan, spaghetti, and grilled chicken.

Sci-Fi Dine-In Theater

Streets of America, near ABC Commissary

CUISINE American. **HOURS** 12pm–park close. **DDP** Yes. **DISCOUNTS** 20% TiW.

PRICES *Breakfast* (8–10:15am, fixed price): $24 adults, $13 kids. Lunch/ Dinner (11am–30 minutes before park close, a la carte): Appetizers: $6–$11. Entrees: $14–$32. Kids: $9.

OVERVIEW Diners sit inside classic car-shaped booths at this indoor "drive-in theater" while old black-and-white movie clips, trailers, and commercials play on a large movie screen ahead. Above, the ceiling is lit up like the night sky, complete with twinkling stars. A fixed-price breakfast is being tested through January 23 with the expectation that it will continue after that. Start with a yogurt parfait or fresh fruit. Entrees include grilled beef tenderloin or a puff pastry filled with scrambled eggs, crab, asparagus, and Gruyère cheese with roasted tomatoes and avocado, in addition to the standard eggs/bacon/sausage/potatoes. The lunch/dinner menu offers several sandwiches and burgers under $16 all day, making this a great value out-of-pocket at dinner. The more expensive steak ($32) and

Jim's Gems
by Jim Korkis

Mama Melrose's Ristorante Italiano was supposed to be an interactive restaurant called The Great Gonzo's Pizza Pandemonium Parlor run by Gonzo and Rizzo the Rat who would make appearances with other Muppets during the dining experience. When Jim Henson passed away in May 1990, the final contracts allowing Disney to acquire the Muppets franchise were never completed. Many Muppets-related projects, including this one, were cancelled. Instead, the Imagineers developed a back story of a fictional young girl who came to Hollywood to open an authentic Italian restaurant to feed the movie stars.

chicken pasta ($24) don't offer as much value. The restaurant is dark, but kids usually love the carhop shtick and campy clips on screen. Kids' meal choices include grilled salmon, cheeseburgers, popcorn chicken, and pasta.

DINING AT MAGIC KINGDOM

Three of the most popular restaurants in all of Walt Disney World are in Magic Kingdom, with the likelihood that a fourth will be added when Skipper Canteen opens in Adventureland in late 2015. Overwhelmingly the most popular is Be Our Guest Restaurant. Not only does it serve upscale, French-inspired fare at (relatively) reasonable prices, but it's also the first (and only) place at the Magic Kingdom to offer wine or beer with dinner. The restaurant operates as a quick service for breakfast from 8–10am and then serves lunch from 10:30am to 2:30pm daily. It's currently the only quick service that not only accepts reservations for breakfast and lunch up to 180 days in advance, but largely requires them if you'd like to dine. They do accept a limited number of walkups if you're unable to secure a reservation, particularly after 2pm. If you're interested in reserving breakfast or lunch, do so as early as possible.

Magic Kingdom is also home to two of the most popular character meals: Crystal Palace and Cinderella's Royal Table. The Crystal Palace buffet features Winnie the Pooh, Tigger, Piglet, and Eeyore in a Victorian solarium setting. Royal Table is located inside Cinderella Castle and includes a picture with Cinderella, in addition to four princesses meeting diners tableside. Both are excellent overall experiences for the target audience, but neither is likely to impress on food quality alone.

Liberty Tree Tavern is best for cash lunch, when entrées like the pot roast and turkey come in under $20 each, in addition to burgers, salads, and sandwiches that are priced around $15. The family-style dinner is similar food, but will run you about $36 per adult. For big appetites, or for those on the Disney Dining Plan, dinner may make more sense. Plaza Restaurant and Tony's Town Square serve one menu all day. We prefer Plaza, where most sandwiches come in under $15 and the quaint Victorian theming charms. We're less enthusiastic about Tony's Town Square after it went to just one menu served all day in June 2015. Many of the less expensive options were eliminated and what's left is generally overpriced and lower quality than most other restaurants, though the remaining pizzas in the $15-$18 range are much better than their quick service counterparts.

The character meals are excellent if you can swing the cost and have members of the group that want to meet the characters. Otherwise, for table service lunch with cash, we like Liberty Tree Tavern. Dinner is best at Be Our Guest and Plaza Restaurant. You'll find more details on each of these table service restaurants in the reviews that follow.

With only a few exceptions, Magic Kingdom quick service is mostly burgers, hot dogs, and chicken nuggets. Josh's recommendation is Columbia Harbour House, where you'll find grilled salmon, lobster rolls, fried shrimp platters, a tuna fish or hummus and broccoli slaw sandwich, and great soups and fresh salads. The second floor seating area is usually quiet because there's no elevator access for strollers and the view of the Rapunzel area is more scenic than most. We also like Pinocchio Village Haus in Fantasyland, which serves interesting flatbread pizzas, salads, and an Italian sub sandwich.

Cosmic Ray's in Tomorrowland offers a lot of options with plenty of air-conditioned seating, but food quality is just average. Ray's also serves a different menu at each of its three "bays", resulting in guests having to wait in multiple lines if they'd like to order different items. Reducing the potential value of the Quick Service Dining Plan, the popular $16+ chicken and rib combo is only available after 4pm. Pecos Bill in Frontierland serves burritos, rice bowls, and fajita platters with choice of chicken, vegetables, or beef. Entrees are a couple of dollars more expensive than most, but portions are on the large side and unlimited toppings from the expansive fixins' bar are included. Casey's Corner, serving up a few variations of the usual hot dog, is the last major quick service. About $10 buys you a chicken/beef dog with your choice of chili/cheese or barbecue pork/coleslaw with fries or apple slices. A polish sausage topped with onions and mustard is available, in addition to a plain hot dog. While filling, they are pricey for a low quality, non-kosher dog.

Several quick service outlets are seasonal, based on expected crowds, or operate with limited hours. Tortuga Tavern, with its burrito and rice bowl fare usually served in Adventureland from 11am–3pm, is worth checking out for lunch. Sleepy Hollow Refreshments in Liberty Square serves excellent, economically priced waffle sandwiches with spicy chicken or ham, prosciutto, and swiss from 11am–5pm. The others, including Diamond Horseshoe, Friar's Nook, and Tomorrowland Terrace, are best skipped.

Overall, we suggest Columbia Harbour House, Be Our Guest, and Pecos Bill for quick service lunch.

Be Our Guest Restaurant

Fantasyland, near Belle's Village

CUISINE French/American. **HOURS** 4pm–park close. **DDP** Yes. **DISCOUNTS** 20% TiW Dinner Only.

PRICES Dinner Appetizers: $5–$16. Entrées: $17–$33. Kids: $9-$11. (Lunch and breakfast are available as reservable quick service meals. Make a reservation as early as you can because they're severely limited.)

OVERVIEW Set inside Beast's enchanted castle, Be Our Guest is Disney's (arguably) most lavishly themed restaurant and currently the hardest reservation to snag. With three elaborately themed rooms, you may find yourself in the dark and mysterious West Wing, the expansive two-story Grand Ballroom, or the bright Rose Gallery complete with a spinning Belle and Beast music box. The menu is French-inspired and includes items like Thyme-scented Pork Rack Chops, Pan-seared Salmon on Leek Fondue, and Herb-crusted Lamb Rack with a Stone-ground Mustard Demi-glace, all under $30 each. The kids' menu may be too refined for the picky eater and includes Grilled Cheese and Tomato Soup, Beast Casserole, Grilled Steak, Chicken Brochette, and Grilled Fish of the Day. Food and service are better than any other Magic Kingdom restaurant, and it's worth going out of your way to book at 180 days if possible.

Cinderella's Royal Table

Princess character meal, in Cinderella Castle with check-in at rear of castle

CUISINE American. **DDP** Yes (2 credits). **DISCOUNTS** 20% TiW.

HOURS AND PRICES *Breakfast* (8–10:40am): $60 adults, $37 kids. *Lunch* (11:45am–2:40pm): $62 adults, $40 kids. *Dinner* (3:50–9:40pm): $74 adults, $44 kids.

OVERVIEW By far the most popular character meal, dining here is ordinarily the only way for guests to see the inside of Cinderella Castle. The pricey affair begins in the Grand Hall waiting area and continues through a personal meet and greet with Cinderella on the ground floor. Continue up the red-carpeted spiraling staircase and enter the banquet hall fit for kings and queens. Four princesses greet tableside–usually Ariel, Aurora, Jasmine, and Snow White, and a picture package with Cinderella is available on PhotoPass. Diners select items from a set menu featuring upscale fare. Breakfast choices include the standard plate of bacon, eggs, and sausage, or the more lavish Lobster and Crab Crêpes, or Grilled Beef Tenderloin. Lunch brings items like Braised Short Rib and Gnocchi with Roasted Vegetables. Dinner offers similar items along with Beef Tenderloin. Food quality and service are decent, but you're paying for the magical atmosphere, princess interaction, and photos. For cash, breakfast is the best and cheapest meal; on the DDP, all meals are two credits. Lunch is the easiest reservation to snag.

The Crystal Palace

Character meal, at end of Main Street on the left, past Casey's Corner

CUISINE American. **DDP** Yes. **DISCOUNTS** 20% TiW.

HOURS AND PRICES *Breakfast* (8–10:45am): $28 adults, $16 kids. *Lunch* (11:30am–2:45pm): $41 adults, $25 kids. *Dinner* (3pm–park close): $45 adults, $27 kids.

OVERVIEW Join Winnie the Pooh, Tigger, Eeyore, and Piglet at this all-you-care-to-enjoy buffet. The bright, airy restaurant is inspired by Victorian greenhouses of the late 1800s, complete with high ceilings, character topiaries, and plenty of natural sunlight. Character interaction is above average, as is the food, which includes Spit-roasted Carved meats, Spice Boiled Shrimp, 20+ salads, and over a dozen desserts. Crystal Palace is often the most over-booked restaurant on property. Even with a reservation, plan to wait 15–30 minutes for your table. For guests paying cash, an early lunch is the best choice—cheaper than dinner, shorter waits, and no rush to get through the meal.

Jungle Navigation Co., Ltd. Skipper Canteen

Adventureland near Sunshine Tree Terrace and Swiss Family Robinson Treehouse

Expected to open in December 2015, Skipper Canteen looks to push the envelope further than Be Our Guest Restaurant in Fantasyland, marrying innovative design details with a menu of authentic flavors born from the adventures of the punny Jungle Cruise skippers just down the road. With several unique dining rooms, including a crew mess hall and a previously secret meeting room used by the famous Society of Explorers and Adventurers, the restaurant will offer new experiences for returning diners as well. Exact details remain slim, but this is sure to be a popular and fun location for years to come.

Liberty Tree Tavern

Liberty Square, near Diamond Horseshoe

CUISINE American. **DDP** Yes. **DISCOUNTS** 20% TiW.

HOURS AND PRICES *Table service Lunch* (11:30am–3pm): Appetizers: $6–$15. Entrees: $13–$24. Kids: $9. *Family-style Dinner* (4pm–park close): $36 adults, $18 kids.

OVERVIEW Lunch is the usual table service gig with an a la carte menu, with entrees that average $15, while dinner is served family style. Liberty Tree is a Colonial-themed tavern, featuring candelabra chandeliers, brick fireplaces, and rooms filled with artifacts from some of America's most famous patriots. Lunch is significantly less expensive, with entrees plenty large enough to fill up the biggest appetites. Guests choosing to pay about

$40/adult for the Thanksgiving-inspired dinner will receive a wider variety of foods, in addition to dessert and non-alcoholic beverages. We prefer a late lunch at this well-air-conditioned, moderately priced restaurant where the turkey, pot roast, and salad are similar to dinner. Other lunch options include pasta, sandwiches, and a burger. Kids choose from turkey, pasta with marinara, macaroni and cheese, and flatbread pizza.

The Plaza Restaurant

End of Main Street, on the right

CUISINE American. **HOURS** 11am–park close. **DDP** Yes. **DISCOUNTS** 20% TiW.

PRICES Lunch/ Dinner Entrees: $13–$19. Kids: $9.

OVERVIEW Continuing the Main Street theme, The Plaza features Art Nouveau touches inside a turn-of-the-century ice cream parlor. By far the least expensive theme park sit-down-restaurant, Plaza is an excellent choice for cash guests on a budget, particularly at dinner, when sandwiches are all under $15 and no item is over $20. Kids' options include a cheese sandwich, burger, chicken strips, turkey sandwich, and PB&J. Food and service are great for the money, but we are not talking highfalutin' dining at this casual eatery.

Tony's Town Square Restaurant

Entry Plaza, on the right

CUISINE Americanized Italian. **HOURS** 11:30am–park close. **DDP** Yes. **DISCOUNTS** 20% TiW.

PRICES Lunch/Dinner Appetizers: $7–$10. Dinner Entrees: $15–$33. Kids: $9.

OVERVIEW Modeled after Tony's from *Lady and the Tramp*, guests have an opportunity to relive the romance at this casual family trattoria that serves Olive-Garden-quality Italian food in a relaxing atmosphere. Since moving to one menu all day, Tony's has eliminated many of the less expensive lunch entrées that presented a good value to diners. Quality on the higher-end items doesn't justify the prices, and we usually recommend that people head elsewhere. Kids' choices include spaghetti, pizzas, and pasta. Service is conspicuously fast, with most meals complete within an hour.

DINING AT DISNEY SPRINGS
....

Construction continues on Downtown Disney's transformation into Disney Springs with the expectation that it will be complete sometime in late 2016. New venues will open intermittently between now and then as work continues.

The Disney Springs ("DS" or occasionally "Springs") shopping and entertainment complex includes more than a dozen third-party-operated table service restaurants and quick services, most on the Dining Plan and reservable on My Disney Experience. Some, like The Boathouse, Paradiso 37, and Raglan Road, have additional capacity that can be reserved directly with the restaurant over the phone or via OpenTable. com. Even more restaurants will come as part of the current expansion. In addition to restaurants, you'll find many stores, some Disney and others of the variety you'd find at the local mall. There's also the AMC movie theater, Splitsville upscale bowling alley, DisneyQuest interactive arcade (expected to close summer 2016 to make way for the NBA Experience), and a Cirque du Soleil show called La Nouba.

Disney Springs features four distinct neighborhoods: The Landing, Marketplace, West Side, and Town Center. The bulk of the new venues are found in The Landing and Town Center, while The West Side and Marketplace remain relatively untouched from their former Downtown Disney days.

The West Side. The West Side is dominated by the Cirque du Soleil, DisneyQuest (expected to close around July 2016 to make way for an NBA Experience), Splitsville, and AMC buildings, with a sprinkling of retail and several restaurants and quick services.

West Side quick service options are diverse, though relatively limited. Bongos Cuban Café includes a small takeout window offering mostly sandwiches with a few traditional Cuban entrees from the kitchen available to-go. With drab outdoor seating as the only option, most guests will bypass it for something more comfortable. House of Blues opened a very good barbecue joint in late 2013 —seating is also outside, but live music permeates the area beginning daily around 4pm and happy hour offers some drink specials from 3pm to 5pm daily. One of two Wolfgang Puck Express locations is attached to the restaurant across from the movie theater. The pizza is excellent, but the menu is far less diverse than the Express location in the Marketplace and seating is again all outdoors. The larger of the two Starbucks locations is here, reliably offering the company's usual beverage and food lineup for about the same cost as your local shop. Beginning at 4pm daily, the menu expands to include wine and additional food offerings. Finally, Disney has gotten into the food truck game with an area dedicated to food trucks between Bongos and Wolfgang Puck. The trucks serve a variety of Disney favorites from around the globe, like a corn dog similar to what's served at Corn Dog Castle in Disneyland, in addition to offerings inspired by Disney World locations like Hollywood Studios and Animal Kingdom Lodge.

On the table service front, Splitsville often has last-minute availability and is an easy walk-up when other restaurants are quoting 45+ minute waits without a reservation, as they often are after 6pm. Its pizza, burgers, and sushi are surprisingly good. House of Blues is economically priced and extremely casual for a nice, no-fuss lunch or dinner. It may be busier if a popular act is scheduled to perform in the club next door. Bongos Cuban Café's menu favors quantity over quality, where you'll find over 50 entrée choices. Grab a mojito from the outdoor bar and look for dinner elsewhere. We don't have a lot of nice things to say about the Wolfgang Puck Café or the Grand Café above it. Food, service, and ambiance are better elsewhere. Coming in last is Planet Hollywood, which is the worst restaurant on just about every front —loud, garish, and expensive.

The Landing. Once home to Pleasure Island, The Landing shifts focus away from the clubs and dance halls that used to permeate the area and replaces them with restaurants, bars, and outdoor music in the evenings. There are some holdovers from the previous era: Paradiso 37, Portobello, Fulton's Crab House, and Raglan Road. For lunch, our favorite is Fulton's Crab House, which is located in a riverboat on the water. The lunch menu replicates the famous dinner menu's focus on fish and seafood, but the lobster is found in a sandwich for $16 instead of on a plate for $50+. Lunch at next-door Portobello is also a good value—the same great Italian food as at dinner for about half the price, but in a forgettable atmosphere. Raglan Road Irish Pub is best at dinner. While prices are a couple dollars higher here and there, the live music and dancing are worth the extra cost. Paradiso is great for appetizers and margaritas, but the south-of-the-border entrees are overpriced and the atmosphere is lackluster considering the other options.

The BOATHOUSE (the capitalization is part of the name), offering mostly upscale seafood and steaks, opened in May 2015 and was the first of the many major new restaurants coming with the expansion to open. Operated by Gibsons out of Chicago, food is usually excellent, but the casual atmosphere may or may not endear diners to the high price points. Morimoto Asia, brought to you by Chef Masaharu Morimoto of Iron Chef fame, opened in September 2015, serving high end seafood, sushi, and Asian cuisine in an upscale atmosphere. Jock Lindsey's Hangar Bar might be the best themed dining venue on property, which is saying something when it's going up against the likes of T-Rex and Trader Sam's Grog Grotto. Visit for a fun cocktail served in one of their souvenir glasses or a casual bite to eat. STK Orlando will probably be the most posh restaurant on property, offering pricy steaks and seafood in a sleek atmosphere when it opens in mid-2016. Themed to a 1920s-period electric company, The Edison is expected to open midway through 2016. Nightly entertainment is expected to include contortionists, palm readers, DJs and more at what should be another exquisitely themed bar and restaurant. Look for reviews of these new venues on our sites and in later updates to this book.

Quick service options at The Landing are slimmer. Your main option is Cookes of Dublin. We like Cookes' Irish food a lot for lunch and early dinners, but it gets backed up in the evenings and there's rarely anywhere to sit. You'll also find a very good, albeit expensive, stop for a cold treat in Vivoli il Gelato and a Tea Traders Café by Joffrey's, which offers a variety of inexpensive snacks and a full menu of teas and other drinks.

The Marketplace. The Marketplace section is predominantly retail with a few restaurants and quick services mixed in. Shoppers looking for Disney items should pay special attention to World of Disney, Tren-D, Once Upon A Toy, The Art of Disney, and the Marketplace Co-Op. You'll find just about every imaginable theme park item in one of these stores.

The Marketplace is home to our favorite Springs' quick services: Earl of Sandwich and Wolfgang Puck Express. Earl of Sandwich serves excellent hot sandwiches for less than seven dollars each, in addition to great tasting sides and desserts. Lines can appear long, but service is surprisingly fast. Wolfgang Puck Express is more expensive than most quick services, but its food is table service quality and a server will deliver your meal and take care of drink refills and other needs. Ghirardelli Ice Cream and Chocolate Shop is one of the best places on property to indulge. Decadent sundaes are $9–$10 and, for those looking to be able to walk out after without assistance, best shared.

Two kid favorites operated by the same parent company are located in the Marketplace: Rainforest Café and T-REX. Rainforest is best known for providing dining in a tropical setting complete with Animatronic animals that rival some of Disney's best. T-REX is similar, but with a dinosaur theme. We give the nod to T-REX, partly because it's more likely to be new to a visitor (there are only two locations worldwide) but also because the food and drinks are slightly more inspired. Rainforest, however, is fun and less intimidating for some youngsters than T-REX.

Town Center. The last piece to open, Town Center is almost entirely new retail and dining. It's situated behind The West Side and The

Landing and will be the future home to outlets like Uniqlo, Pandora, Ugg, Zara, Lilly Pulitzer, Tommy Bahama and more, in addition, we expect, to Blaze Fast Fire'd Pizza and Sprinkles cupcakes. Disney has been mum about the majority of new tenants, but expect some major players when all is said and done.

Visiting Disney Springs. A visit to Disney Springs is not an essential part of a first vacation, particularly with all the other things to do at Disney World. Ongoing construction will detract from the experience and make travel more difficult well into 2016. If you do go, plan a single afternoon or evening perusing the shops and grabbing a meal. Crowds are considerably lower in the afternoon. If you arrive after 5pm, don't expect to eat without very long waits unless you have secured a dinner reservation.

Disney Springs is served by buses to and from the Disney resort hotels (but not to and from the parks). These buses are slow and can have many stops, so allow more time than you'd think. DS is also served by slow, low-capacity boats from the Port Orleans resorts, Old Key West, and Saratoga Springs, and there's a walking path from Saratoga Springs.

Driving to Disney Springs after 5pm is often arduous as Disney expands Buena Vista Drive, the road that surrounds Disney Springs, to ten lanes. Parking is complimentary in the garages or in one of the lots that surround the complex. Unfortunately, driving your vehicle and relying on Disney transportation both suffer from their own set of problems. Driving is often stop and go in the evening. Disney transportation often stops at Typhoon Lagoon on the way, in addition to taking indirect routes to keep buses off the main roadways, both of which add transit time. Our recommendation is to rely on Disney transportation, particularly if you can take the watercraft from Port Orleans, Old Key West, or Saratoga Springs.

The BOATHOUSE

In between Paradiso 37 and Raglan Road

CUISINE Seafood and steaks. **HOURS** 11am–11pm. **DDP** Yes (2 credits). **DISCOUNTS** 15% AP; 15% DVC.

PRICES Lunch/Dinner Appetizers: $12–$19. Entrées: $20–$115. Kids: $10.

OVERVIEW Offering picturesque waterfront dining, multiple bars inside and out, and a number of diversely themed dining areas, The BOATHOUSE brings upscale cuisine wrapped up in a casual atmosphere to Disney Springs. Entrees vary wildly in price, from the $20 hamburger and $29 lobster roll all the way up to $62 for a 12-ounce filet mignon or well over $100 for the dry-aged tomahawk steak and lobster for two, neither of which include a side. Fortunately, the kitchen reliably executes the pricier steak and seafood options perfectly, and the quality is a step above just about any Disney-operated restaurant. Those who want to spend considerably less can stick with the bar menu, which includes about a dozen entrées under $25 like the $15 club sandwich, $19 coconut shrimp, and $23 steak sandwich. Despite the high price point on most entrées, the atmosphere is decidely casual and service is largely unrefined. If you're looking for a quiet, intimate steak dinner, this isn't it, but some people may prefer the lack of pretention.

Bongos

West Side, across from Splitsville

CUISINE Cuban. **HOURS** 11am–11pm or Midnight. **DDP** Yes. **DISCOUNTS** None.

PRICES Lunch/Dinner Appetizers: $3–$23. Lunch Entrées: $8–$40. Dinner Entrées: $15–$40. Kids: $8–$10.

OVERVIEW Enter this two-story 1950s-era Havana nightclub and dine on one of over 50 Cuban specialties, including Cuban Style Skirt Steak, Shrimp Cuban Criolla, and Bongos Famous Fried Shredded Beef. Or pull up a seat at one of three bars, including one housed inside of a 75-foot tall pineapple sculpture, and select from a cocktail list including everything from Bongos Original Mojito to a 45-ounce Cuban Rum Runner. Kids are welcome all day, but it's a loud and boisterous crowd on weekends and late nights when live music is prevalent and dancing encouraged. Service is spotty, but food is prepared well and drinks are excellent.

Fulton's Crab House

The Landing, between Portobello and T-REX

CUISINE Seafood and Steak. **HOURS** 11am–Midnight. **DDP** 2 credits. **DIS-COUNTS** 20% TiW; 20% AP Lunch, 10% AP Dinner; 20% DVC Lunch, 10% DVC Dinner.

PRICES Lunch/Dinner Appetizers: $8–$20. Lunch Entrées: $11–$24. Dinner Entrées: $27–$59. Kids: $8–$14.

OVERVIEW Set inside of a majestic full-size replica of a riverboat anchored in Lake Buena Vista Lagoon, Fulton's imports fresh seafood daily. While no longer the most upscale Disney Springs restaurant for dinner, it's still expensive, with lobster coming in over $50 and steaks that start around $45. Visit for lunch when a soup/sandwich combo is under $15 and Fish and Chips cost $13 and you'll be able to enjoy the same atmosphere for a lot less money. Kids' entrees include filet mignon, snow crab legs, shrimp pasta, chicken fingers, and burgers. The high prices aren't justified for dinner, but this is a venue worth checking out.

Crossroads at House of Blues

West Side, across from DisneyQuest

CUISINE Southern American. **HOURS** 11am–11pm on weekdays, 1am on weekends. **DDP** Yes. **DISCOUNTS** 20% TiW. 20% AP Lunch; 10% AP Dinner; 10% DVC; 20% DVC Sunday brunch only.

PRICES Lunch/Dinner Appetizers: $6–$16. Entrées: $12–$29. Kids: $7–$9. Sunday Gospel Brunch: $41 adults, $21 kids.

OVERVIEW Celebrity Chef Aaron Sanchez took over the menu in July 2011, "incorporating flavors from around the world" in the process. The menu still favors southern favorites like jambalaya, voodoo shrimp, and buttermilk fried chicken, but you'll find inexpensive flatbread pizzas, sandwiches, and pastas, too. Heavy on edgy religious artwork that may appeal to some more than others, Blues is supposed to be themed to a shack on the side of a road down in the New Orleans bayou. Free live music inside the restaurant on weekends after 10pm. Calmer and kid friendly until then.

Paradiso 37

Old Pleasure Island, between Portobello and West Side

CUISINE North/South American. **HOURS** 11am–Midnight on weekdays, 1am on weekends. **DDP** Yes. **DISCOUNTS** 20% TiW. 15% AP; 20% DVC.

PRICES Lunch/Dinner Appetizers: $4–$17. Entrées: $14–$27. Kids: $8.

OVERVIEW The appetizers and margaritas are better than the entrées at this waterfront restaurant that focuses on cuisine of the Americas. Much busier after 6pm when the live music starts outside, Paradiso is best experienced without kids, who are unlikely to be impressed by the Latin flair or tequila tower stacked with 37 varieties. Walk-up tables are usually available, as are seats at one of the three bars.

Planet Hollywood

West Side, across from entrance to AMC Fork-and-Screen Theater

CUISINE American. **HOURS** 11am–1am. **DDP** Yes. **DISCOUNTS** 20% TiW. 10% AP; 10% DVC.

PRICES Lunch/Dinner Appetizers: $9–$25. Entrées: $14–$30. Kids: $8.

OVERVIEW One of very few remaining restaurants in this dwindling franchise, it should come to the surprise of no one other than Sylvester Stallone and Arnold Schwarzenegger that lousy, overpriced food in a deafeningly loud restaurant is not the key to long-term success. Yes, a few pieces of memorabilia are neat, but that won't make up for everything else wrong here. Diners that must visit should stick to burgers, salads, and beer, and be certain they have nowhere else to be. Advil not included.

Portobello

The Landing, between Fulton's and Paradiso 37

CUISINE Italian. **HOURS** 11am–11pm. **DDP** Yes. **DISCOUNTS** 20% TiW. 20% AP Lunch; 10% AP Dinner; 20% DVC Lunch; 10% DVC Dinner.

PRICES Lunch/Dinner Appetizers: $6–$16. Lunch Entrées: $9–$17. Dinner Entrées: $10–$29. Kids: $5–$11.

OVERVIEW With virtually no name recognition, a rather mundane dining atmosphere, and a menu that doesn't do much to draw in guests, this Italian restaurant is the least popular in Disney Springs. It's a great value before 4pm for lunch, when virtually the same menu as dinner is offered for half the price, but meals here are not particularly memorable. Visit when other restaurants are full and your party doesn't have a reservation elsewhere, or for lunch when it's cool enough for the patio and seating overlooking the water is available. Pizzas come in under $15 and are a great value for lunch or dinner.

Raglan Road

The Landing, near Fulton's and Portobello

CUISINE Irish. **HOURS** 11am–1am. **DDP** Yes. **DISCOUNTS** 20% TiW; 10% DVC.

PRICES Lunch/Dinner Appetizers: $6–$27. Lunch Entrées: $10–$25. Dinner Entrées: $15–$29. Kids: $8–$14.

OVERVIEW The restaurant features a live band playing Irish songs, popular ballads, and pub classics alongside traditional Irish jigs beginning at 6pm nightly (except for Sunday, when the live band plays only during brunch). Each of the four bars, some over 130 years old, were imported directly from Ireland. Celebrity Chef Kevin Dundon oversees the menu, which includes favorites like Shepherd's Pie, Guinness & Onion Bangers on Mash, and Roasted Chicken all under $20 for lunch or dinner. Add Guinness, Smithwick's, and a dozen more beers on draft, and you have yourself an authentically Irish good time. Kids' entrees at this family-friendly, highly-recommended restaurant include steak, shepherd's pie, burgers, and macaroni-and-cheese. Nearly everything, from the food to the service to the beer, is excellent. A cult favorite among Disney World guidebook authors.

Rainforest Café

Marketplace, near Earl of Sandwich

CUISINE American. **HOURS** 11am–11pm or 12am. **DDP** Yes. **DISCOUNTS** No TiW; DVC: 10% on up to four entrees; AP: 10% on up to four entrees.

PRICES Lunch/Dinner Appetizers: $7–$19. Entrées: $13–$26. Kids: $6–$7.

OVERVIEW See the Animal Kingdom table service reviews for background info on this raucous chain restaurant. The Disney Springs location is extremely popular with kids and online reservations are hard to come by because only part of the inventory is released to Disney. Call the restaurant directly at 407-827-8500 to book, or visit before 4pm when walk-ups don't require 60+ minute waits. The Lava Lounge next door offers the same menu without any of the restaurant's antics. The water view at the lounge is pleasant for couples, but most families will want to eat inside where the action is.

Splitsville Luxury Lanes

West Side, across from Bongos

CUISINE American, Sushi, Pizza. **HOURS** 11:30am–11pm or later. **DDP** Yes. **DISCOUNTS** 20% TiW; 10% AP.

PRICES Lunch/Dinner Appetizers: $6–$15. Entrées: $12–$25. Kids: $7.

OVERVIEW The food at Splitsville is not quite as luxurious as the bowling setup (your've never read a sentence like that before, we bet), but it does offer a bevy of options, including a dozen freshly made sushi rolls, a half-dozen pizzas, a dozen sandwiches and salads, rice bowls, and more. The pricier entrées are best skipped in favor of sushi and pizza, which are executed quite well. The nicest part of dining in this 50,000 square foot complex loosely themed to 1960s kitsch is the lack of a wait for a table when Disney Springs is crawling with people. Eat outside to get away from the bowling noise and stick to beer—the cocktails are overpriced and watered down.

T-REX Café

Marketplace, near the Lego Store

CUISINE American. **HOURS** 11am–11pm or 12am. **DDP** Yes. **DISCOUNTS** No TiW; DVC: 10% on up to four entrees; AP: 10% on up to four entrees.

PRICES Lunch/Dinner Appetizers: $7–$17. Entrées: $14–$33. Kids: $7–$8.

OVERVIEW Operated by the same parent company as Rainforest Café, T-REX replaces Rainforest's drizzle with thundering meteor showers and singing birds with a massive undulating octopus and life-sized Animatronic dinosaurs. The T-REX menu offers a staggering number of items, mostly of decent quality and universally in large amounts. Stick with the lower-priced fare or chance a regrettable $30 steak. Younger kids may be scared of the dinosaurs, noise, fire, and occasional darkness, but most kids between the ages of six and twelve love the atmosphere. With apprehensive kids, consider a walk through the restaurant before committing to a meal, or request a table near the entrance. Call the restaurant directly at 407-828-8739 to book because few slots are offered to Disney Reservations.

Wolfgang Puck Grand Café

West Side, across from DisneyQuest

CUISINE American. **HOURS** 11:30am–11pm. **DDP** Yes. **DISCOUNTS** 20% TiW; 20% AP Lunch; 10% AP Dinner; 20% DVC Lunch; 10% DVC Dinner.

PRICES Lunch/Dinner Appetizers: $8–$15. Entrées: $13–$30. Kids: $7–$9.

OVERVIEW Wolfgang Puck has nothing to do with this restaurant that bears his name, which is now operated by the same company that runs Portobello and Fulton's. The restaurant is reminiscent of "The Max" from *Saved by the Bell* and the menu features an assortment of fresh pizzas, salads, pastas, sushi, and traditional entrees like steak and chicken. Kids are unlikely to connect with the art-deco style, though their menu includes spaghetti, cheese pizza, chicken tenders, and sushi. Wolfgang Puck Express next door serves pizzas that come out of the same oven for less money, and is a better choice.

Dining Reviews: The Disney Resorts

Disney's resorts offer the majority of the best restaurants on property, whether we're discussing five-star dining at Victoria & Albert's at the Grand Floridian or the rootin' tootin' good time that is hollering along to Hoop-Dee-Doo Revue at Fort Wilderness. We provide reviews of all these meals in the material that follows.

Unfortunately, resort-to-resort travel is often inconvenient because Disney does not offer resort-to-resort buses. Guests relying on Disney transportation from the values and moderates in particular will need to wait for a bus to a theme park or Disney Springs, then wait for a bus for the resort they're headed to, and then take the time to ride the bus over to the resort and find the restaurant. Disney recommends allowing 90 minutes each way for such travel. And they're not wrong. Travel is particularly taxing for early morning breakfasts when buses run less frequently (check with your concierge for the schedule) and for late night dinners when the theme parks may already be closed, limiting transfer options.

There are some alternatives. Taxis are usually stationed outside the resort or bell services will be glad to call, but they add $25-$60 roundtrip to the cost of the meal. Guests already renting cars have it easiest and can drive directly to the resort with the help of signs and GPS.

We have some tips on reducing the hassle using Disney transportation.

- Guests staying at the monorail resorts—Contemporary, Polynesian, and Grand Floridian—are connected by the resort monorail and visiting any of the resorts from any other will only take about 15 minutes each way.
- Guests staying at the Contemporary, Wilderness Lodge, or Fort Wilderness are connected by boat and visiting any of the resorts

from any other will only take about 15-30 minutes each way.

- Guests staying at the Epcot resorts—Beach Club, Yacht Club, BoardWalk Inn, Swan, and Dolphin—are all within a 15-minute walk from each other and watercraft transportation is also available between the resorts.

- If you find yourself at Magic Kingdom, you can take the resort monorail to any of the monorail resorts, or watercraft to Fort Wilderness or Wilderness Lodge.

- If you find yourself at Epcot, you can exit the park via the International Gateway between the United Kingdom and France Pavilions and either walk or take the boat to any Epcot resorts.

Particularly for first-time visitors relying on Disney transportation away from the monorail or Epcot area, our strong advice is eat where you otherwise plan to be in order to reduce the time commitment of transferring from one place to another. If you simply can't resist a breakfast with Mickey at the Contemporary or a romantic dinner at the Grand Floridian, that's fine, too. But take a cab and consider it the low cost of doing business versus the high cost of your time.

DINING AT DISNEY'S ANIMAL KINGDOM LODGE

Boma - Flavors of Africa

Take the elevator to the first floor

CUISINE African-inspired. **DDP** Yes. **DISCOUNTS** 20% TiW; 10% AP; 10% DVC; 10% Disney Visa.

HOURS AND PRICES *Breakfast* (7:30–11:00am): $25 adults, $13 kids. *Dinner* (4:30-9:30pm): $41 adults, $22 kids.

OVERVIEW Featuring a robust dinner menu of over 50 African-inspired specialties, Boma is a favorite of many for its wide selection and high quality, unique options. Best are the soups and roasted meats, but just about everything from the seasonal salads to the zebra dome desserts are excellent. Kids enjoy the full buffet in addition to items like macaroni-and-cheese, mashed potatoes, pasta, and baked chicken legs. Breakfast is more pedestrian with the usual selection of French toast, Mickey waffles, bacon, sausage, and the like. The only downside is that very few tables in the African-marketplace-themed dining room have views of the savannas outside.

Jiko - The Cooking Place

Take the elevator to the first floor

CUISINE African. **HOURS** 5:30–10pm. **DDP** 2 credits. **DISCOUNTS** 20% TiW; 10% AP; 10% DVC; 10% Disney Visa.

PRICES Appetizers: $9–$19. Dinner Entrées: $30–$49. Kids: $8–$16.

OVERVIEW Jiko isn't afraid to use a liberal amount of exotic spices on many of its constantly changing menu items. Flatbreads, like the KG's Peri-Peri Roasted Chicken with Lime Chakalaka, Lamb Chopper Cheese, and Pickled Sweet Bell Peppers are excellent. Filet mignon, scallops, and short ribs are menu mainstays. Kids have a wide range of options from macaroni-and-cheese or cheese pizza to pan-seared scallops and grilled steak. The main dining room, themed to the opening scenes from *The Lion King*, is elegant and reserved. This is one of the best date-night restaurants on property. Request a window table deep inside the restaurant to get away from the lobby noise.

Sanaa

In the Kidani Village wing (at Kidani, take the elevator to the first floor)

CUISINE African/Indian. **HOURS** *Lunch* 11:30am-3pm; *Dinner* 5–9:30pm. **DDP** Yes. **DISCOUNTS** 20% TiW; 10% AP; 10% DVC; 10% Disney Visa.

PRICES Lunch/Dinner Appetizers: $6–$15. Lunch Entrées: $12–$22. Dinner Entrées: $15–$30. Kids: $9.

OVERVIEW Sanaa features expansive savanna views in a fun, low-key dining room themed to an African spice market. The Indian Bread Service with nine accompaniments is not to be missed. Excellent Tandoori options reliably come in under $20, in addition to slightly more expensive chicken and steak. Kids' options are a little out there and include items like Tandoori Chicken Pot Pie and Fish of the Day served with Pearl Pasta, Green Beans, Carrots, and Sliced Apples. The lounge is open until midnight. Request a window table during daylight for the best views.

DINING AT DISNEY'S BEACH CLUB RESORT

Beaches and Cream Soda Shop

Behind Stormalong Bay

CUISINE American burgers, sandwiches, and ice cream. **HOURS** 11am–11pm. **DDP** Yes. **DISCOUNTS** 20% TiW.

PRICES Lunch/Dinner Entrées: $9–$17. Kids: $9.

OVERVIEW Themed to a boardwalk-style ice cream shop, Disney's smallest table service restaurant offers inexpensive burger and sandwich fare in a fun, bright setting. The restaurant began accepting reservations for the first time in late 2013, cutting down waits from as much as two hours to just a few minutes. The $29 Kitchen Sink Dessert, featuring eight scoops of ice cream and an entire bottle of whipped cream, is a favorite tradition of many returning visitors. An ice-cream to-go window is also available.

Cape May Café

Character meal (breakfast only); inside the lobby to the left of check-in

CUISINE American character breakfast with Minnie, Goofy, Donald in beach outfits. Dinner buffet is heavy on seafood. **DDP** Yes. **DISCOUNTS** 20% TiW.

HOURS AND PRICES *Breakfast* (7:30–11:00am): $32 adults, $19 kids. *Dinner* (4:30–9:30pm): $43 adults, $24 kids.

OVERVIEW Like the rest of the resort, Cape May Café is themed to a comfortable beachside setting with inviting pastel colors. Breakfast is a character affair with the usual suspects like waffles and pancakes, in addition to elevated offerings like smoked salmon, creamy cheddar grits, and sliced capicola. Dinner is more expensive and characterless, with an emphasis on seafood paella, peel-and-eat shrimp, snow crab legs, salmon, clams, and mussels, in addition to salads and roasted meats. Kid options include chicken nuggets and macaroni. Both meals are above average, though the lack of Mickey at breakfast is disappointing.

DINING AT DISNEY'S BOARDWALK

Big River Grille and Brewing Works

On the end, near Jellyrolls

CUISINE American. **HOURS** 11am–11pm. **DDP** Yes. **DISCOUNTS** 20% TiW; 10% DVC.

PRICES Lunch/Dinner Appetizers: $5–$13. Entrées: $10–$26. Kids: $8.

OVERVIEW Big River is the only working brewpub on property, offering five beers brewed on-site, in addition to a robust menu featuring less expensive sandwich fare along with more expensive steaks and ribs. The less expensive burgers and sandwiches are more reliable than the more expensive items. Beer is unique and decent, but not up to snuff compared to some of the better bottled craft brews available at other restaurants. Diners can sit inside the family-friendly restaurant or outside on the boardwalk overlooking Crescent Lake. Most sports and beer fans will want to take a look at ESPN Club a few hundred feet away. The restaurant otherwise has very little kid appeal, though its menu includes similar burgers and sandwiches.

ESPN Club

Closest to Epcot

CUISINE American. **HOURS** 11:30am–11:30pm. **DDP** Yes. **DISCOUNTS** 20% TiW; 10% AP; 10% DVC; 10% Disney Visa.

PRICES Lunch/Dinner Appetizers: $8–$15. Entrées: $14–$24. Kids: $9–$11.

OVERVIEW With around 100 video monitors showing just about every televised sporting event imaginable, ESPN is heaven for anyone looking to catch a game while on vacation. Food and drinks are better and more varied than you might expect, including appetizers like the very good tuna tartare. Entrees are almost entirely burgers and sandwiches that are relatively inexpensive at $12–$18. ESPN Club is extremely popular during major sporting events and all day Saturday and Sunday during football season. Arrive early or take advantage of the $50+ reserved seats, which includes $50+ toward food and drink.

Flying Fish

Nearest entrance to the BoardWalk Inn (Expected to be closed for refurbishment from February through November 2016)

CUISINE Seafood. **HOURS** 5:30–10pm. **DDP** 2 credits. **DISCOUNTS** 20% TiW; 10% AP; 10% DVC; 10% Disney Visa.

PRICES Dinner Appetizers: $10–$19. Entrées: $31–$47. Kids: $6–$15.

OVERVIEW Reliably serving the best food in the BoardWalk area, Flying Fish is an upscale restaurant with a playful boardwalk theme. Specialties include the excellent Potato-wrapped Red Snapper and Char-crusted Angus New York Strip Steak which can be ordered together as part of an entrée duo. Seafood and salads featuring Florida produce are otherwise highlighted at this restaurant with a more discerning eye for detail than most. Kids' choices include fish sticks, grilled cheese, and steak skewers. While expensive, the fresh, high ingredient quality and seasonal menu changes keep locals and vacationers alike returning time and time again.

Trattoria al Forno

In between Flying Fish and ESPN Club

CUISINE Italian. **HOURS** *Breakfast* 7:30–11:00am; *Dinner* 5–10pm. **DDP** Yes. **DISCOUNTS** 20% TiW; 10% AP; 10% DVC.

PRICES Breakfast Entrees: $11–$13. Kids: $7. Dinner Appetizers: $7–$16. Personal Pizzas: $17–$19. Dinner Entrées: $19–$37. Kids: $9–$12.

OVERVIEW Trattoria al Forno replaced Kouzzina by Cat Cora in December 2014, bringing the number of Italian restaurants in the area to four. The menu focuses on Italian classics like fried calamari, shaved Italian carved meats, baked lasagna, and chicken breast alla parmigiana, in addition to T-bone steak Florentine and innovative pizzas like the one topped with fennel sausage, salame piccante, and house pickled peppers. Breakfast includes some unique touches like waffles with whipped tiramisu mascarpone and cocoa powder or Frittata with roasted red peppers, prosciutto, onions, potatoes, pecorino-romano cheese topped with arugula. Overall, the restaurant is just fine, but it doesn't do anything to stick out from a sea of more interesting options.

DINING AT DISNEY'S CARIBBEAN BEACH RESORT

Shutters

Old Port Royale, on the far end of the food court

CUISINE American with a Caribbean twist. **HOURS** 5–10pm. **DDP** Yes. **DISCOUNTS** 20% TiW; 10% AP; 10% Disney Visa.

PRICES Dinner Appetizers: $7–$12. Entrées: $18–$34. Kids: $9–$11.

OVERVIEW While not a destination restaurant by any stretch of the imagination, Shutters has improved significantly recently with the arrival of a fantastic chef from the Disney Cruise Line. A pastel-pink dining room lined with sea-green shutters invites guests inside the restaurant that offers a menu heavy on steak, pork, and chicken. The Caesar Salad with Cornbread Croutons and Barbecue Pork Brisket are best alongside one of the unique rum flights. Kids may enjoy chicken nuggets, pasta, fish, cheese pizza, or grilled chicken or steak.

DINING AT DISNEY'S CONTEMPORARY RESORT

California Grill

Check in on 2nd floor, ride designated elevator to the restaurant on the 15th floor

CUISINE American, Sushi. **HOURS** 5–10pm. **DDP** 2 credits. **DISCOUNTS** 20% TiW.

PRICES Appetizers: $12–$18. Sushi: $22–$26. Dinner Entrées: $35–$55. Kids: $9–$18.

OVERVIEW Best known for its wide angle views of Magic Kingdom from the 15th floor of the Contemporary, California Grill underwent renovations throughout much of 2013. The restaurant retains its emphasis on $50 steaks, in addition to many of the same excellent, albeit pricey, sushi dishes. Schedule a meal about an hour before Wishes begins. Guests may watch the show from their table or head outside to the balcony. It's first come, first served at the large bar and lounge area in the middle of the restaurant, making it perfect for drinks and appetizers closer to when the restaurant opens. Check on the second floor for availability. California Grill is great for a date night, but kids are more common than at other signature restaurants due to the excellent fireworks view. Kids may choose between cheese pizza, pasta, chicken, or grilled beef tenderloin.

Chef Mickey's

Character meal, 4th floor Concourse

CUISINE American. Character meal with Mickey, Minnie, Goofy, Donald, and Pluto in chef gear. **DDP** Yes. **DISCOUNTS** 20% TiW.

HOURS AND PRICES *Breakfast* (7:30–11:30am): $40 adults, $21 kids. *Brunch* (11:30am–2:30pm): $40 adults, $21 kids. *Dinner* (5pm–9:30pm): $50 adults, $25 kids.

OVERVIEW Consistently the most popular and one of the most expensive single-credit character meals on property, this is the only place you'll find Mickey, Minnie, Donald, Goofy, and Pluto together greeting diners tableside. Meals are a crowded, raucous affair with the monorail whizzing by just one floor up, but kids don't seem to mind and parents are happy to take pictures of the Fab Five without having to wait an hour in the sun. Breakfast is the strongest and less expensive meal with all of the usual suspects, in addition to Pixie-Dusted Challah French Toast, Minnie's Breakfast Pizza, and Pluto's Cheese Blintz. Brunch swaps things like oatmeal for peel-and-eat shrimp and salads in place of cereals, in addition to carved ham instead of bacon and ribs and salmon instead of biscuits and pancakes. Dinner food quality is below average, but there's a wide variety of roasted meats, soups, and salads, in addition to an all-you-can-eat ice cream bar. Brunch may be a good option for those looking to take some time away from the parks during the busy afternoons and also makes securing a reservation easier. Visit only if the characters are important.

The Wave of American Flavors

First floor on the left, past the check-in area

CUISINE American. **HOURS** Breakfast 7:30–11am; Lunch 12–2pm; Dinner 5–9:30pm. **DDP** Yes. **DISCOUNTS** 20% TiW; 10% AP; 10% DVC; 10% Disney Visa.

PRICES Breakfast Entrées: $8–$17. Breakfast Buffet: $22 adult, $12 kid. Lunch/Dinner Appetizers: $8–$19. Lunch Entrées: $14–$20. Dinner Entrées: $17–$34. Kids: $9–$11.

OVERVIEW With more emphasis on healthy food and fresh, locally sourced ingredients than almost any other restaurant on property, The Wave offers an innovative menu for all three meals. The breakfast buffet is excellent, with a wide array of fresh fruit, made-to-order omelets, a smoked salmon bar, and all the traditional accompaniments like pancakes, sausage, and waffles. Less hungry patrons can order a la carte for not much more than the counter-service Contempo Café upstairs. Lunch focuses mostly on sandwiches, burgers, and salads under $20. Only a few tables are usually occupied unless convention goers take over the space. Dinner brings signature quality fare at one-credit prices, including items like the $29 Grilled

Hanger Steak with Ginger-Soy Marinade, Udon Noodles, Baby Bok Choy, Carrots, and Snow Peas and the Curry Vegetarian Stew with Butternut Squash, Asparagus, Pink Lady Apples, Fire Roasted Peppers, and Jade Rice. Same-day reservations are usually easy to secure.

DINING AT DISNEY'S CORONADO SPRINGS RESORT

Maya Grill

Inside the main building, down the hall to the right of Pepper Market

CUISINE Mexican. **HOURS** 5–10pm. **DDP** Yes. **DISCOUNTS** 20% TiW.

PRICES Appetizers: $7–$12. Dinner Entrées: $20–$33. Kids: $7–$10.

OVERVIEW Operated by the same company as the so-so restaurants in Epcot's Mexico Pavilion, Maya Grill recently updated its menu to be more in line with La Hacienda de San Angel. In fact, it offers two of the same platters – one featuring steak, chicken al pastor, and chorizo and the other with shrimp, fish, scallops, and vegetables. Other Tex-Mex-style entrées include Beef Short Ribs with Oaxacan Mole Coloradito and Menonita Cheese and Chili-Battered Shrimp Tacos with Pico de Gallo and Avocado Crema Salsa. Kids are unlikely to connect with the restaurant's loosely themed Mayan motifs of fire, sun, and water, but their menu includes some interesting options like the Quesadilla, Beef or Chicken Tacos, and Grilled Fish, in addition to Chicken Nuggets and Mac 'n Cheese.

DINING AT DISNEY'S
FORT WILDERNESS RESORT AND CAMPGROUND

Hoop-Dee-Doo Musical Revue

Dinner show at Pioneer Hall, near the boat dock

CUISINE Fried chicken, ribs, and all the fixins. Includes unlimited beer and wine for those 21 and older. **HOURS** Usually three shows daily: 4pm, 6:15pm, and 8:30pm. **DDP** 2 credits. **DISCOUNTS** 20% TiW for final show only.

PRICES Hoop Dee Doo offers tables in three price categories. Category 1, which we recommend, is $66-$70 for adults, and $34-$36 for kids. Category 2 and 3 tables ($7/$11 less for adults and $5/$6 less for kids) are distant from the main stage.

OVERVIEW Run more than 35,000 times over the last 40-or-so years, Hoop-Dee-Doo is as much of a Walt Disney World institution as chicken nuggets and Peter Pan's Flight. While expensive at first blush, your admission includes all-you-care-to-eat fried chicken, ribs, corn, salad, baked beans, corn bread, and strawberry shortcake, in addition to unlimited soft drinks, sangria, house wine, and beer. And, of course, the two-hour, kid-friendly Western musical remains the star of the show. Expect a lot of banjos, sing-a-longs, and audience participation in what ends up being a hokey, joke-filled experience where nobody takes themselves seriously. Take the boat from Magic Kingdom if possible for an easy walk to Pioneer Hall. Those arriving via Disney bus will need to transfer to the internal shuttle for transportation to the show, which can take an extra 20 minutes.

Mickey's Backyard Barbecue

Dinner show and character meal, near Pioneer Hall on the stables side

CUISINE Fried chicken, ribs, hot dogs, hamburgers, and the like. Includes unlimited beer and wine for those 21 and over. **HOURS** Now a year-round offering, shows are usually scheduled at 6:30pm on Thursdays and Saturdays, with the possibility that additional days will be available from June through August. **DDP** 2 credits. **DISCOUNTS** 20% TiW.

PRICES $63 adults, $37 kids.

OVERVIEW Mickey's Backyard Barbecue takes place in a roofed but otherwise open-air (thus not air-conditioned) space. The show features a country band, line dancing, and interactions with Mickey, Minnie, Chip, Dale, and Goofy. Most guests will get more entertainment for their money from Hoop-Dee-Doo, and any number of other meals provide better (and less expensive) chances to meet Mickey and friends. Line-dancers and families with young, excitable kids enjoy the experience most. Take the boat from Magic Kingdom if possible for an easy walk to the Barbecue. Those arriving via Disney bus will need to transfer to the internal shuttle for transportation to the show, which can take an extra 20 minutes.

Trail's End

Pioneer Hall, near the boat dock

CUISINE American/BBQ. **HOURS** Breakfast 7:30–11:25am; Lunch 11:30am–2pm; Dinner 4:30–9:30pm. **DDP** Yes. **DISCOUNTS** 20% TiW; 10% AP; 10% DVC; 10% Disney Visa.

PRICES Breakfast Buffet: $18 adult, $11 kid. Lunch Appetizers: $3–$10. Entrées: $13–$18. Dinner Buffet: $28 adult, $16 kid.

OVERVIEW Consistently the cheapest Disney World buffet at breakfast and dinner, with an inexpensive a la carte lunch served in between, Trail's End serves up country cooking in Disney's most casual sit-down restaurant. Breakfast is satisfying with a spread of the usual Mickey waffles, pancakes, pastries, bacon, sausage, etc., in addition to unique items like Pulled Pork Eggs Benedict and Brisket Mash. Lunch is a nice selection of southern favorites like Shrimp and Grits and Pulled Pork Sandwiches, in addition to burgers and sandwiches that cost only a dollar or two more than quick service. The dinner buffet consists of much of the same food as the much more expensive family-style dinner at Whispering Canyon Café at Wilderness Lodge. Enjoy all-you-care-to-eat peel and eat shrimp, pulled pork, baked beans, chili, brisket, and more. While not necessarily a destination restaurant, Trail's End is a fantastic, economical choice for those staying at the campground.

DINING AT DISNEY'S GRAND FLORIDIAN RESORT & SPA

1900 Park Fare

Character meal, just inside the first-floor entrance on the left

CUISINE American. Character meal with Mary Poppins, Mad Hatter, Alice, Winnie the Pooh, and Tigger for breakfast. Dinner has Cinderella, Prince Charming, Lady Tremaine, Anastasia, and Drizella. All characters may not appear. **DDP** Yes. **DISCOUNTS** 20% TiW.

HOURS AND PRICES *Breakfast Buffet* (8–11:15am): $32 adults, $19 kids. *Dinner Buffet* (4:30–8:30pm): $45 adults, $22 kids.

OVERVIEW 1900 Park Fare's Victorian theme is carried out subtly throughout the restaurant with carousel animals placed around the massive dining room. A calliope, or steam organ, is the focal point, hanging high above the buffet area. The restaurant is otherwise nondescript for the most part—loud, and without windows. Food is quite good for a buffet. Breakfast includes specialties like Lobster Benedict, Smoked Salmon Lox, and Hickory-smoked Ham, in addition to the usual. Dinner brings a large selection of salads and roasted meats, as well as Spice-crusted Salmon, sushi, and Roasted Root Vegetable Gratin. Don't forget the Strawberry Soup. The five very different characters present at each meal otherwise steal the show, as they visit every table taking pictures and mingling with guests.

Citricos

Second floor of the main building, near Mizner's

CUISINE American/Mediterranean. **HOURS** 5:30–10pm. **DDP** 2 credits. **DISCOUNTS** 20% TiW; 10% AP; 10% DVC; 10% Disney Visa.

PRICES Appetizers: $13–$17. Dinner Entrées: $30-$49. Kids: $8–$17.

OVERVIEW Citricos is Grand Floridian's best signature restaurant, serving inspired steak and seafood with a Mediterranean twist. Old World furnishings and mosaic-tiled floors invite guests into a restaurant that is just fancy enough that everyone feels welcome, yet an air of glamour and prestige permeates throughout. Shrimp, pork, and veal are done best here with seasonal changes that bring out the freshest flavors. Kids can choose from basics like cheese pizza and macaroni-and-cheese, or go big with Grilled Berkshire Pork Tenderloin or Grilled Steak. Views out the expansive windows are pleasant, but don't provide much of a theme park or Wishes view.

Grand Floridian Café

First floor, all the way back on the left

CUISINE American. **HOURS** Breakfast 7–11am; Lunch 11:30am–2pm; Dinner 5–9pm. **DDP** Yes. **DISCOUNTS** 20% TiW; 10% AP; 10% DVC; 10% Disney Visa.

PRICES Breakfast Entrées: $9–$19. Lunch/Dinner Appetizers: $6–$14. Lunch Entrées: $12–$29. Dinner Entrées: $20–$33. Kids: $9.

OVERVIEW It's usually easy to secure reservations at Grand Floridian's least expensive, most casual restaurant, subtly themed to the Victorian era with charming views of the rose gardens outside. Unlike the signature restaurants, nobody will bat an eye if you arrive wearing fanny packs and Mickey ears. Breakfast is best, with upscale items like Lobster Eggs Benedict and Citrus Pancakes stealing the show. Lunch is a relatively inexpensive affair with sandwiches, salads, and burgers all coming in under $20. Still, upscale touches remain, with butter-poached lobster topping the burger and roasted garlic aioli, balsamic onions, spinach, and fennel salad adorning the chicken sandwich. Don't miss the gigantic Grand Sandwich. Dinner isn't great, with just six or seven entrees on the menu, but the Shrimp & Grits, Grilled Pork Chop, and Chicken Breast all arrive under $24 with large portions and fresh ingredients. Kids won't be impressed by the ambiance, but they can get in on the action with salmon, cheese pizza, chicken, and meaty mac 'n cheese.

Narcoossee's

Located outside, near the boat dock

CUISINE Steak and Seafood. **HOURS** 5:30–10pm. **DDP** 2 credits. **DISCOUNTS** 20% TiW.

PRICES Appetizers: $11–$19. Dinner Entrées: $33–$75. Kids: $7–$15. Brunch (Sundays only from 10am–2pm): $69 adults, $41 kids.

OVERVIEW Disney's most expensive signature restaurant is not its best in food quality, service, or ambiance. The windows and waterfront veranda do provide decent, albeit off-centered views of Magic Kingdom and Wishes, but it's far less impressive than California Grill's 15th floor observation deck. Food is generally on point, but the menu is far less innovative than Citricos, and it's hard to justify a $70+ filet mignon/lobster tail combo when the beef isn't even certified Choice. The atmosphere is otherwise bland at what Disney describes as an "elegant waterfront retreat" with basic wood furniture and standard wood floors. Book about an hour before Wishes begins and request a window table at check-in, or consider other options.

Sunday brunch is an expensive fixed price affair. It does include a mimosa, champagne, or bloody mary for adults and a fruit smoothie for kids, but it's hard to justify these prices when the entrees include the likes of brioche French toast and chicken and waffles. Still, those looking for some pomp and circumstance may find some value here, particularly if you enjoy a morning cocktail and choose the lobster eggs benedict or steak and eggs as an entrée.

Victoria and Albert's

Second floor of the main building, near Citricos

CUISINE Fine Dining; **HOURS** Two seatings nightly: first between 5–6:05pm and second from 8:30–9:20pm. **DDP** No. **DISCOUNTS** None.

PRICES $185/person seven–course Prix Fixe menu.

OVERVIEW Victoria & Albert's, boasting the AAA Five Diamond Award every year since 2000, is unlike any other restaurant on property. With a seven-course menu that starts at $185 per person, it's also the most expensive. The restaurant does not serve children under the age of ten in the main dining room and there is a strict dress code: men must wear dinner jackets with dress pants or slacks and shoes. Ties are optional. Women may wear a cocktail dress, nice dress, dressy pant suit, or a skirt with a blouse. The 18-table restaurant is otherwise equal parts intimate and opulent, with reliably impeccable service from the inviting staff. Menus change daily, but Chef Hunnel reliably offers Australian Kobe-style beef tenderloin, Holland white asparagus, braised oxtail, Imperial osetra caviar, and other fine ingredients. Desserts, overseen by the venerable Erich Herbitschek, are excellent. While expensive, Victoria & Albert's may be the best value on property. Strongly consider the $65 wine pairings with seven healthy pours of fine wines perfectly paired to each selection. V&A's is not for everyone, but it doesn't get any better than this for those celebrating something special.

DINING AT DISNEY'S OLD KEY WEST RESORT

Olivia's

Next to the gift shop, across the way from check-in

CUISINE American. **HOURS** Breakfast 7:30–10:30am; Lunch 11:30am–4:55pm; Dinner 5–10pm. **DDP** Yes. **DISCOUNTS** 20% TiW; 10% AP; 10% DVC; 10% Disney Visa.

PRICES Breakfast Entrées: $10–$16. Lunch/Dinner Appetizers: $6–$13. Entrées: $18–$33. Kids: $9.

OVERVIEW Nautically themed with wooden fish and pictures of past guests adorning the walls, Olivia's is one of the friendliest restaurants on property. Breakfast is excellent with specialties like Crab Cake Eggs Benedict and the Conch Republic Omelet with Shrimp, Avocado, and Pepper Jack Cheese. Standard fare includes pancake, waffle, and egg platters. Lunch and dinner both feature inexpensive burger and sandwich fare, in addition to more expensive steak, scallops, and prime rib. Order at least one Conch Fritters. Kids enjoy this colorful, boisterous restaurant with their menu of pasta, salmon, pizza, chicken, hamburgers, and grilled fish. While not a destination restaurant for first time-visitors, anyone staying here should plan at least one meal back at the resort. Outdoor patio seating is available.

Jim's Gems
by Jim Korkis

Olivia's Café at the Old Key West Resort was designed by WDW Imagineers to tell the story of a poor young woman in the Florida Keys who was an outstanding cook but lacked the needed money to open her own restaurant. To raise money, she opened up part of her house as an occasional make-shift eatery, but even then she lacked the cash for matching sets of silverware, plates, and chairs. Friends brought their own plates and chairs when they came to dine and left them for others, which explains why everything at Olivia's is mismatched.

DINING AT DISNEY'S POLYNESIAN VILLAGE RESORT

'Ohana

Character meal (breakfast only), on second floor of main building

CUISINE Character breakfast with Mickey, Pluto, Lilo, and Stitch. Dinner (served family style) is heavy on meat. **DDP** Yes. **DISCOUNTS** 20% TiW.

HOURS AND PRICES *Breakfast* (7:30–11:00am): $32 adults, $19 kids. *Dinner* (5–10pm): $42 adults, $22 kids.

OVERVIEW Characters stop by for the Polynesian-themed breakfast served family-style. Scrambled eggs, Mickey waffles, fried potatoes, pork sausage, bacon, and biscuits will all be delivered in copious quantities throughout the meal. It's a limited selection compared to buffets, but it does the trick and the characters are friendly. Dinner starts with pineapple-coconut bread and salad and continues with honey-coriander chicken wings and potstickers. Skewers with sweet-n-sour chicken, marinated sirloin steak, and spicy grilled peel-n-eat shrimp follow with stir-fried vegetables and lo mein as accompaniments. The restaurant is incredibly loud, particularly at dinner when staff members lead kids in games and parades throughout the meal. Very few tables have window views of Magic Kingdom. (Protip: It's 'Ohana. Not O'hana. Or O'hana's. Just, 'Ohana. It means "family".)

Kona Café

Second floor of main building

CUISINE American, Pan-Asian. **HOURS** Breakfast: 7:30–11:15am; Lunch: 12–2:45pm; Dinner; 5–10pm. **DDP** Yes. **DISCOUNTS** 20% TiW.

PRICES Breakfast Entrées: $9–$15. Lunch/Dinner Appetizers: $8–$15. Lunch Entrées: $12–$19. Dinner Entrées: $19–$33. Kids: $9.

OVERVIEW Kona is too many people's "best kept secret" to count as a secret anymore, but it remains one of Disney's hidden gems, particularly for its relatively inexpensive, high-quality lunch. Although most famous for its Tonga Toast (banana-stuffed sourdough French toast rolled in cinnamon sugar and served with a strawberry compote), the Macadamia-Pineapple Pancakes with macadamia nut butter and pineapple sauce might be even better. Lunch is sandwiches, Pan-Asian noodle bowls, tacos, and satisfying plated lunches featuring grilled steak or chicken for under $16 each. Dinner remains reasonably priced with many entrees under $25 and an emphasis on steak, ahi tuna, chicken, and the like. Excellent sushi is served inside the restaurant and next door at the Sushi Bar after 5pm. Just off the main lobby, Kona is extremely loud and not private for dinner, but it's a casual affair and guests can fill up for about half as much as 'Ohana next door.

Spirit of Aloha

Dinner show, in dedicated space on the Grand Floridian side

CUISINE American/Polynesian. **HOURS** Usually two shows Tuesday-Saturday at 5:15pm and 8pm. **DDP** 2 credits. **DISCOUNTS** 20% TiW, for final show only.

PRICES The Spirit of Aloha show offers tables in three price categories. Category 1, which we recommend, is $70–$74 for adults, and $36–$40 for kids. Category 2 and 3 tables ($7/$11 less for adults and $5/$6 less for kids) are distant from the main stage.

OVERVIEW Food is okay at this Polynesian luau and dinner show, which follows the story of a young woman returning home after spending time as a city girl on the mainland. All-you-care-to-enjoy Island pulled pork, BBQ ribs, roasted chicken, and Polynesian rice are served family-style alongside fresh salad with honey-lime vinaigrette, seasonal vegetables, and pineapple-coconut bread. Complimentary beer and wine are served, though it may be difficult to flag down a server for a refill. Kids receive chicken nuggets with tater tots, cheese pizza, and either grilled chicken or mahi mahi with rice and green beans. The show has its moments, with an outstanding fire-dancing and sword-eating finale, but at over two hours, it drags in places. With the amount of better entertainment already seen at the parks, the Luau is going to be superfluous for many, and, at $70/adult, is an expensive proposition.

Trader Sam's Grog Grotto

Past Captain Cook's in the main building and outside on the patio

CUISINE Polynesian, Sushi. **HOURS** 4pm–12am; 21+ only after 8pm. **DDP** No. **DISCOUNTS** None.

PRICES Appetizers/Small Plates: $9–$15.

OVERVIEW Trader Sam's Grog Grotto features two distinct areas married under a single banner. The outdoor, open air Tiki Terrace offers a surprisingly relaxing atmosphere among swaying palm trees, fountains, and live ukulele music. Inside, the bar that officially seats just about 50 people is whimsically themed and full of interactive artifacts from around the mysterious South Seas. Due to the bar's low capacity, Sam's usually uses a pager system to alert prospective imbibers that space is available inside. Wait times can be quoted as high as two or more hours on the weekends, but are usually short or nonexistent on weeknights, particularly after 9pm. Staff will remind those under 21 that they should prepare to leave by the 8pm cutoff. Food tends to be better and more varied upstairs at Tambu Lounge and Kona Café, though you might want to order one of the small bites with drinks inside or out on the patio. Our favorite drink is the souvenir HippopotoMai-Tai, which includes a take-home tiki glass for $15. Be careful with the souvenir Uh-Oa, which will run you north of $40, and the Nautilus, which arrives over $50. Other drinks like the Tropical Dark and Stormy are closer to $8, but don't include a souvenir glass.

DINING AT DISNEY'S PORT ORLEANS RIVERSIDE RESORT

Boatwright's

Inside the main building, near the quick service

CUISINE Cajun/American. **HOURS** 5–10pm. **DDP** Yes. **DISCOUNTS** 20% TiW; 10% AP; 10% Disney Visa.

PRICES Appetizers: $7–$12. Dinner Entrées: $17–$34. Kids: $9.

OVERVIEW Loosely themed to a shipyard warehouse with the skeletal hull of a fishing boat suspended overhead, Boatwright's is a casual restaurant just off the main lobby. The menu revolves around typical New Orleans favorites like Jambalaya, Crawfish Ètouffée, and Andouille-crusted Catfish with Dirty Rice, but the usual American steaks, prime rib, short ribs, and pork chop are also present. Most of the Cajun entrees are under-seasoned and bland. Boatwright's is excellent for guests who unexpectedly find themselves back at the resort, but do make sure you have reservations because waits can be surprisingly long, particularly on weekends in lousy weather.

DINING AT DISNEY'S SARATOGA SPRINGS RESORT & SPA

The Turf Club Bar & Grill

Inside the main building, beyond the quick service

CUISINE American. **HOURS** 5–10pm. **DDP** Yes. **DISCOUNTS** 20% TiW; 10% AP; 10% DVC; 10% Disney Visa.

PRICES Appetizers: $7–$13. Dinner Entrées: $18–$35. Kids: $9.

OVERVIEW Turf Club is themed to a turn-of-the-century, upstate New York racetrack clubhouse. Wood-paneled walls and dark wood furniture provide a gentlemanly ambiance with views of Lake Buena Vista Golf Club down below and Disney Springs in the distance. It's not the most inviting restaurant, particularly with kids, but it's a great choice for couples staying at the resort who are looking for a more intimate experience, and riders will find the displayed horse tack delightful. Kids may enjoy the covered patio seating outside more. The menu leans toward steak, lamb, and pork. The Spice-rubbed Pork Tenderloin and the Grilled Lamb Chops are best. Start with the Turf Club Signature Grilled Romaine Salad and Buffalo Chicken Dip. Kids have the usual burger/nugget/pizza/fish/chicken/pasta options. The Saratoga Cocktail with Maker's Mark Bourbon and Mint Julep with Woodford Reserve are a nice departure from most cocktail menus heavy on flavored vodkas and light rum.

DINING AT DISNEY'S WILDERNESS LODGE

Artist Point

Back of main building

CUISINE American. **HOURS** 5:30–9:30pm. **DDP** 2 credits. **DISCOUNTS** 20% TiW; 10% AP; 10% DVC; 10% Disney Visa.

PRICES Appetizers: $10-$15. Dinner Entrées: $28–$49. Kids: $7–$14.

OVERVIEW Specialties of the Northwest are served as guests take in the large, open dining room inspired by national park lodges. Two-story high murals capture the heart and romance of the American frontier as iron lanterns provide the only light. Be sure to request a window table overlooking Bay Lake and Silver Creek Falls, or you risk a lousy view of a walkway or the lobby. The restaurant welcomes kids, but they are unlikely to be transfixed with the restaurant's subtle charm. The restaurant is best enjoyed as a romantic rendezvous. Best are the Smokey Portobello Soup appetizer and anything with buffalo strip or venison loin paired with one of the Northwest wine flights. Don't miss the Artist Point Cobbler for dessert.

Whispering Canyon Café

Just inside the main entrance, on the left

CUISINE American. **HOURS** Breakfast: 7:30–11:15am; Lunch: 11:45am–2:30pm; Dinner: 5–10pm. **DDP** Yes. **DISCOUNTS** 20% TiW; 10% AP; 10% DVC; 10% Disney Visa.

PRICES Breakfast Entrées: $10–$17. Lunch/Dinner Appetizers: $6–$12. Lunch Entrées: $12–$22. Dinner Entrées: $18–$33. Kids: $9–$12.

OVERVIEW Whispering Canyon Café is like a Western-themed 50's Prime Time Café. While the antics have been toned down in recent years, guests requesting a bottle of ketchup will find that 25 bottles from around the restaurant appear. Don't be surprised if your drink refill comes in a gallon jug or a two-ounce miniature jar, depending on how generous your server is feeling. All-you-care-to-enjoy platters are the most popular here. Breakfast brings scrambled eggs, Western home fries, bacon, sausage, waffles, buttermilk biscuits, and sausage gravy. A la carte choices include the usual. Lunch and dinner platters include family-style mixed greens tossed in an apple-vinaigrette dressing and freshly baked cornbread. Start with three: smoked pork ribs, barbecue-pulled pork, herb-baked chicken, beef strip loin, market fish, or sausage, along with vegetables, mashed potatoes, cowboy-style baked beans, and corn on the cob. Bring your sense of humor to enjoy this loud, raucous restaurant, particularly at dinner.

DINING AT DISNEY'S YACHT CLUB RESORT

Captain's Grille

Off the main lobby

CUISINE American. **HOURS** Breakfast: 7:30–11:25am; Lunch: 11:30am–2pm; Dinner: 5–9pm. **DDP** Yes. **DISCOUNTS** 20% TiW; 10% AP; 10% DVC; 10% Disney Visa.

PRICES Breakfast Entrées: $9–$16. Breakfast Buffet: $21/adults, $13 kids. Lunch/Dinner Appetizers: $4–$15. Lunch Entrées: $13–$23. Dinner Entrées: $18–$33. Kids: $9–$12.

OVERVIEW Serving seafood classics in a bland dining room, Captain's Grille had its menu and décor revamped in early 2014. New breakfast items include the $14 Butter-poached Lobster, Asparagus, Chive Cream, and Savory Hash Brown, in addition to the excellent breakfast buffet that includes fruit, pastries, eggs, bacon, sausage, smoked salmon, bread pudding, and more. It's an excellent value. Lunch is sandwich and burger fare, with the New England-style Lobster Roll on Butter-toasted Parker House Roll leading the way. Dinner brings more expensive items like the classic New York strip steak, snow crab legs with new potatoes and corn on the cob, and cabernet-braised short ribs. Kids may enjoy a burger, chicken nuggets, beef kebabs, baked fish, or shrimp skewers. Décor remains forgettable, but it's easy to secure a last-minute reservation, and food and service are excellent.

Yachtsman Steakhouse

Back of lobby

CUISINE American. **HOURS** 5–9:30pm. **DDP** 2 credits. **DISCOUNTS** 20% TiW.

PRICES Appetizers: $12–$19. Dinner Entrées: $31–$119 (for a 32 oz. Porterhouse for two). Kids: $8–$15.

OVERVIEW Yachtsman takes its meat more seriously than any other Disney resort restaurant on property, though recent additions like The BOATHOUSE, STK Orlando, and Morimoto Asia to Disney Springs make it much more difficult to definitively award it "best steak". Steaks are aged, trimmed, and hand cut on site before being prepared on an oak-fired grill in the open kitchen. The traditional steakhouse setting is heavy on wood with elegant white linens topping every table. While all steaks come in over $40, their quality is higher than at any other Disney-operated signature restaurant on property. The restaurant is not the best with young kids in tow, as there's little about the restaurant that will keep them occupied, but they may choose from mac 'n cheese, baked fish, grilled chicken, pasta and meatballs, or a steak skewer. Consider the restaurant for an intimate meal or special occasion, particularly with someone who knows their meat.

Which Tickets To Buy and How Much to Budget

8

"What should we budget?" is the hardest simple question for this book to answer. This is because smaller families, families whose kids are younger, families staying at a less expensive hotel, families going during a less expensive week, and families on shorter trips will pay less. Larger families, families where everyone is over nine, families staying at a more expensive hotel, families going during a more expensive week, and families on longer trips will pay more.

- A parent and one younger child, with three days of tickets and three nights in a value resort during one of the less expensive price seasons, could spend as little as $1,300 in Orlando.
- Add another parent and another younger child and this trip jumps to $2,100.
- Stretch the visit out to the 8 nights we recommend for "only visits" and the in-Orlando price exceeds $4,000.
- Stay this long in one of the more expensive deluxe resorts instead, and the price is more than $7,500.
- Shift to the most expensive times to visit at this deluxe resort and add $1,700 more.

(Prices will likely increase 3-5% during 2016. All the figures are before transportation costs and souvenirs.)

The good news is that budgeting for a specific trip is relatively straightforward, with most costs set and paid far in advance of arrival.

This chapter discusses the ins and outs of budgeting. More precisely, we'll walk you through how to establish what you can expect to pay for each component of your trip, whether it includes just one adult and one child on a tight budget over a few days, or a week-long extended family blow-out.

We open with a discussion of the one major budget issue we haven't discussed yet: theme park tickets with their various add-ons and related costs. The section that follows covers estimating your budget based on your dates, resort hotel, group, etc. Then we cover budgets for "only" trips, several ways to reduce costs, and even a few reasons to spend even more!

Disney World Tickets and Prices

Like most of our budgetary concerns thus far, deciding on the right theme park tickets for your group is simple at first blush and a bit more complicated once we delve into the specifics. Let's break it down.

The Magic Your Way base ticket is the name of the basic theme park admission ticket that Disney offers. The great majority of Disney World visitors will purchase a Magic Your Way ticket, although some guests return with Annual Passes (good for unlimited admissions throughout the year, sometimes with blackout dates) or have a promotional ticket of some kind. You may purchase a Magic Your Way ticket with one to ten days of theme park admissions. The tickets expire 14 days from their first use at Disney World (the day of first use plus 13 additional days), not from the date of purchase or the date of receipt in the mail.

International visitors, particularly those visiting from the United Kingdom and Europe, may have additional ticket options. For example, Disney offers a 7, 14, and 21-day Ultimate Ticket to UK and some European visitors, good for admission into all four major theme parks, in addition to the water parks and each of the minor parks discussed later in this chapter. The 21-day tickets cost more than $500 each, but for those eligible may be the best option on a long vacation as the only other options for those visiting longer than ten days are Annual Passes or two individual tickets, both of which would likely be even more expensive.

COST OF MAGIC YOUR WAY BASE TICKETS

While the cost always goes up to add more days to your base ticket, the cost per day goes down as you add days.

Disney charges more for a one-day ticket to Magic Kingdom than a one-day ticket to the other three major theme parks. Current pricing for tickets of all lengths is shown in the facing chart, which includes 6.5% sales tax (expect prices to increase in early 2016).

As you can see, the cost to add the fourth day is about $32 and each day after that is $10.65. Disney prices their tickets in this way so it is cost-effective to visit the parks for additional days, which means you will be spending more money on food, souvenirs, and hotel rooms, which is where the Walt Disney Company makes even more money than on admission. It also dissuades people from purchasing tickets to other theme parks. After all, the cost to add the 7th day to your Disney vacation is

Number of Ticket Days	Adult Price	Price to Add Day	Child Price	Price to Add Day
1 (Magic Kingdom)	$111.83	n/a	$105.44	n/a
1 (Any Park but Magic Kingdom)	$103.31	n/a	$96.92	n/a
2	$204.48	$92.66	$190.64	$85.20
3	$292.88	$88.40	$272.64	$82.01
4	$324.83	$31.95	$303.53	$30.89
5	$335.48	$10.65	$314.18	$10.65
6	$346.13	$10.65	$324.83	$10.65
7	$356.78	$10.65	$335.48	$10.65
8	$367.43	$10.65	$346.13	$10.65
9	$378.08	$10.65	$356.78	$10.65
10	$388.73	$10.65	$367.43	$10.65

"only about $10", compared to $90+ for a one-day ticket to SeaWorld, Universal Studios, etc. Disney keeps its single-day tickets expensive in order to capitalize on those only spending one day at Disney World.

ADDING DAYS TO YOUR TICKET

The Magic Your Way ticket is the bare minimum ticket that can be purchased, but that doesn't necessarily mean you need "more ticket". There are a few rules for upgrading base tickets. First, all upgrades must be done within 14 days of the first use of the ticket. You may also add days to your ticket as needed at the same price as it would have cost had you originally added them. For example, if you're unsure whether you need six, seven, or eight days of admission, you can purchase a six-day ticket and add a seventh or eighth day if you decide that you need them, even after using the tickets. You would only pay the additional cost per day at the same rate had you originally purchased a seven-day ticket ($10.65 per day, as noted in the chart above). These upgrades must be made before the end of the last day on the ticket. For example, if you've purchased a five-day ticket and would like to add a sixth, you must add it before the end of your fifth day spent in the theme park. Disney uses this policy to cut down on ticket resellers that offer unsuspecting visitors money for their used tickets. The resellers used to take these used tickets to Disney, add extra days for the $10.65 per day cost, and then turn around and resell them as "new" one-day tickets for $50 or more. Reselling used tickets is illegal in Florida, and if you find yourself in the unfortunate situation of trying to use bogus tickets, you'll be refused admission to the parks. Stick with Disney directly or a trusted third party, not the various resellers with strip mall storefronts.

ADDING PARK HOPPERS

The Park Hopper ticket add-on allows the user to visit more than one theme park on the same day. For example, the Animal Kingdom might close at 5pm on the day you choose to visit. With the Park Hopper upgrade, you could exit the Animal Kingdom at any time and travel to and enter any of the other three theme parks to take advantage of evening Extra Magic Hours, a late dinner reservation, or anything else.

For both kids and adults, the current cost of the hopper on a one-day Magic Kingdom ticket is $53.25 with tax. A hopper on a one-day, non-Magic Kingdom ticket is $61.77. For two- or three-day tickets, the cost is $53.25. With a four- to ten-day ticket, the cost is a flat $68.16 per ticket with tax. On a six-day ticket, the cost for the upgrade comes out to $11.36 per day. Guests adding both Park Hopper and Water Park Fun & More (described next) at the same time receive a discount of about $40 versus adding them separately. The cost to add both upgrades is $95.85. (Expect prices to increase in early 2016.)

Many guests have what they think is the bright idea of bypassing the expensive Park Hopper upgrade and instead purchase more days of theme park admissions than they need with the idea that they will visit a second theme park on the same day and simply use a second day's admission. For example, a family might be visiting the parks on five days and purchase seven days of admission with the idea that on day five they'll visit Animal Kingdom in the morning and then use a sixth day of admission on the same day to visit Epcot at night. This will not work. Disney is wise to the fact that adding Park Hopper would be over $60 per ticket, while adding two additional days is only about $20. In our example, the Cast Member at Epcot would explain the benefits of upgrading to Park Hopper after the ticket was rejected at the scanner.

In most situations, we don't recommend spending the money on the Park Hopper upgrade, at least not until you experience Walt Disney World for the first time and realize how big it is, how much there is to do everywhere, and how long it takes to get from park to park. Remember, Disney will very rarely not take your money and they are more than happy to add the Park Hopper upgrade to your ticket should you deem the cost necessary, even after you've started using the ticket.

Remember that the regular base ticket allows unlimited re-entries to the same theme park on the same day. Should you take a recommended afternoon break, you can return to the same theme park later for dinner, additional attractions, and the night-time entertainment. It's true that Animal Kingdom routinely closes around 5 or 6pm, and it may seem like there's a lot of time after it closes to do *something*. Instead of pushing on to another theme park, consider making a dinner reservation and exploring a nearby resort. In Animal Kingdom's case, Animal Kingdom Lodge is just a few minutes away. It's a beautiful resort where anyone is free to use the observatories to check out the giraffes, zebras, and other animals on the savannas. The restaurants and quick service are all excellent as well.

Park Hopper does have its uses, particularly for guests staying at Epcot area resorts or guests visiting for a special event. Guests staying at a resort like the Beach or Yacht Club may wish to start their day at Magic Kingdom, take a break back at the resort, and then simply walk the five minutes to Epcot for drinks, dinner, rides, entertainment, or whatever else.

If you are considering the Park Hopper upgrade, calculate how much it's going to cost and then divide that by the number of times you plan to hop. That's the cost per hop and will give you a better idea if the real additional theme park time is worth the money.

ADDING WATER PARK FUN & MORE

The Water Park Fun & More add-on includes an allotment of entrances to the following "minor parks" in Disney World: Typhoon Lagoon water park, Blizzard Beach water park, Disney's Wide World of Sports Complex,

Magic Your Way Base Ticket Days	Water Park Fun Admissions
1	2
2	2
3	3
4	4
5	5
6	6
7	7
8	8
9	9
10	10

DisneyQuest (which will be closing in 2016), one round of golf at 9-hole Oak Trail, Disney's Fantasia Gardens Mini Golf (before 4:00 pm), or Disney's Winter Summerland Mini Golf (before 4:00 pm). The number of entrances you will receive to the minor parks is based on the number of days your Magic Your Way Base Ticket is valid. The following chart illustrates this:

For example, if your ticket is good for five days, then you will receive five entrances to any of the minor parks. Note that guests with both one- and two-day theme park tickets receive two minor theme park admissions.

With tax, the current cost to add the Water Park Fun & More upgrade is $68.16, for any ticket except one-day non-Magic Kingdom tickets, where it is $76.68. The cost is $95.85 with tax to add both Park Hopper and Water Park fun & More.

Water Park Fun & More is a great value if you plan to visit the water parks at least twice.

Here are the current costs (with tax) of a one-day ticket to the minor parks that you can visit with the Water Park Fun & More upgrade (expect prices to go up in 2016):

- DisneyQuest (closing in 2016): $47.93 Adult, $41.54 Child (3–9)
- Blizzard Beach or Typhoon Lagoon: $61.77 Adult, $53.25 Child (3–9)
- Disney's Wide World of Sports: $17.57 Adult, $12.25 Child (3–9)
- Round of Golf at Oak Trail: $40.49 Adult, $21.32 Junior (17 and under)
- Fantasia Gardens Mini Golf: $14.91 Adult, $12.78 Child (3–9)
- Winter Summerland Mini Golf: $14.91 Adult, $12.78 Child (3–9)

As you can see, the cost of a one-day ticket to Blizzard Beach, Typhoon Lagoon, or Oak Trail is just a little less expensive than adding the Water Park Fun & More upgrade. The upgrade becomes cost effective if you're planning to visit at least two of the more expensive minor parks. If you're unsure of whether you'll be visiting a second time, you can apply the cost of one day's admission to the water parks, DisneyQuest, golf, or one of the other minor parks toward the full cost of the upgrade so long as you present the receipt at the time of upgrade.

While the water parks and other minor attractions are a lot of fun, we don't usually recommend the add-on for a first visit because the major theme parks offer so much to see and do. For return trips or vacations lasting more than eight days, it is potentially a great value for those planning several visits to the minor parks.

Estimating Budgets

Now that we've determined the cost of theme park tickets, let's add them to the resort and dining costs discussed in Chapters 5 and 7, and consider the following variables:

- **DATES OF THE VISIT** Walt Disney World price seasons for hotel rooms vary tremendously over the year.

- **GROUP SIZE AND AGE STRUCTURE AT PLANNED CHECK-IN DATE** Kids less than three years old don't require theme park admission and aren't charged at buffets. Kids from three to nine are charged a little less than older folk for theme park tickets, and a lot less for kids' meals and kids' buffets. Kids ten and older as of the check-in date are charged the same as adults for theme park tickets and the Dining Plan. With the exception of the Disney Vacation Club rooms and the Fort Wilderness campground, Disney includes two guests age 18 or older in the room at the base price. Additional guests over the age of 18 will be charged $10–$25 per night extra, depending on the resort level.

- **TARGETED HOTEL** Walt Disney World hotel rooms are available for prices just south of $100 per night to well over $600 per night.

- **TRANSPORTATION COSTS** These vary greatly depending on mode and length of travel.

- **TIPS, SNACKS, SOUVENIRS, AND OTHER EXTRAS** Add about $25 per person, per night.

Now that we have an idea about when and for how long we want to visit, let's input our information and get an idea of how much it's all going to cost. Visit DISNEYWORLD.COM and input your check-in date, check-out date, and desired hotel, and then select Find Prices. Select Room-only, Package, or one of the special offers (if available), and then scroll down and select the room type. The next page lists tickets and the add-ons discussed previously in the chapter. Select the tickets and then click Dining Plan. Note the cost with and without the Plan. While we don't recommend the Dining Plan in most situations, it does give a general idea about what it will cost to eat one quick service and one table service meal per day, in addition to a snack or two. Don't worry if this number seems too high—we'll cover discounts and ways to save money shortly.

Budgeting an Only Visit

For a nine-day itinerary during the Fall 2016 price season, assuming a family of four with two adults, one child younger than ten and one older, budget if possible:

- $7,900+ if you are staying at a deluxe resort
- $5,450 if you are staying at a moderate
- $4,700 if you are staying at a value

Add to this budget the costs of getting the group to and from Orlando.

We suggest that a day or two shorter can also work for an "only" visit. For shorter visits, subtract about $400/day if you are staying at a value resort, $500/day at a moderate, and $850/day at a deluxe.

Saving Money on a Disney World Visit

The money-saving opportunities available depend greatly on when you go and where you stay:

- When you go matters because Disney changes seasonal pricing roughly 25 times over the course of the year. Staying in the same exact standard-view room at the Polynesian for eight nights during the most expensive time of the year can cost $2,200 more than it would cost during the cheapest period.
- Where you stay matters because Walt Disney World has resorts priced at many different levels. Staying eight nights at the Polynesian instead of Art of Animation during the lower cost season will cost almost $3,000 more.
- Combining these effects—staying eight nights at the Poly during the highest cost time of the year instead of at Art of Animation during the lowest cost time of the year—costs a whopping $5,200 more for the same family with the same theme park tickets!

So the takeaways for the first-time family visitor:

- On a tight budget, consider sticking with one of Disney's less expensive on-property resorts like Art of Animation or Pop Century.
- Think carefully about what is really getting in the way of going during one of the less expensive seasons. Is it possible to pull the kids out of school to visit when crowds and prices are much lower?

Because Disney controls the entire supply of theme park tickets, discounts from reputable sources are slim. Check UNDERCOVERTOURIST. COM for some of the best discounts on multi-day tickets.

Fortunately, major savings may be available on other aspects of your vacation:

- Keep an eye out for deals available to the general public—typically room rate discounts, but sometimes a version of the Dining Plan for free—especially in September. Find them at YOURFIRSTVISIT. NET/DEALS or at Disney World's Special Offer web page as they are announced. These discounts are usually available to Disney Visa card holders a few days before they become available to everyone else. Visit DISNEYREWARDS.COM for more information.

- Use special discounts that you quality for, the most valuable of which is the Armed Forces Salute. See MILITARYDISNEYTIPS. COM for more. There may also be discounts for Florida residents, Annual Passholders, international guests, and others.

- Access Disney Vacation Club rooms for a lot less by renting points from owners who won't be using them—this is a particular boon for large families, who have the most difficulty finding Disney-owned accommodations at reasonable prices. Visit DVCREQUEST.COM for pricing and options.

- Consider staying offsite, especially with large groups. As noted in Chapter 5, there are some takeaways on the convenience side of things, but it may be the most viable option for some groups, and the savings can be substantial. It's hard to find reasonably priced Disney-owned options on-site for groups larger than four people, and even more difficult for groups larger than five. You'll find lots of ideas at YOURFIRSTVISIT.NET/LARGE-FAMILIES, but the least expensive way to stay will be offsite.

Art of Animation Nights	1	2	3	4
Base Ticket Days	2	3	4	5
Hotel	$ 173	$ 346	$ 494	$ 642
Dining Plan/Other Food*	$ 414	$ 669	$ 925	$ 1,181
Park Tickets*	$ 844	$ 1,209	$ 1,342	$ 1,387
Extras, Souvenirs, etc*	$ 210	$ 245	$ 327	$ 408
TOTAL: No Extras	$ 1,431	$ 2,223	$ 2,761	$ 3,210
TOTAL: With Extras	$ 1,641	$ 2,468	$ 3,088	$ 3,619

Art of Animation Nights	5	6	7	8
Base Ticket Days	6	7	8	9
Hotel	$ 790	$ 938	$ 1,086	$ 1,259
Dining Plan/Other Food*	$ 1,437	$ 1,694	$ 1,949	$ 2,205
Park Tickets*	$ 1,431	$ 1,476	$ 1,520	$ 1,566
Extras, Souvenirs, etc*	$ 490	$ 571	$ 653	$ 735
TOTAL: No Extras	$ 3,659	$ 4,108	$ 4,555	$ 5,030
TOTAL: With Extras	$ 4,149	$ 4,679	$ 5,208	$ 5,765

*4 Person "Little Mermaid" room; Friday arrival Fall 2016 price season
Family of four with one younger than ten. Assumes 5% increase in non-hotel costs

For groups that will fit into a four person standard Little Mermaid room at Disney's value resort Art of Animation, the chart above illustrates what it will cost two adults, one kid older than ten, and one aged from three to nine, to stay for various trip lengths during the Fall 2016 price season.

Spending Even More at Disney World

There's almost no limit to what could be spent on a first visit to Walt Disney World, with a fat enough wallet and sufficient desire to thin it. For example, how about a couple of newly-published authors as really expensive tour guides?

For a fuller list, see "The Comfortable Guide to Walt Disney World" on YOURFIRSTVISIT.NET/COMFORTABLE. But a shorter list of extra spending that may significantly increase comfort levels on a first visit includes the following:

- **RENTING A CAR** Disney's Magical Express (discussed in Chapter 9) will transport your group back and forth from the airport, but it requires that guests return to their resort for pickup no later than three hours before the flight is scheduled to leave. With a car, you can potentially leave for the airport directly from the theme park. On property, Disney's transportation system will get you from your Disney hotel to the parks, but a rental car reduces waits, increases flexibility, and offers a more comfortable, private ride. Transport to all the parks but the Magic Kingdom is faster by car than by Disney bus: it's the only simple way to get from most resort hotels—especially values and moderates—to another for dining, etc.; it's the only easy way to get to the non-Disney parks; and it makes shopping, off-site dining, and other activities much easier.

- **STAYING A FEW DAYS LONGER** Adding two or three days to a trip—and planning on relaxing those days—can make your vacation much more comfortable. A Disney World trip is like a backpacking expedition—lots of walking, lots of energy used, lots of early mornings. A few more days off can make a world of difference.

- **GETTING A MULTI-SPACE ROOM** Even the happiest families can tire of staying together in a single room. Several Disney lodging options—mostly at the expensive deluxe resorts—give you more space. Consider (in order of increasing prices) deluxe rooms at the Wilderness Lodge, one and two bedroom villas at the Disney Vacation Club resorts, and suites at all the deluxe resorts. Much lower priced—but still expensive—multi-room options are Family Suites at All-Star Music and at Art of

Animation, and the Cabins at Fort Wilderness. Many—but not all—of these options include full kitchens as well.

None of these are inexpensive...but they might make a real difference to comfort!

Pricing out a Walt Disney World vacation is daunting. The good news is that once you've arrived, most everything is already taken care of and you can let loose and enjoy your trip. In fact, if you've added the Dining Plan, the only additional costs most guests encounter in Orlando is souvenirs (and there will be souvenirs), tips, and a few treats. With the ability to save a substantial amount of money on resort costs and a few dollars on tickets, it's easy to design around just about any budget.

How to Set Everything Up and Get Everything Done

9

There are three key dates to consider:

- Restaurant reservations open for booking 180 days before a potential dining date
- For those staying at a Disney-owned resort or the Swan or Dolphin, FastPass+ reservations can be booked beginning 60 days before their arrival date
- For everyone else, FastPass+ reservations can be booked beginning 30 days before planned use

Building a To-Do List is keyed to these three dates because booking as early as possibly will result in the widest selection of experiences being available.

The first section of this chapter outlines how to sign up for and use Disney's new My Disney Experience mobile app and website. From there, we'll walk through customizing MagicBands and setting up FastPass+.

Tailored to-do lists are available for each of the sample itineraries available at YOURFIRSTVISIT.NET/ITINERARIES. For guests building custom itineraries, the second section of this chapter discusses putting together a to-do list to make sure everything is booked as easily and conveniently as possible.

My Disney Experience, FastPass+, and MagicBands

MY DISNEY EXPERIENCE

If you don't already have a My Disney Experience (MDE) account, sign up for one by visiting DISNEYWORLD.COM and clicking the "sign in or create account" button on the top right of the screen. An account is required to make dining and FastPass+ reservations, in addition to customizing MagicBands and keeping track of each component of your vacation online.

If you already have an account and booked a trip through the website while logged in, you should already see these reservations upon signing in. If not, link them manually by clicking "My Reservations and Tickets" under the My Disney Experience dropdown menu (located in the top right under the search box) and input the confirmation numbers and ticket IDs.

If people on the reservation are missing, click from the same MDE dropdown menu, "My Family and Friends". Once the new screen opens, click the little "Add a Guest" button at the upper right. Type the names of the missing people, and, if applicable, their ticket IDs. If you have trouble, try tech support—at (407) 939-5277—and have the ticket and reservation numbers of the missing elements at hand.

BOOKING FASTPASS+ AHEAD OF YOUR ARRIVAL

FastPass+ can be booked in advance by everyone with a valid "Magic Your Way" ticket or annual pass. Guests staying in Disney-owned resorts or the Swan or Dolphin can begin booking FastPass+ 60 days before their arrival date. Guests staying elsewhere can book up to 30 days before planned use. FastPass+ strategy is covered in depth back in Chapter 6.

Booking FastPass+ as soon as eligible is advantageous because the most attractions and times will be available. Each FastPass+ experience has a limited number of slots. Fewer and fewer experiences will be available as a specific visit date approaches because more and more people have gone online and secured their choices.

Read Chapter 6, if you haven't already, and decide which FastPass+ experiences and times you'd like to book. Beginning at midnight exactly 60 days out, you can sign into your MDE account on DISNEYWORLD.COM and complete the following steps:

- From the My Disney Experience drop down, pick FastPass+.
- On the next screen, select New FastPass+.
- Not all members of the group are required to select the same FastPass+ experiences. Some groups with younger and older children may want to book two separate sets of FastPass+ experiences because the little ones want to ride Winnie the Pooh and Tomorrowland Speedway with Dad while the older kids prefer Space Mountain and Big Thunder Mountain with Mom. On the next screen, select the members of the party for whom you'd like to reserve the same experiences and times. This may be the entire group or just a few people. Simply repeat the FastPass+ booking process for each group if booking two or more separate groups.

- Then pick both the park and the date. One of two types of screens then opens here, depending on whether or not the park is tiered. In the tiered parks, the FastPass+ rides are split into two groups. In the first group (Tier One) pick only one ride from among those offered, and in the second group (Tier Two), pick only two. At the non-tiered parks, pick any three experiences from the options listed.

- Then click Next to be offered four different options, labeled 1, 2, 3 and 4, one of which will also be labeled "Best!". Not all options may include all of your selections. Pick the one that includes all of your selections but starts latest in the evening. This will make it easier to change times to the afternoon later because it reduces overlapping experiences. Save it.

- As we learned in Chapter 6, booking FastPass+ times in the late morning and early afternoon is advantageous because lines and crowds will have peaked and FastPass+ will save us the most time. There's no reason to use most FastPass+ experiences in the early morning when standby waits are short. We originally selected evening times so we have the entire afternoon free to change the times without any worry that My Disney Experience will say that times are unavailable because we already have an experience booked in that slot. Unless it's your departure day or you have afternoon/evening plans elsewhere, we'll change the times so they're convenient in the late morning and afternoon. On the confirmation screen, click "Modify". (If you're modifying selections at a later date, click the My Disney Experience drop-down menu and choose "FastPass+" and then "Update FastPass+.)

- Click the party members to make the change for, then move the FastPass+ around based on your desired timing. Because FastPass+ can't be double-booked at any time that overlaps, a couple of changes may have to be made to a single ride—first to move it out of the way of another FastPass+, then to move it back to a time newly vacated. You'll be offered the most desirable times if you initially book your experiences first thing in the morning or at the very end of the night.

- Then, if needed, move on to the rest of the party for that day. When done with the day, move on to the next day.

Times and experiences may be changed as often as wished (limited, though, to what is available at the time you change them), up through the last hour the theme park is open on the day you're visiting. If you run into problems, try tech support at (407) 939-5277.

MAGICBANDS

For those staying at a Disney-owned resort, MagicBands play many roles on a trip. Most importantly, they are room keys, park tickets, the link to using your Dining Plan credits, the link to FastPass+, and, if charging privileges are enabled, a means to charge back to the room.

They contain no personal data—rather, all they have encoded within them is a unique numeric identifier which Disney uses to link up databases in its own systems behind the scenes.

MagicBands are waterproof and hypoallergenic, and don't even need to be worn on a wrist—you can stick them in a pocket or purse and just wave them about when needed. Many need to take them off and wave them about anyway since not all the readers work perfectly when they are on a wrist, especially hotel room locks.

The color and names printed on the MagicBands can be customized online at DISNEYWORLD.COM after booking. Disney will email you when you can begin customization. To do so, log in to your MDE account at DISNEYWORLD.COM and select MagicBands and Cards from the My Disney Experience dropdown menu. Confirm the shipping address, then select MagicBands one by one for the people in your party. For each MagicBand, pick a color and customize the name, which is limited to nine characters including spaces. So "easyWDW" fits, but not "yourfirstvisit.net". Colors can be the same among your group, so long as the names are different. Well, names can be the same, too...but why would you do that? Haven't we already helped you cause enough confusion?

MagicBands will be shipped directly to the U.S. address of your choice if they're customized at least 10 days (at press time) before the arrival date. MagicBands customized closer to the check-in date will be available at check-in at the resort. Disney does not ship MagicBands internationally, which means all visitors without a U.S. address will pick up their MagicBands at check-in. If you fail to customize the MagicBands at all, grey MagicBands with or without the names listed on the reservation will be waiting at the resort at check-in.

Those not staying at a Disney-owned resort can purchase MagicBands on site, with current pricing at $12.95 each. The MagicBands of such visitors are linked at the time of purchase to a theme park ticket, and the MagicBand can then be used for FastPass+. Note that a MagicBand is not required to use FastPass+ (a ticket, of course, is required) and off-site guests can simply scan their ticket instead of a Band. There are no charging privileges for off-site guests, so you'll need to keep cash or a credit card handy.

Disney World To-Do List

Tailored To-Do lists are available for each of the itineraries located at YOURFIRSTVISIT.NET/ITINERARIES. For more general guidelines, see below:

More Than 181 Days Before Your Planned Arrival Date

1. Double-check budget (Chapter 8), dates (Chapter 4), intended hotel (Chapter 5), intended dates in each park (Chapter 6), intended dining venues (Chapter 7), and transportation choices and their availability for the planned dates.

2. Make transportation arrangements as necessary, including any flight or rental car reservations.

3. Create your My Disney Experience account and add your group members to it.

4. If staying at a Disney-owned hotel, book your hotel and purchase your tickets. Call 407-939-7675 to book by phone (optimal, because this allows you to tell the reservationist which area at a resort you want to be in, if you have a preference) or go to DISNEYWORLD.COM/PLAN to use Disney's online system. At the same time, you'll have the opportunity to sign up for Disney's Magical Express service that transports Disney-owned hotel guests from Orlando International (but not Sanford) Airport directly to their hotel. Don't worry if you don't have your flight details set. You can come back to this page later or call 866-599-0951 to set it up. Disney hotel reservations can be made over the phone up to 500 days before an arrival date. Online, the system may only show reservations available through the end of the calendar year, particularly if you try to book for the next year more than six months in advance. Call Disney reservations at 407-939-7675 if your dates aren't available online but you are within 500 days of your arrival date.

5. If not staying at a Disney resort, buy your tickets from within your My Disney Experience account—this increases the chance that they will be properly linked. Alternatively, purchase tickets from an authorized reseller and link them manually.

Exactly 6am EST, Exactly 180 Days Before Arrival Date

Log on to DisneyWorld.com/dining by at least 5:50am EST, and have your highest priority reservation all set up on the page. Keep refreshing, as you will be let in as soon as Disney's system decides it is 6am. Make as many of the following hardest-to-get reservations that are on your itinerary, in the order listed:

- Be Our Guest Restaurant [Magic Kingdom]
- Cinderella's Royal Table [Magic Kingdom]

- Chef Mickey's [Contemporary Resort]
- 'Ohana [Polynesian Resort]
- Akershus Royal Banquet Hall [Epcot]
- 1900 Park Fare Dinner [Grand Floridian Resort]
- California Grill [Contemporary Resort]
- Crystal Palace [Magic Kingdom]
- Hoop-Dee-Doo Revue [Fort Wilderness Campground and Resort]

For other restaurants, booking at 6am 180+ days in advance isn't necessary, but doing so will guarantee a desired day and time.

If you have trouble online, call (407) WDW-DINE (939-3463) to book reservations offline, beginning at 7am EST on the same date.

60 Days Before Arrival Date (If Staying at Disney-Owned Resort, the Swan, or the Dolphin)

1. Beginning (if you choose) at midnight, go to your My Disney Experience account and set up your FastPass+ selections
2. Do online resort check in, requesting any special location or amenity preferences
3. Customize MagicBands

30 Days Before First Park Visit (If Staying Anywhere Else)
Beginning (if you choose) at midnight, go to your My Disney Experience account and set up your FastPass+.

Notes on Packing, Etc., Before You Leave

1. If you have them, bring your MagicBands in your carry-ons or wear them on your wrists.
2. If you use Disney's Magical Express, you do not need to collect your bags at the Orlando airport unless you choose to, arrive late in the evening/at night (between 10 pm and 5 am), or are an international traveler. Disney will obtain them for you (without the bags ever going to baggage claim) and deliver them directly to your room. Your bags will likely arrive at your hotel hours after you do. Plan to pack an appropriate change of clothes for Orlando weather, medications, etc., in a carry-on. Follow the instructions in the Magical Express packet you will receive in the mail regarding both tagging your bags pre-departure and where to go at the Orlando airport to find the bus to your resort. Magical Express check-in is located on the B side of Level 1. If you arrive on the A side or pick up your luggage yourself on the A side, you will need to walk over to the B side. Note that this is only possible on Level 3. There is no way to walk from the A side to the B side on any other level.

3. Bring copies/printouts of your room reservation, confirmation numbers, and any tickets for special events you may have received in the mail.

4. When you arrive at the hotel, if you used Online Check-in, look for the special Online Check-in line, and get into it.

We're almost there! Setting up dining and FastPass+ reservations can be stressful and frustrating, but you're armed with the best possible strategy. Once the reservations are booked, there's little to worry about.

Where to Go Next

Congratulations! You either skipped to the end of the book to find out if the princess really does end up with the prince, or have now read so much great Disney World information that there's really no need to actually go on the vacation. And this book isn't even billed as a money saver. Oh, you still want to go, and you want to be kept up to date on any changes? We weren't expecting that, but we might still be able to help.

First of all, bookmark YOURFIRSTVISIT.NET/EASY-GUIDE-2016-CHANGES and EASYWDW.COM/EASY-GUIDE for anything in the book that's changed since the publication date. As FastPass+ continues its rollout, there are bound to be some details that change in the coming months – not to mention potential price increases, character switcheroos, and whatnot. The latest scoop will always be at those links.

From there, easyWDW.com is your best chance to see what's going on inside the theme parks as it happens. With weekly visits, thousands of pictures, up-to-date info on operating schedule changes, crowd calendars, and ideal touring strategies, there's no other website in the world like it. If you'd like to join other WDW fans and have an opportunity to ask Josh questions about your trip directly, sign up for the forums at WWW.EASYWDW.COM/FORUMS.

Pay close attention to YOURFIRSTVISIT.NET for new material aimed squarely at first-timers who both may never return and also don't necessarily want to spend a lot of time planning. Advice there for such visitors is very specific, but always comes with next best options ranked in order for those who can't, or won't, follow Dave's specific advice. The site is particularly helpful for choosing among hotels. Read it, and EASYWDW.COM, too, and your life will be fulfilled.

We sincerely hope this book helped you plan a special trip full of the best that Walt Disney World offers. Get out there and put everything you learned into action. And after you've left Disney World and come back home—leave us comments at YOURFIRSTVISIT.NET/EASY-GUIDE-2016-CHANGES and EASYWDW.COM/EASY-GUIDE to let us know how it went!

Acknowledgments

Dave would like to thank those who helped with this book and the years of work that led up to it:

- This book would not have been possible without the encouragement and skills of Bob McLain and Theme Park Press.
- And it wouldn't have been too good without my co-author Josh Humphrey. The best Disney World thinker of his generation, Josh has made this book more than twice as good as it would have been without him, thanks to his capability and stubbornness.
- Gratitude to my family—Amy, Ted, and Alex—who once again let a Walt Disney World project divert my time and attention.
- Many thanks to a list of people whose support over the years made the work that led to this book possible: Steve Bell, Joe Black, Tom Bricker, Lee Cockerell, Mary Conor DeFazio, Beth Pickel Doda, Faith Dority, Mike Ellis, Kristen Hoetzel-Go, Jackie Hutnik, Allison Jones, Linda Stevens Jones, Kathleen Kelly, Karen Landry, Kuleen Lashly, Sarah Harvey Mitchell, Julie Neal, Steve Seifert, Len Testa, Carl Trent, and Jodi Whisenhunt.
- Last, but not least, thanks to the readers of YOURFIRSTVISIT. NET—coming up on ten million of them—you all inspire me every day.

Josh would like to thank:
- My mom and dad for smiling as their (favorite) son crossed the country to try and chase down yet another dream.
- The lovely Miss Lisa Taylor for her love and generosity through all of this nonsense. And for taking me where I need to go.
- Dave Shute for bringing me this posh book deal, in addition to providing the foundation and structure for everything in it.
- Everyone that's ever recommended easyWDW to a friend, colleague, family member, or fellow DISboards member. Your continued support is what drives everything I do. Thank you.

About the Authors

Dave by day is a strategist and problem solver for clients ranging from the Fortune 500 to local not-for-profits. At night and on weekends he writes yourfirstvisit.net, and, lately, Disney World guidebooks. All the time he's a husband, dad, son, and brother. He has a BA from the University of Chicago, and both an MA in English Literature and MBA from the University of Virginia, where he also completed the majority of work for a PhD in English Literature. He spent almost a decade as a strategy consultant at McKinsey & Co., Inc., and since then has largely operated as an independent strategy consultant. He founded yourfirstvisit.net more than six years ago—the first Disney World site aimed squarely at first-time visitors who may never return. He visits Disney World six to ten times a year, and in 2014 he stayed in his hundredth different Disney World hotel room.

Josh grew up in Seattle, Washington, the only known city to adequately prepare a person for Orlando's wet summers. He was fascinated by Disney theme parks long before his first visit to Disneyland at age eight. He started easyWDW.com in the spring of 2010 as an outlet to help visitors maximize their theme park experience with practical, hands-on advice. He lives just 15 minutes from Magic Kingdom's gates and records more than a hundred theme park visits every year, each with the express intent of uncovering ways to better enjoy everything the parks offer. In his spare time, he enjoys dressing his Duffy the Disney Bear in fabulous outfits, taking his dog to the park, and the occasional single malt scotch.

Jim Korkis is a noted Disney historian and author of seven books about Disney and animation, including the best-selling *Vault of Walt* series, the definitive "biography" of Mickey Mouse, and a business handbook drawn from Walt Disney's leadership principles (*Who's the Leader of the Club?*). All of Korkis' books are published by Theme Park Press. His "Jim's Gems" content is exclusive to *The easy Guide*.

More Books from Theme Park Press

Theme Park Press publishes dozens of books each year for Disney fans and for general and academic audiences. Here are just a few of our titles. For the complete catalog, including book descriptions and excerpts, please visit:

ThemeParkPress.com

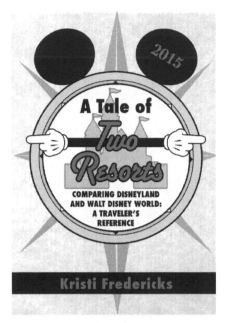

A Tale of *Two Resorts*

COMPARING DISNEYLAND
AND WALT DISNEY WORLD:
A TRAVELER'S
REFERENCE

2015

Kristi Fredericks

THE
RIDE DELEGATE
Memoir of a Walt Disney World VIP Tour Guide

Annie Salisbury

INSIDE THE DISNEY
MARKETING
MACHINE

In the Era of
Michael Eisner & Frank Wells

Lorraine Santoli

Foreword by Sam Tuchman, Ph.D.

MURDER
IN THE MAGIC KINGDOM

Annie Salisbury

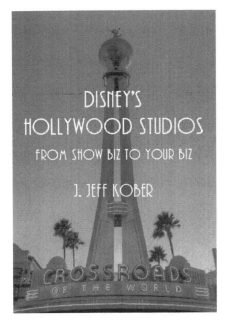

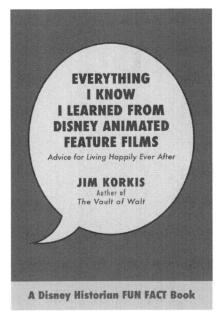

Disneyland SECRETS

GAVIN DOYLE

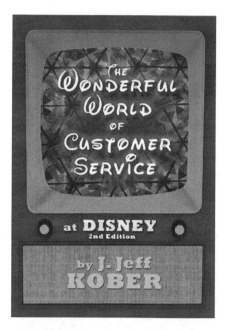

THE WONDERFUL WORLD OF CUSTOMER SERVICE

at **DISNEY**
2nd Edition

by **J. Jeff KOBER**

D

is for
Disneyland

**THE UNOFFICIAL KIDS GUIDE TO
THE HAPPIEST PLACE ON EARTH**

Kelly Pope Adamson

Brittany

EARNS
HER EARS

My Secret Walt Disney World
Cast Member Diary

BRITTANY DICOLOGERO
Earning Your Ears: Volume Five

Made in the USA
Middletown, DE
27 November 2015